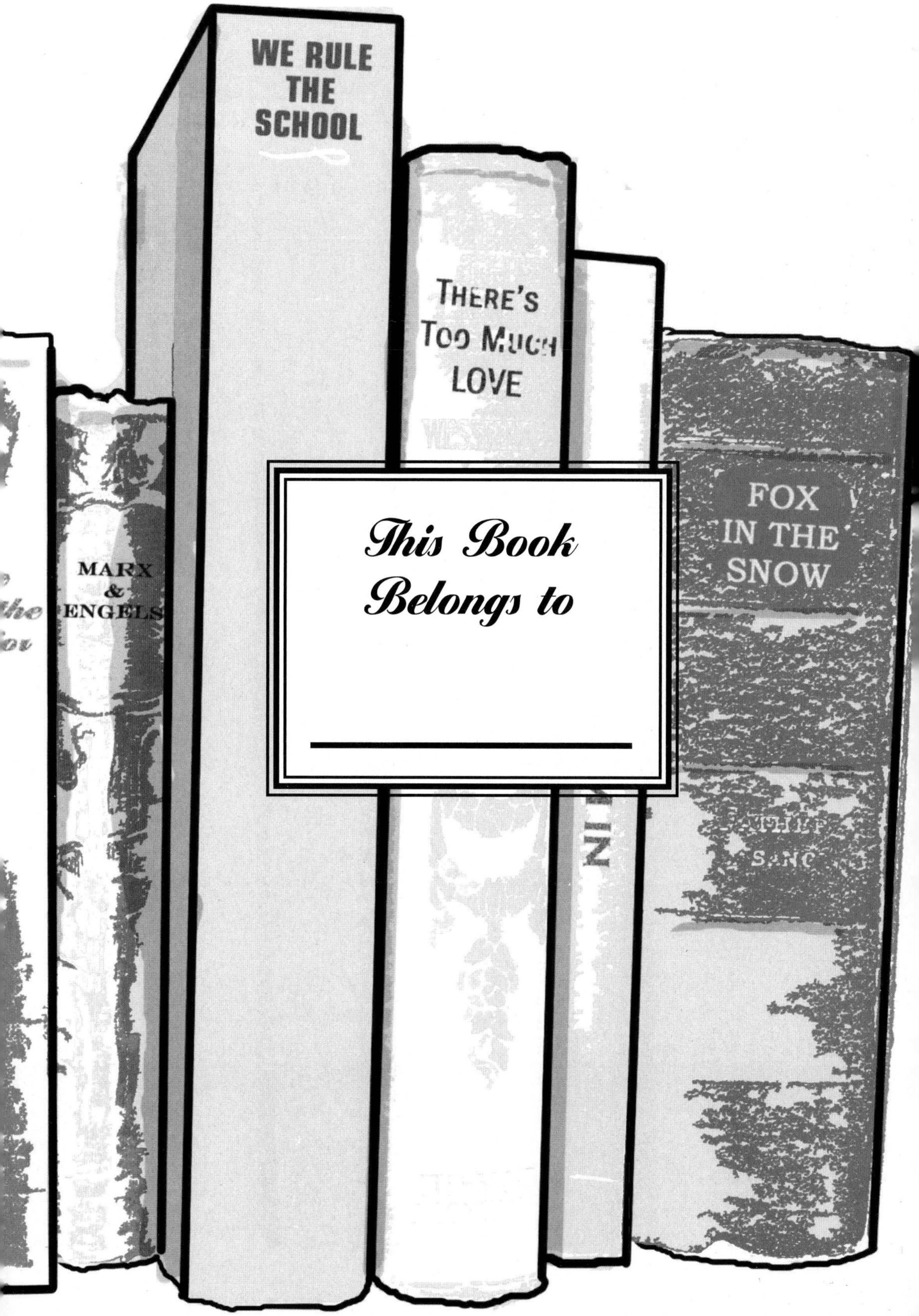
WE RULE THE SCHOOL
THERE'S TOO MUCH LOVE
MARX & ENGELS
This Book Belongs to
FOX IN THE SNOW

PUT THE BOOK BACK
ON THE SHELF:
A BELLE AND
SEBASTIAN
ANTHOLOGY
copyright
© Image Comics and
Belle and Sebastian,
2006
All stories are ™ and ©
their repective creators
All songs written by
Belle & Sebastian,
published by Sony/ ATV

Image Comics ® and
the Image logo are
registered trademarks
of Image Comics.

Second Printing

Image Comics
1942 University Ave.
Suite 305
Berkeley, CA 94704

ISBN#1-58240-600-6

Printed in Canada

IMAGE COMICS

Publisher
Erik Larsen

President
Todd McFarlane

CEO
Marc Silvestri

Vice-President
Jim Valentino

Executive Director
Eric Stephenson

PR & Marketing
Coordinator
Jim Demonakos

Accounts Manager
Mia MacHatton

Art Director
Laurenn
McCubbin

Production Artist
Allen Hui

Traffic Manager
Joe Keatinge

Production Assistant
Jonathan Chan

Production Assistant
Drew Gill

Administrative Assistant
Traci Hui

www.imagecomics.com

*Special
thanks
to Stuart
Murdoch,
Neil
Robertson
and B. Clay
Moore*

PUT THE BOOK BACK ON THE SHELF

A Belle and Sebastian Anthology

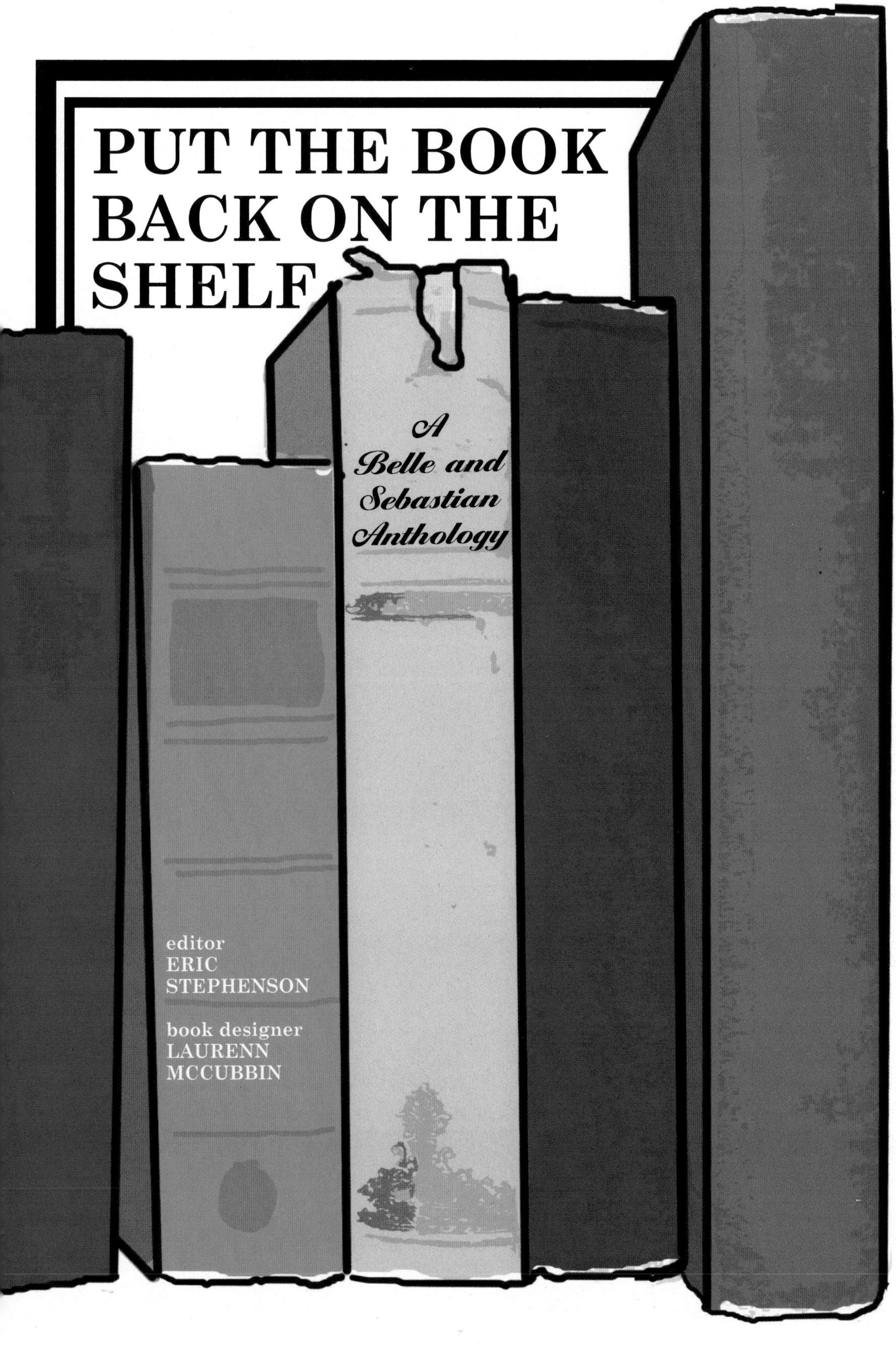

editor
ERIC STEPHENSON

book designer
LAURENN MCCUBBIN

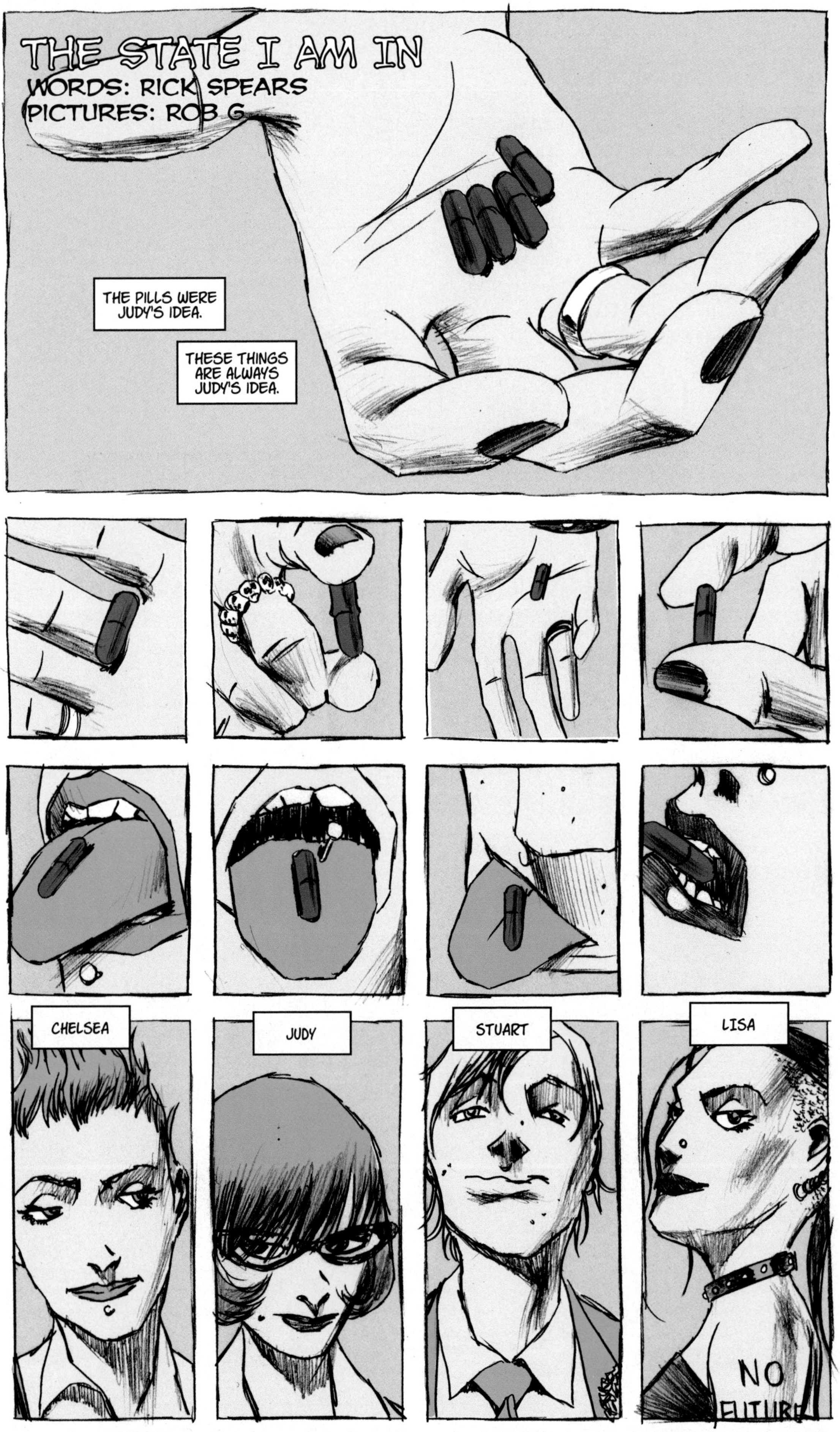

THE STATE I AM IN
WORDS: RICK SPEARS
PICTURES: ROB G
THE PILLS WERE JUDY'S IDEA.
THESE THINGS ARE ALWAYS JUDY'S IDEA.
CHELSEA
JUDY
STUART
LISA
NO FUTURE

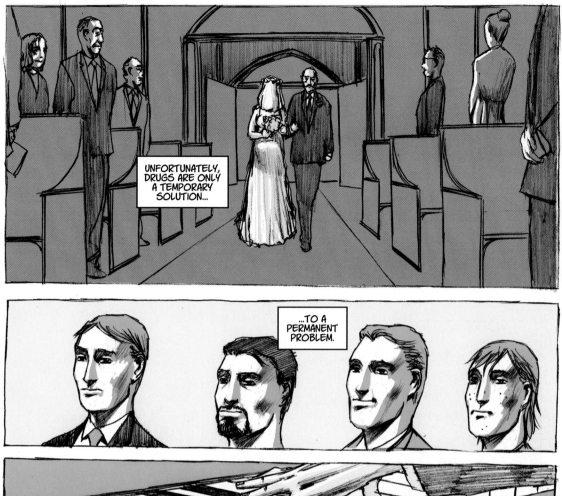

UNFORTUNATELY, DRUGS ARE ONLY A TEMPORARY SOLUTION...

...TO A PERMANENT PROBLEM.

MY SISTER'S WEDDING DAY.

LOOK AT HER... DYING FOR A CIGARETTE AND VICE.

SECOND MARRIAGE IN AS MANY YEARS.

AND A BIT OF OVERLAP IF I DO THE MATH RIGHT.

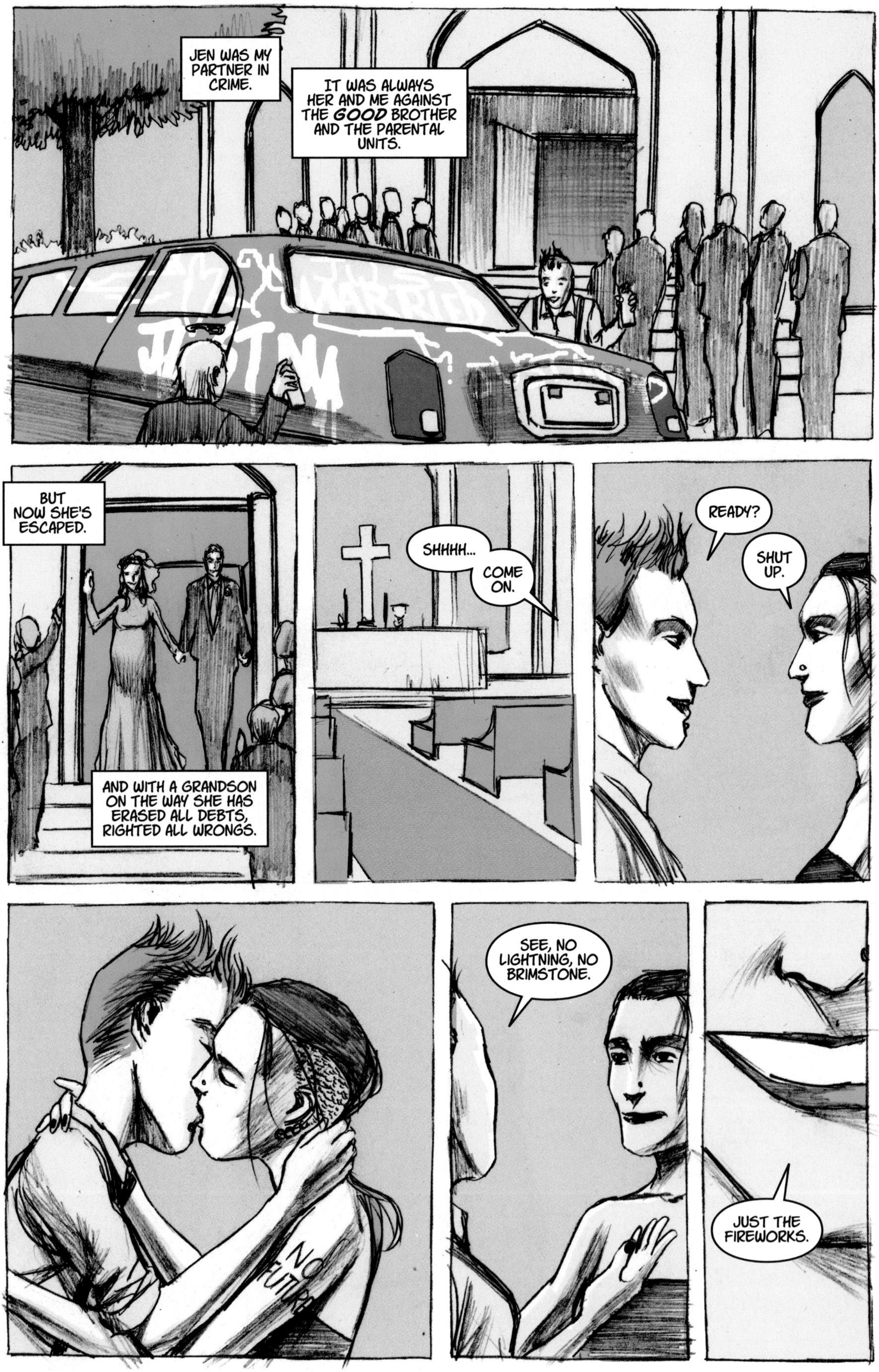
JEN WAS MY PARTNER IN CRIME.
IT WAS ALWAYS HER AND ME AGAINST THE GOOD BROTHER AND THE PARENTAL UNITS.
JUST MARRIED
BUT NOW SHE'S ESCAPED.
AND WITH A GRANDSON ON THE WAY SHE HAS ERASED ALL DEBTS, RIGHTED ALL WRONGS.
SHHHH...
COME ON.
READY?
SHUT UP.
SEE, NO LIGHTNING, NO BRIMSTONE.
JUST THE FIREWORKS.

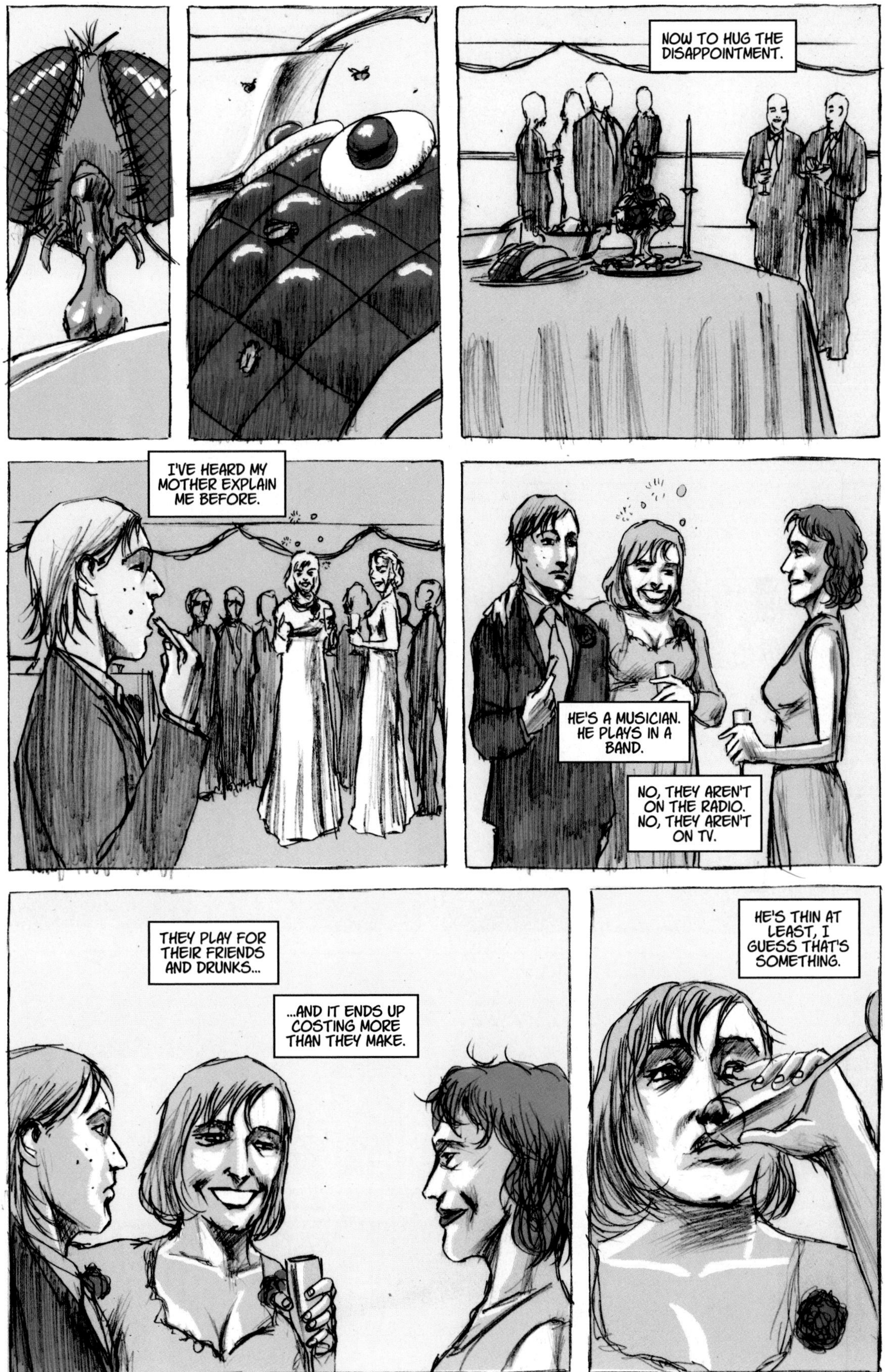
NOW TO HUG THE DISAPPOINTMENT.
I'VE HEARD MY MOTHER EXPLAIN ME BEFORE.
HE'S A MUSICIAN. HE PLAYS IN A BAND.
NO, THEY AREN'T ON THE RADIO. NO, THEY AREN'T ON TV.
THEY PLAY FOR THEIR FRIENDS AND DRUNKS...
...AND IT ENDS UP COSTING MORE THAN THEY MAKE.
HE'S THIN AT LEAST, I GUESS THAT'S SOMETHING.

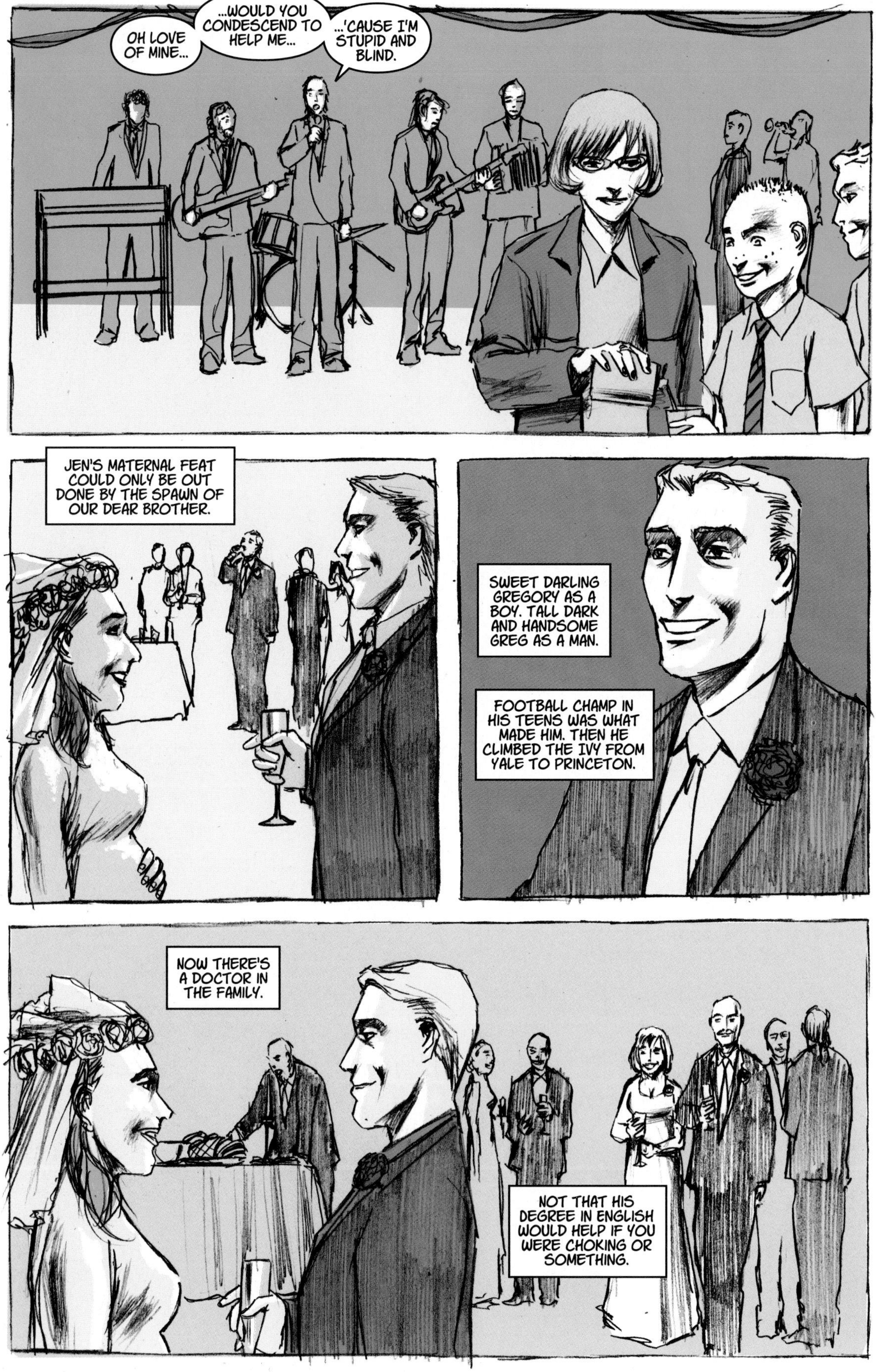
OH LOVE OF MINE...
...WOULD YOU CONDESCEND TO HELP ME...
...'CAUSE I'M STUPID AND BLIND.
JEN'S MATERNAL FEAT COULD ONLY BE OUT DONE BY THE SPAWN OF OUR DEAR BROTHER.
SWEET DARLING GREGORY AS A BOY. TALL DARK AND HANDSOME GREG AS A MAN.
FOOTBALL CHAMP IN HIS TEENS WAS WHAT MADE HIM. THEN HE CLIMBED THE IVY FROM YALE TO PRINCETON.
NOW THERE'S A DOCTOR IN THE FAMILY.
NOT THAT HIS DEGREE IN ENGLISH WOULD HELP IF YOU WERE CHOKING OR SOMETHING.

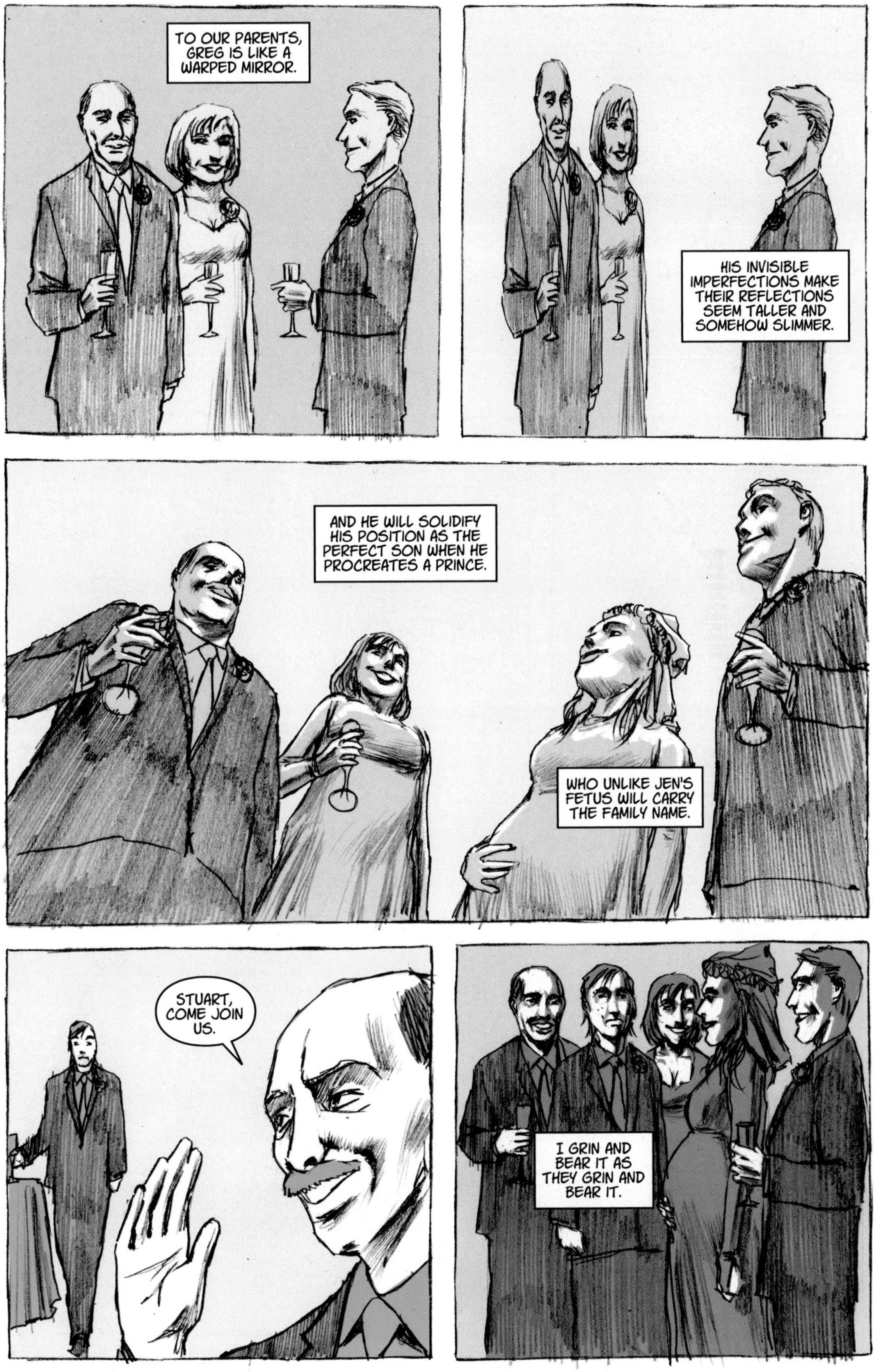
TO OUR PARENTS, GREG IS LIKE A WARPED MIRROR.
HIS INVISIBLE IMPERFECTIONS MAKE THEIR REFLECTIONS SEEM TALLER AND SOMEHOW SLIMMER.
AND HE WILL SOLIDIFY HIS POSITION AS THE PERFECT SON WHEN HE PROCREATES A PRINCE.
WHO UNLIKE JEN'S FETUS WILL CARRY THE FAMILY NAME.
STUART, COME JOIN US.
I GRIN AND BEAR IT AS THEY GRIN AND BEAR IT.

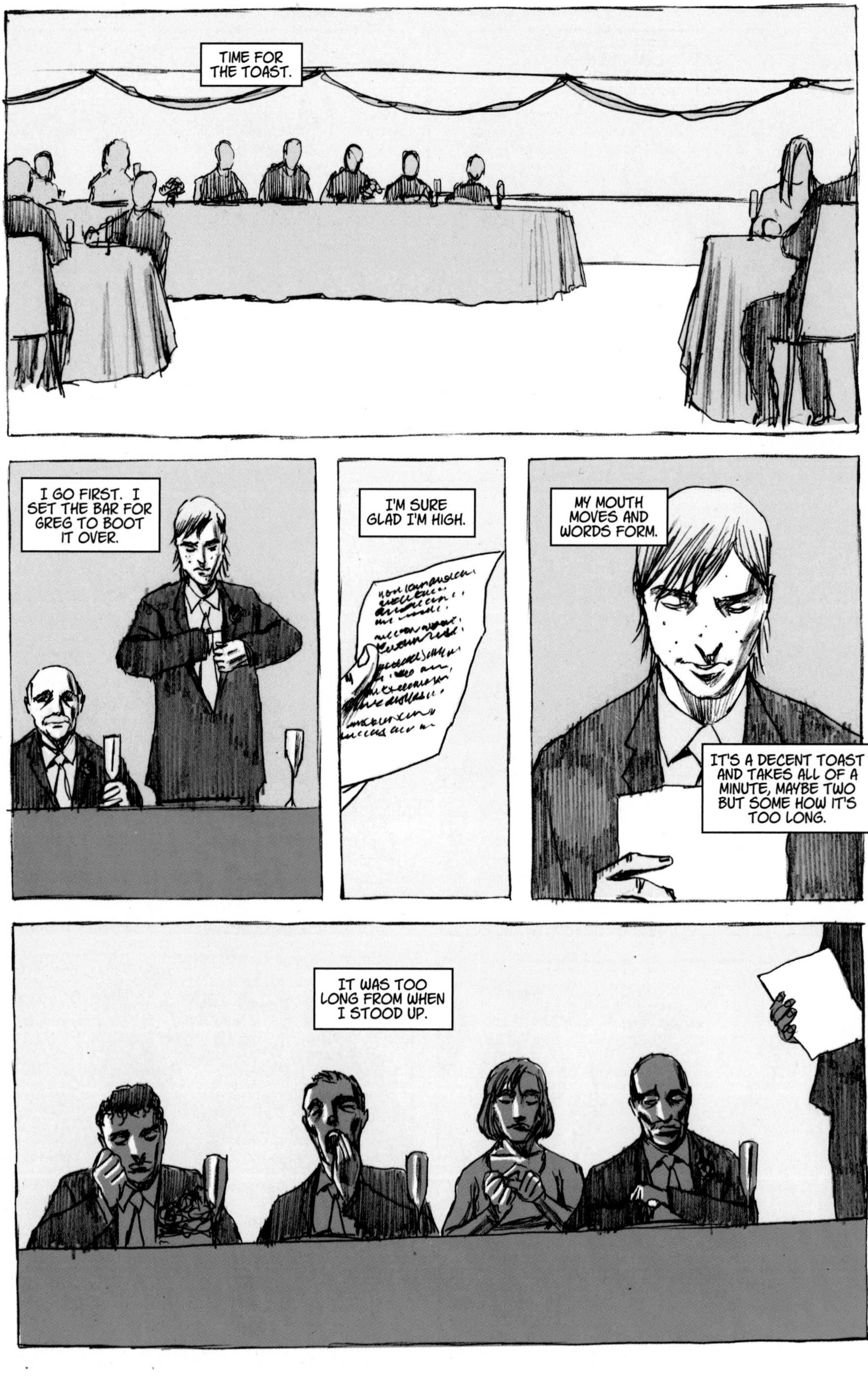
TIME FOR THE TOAST.
I GO FIRST. I SET THE BAR FOR GREG TO BOOT IT OVER.
I'M SURE GLAD I'M HIGH.
MY MOUTH MOVES AND WORDS FORM.
IT'S A DECENT TOAST AND TAKES ALL OF A MINUTE, MAYBE TWO BUT SOME HOW IT'S TOO LONG.
IT WAS TOO LONG FROM WHEN I STOOD UP.

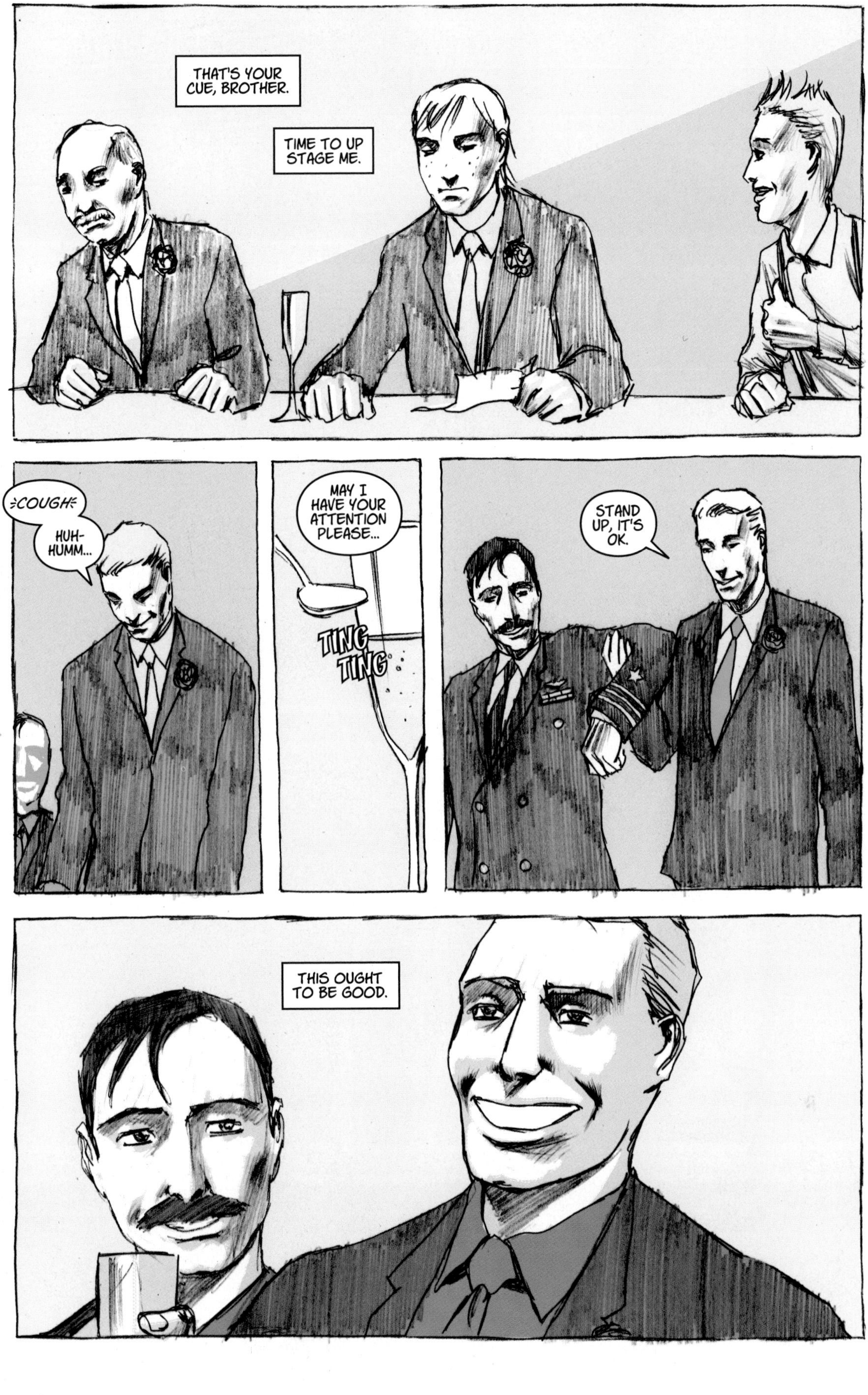
THAT'S YOUR CUE, BROTHER.
TIME TO UP STAGE ME.
COUGH
HUH-HUMM...
MAY I HAVE YOUR ATTENTION PLEASE...
TING TING
STAND UP, IT'S OK.
THIS OUGHT TO BE GOOD.

"Expectations"

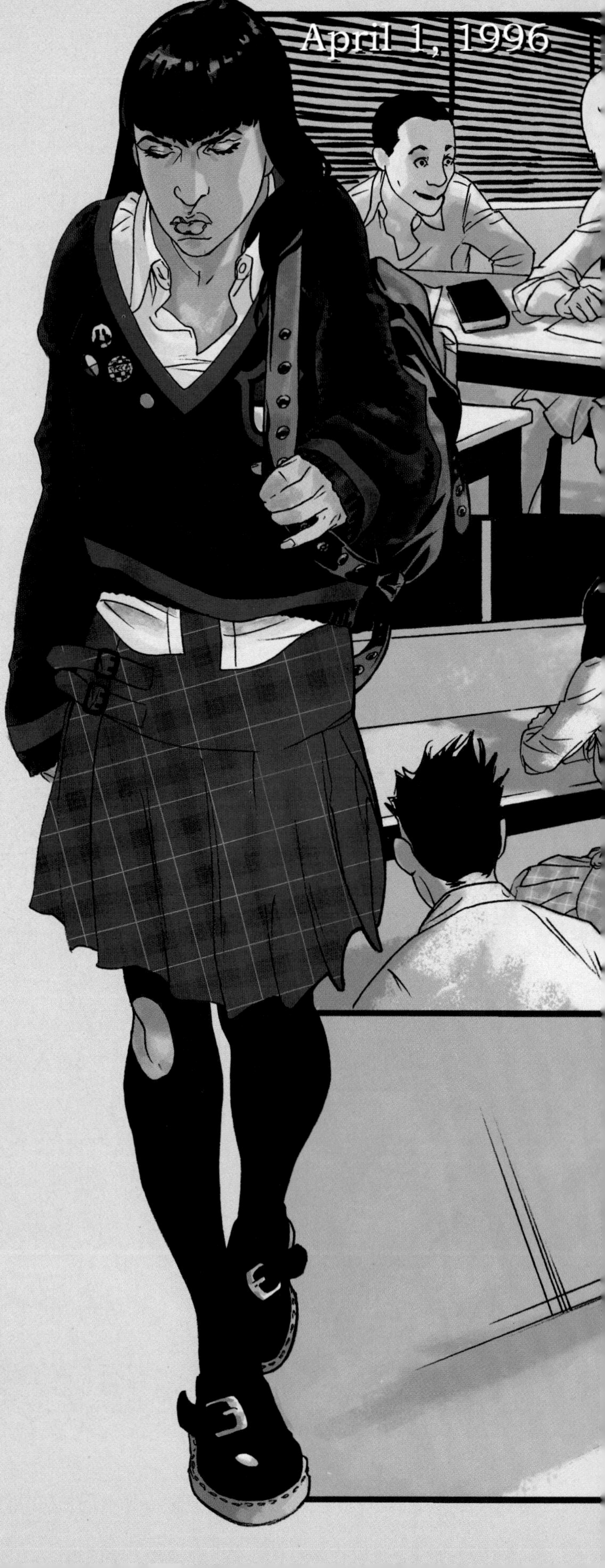
April 1, 1996

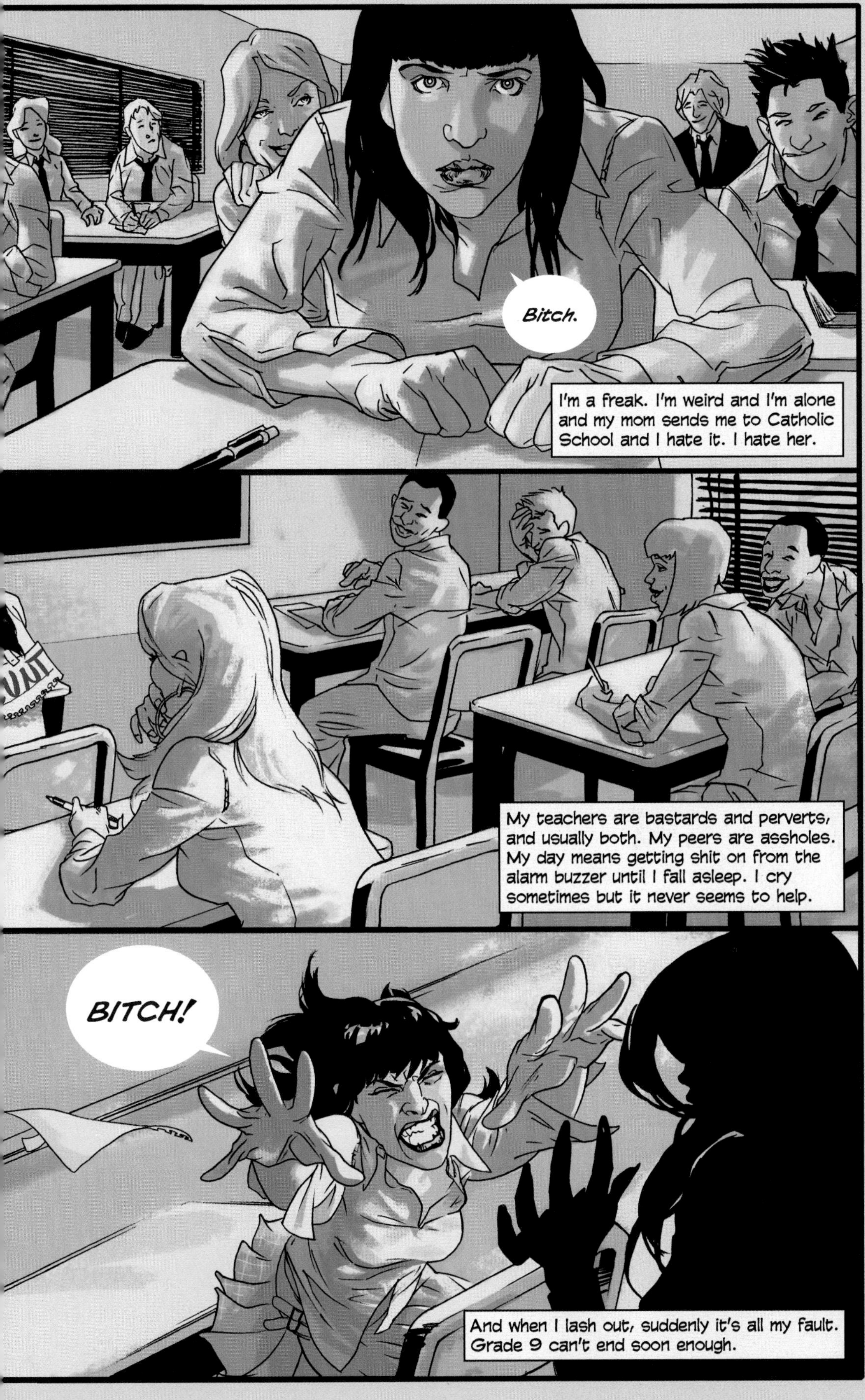
Bitch.
I'm a freak. I'm weird and I'm alone and my mom sends me to Catholic School and I hate it. I hate her.
My teachers are bastards and perverts, and usually both. My peers are assholes. My day means getting shit on from the alarm buzzer until I fall asleep. I cry sometimes but it never seems to help.
BITCH!
And when I lash out, suddenly it's all my fault. Grade 9 can't end soon enough.

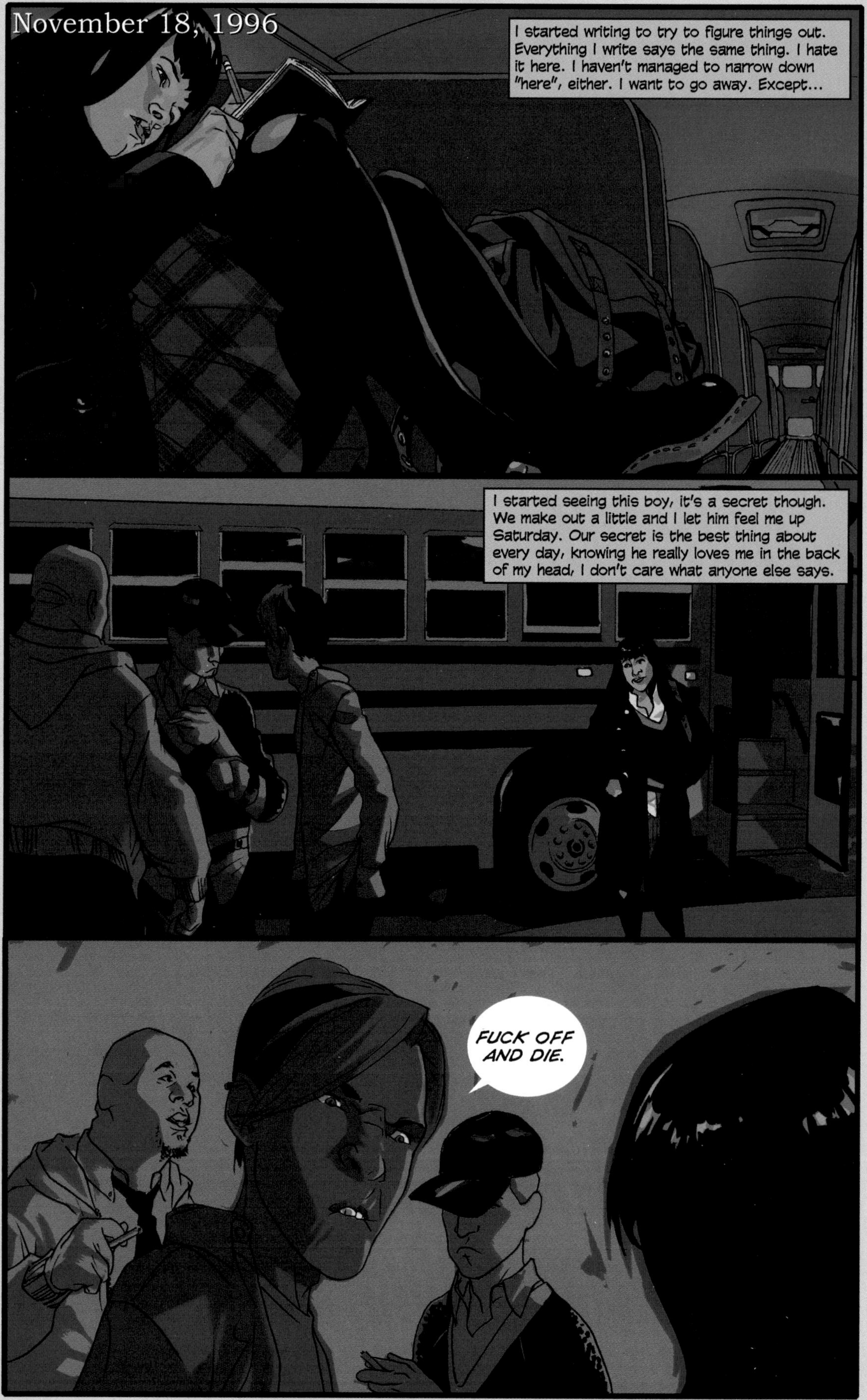
November 18, 1996
I started writing to try to figure things out. Everything I write says the same thing. I hate it here. I haven't managed to narrow down "here", either. I want to go away. Except...
I started seeing this boy, it's a secret though. We make out a little and I let him feel me up Saturday. Our secret is the best thing about every day, knowing he really loves me in the back of my head, I don't care what anyone else says.
FUCK OFF AND DIE.

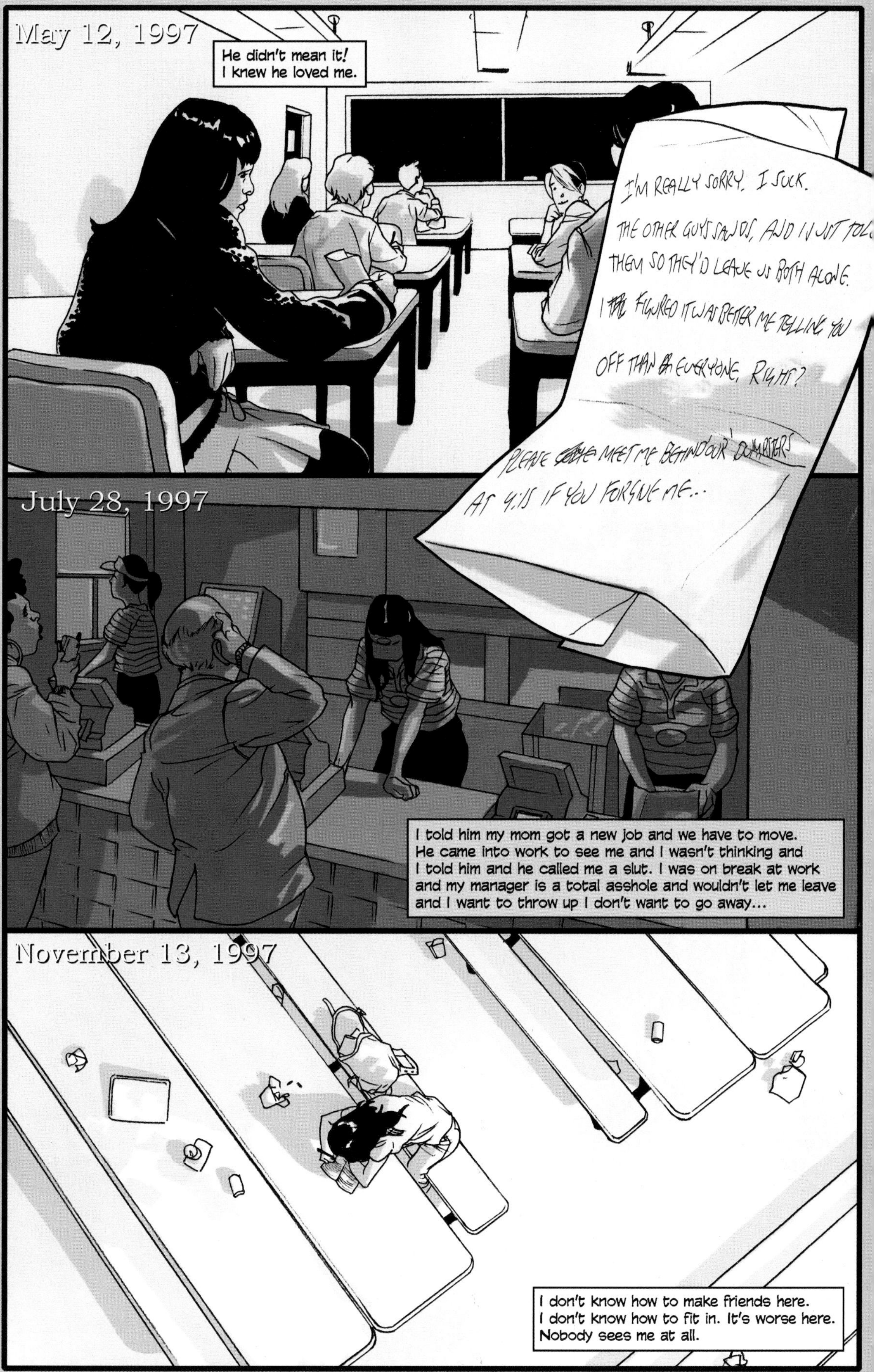
May 12, 1997
He didn't mean it! I knew he loved me.
I'M REALLY SORRY. I SUCK.
THE OTHER GUYS SAW US, AND I JUST TOL
THEM SO THEY'D LEAVE US BOTH ALONE.
I FIGURED IT WAS BETTER ME TELLING YOU
OFF THAN EVERYONE, RIGHT?
PLEASE MEET ME BEHIND OUR DUMPSTERS
AT 4:15 IF YOU FORGIVE ME...
July 28, 1997
I told him my mom got a new job and we have to move. He came into work to see me and I wasn't thinking and I told him and he called me a slut. I was on break at work and my manager is a total asshole and wouldn't let me leave and I want to throw up I don't want to go away...
November 13, 1997
I don't know how to make friends here. I don't know how to fit in. It's worse here. Nobody sees me at all.

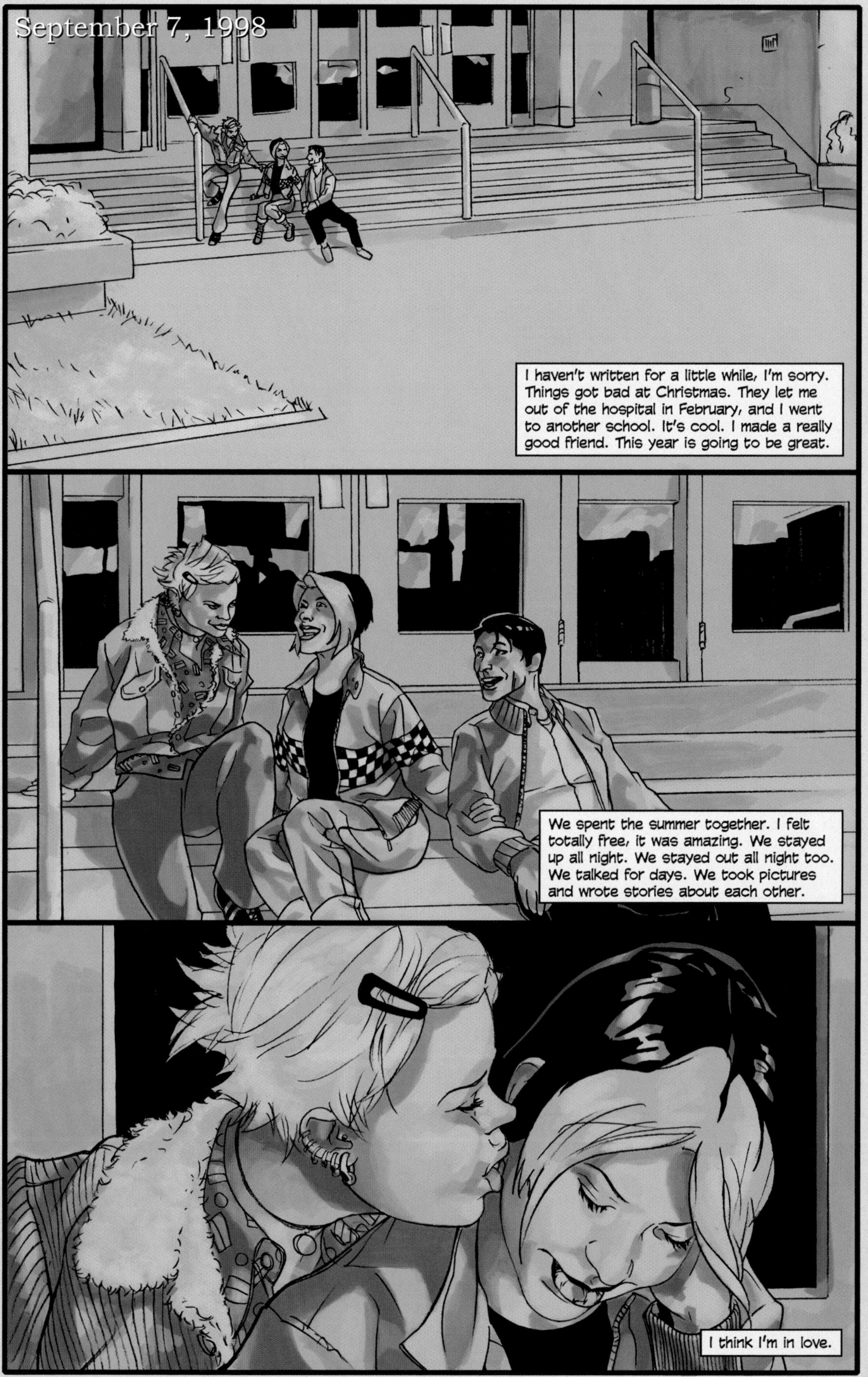

September 7, 1998
I haven't written for a little while, I'm sorry. Things got bad at Christmas. They let me out of the hospital in February, and I went to another school. It's cool. I made a really good friend. This year is going to be great.
We spent the summer together. I felt totally free, it was amazing. We stayed up all night. We stayed out all night too. We talked for days. We took pictures and wrote stories about each other.
I think I'm in love.

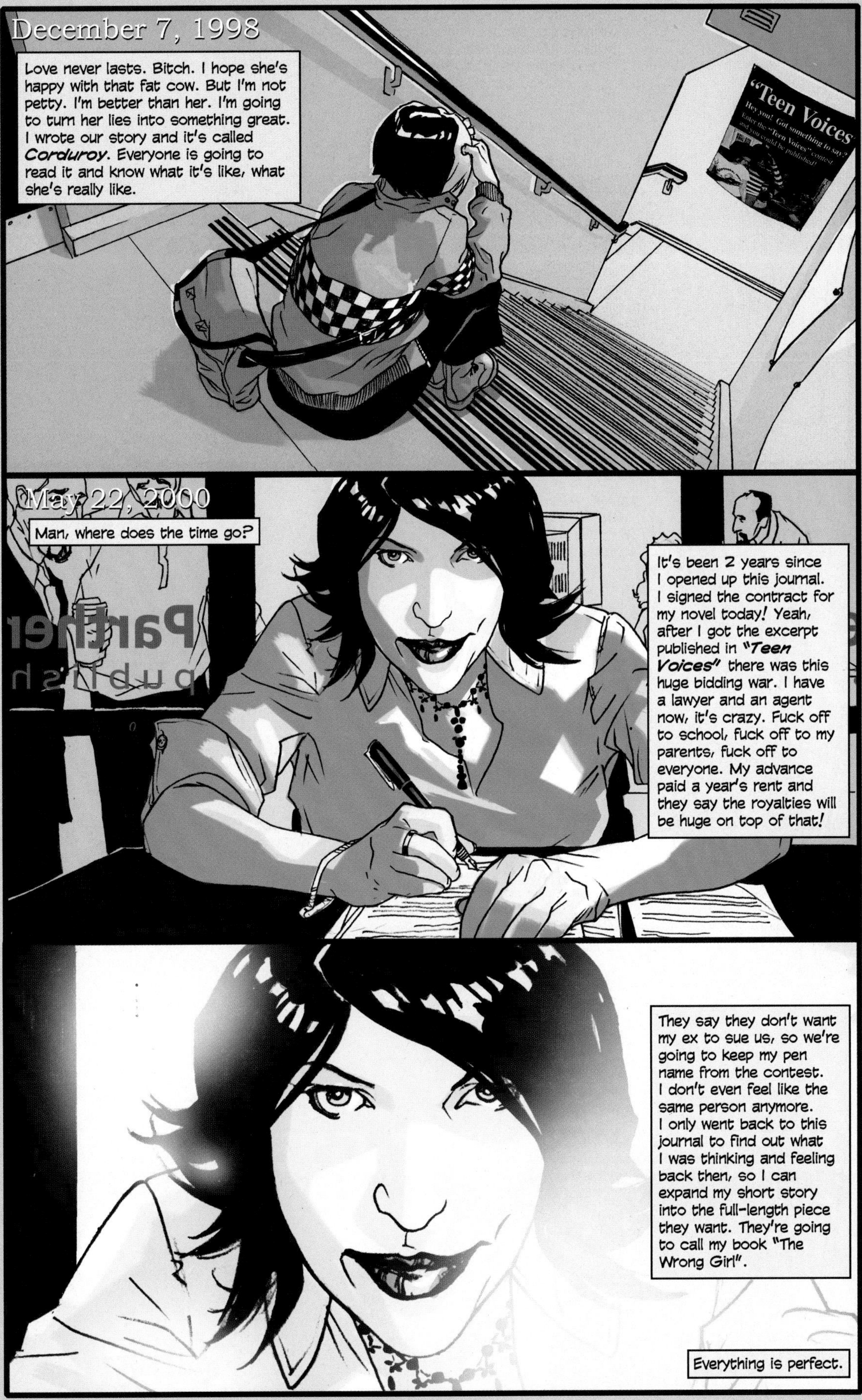
December 7, 1998
Love never lasts. Bitch. I hope she's happy with that fat cow. But I'm not petty. I'm better than her. I'm going to turn her lies into something great. I wrote our story and it's called *Corduroy*. Everyone is going to read it and know what it's like, what she's really like.
"Teen Voices"
Hey you! Got something to say?
Enter the "Teen Voices" contest and you could be published!
May 22, 2000
Man, where does the time go?
It's been 2 years since I opened up this journal. I signed the contract for my novel today! Yeah, after I got the excerpt published in *"Teen Voices"* there was this huge bidding war. I have a lawyer and an agent now, it's crazy. Fuck off to school, fuck off to my parents, fuck off to everyone. My advance paid a year's rent and they say the royalties will be huge on top of that!
They say they don't want my ex to sue us, so we're going to keep my pen name from the contest. I don't even feel like the same person anymore. I only went back to this journal to find out what I was thinking and feeling back then, so I can expand my short story into the full-length piece they want. They're going to call my book "The Wrong Girl".
Everything is perfect.

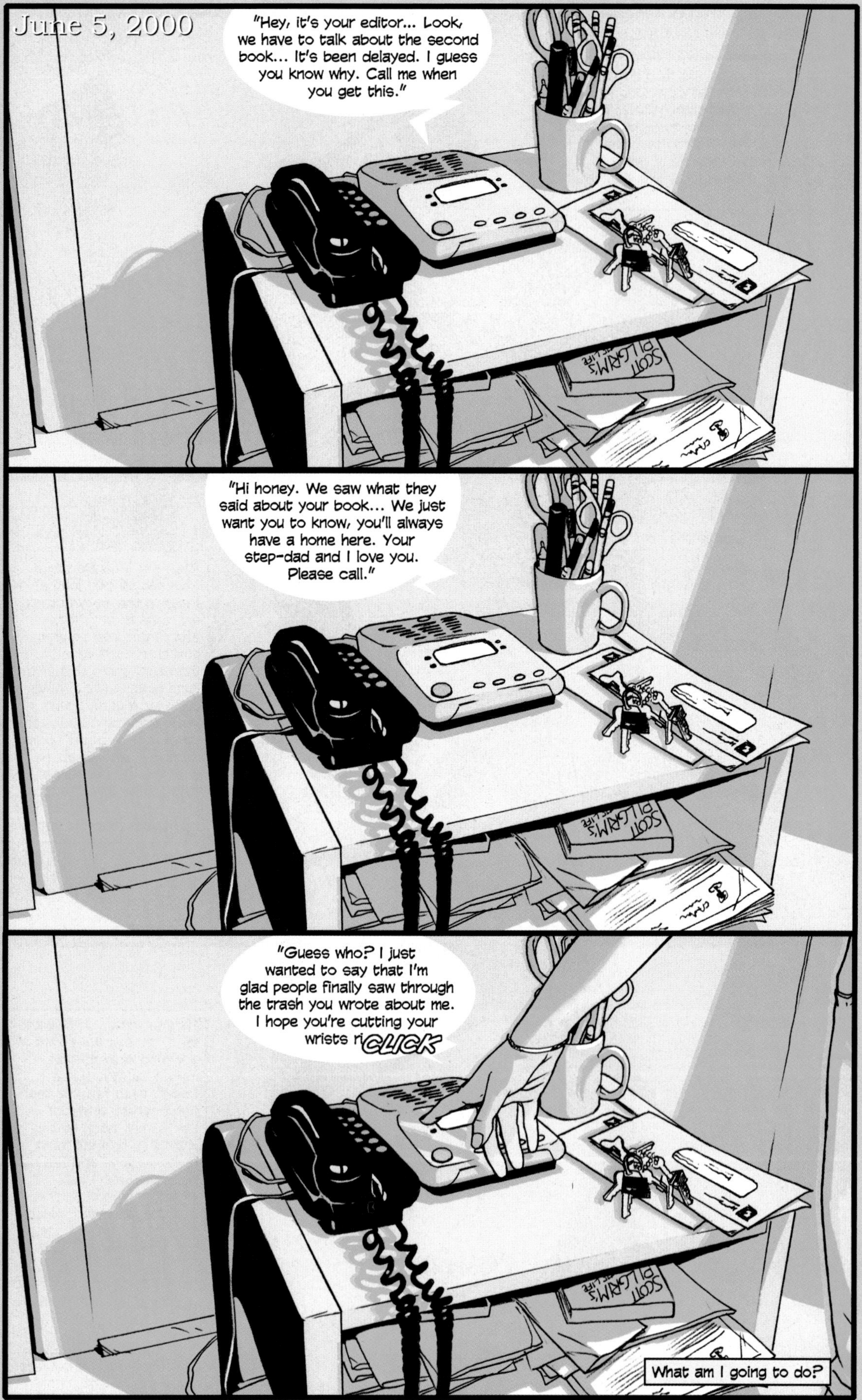

June 5, 2000
"Hey, it's your editor... Look, we have to talk about the second book... It's been delayed. I guess you know why. Call me when you get this."
"Hi honey. We saw what they said about your book... We just want you to know, you'll always have a home here. Your step-dad and I love you. Please call."
"Guess who? I just wanted to say that I'm glad people finally saw through the trash you wrote about me. I hope you're cutting your wrists ri
CLICK
What am I going to do?

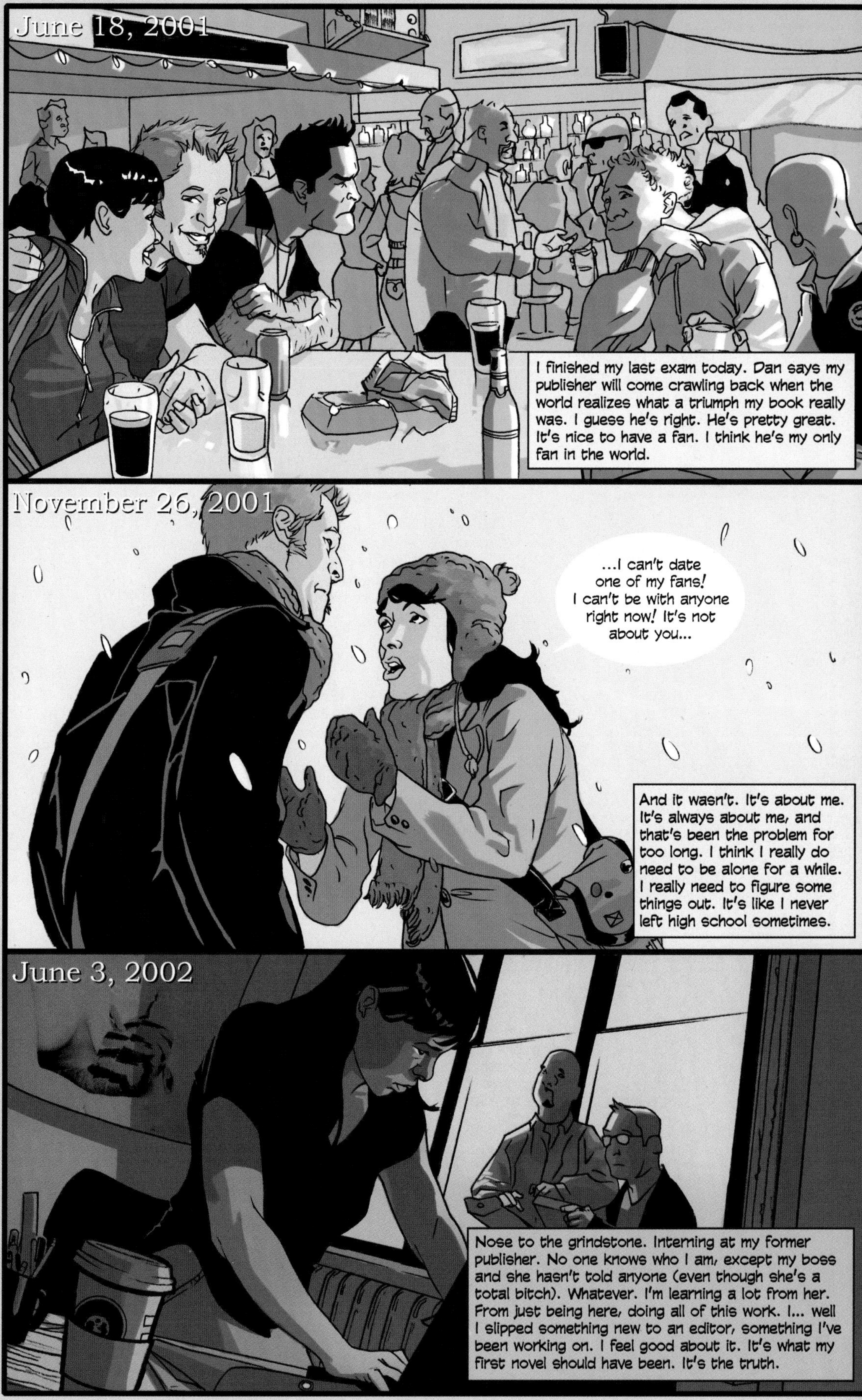
June 18, 2001
I finished my last exam today. Dan says my publisher will come crawling back when the world realizes what a triumph my book really was. I guess he's right. He's pretty great. It's nice to have a fan. I think he's my only fan in the world.
November 26, 2001
...I can't date one of my fans! I can't be with anyone right now! It's not about you...
And it wasn't. It's about me. It's always about me, and that's been the problem for too long. I think I really do need to be alone for a while. I really need to figure some things out. It's like I never left high school sometimes.
June 3, 2002
Nose to the grindstone. Interning at my former publisher. No one knows who I am, except my boss and she hasn't told anyone (even though she's a total bitch). Whatever. I'm learning a lot from her. From just being here, doing all of this work. I... well I slipped something new to an editor, something I've been working on. I feel good about it. It's what my first novel should have been. It's the truth.

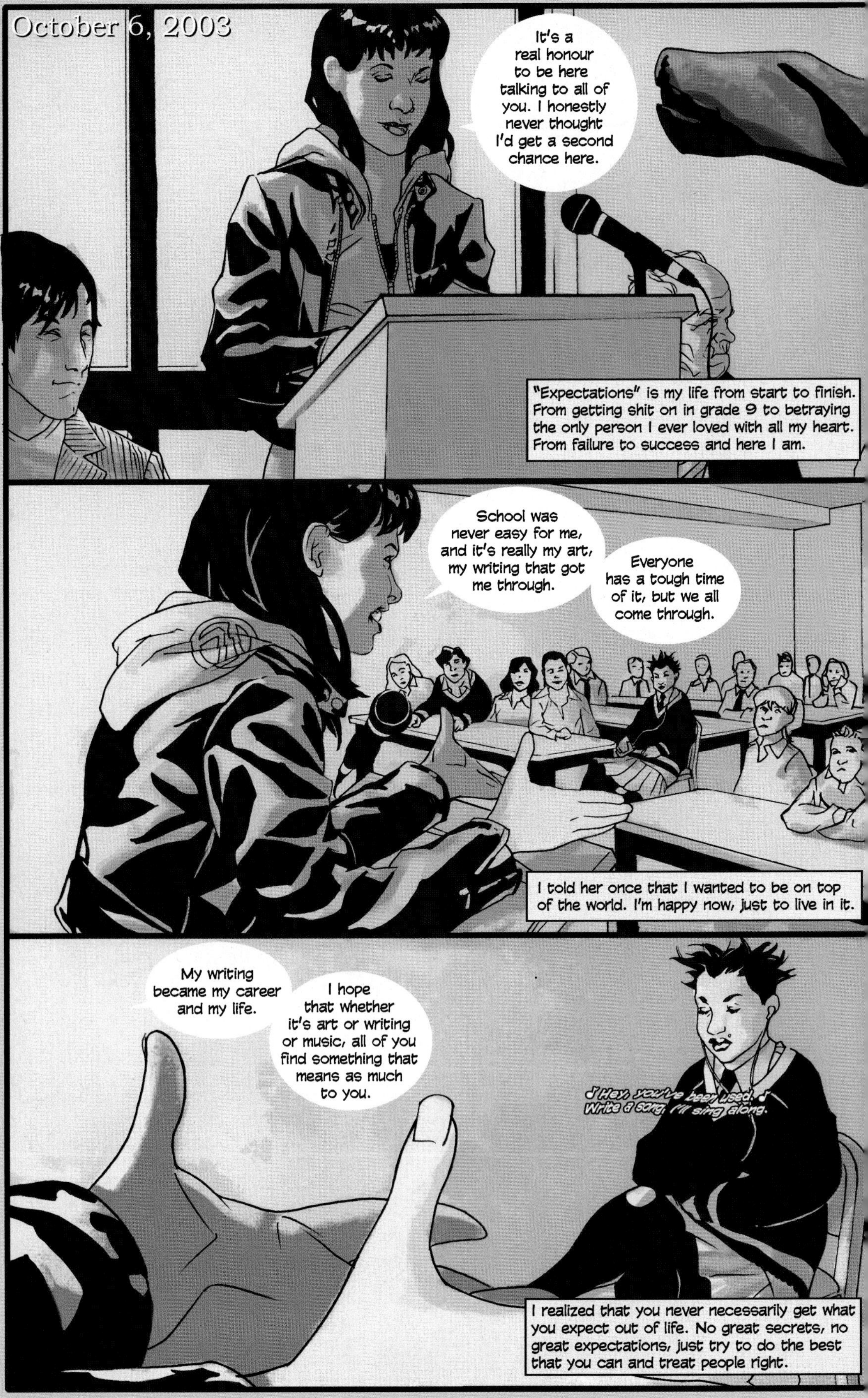
October 6, 2003
It's a real honour to be here talking to all of you. I honestly never thought I'd get a second chance here.
"Expectations" is my life from start to finish. From getting shit on in grade 9 to betraying the only person I ever loved with all my heart. From failure to success and here I am.
School was never easy for me, and it's really my art, my writing that got me through.
Everyone has a tough time of it, but we all come through.
I told her once that I wanted to be on top of the world. I'm happy now, just to live in it.
My writing became my career and my life.
I hope that whether it's art or writing or music, all of you find something that means as much to you.
♪Hey, you've been used. ♪ Write a song, I'll sing along.
I realized that you never necessarily get what you expect out of life. No great secrets, no great expectations, just try to do the best that you can and treat people right.

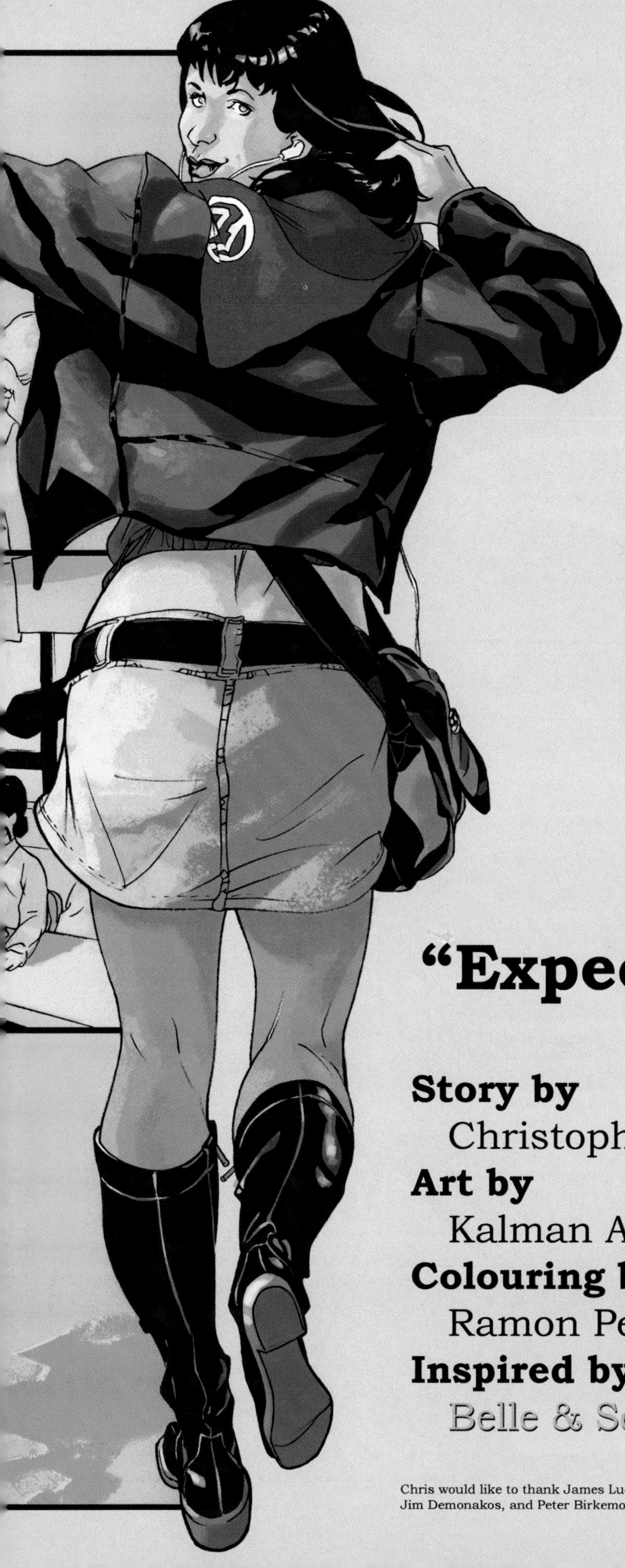

“Expectations”

Story by
Christopher Butcher
Art by
Kalman Andrasofszky
Colouring by
Ramon Perez
Inspired by
Belle & Sebastian

Chris would like to thank James Lucas Jones, Hope Larson, Eric Stephenson, Jim Demonakos, and Peter Birkemoe for their help.

I Could Be Dreaming

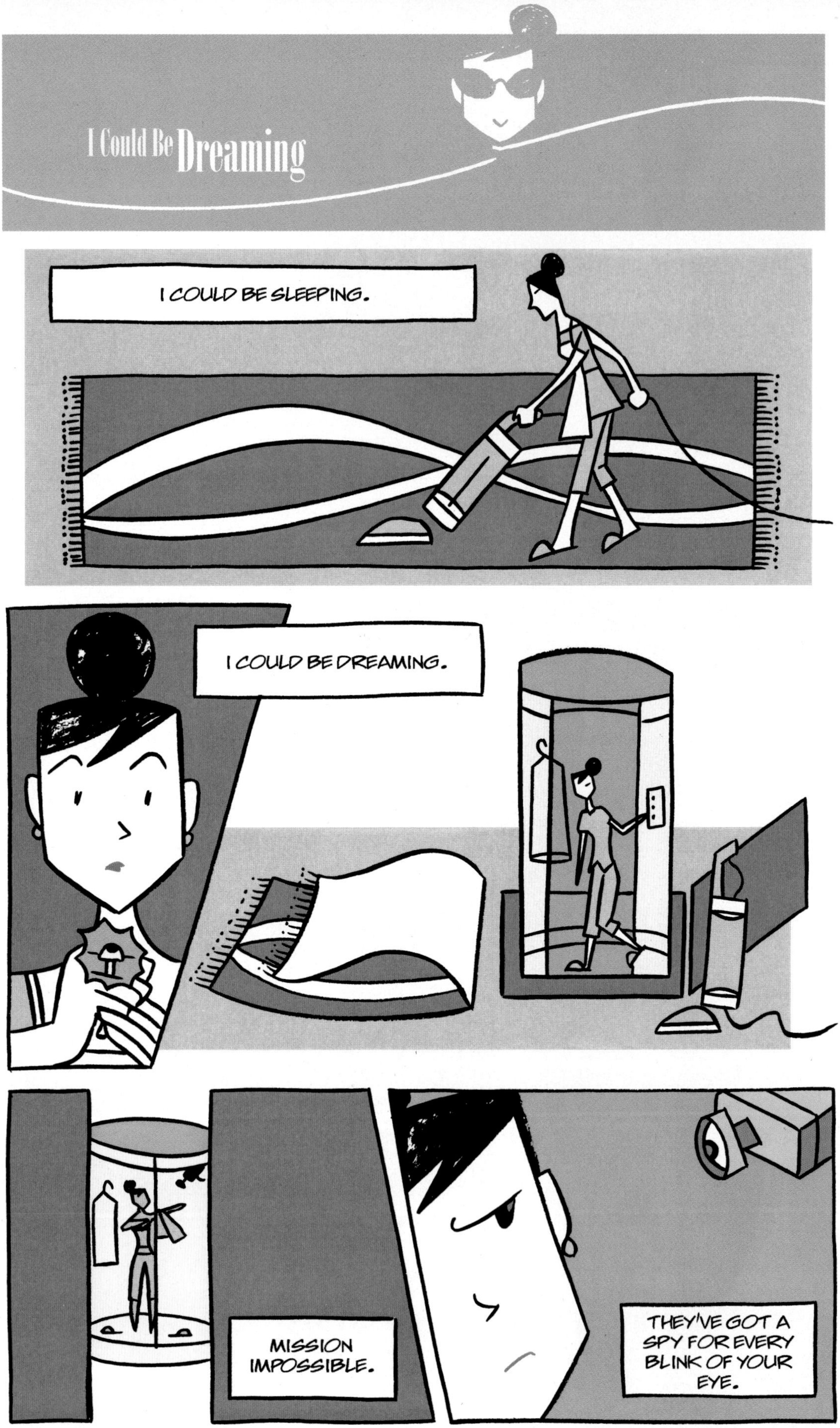

I COULD BE SLEEPING.
I COULD BE DREAMING.
MISSION IMPOSSIBLE.
THEY'VE GOT A SPY FOR EVERY BLINK OF YOUR EYE.

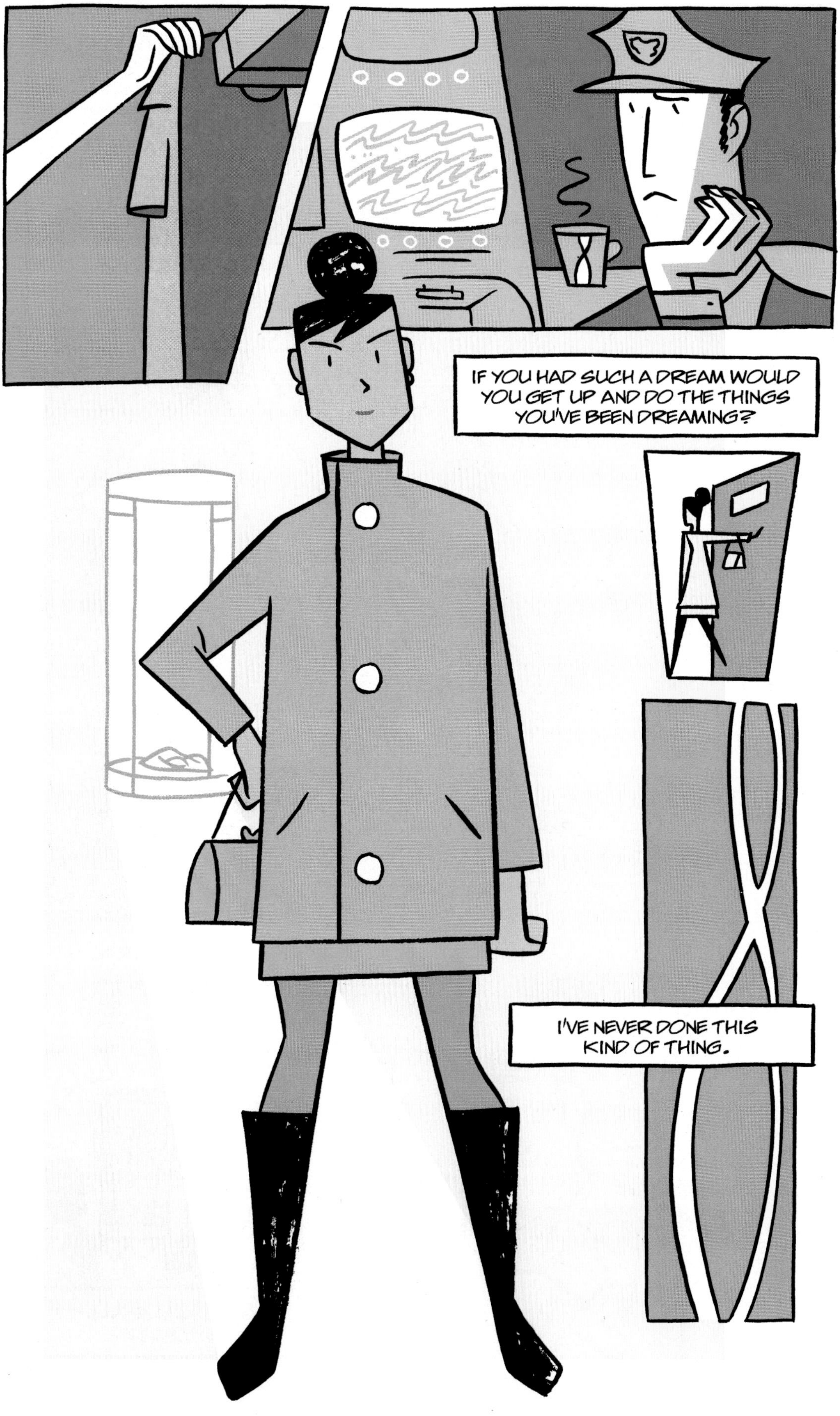
IF YOU HAD SUCH A DREAM WOULD YOU GET UP AND DO THE THINGS YOU'VE BEEN DREAMING?
I'VE NEVER DONE THIS KIND OF THING.

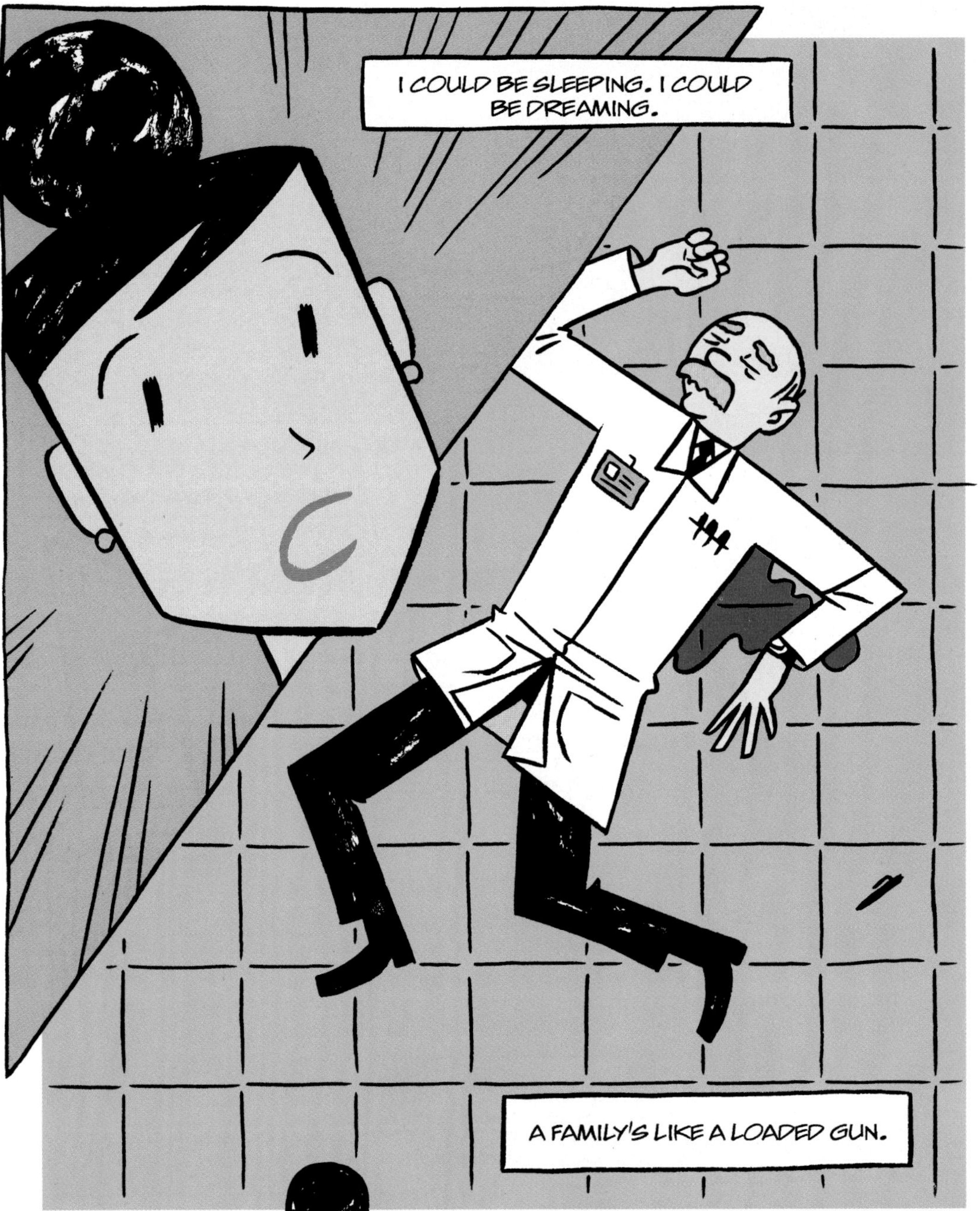
I COULD BE SLEEPING. I COULD BE DREAMING.
A FAMILY'S LIKE A LOADED GUN.

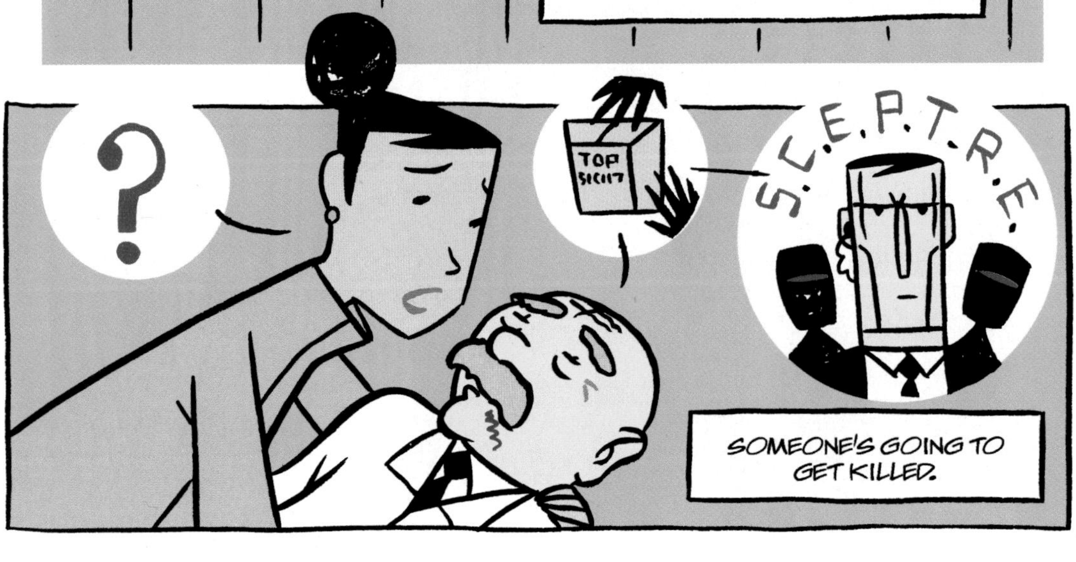
?
TOP SECRET
S.C.E.P.T.R.E.
SOMEONE'S GOING TO GET KILLED.

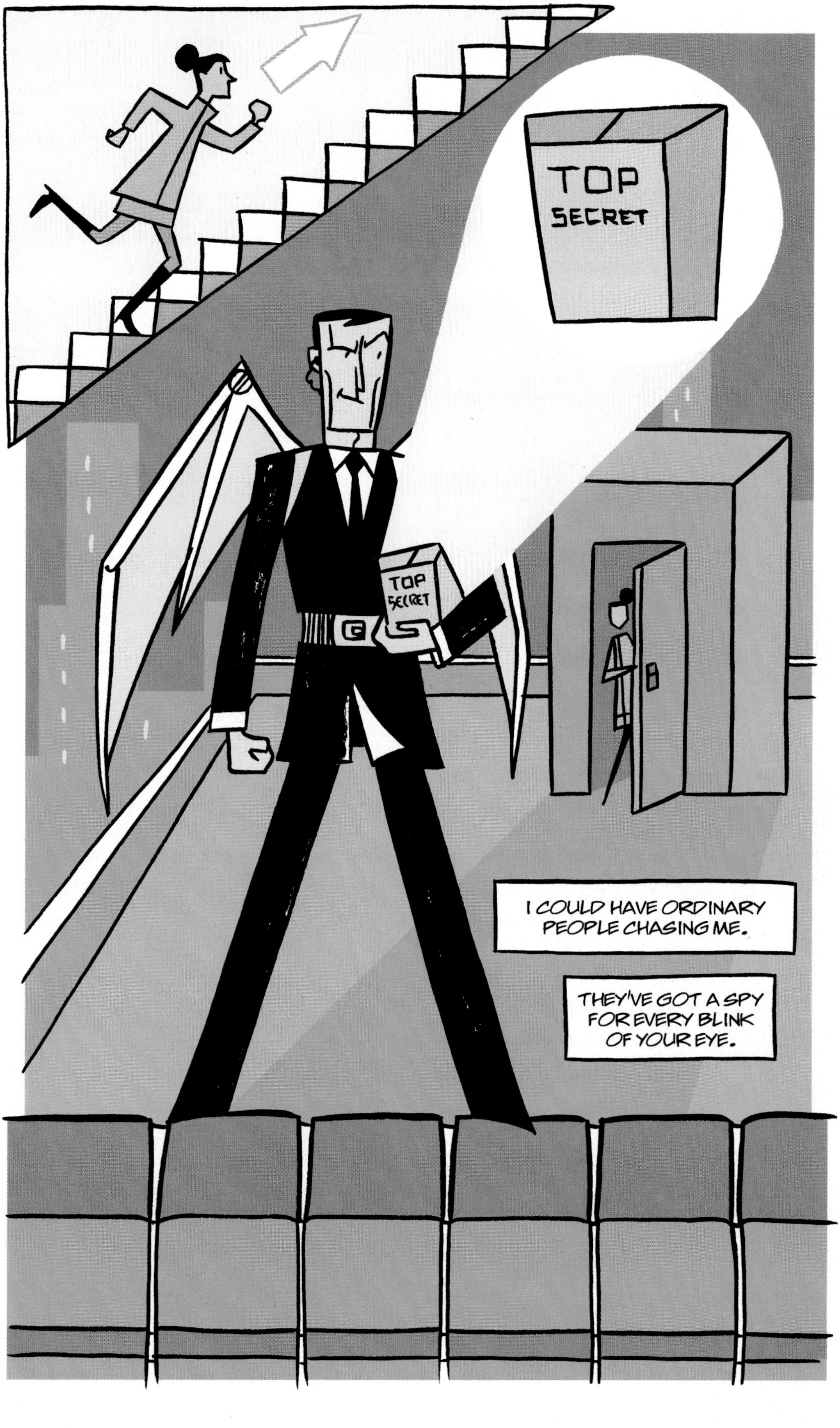
TOP SECRET
TOP SECRET
I COULD HAVE ORDINARY PEOPLE CHASING ME.
THEY'VE GOT A SPY FOR EVERY BLINK OF YOUR EYE.

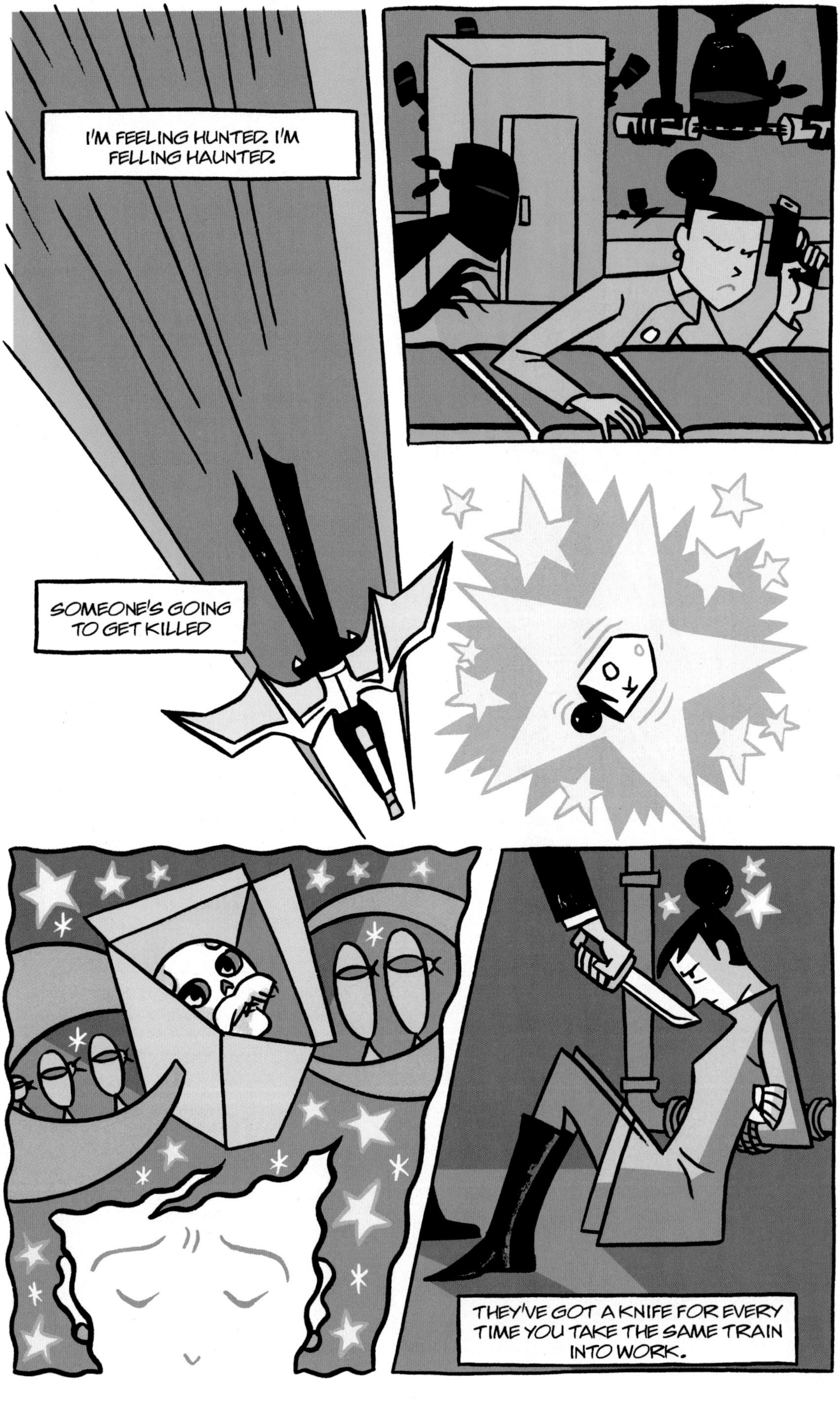
I'M FEELING HUNTED. I'M FELLING HAUNTED.
SOMEONE'S GOING TO GET KILLED
OK
THEY'VE GOT A KNIFE FOR EVERY TIME YOU TAKE THE SAME TRAIN INTO WORK.

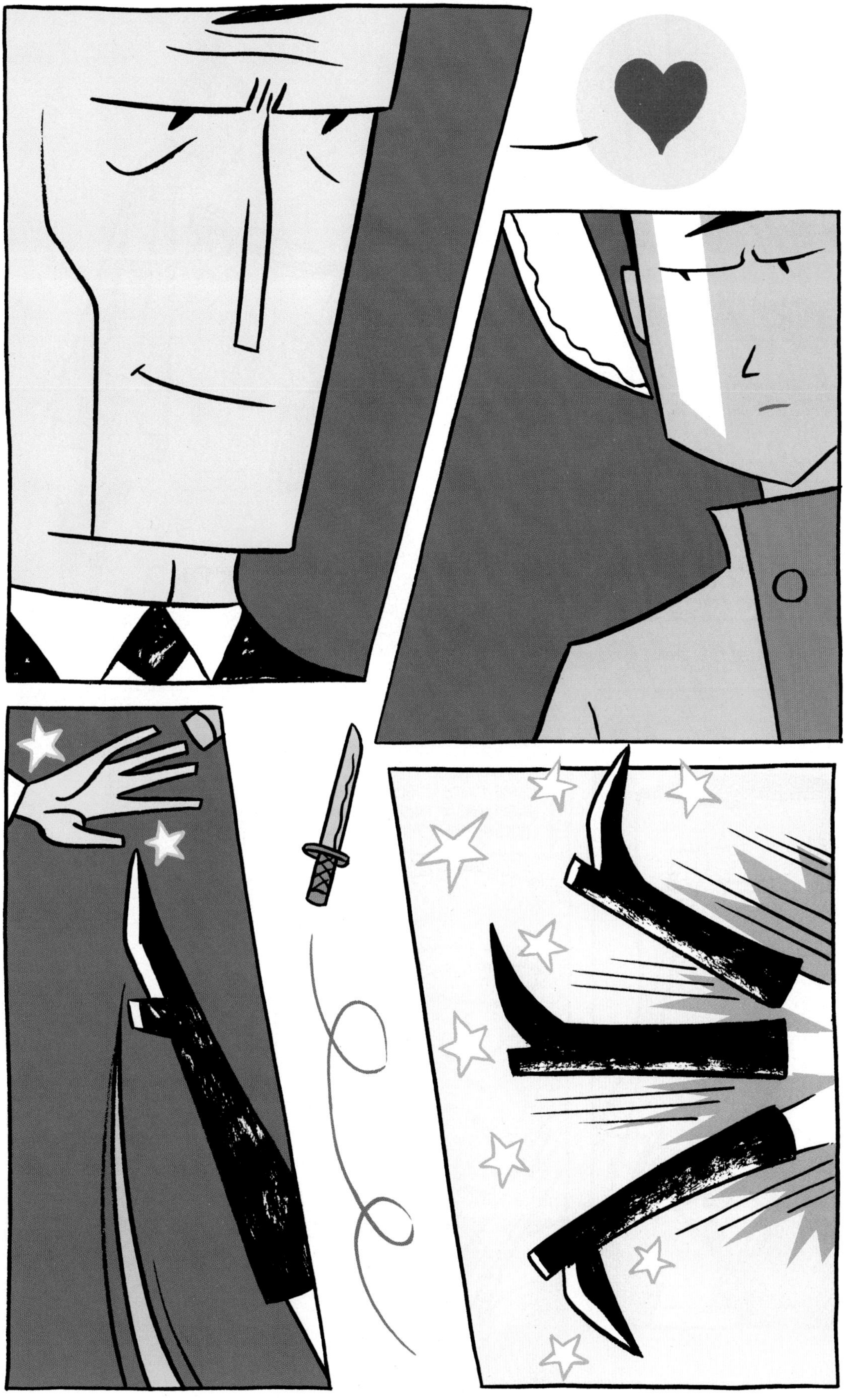

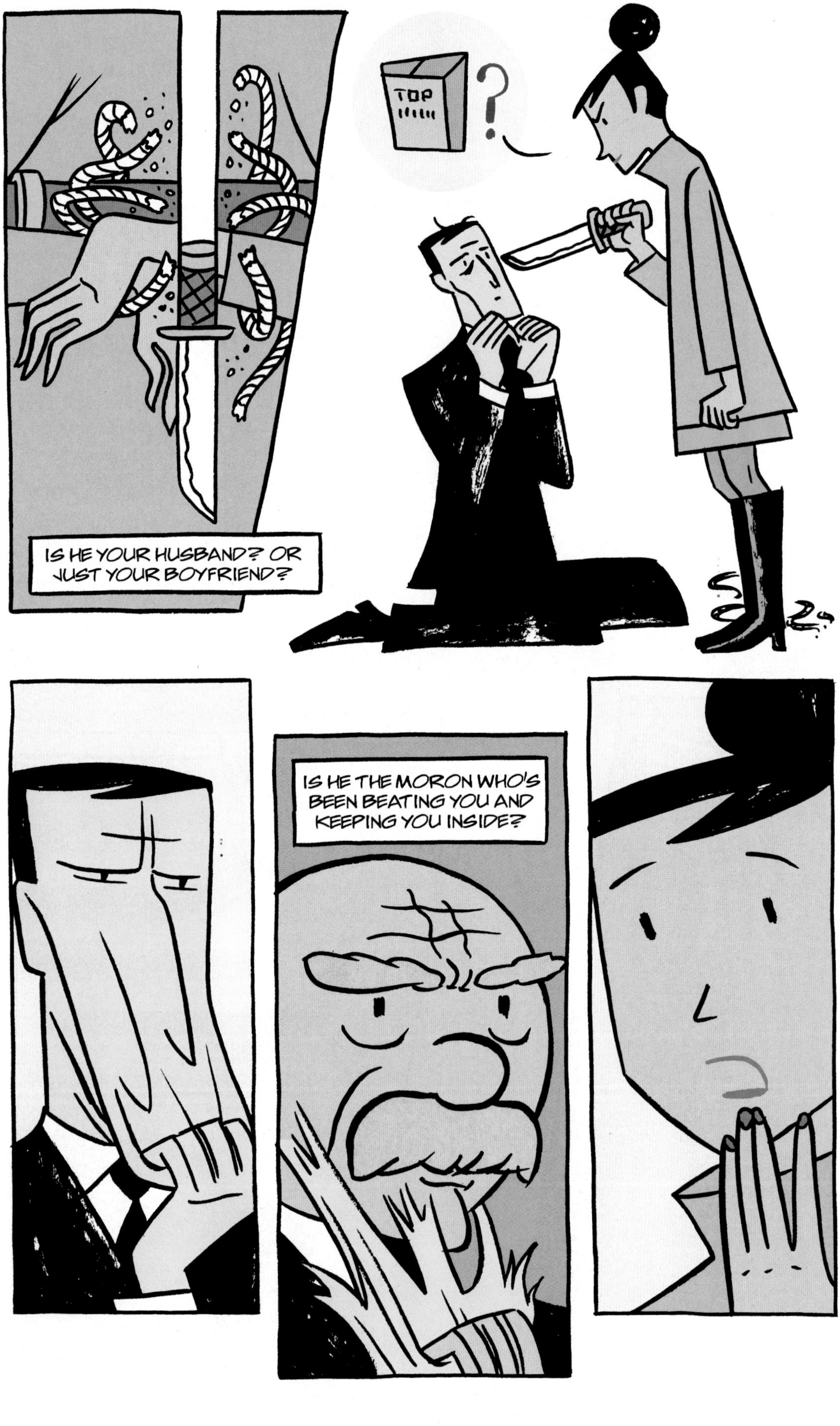
TOP
IS HE YOUR HUSBAND? OR JUST YOUR BOYFRIEND?
IS HE THE MORON WHO'S BEEN BEATING YOU AND KEEPING YOU INSIDE?

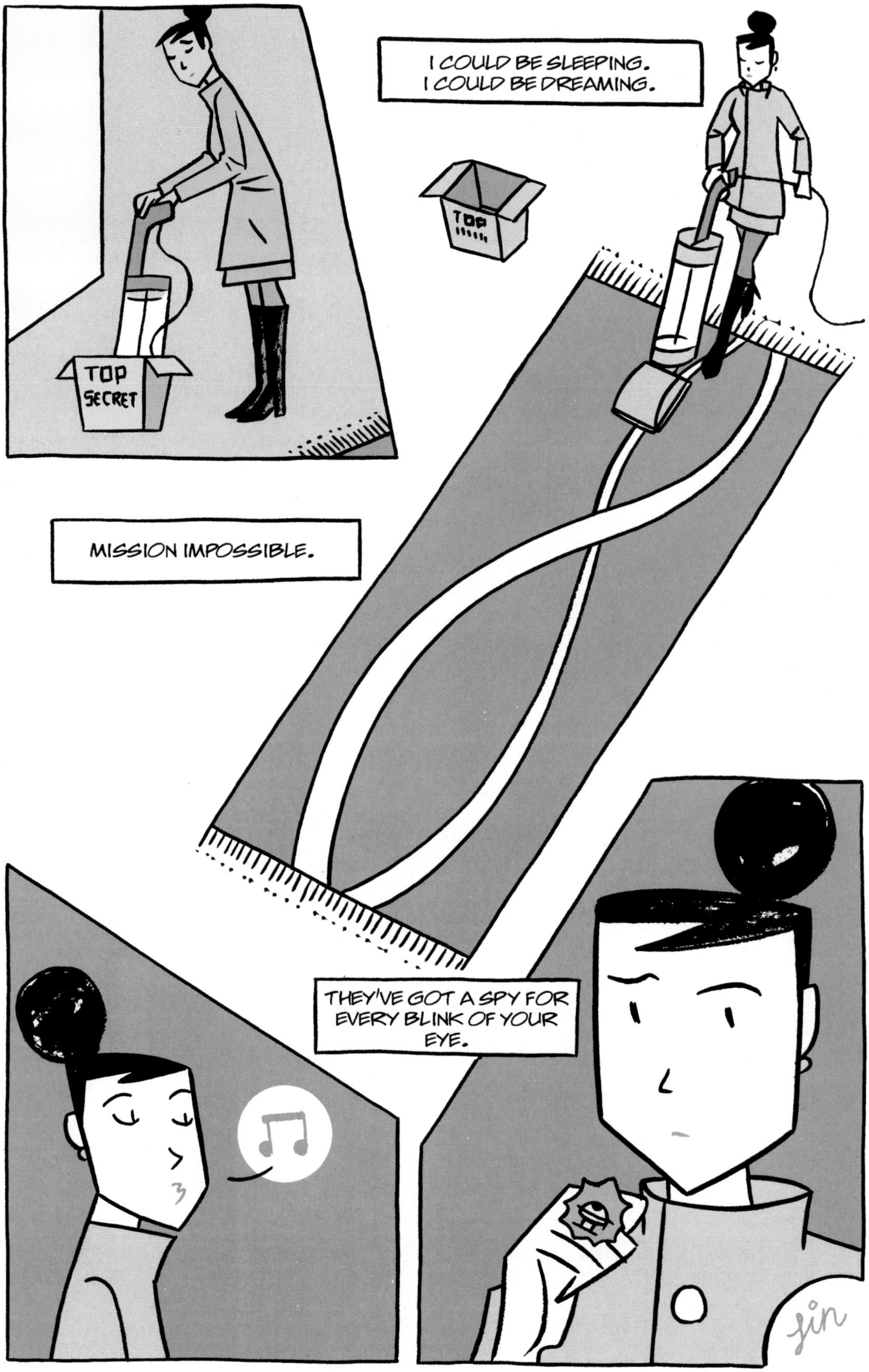
TOP
SECRET
I COULD BE SLEEPING.
I COULD BE DREAMING.
TOP
MISSION IMPOSSIBLE.
THEY'VE GOT A SPY FOR EVERY BLINK OF YOUR EYE.
Jin

words Belle & Sebastian pictures Andi Watson

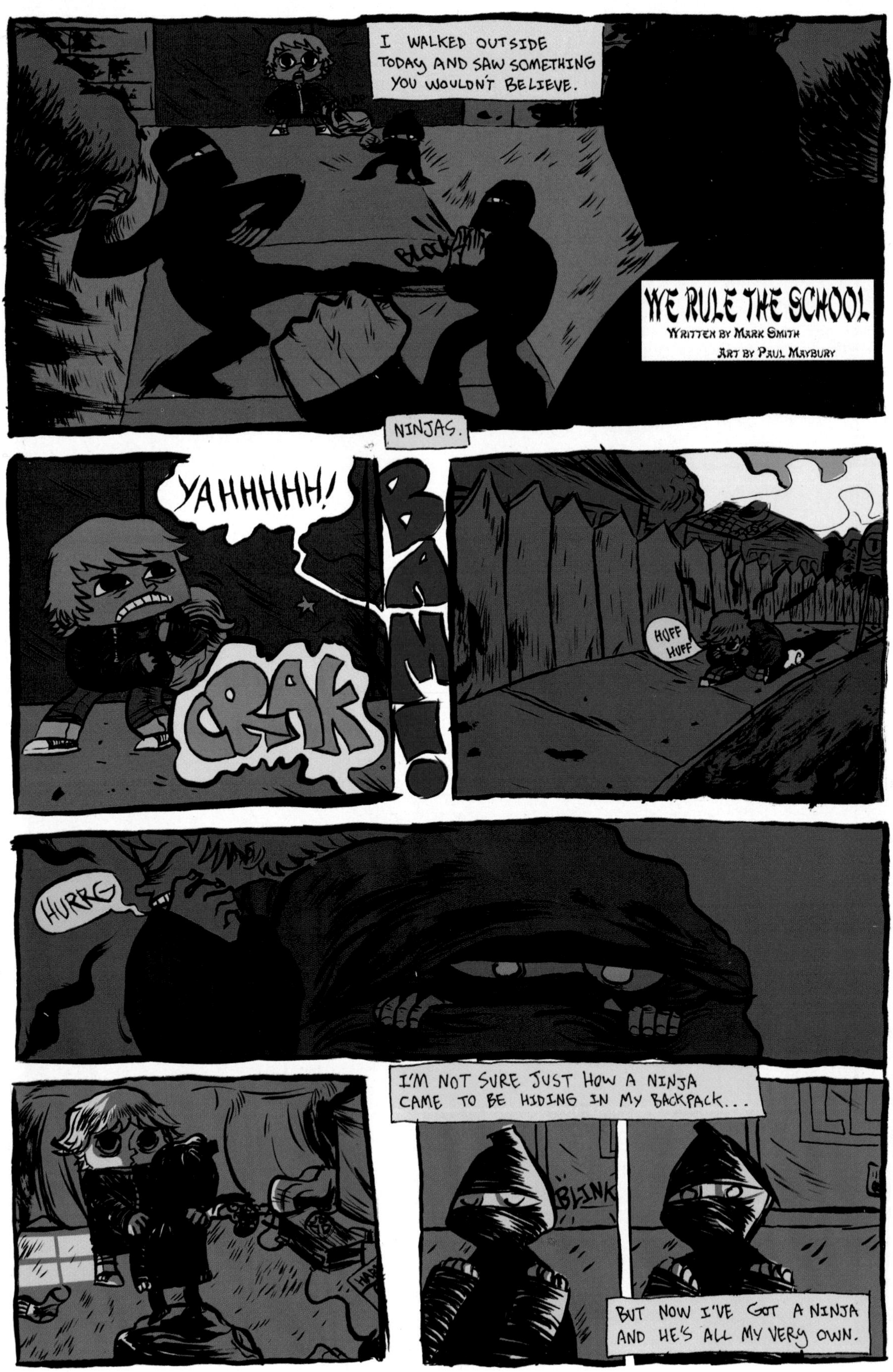
I WALKED OUTSIDE TODAY AND SAW SOMETHING YOU WOULDN'T BELIEVE.
BLOCK
WE RULE THE SCHOOL
WRITTEN BY MARK SMITH
ART BY PAUL MAYBURY
NINJAS.
YAHHHHH!
CRAK
BAM!
HUFF HUFF
HURRG
I'M NOT SURE JUST HOW A NINJA CAME TO BE HIDING IN MY BACKPACK...
BLINK
BUT NOW I'VE GOT A NINJA AND HE'S ALL MY VERY OWN.

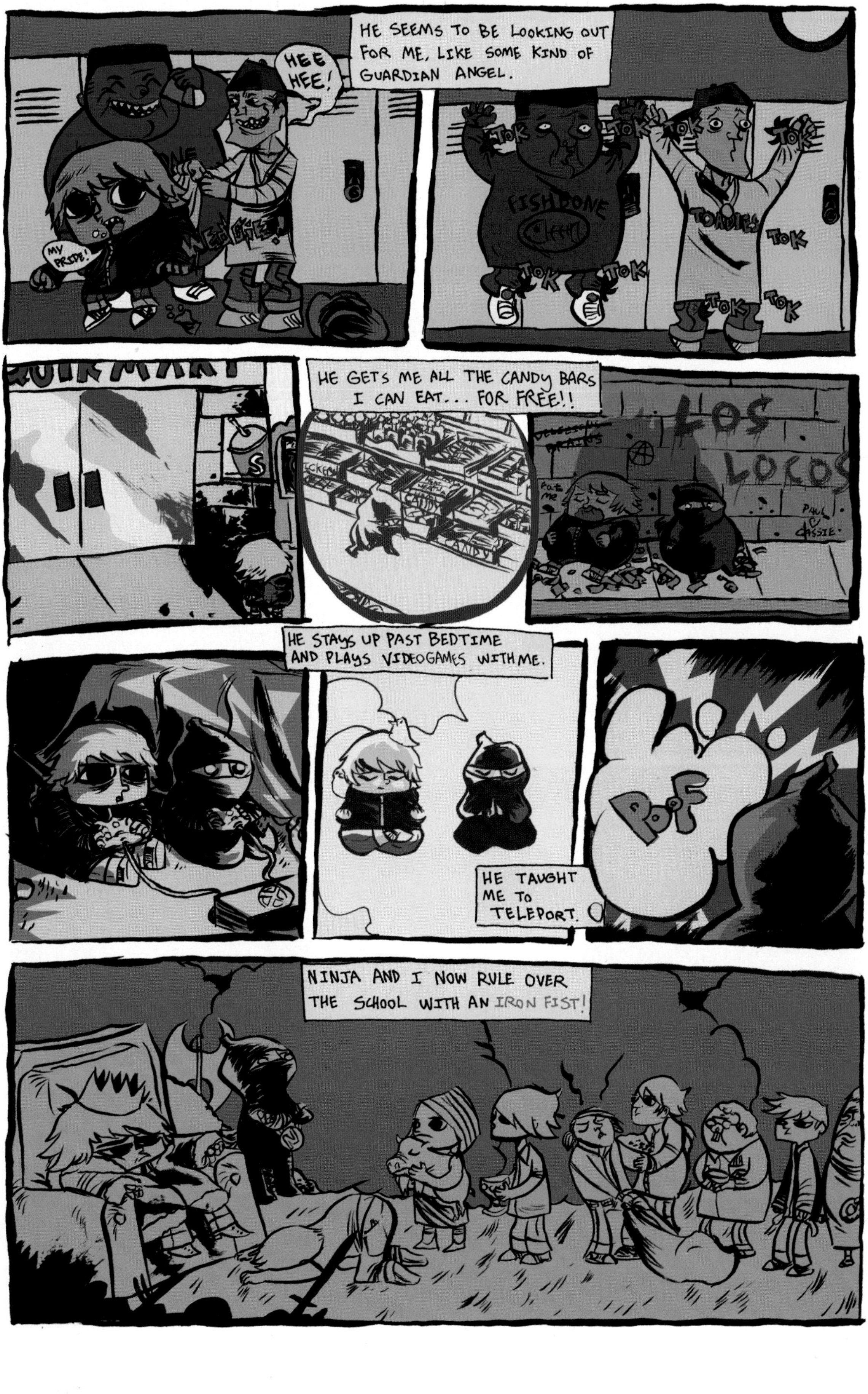
HEE HEE!
WEDGIE!
MY PRIDE!
HE SEEMS TO BE LOOKING OUT FOR ME, LIKE SOME KIND OF GUARDIAN ANGEL.
TOK TOK TOK TOK
FISHBONE
TOADIES
TOK
TOK TOK
TOK TOK
HE GETS ME ALL THE CANDY BARS I CAN EAT... FOR FREE!!
CANDY
LOS LOCOS
Eat me
PAUL ♥ CASSIE
HE STAYS UP PAST BEDTIME AND PLAYS VIDEOGAMES WITH ME.
HE TAUGHT ME TO TELEPORT.
POOF
NINJA AND I NOW RULE OVER THE SCHOOL WITH AN IRON FIST!

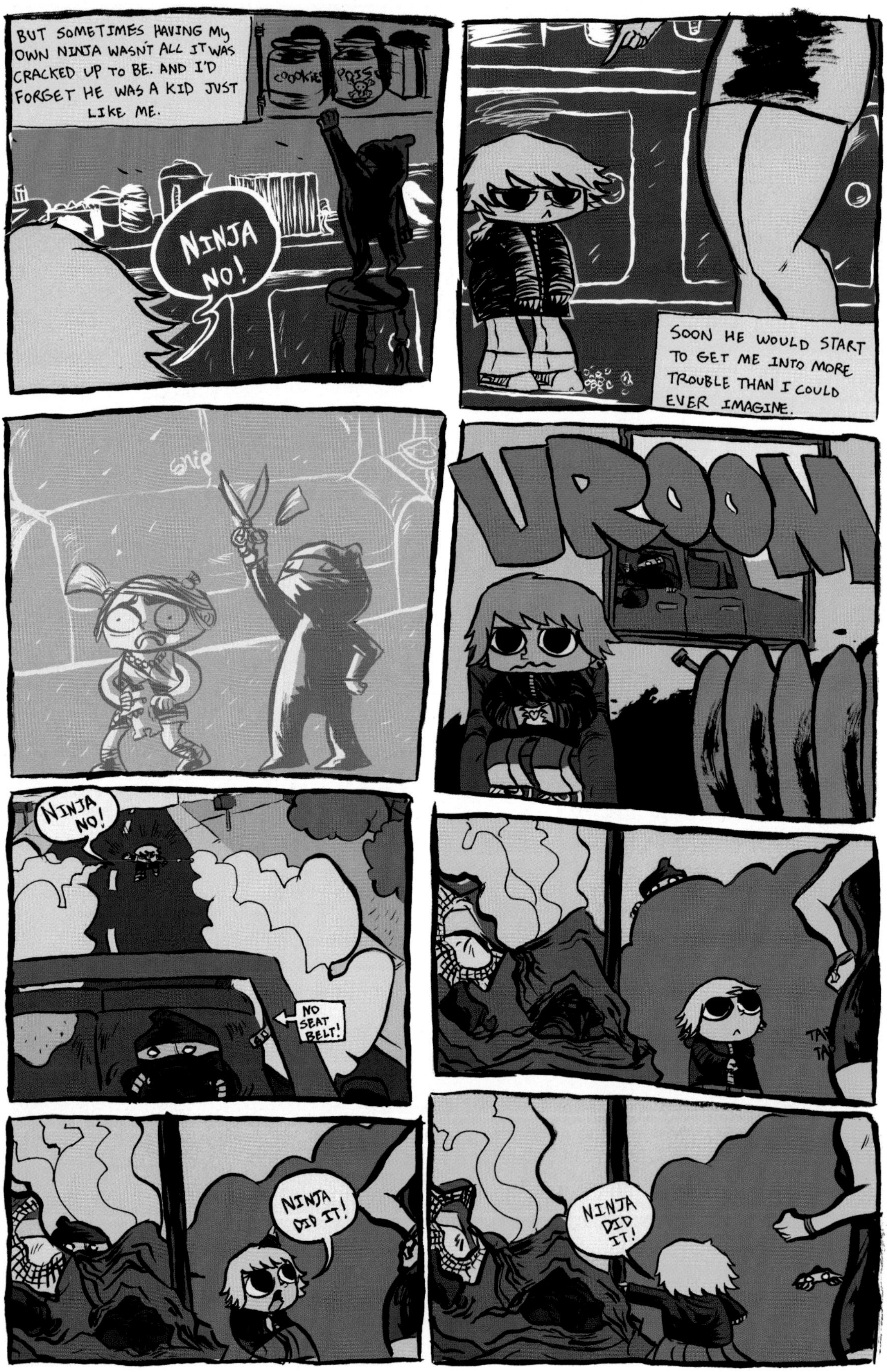

BUT SOMETIMES HAVING MY OWN NINJA WASN'T ALL IT WAS CRACKED UP TO BE. AND I'D FORGET HE WAS A KID JUST LIKE ME.
COOKIES
NINJA NO!
SOON HE WOULD START TO GET ME INTO MORE TROUBLE THAN I COULD EVER IMAGINE.
snip
VROOM
NINJA NO!
NO SEAT BELT!
NINJA DID IT!
NINJA DID IT!

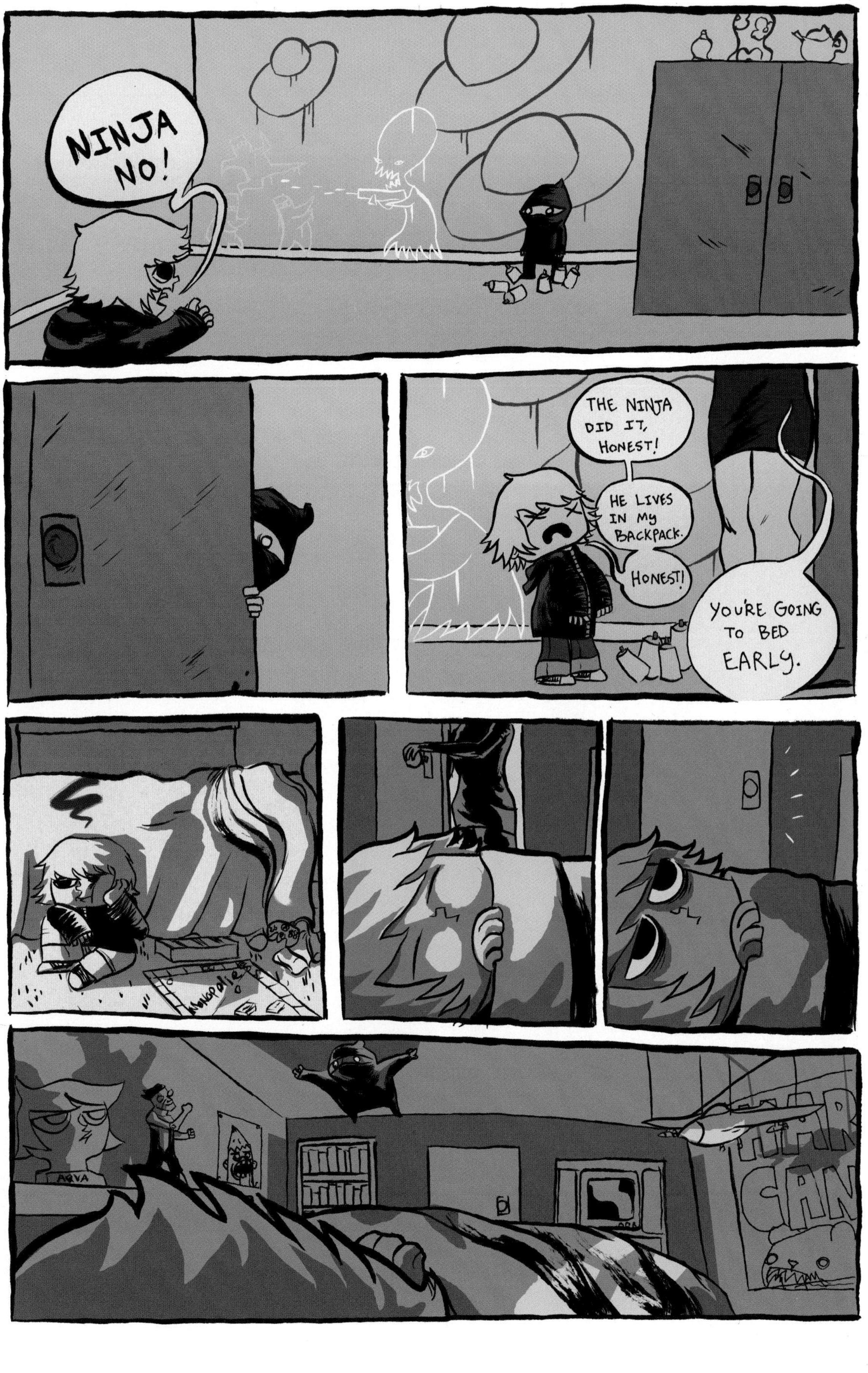
NINJA NO!
THE NINJA DID IT, HONEST!
HE LIVES IN MY BACKPACK.
HONEST!
YOU'RE GOING TO BED EARLY.

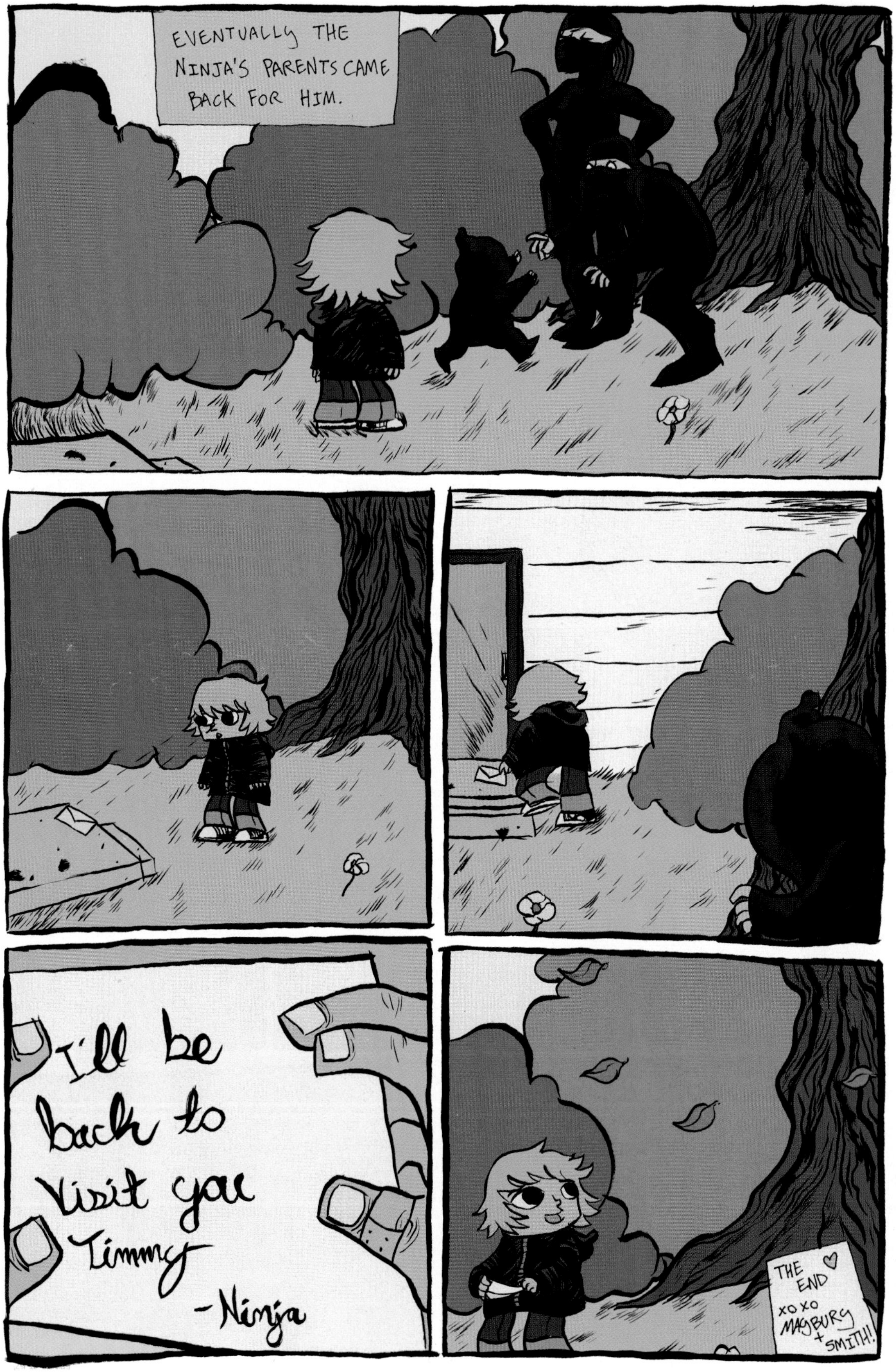
EVENTUALLY THE NINJA'S PARENTS CAME BACK FOR HIM.
I'll be back to visit you Timmy -Ninja
THE END ♥ xoxo MAGBURY + SMITH!

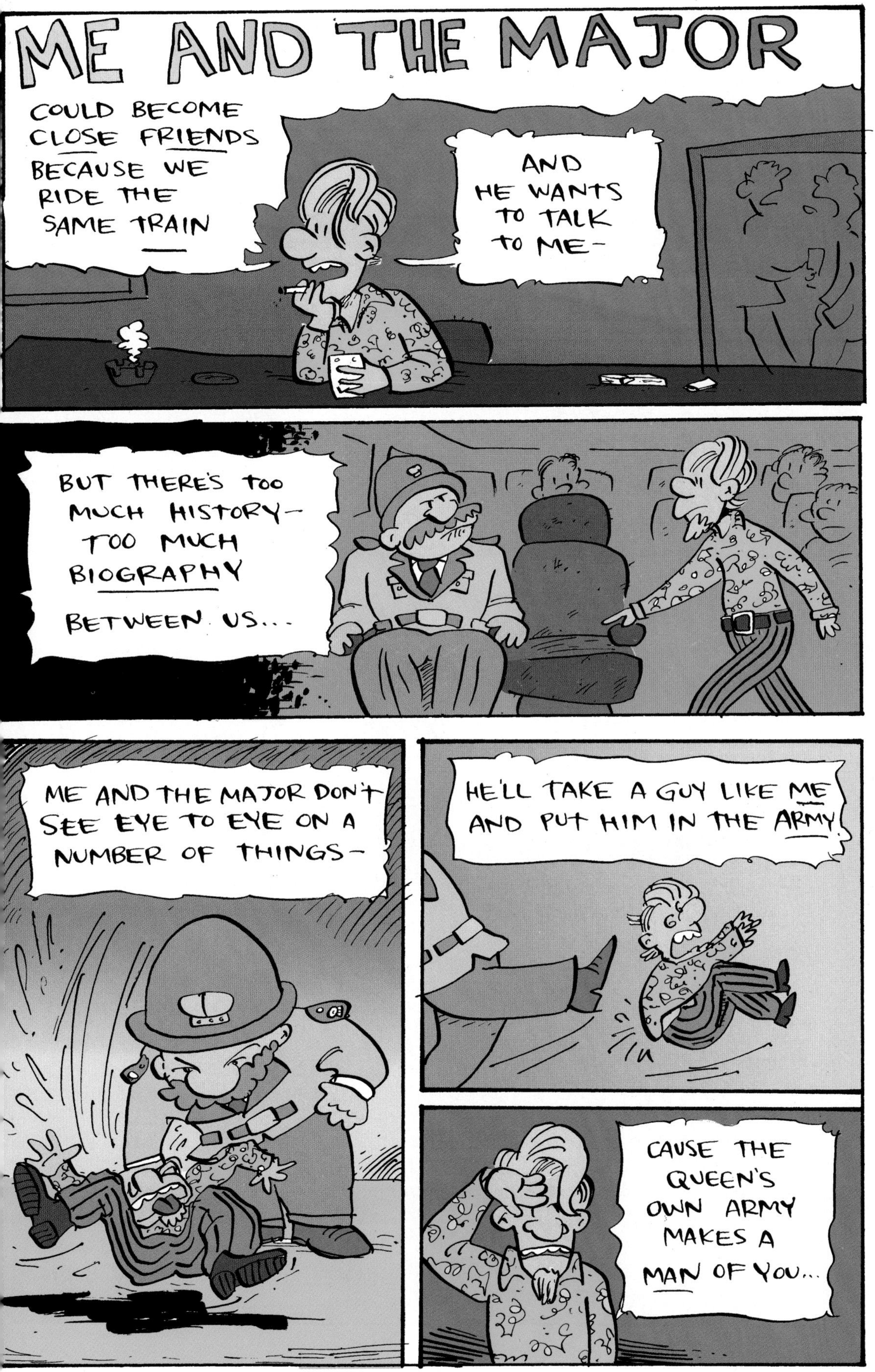
ME AND THE MAJOR
COULD BECOME CLOSE FRIENDS BECAUSE WE RIDE THE SAME TRAIN
AND HE WANTS TO TALK TO ME-
BUT THERE'S TOO MUCH HISTORY- TOO MUCH BIOGRAPHY BETWEEN US...
ME AND THE MAJOR DON'T SEE EYE TO EYE ON A NUMBER OF THINGS-
HE'LL TAKE A GUY LIKE ME AND PUT HIM IN THE ARMY!
CAUSE THE QUEEN'S OWN ARMY MAKES A MAN OF YOU...

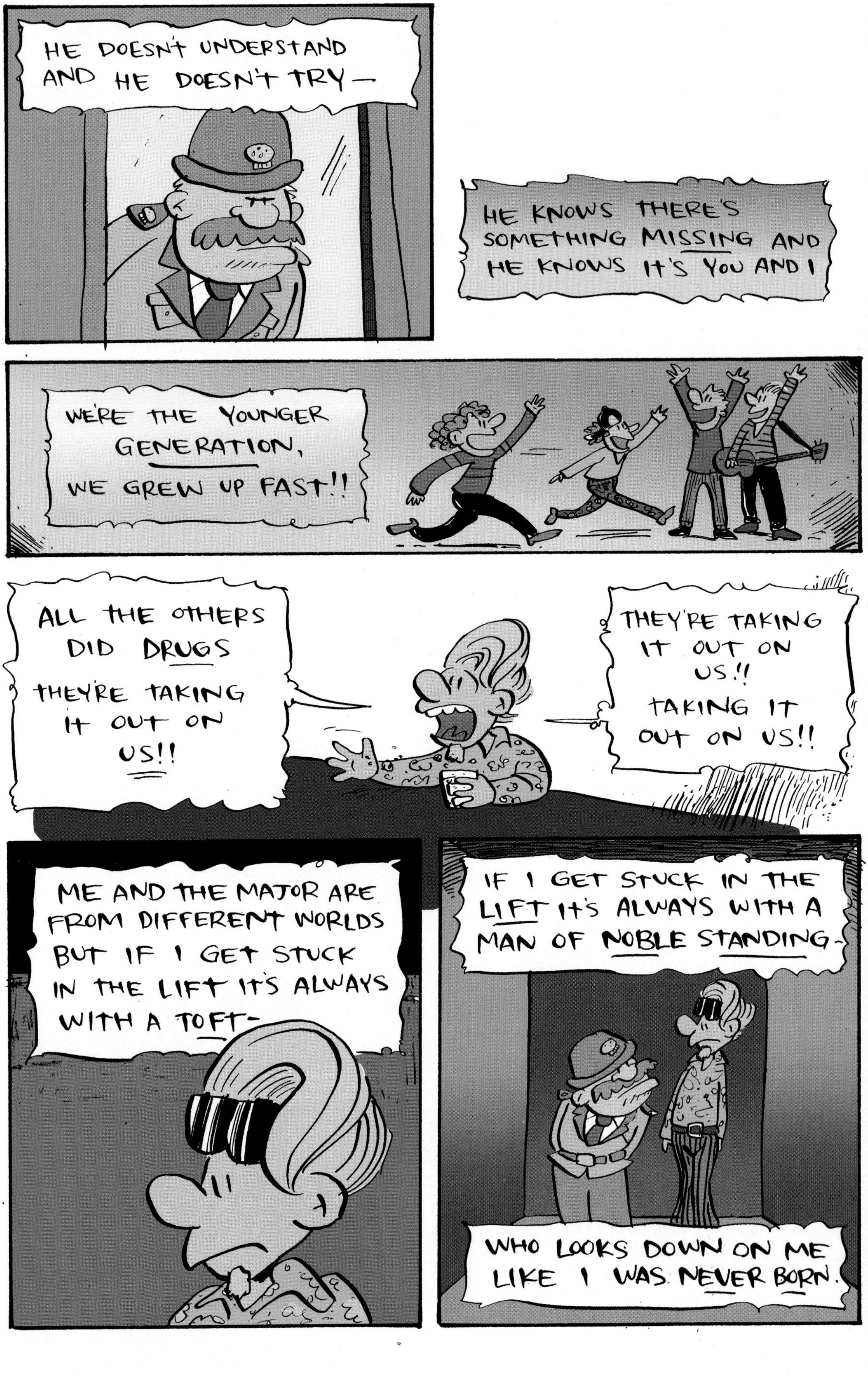
HE DOESN'T UNDERSTAND AND HE DOESN'T TRY—
HE KNOWS THERE'S SOMETHING MISSING AND HE KNOWS IT'S YOU AND I
WE'RE THE YOUNGER GENERATION, WE GREW UP FAST!!
ALL THE OTHERS DID DRUGS THEY'RE TAKING IT OUT ON US!!
THEY'RE TAKING IT OUT ON US!! TAKING IT OUT ON US!!
ME AND THE MAJOR ARE FROM DIFFERENT WORLDS BUT IF I GET STUCK IN THE LIFT IT'S ALWAYS WITH A TOFT-
IF I GET STUCK IN THE LIFT IT'S ALWAYS WITH A MAN OF NOBLE STANDING-
WHO LOOKS DOWN ON ME LIKE I WAS NEVER BORN.

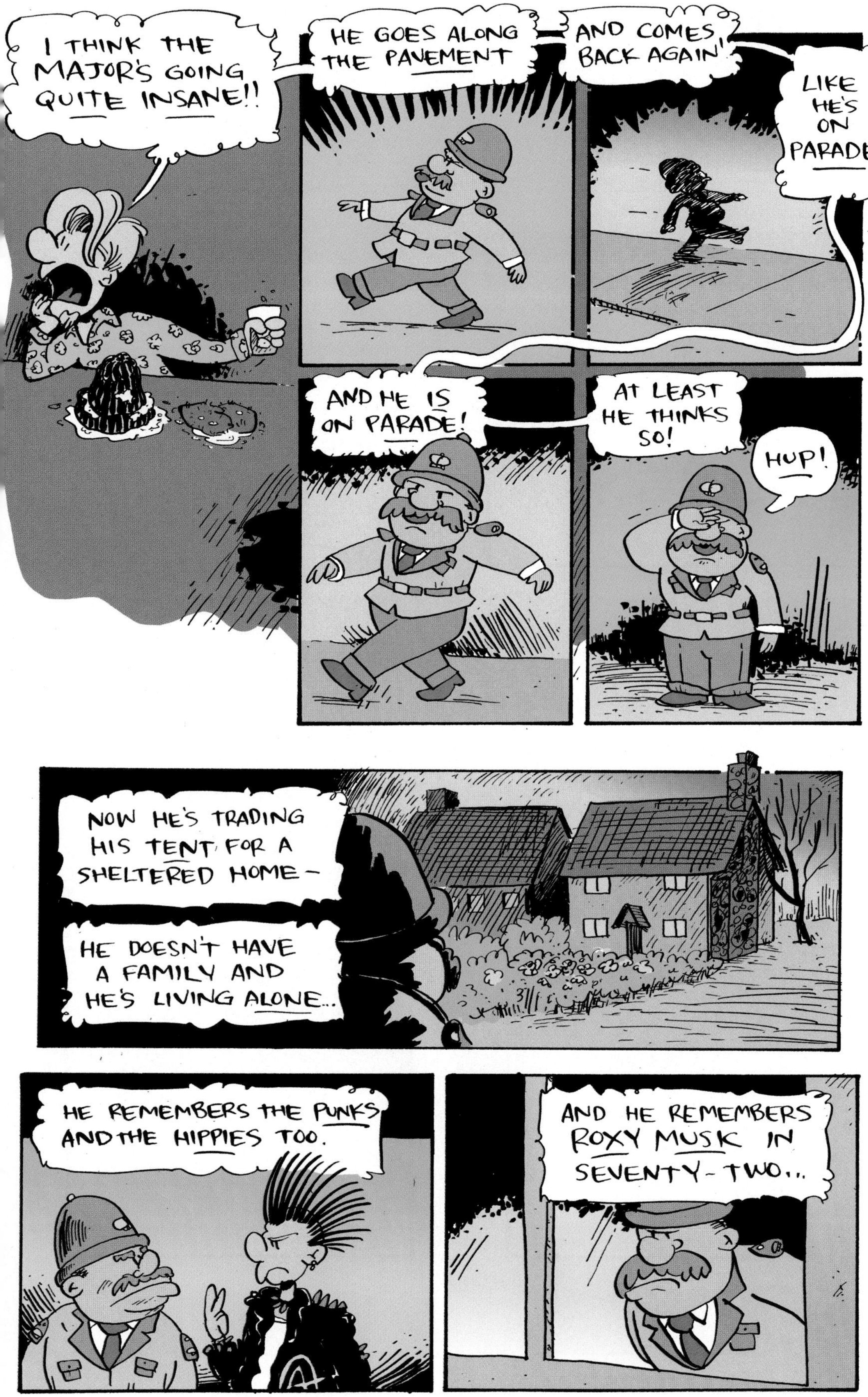
I THINK THE MAJOR'S GOING QUITE INSANE!!
HE GOES ALONG THE PAVEMENT
AND COMES BACK AGAIN!
LIKE HE'S ON PARADE!
AND HE IS ON PARADE!
AT LEAST HE THINKS SO!
HUP!
NOW HE'S TRADING HIS TENT FOR A SHELTERED HOME-
HE DOESN'T HAVE A FAMILY AND HE'S LIVING ALONE...
HE REMEMBERS THE PUNKS AND THE HIPPIES TOO.
AND HE REMEMBERS ROXY MUSK IN SEVENTY-TWO...

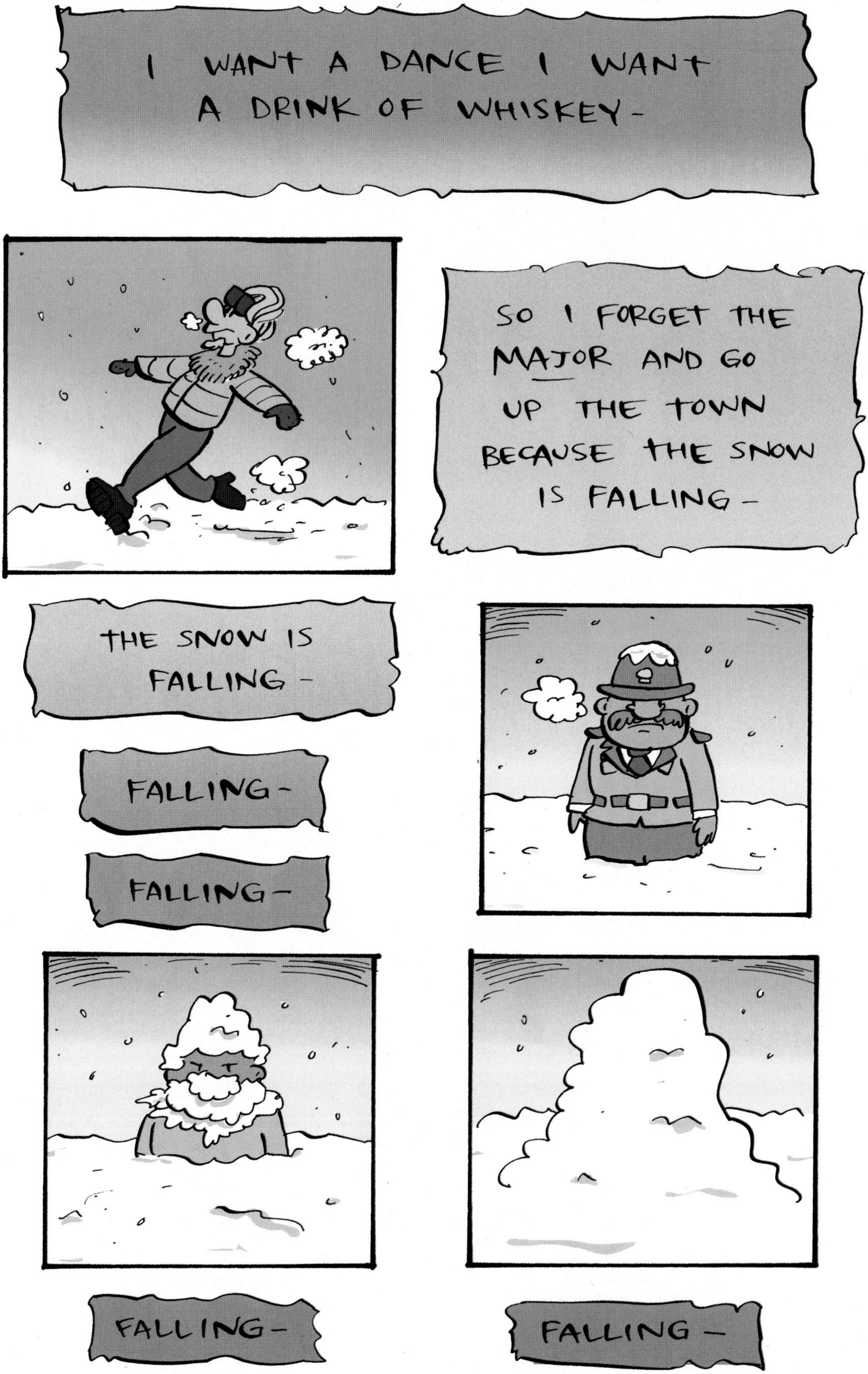
I WANT A DANCE I WANT A DRINK OF WHISKEY-
SO I FORGET THE MAJOR AND GO UP THE TOWN BECAUSE THE SNOW IS FALLING-
THE SNOW IS FALLING-
FALLING-
FALLING-
FALLING-
FALLING-

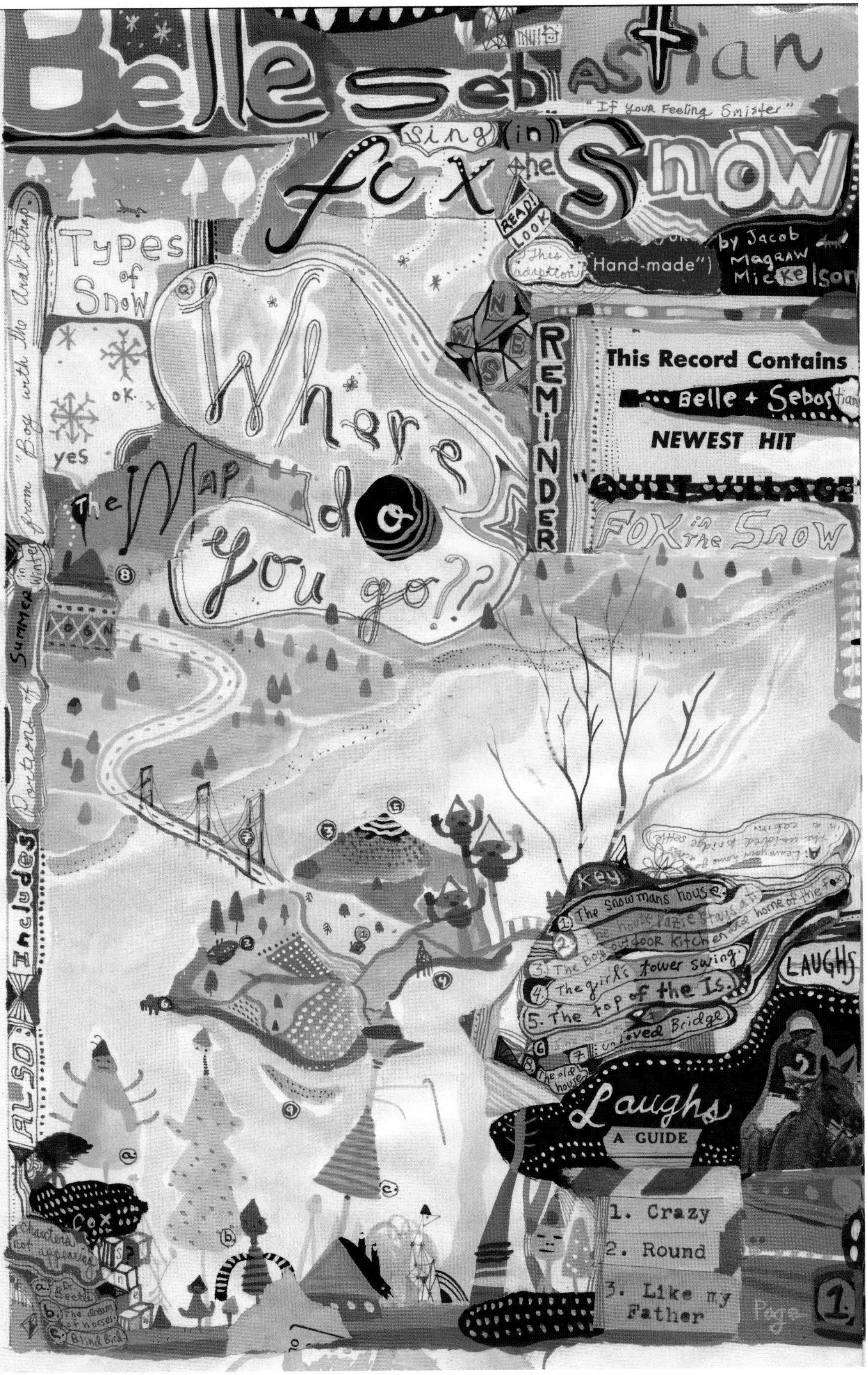

Belle Sebastian
"If your Feeling Sinister"
sing in the Fox Snow
READ! LOOK
This adaption
"Hand-made")
by Jacob Magraw Mickelson
Types of Snow
OK.
yes
Where do you go??
The Map
REMINDER
This Record Contains
Belle + Sebastians
NEWEST HIT
"QUIET VILLAGE"
FOX in the SNOW
from "Boy with the Arab Strap"
Summer in Winter
Portions of
ALSO Includes
key
1. The snow mans house.
2. The Boy outdoor kitchen and home of the Fox
3. The girl's tower swing.
4. The top of the Is.
5. The top
7. unloved Bridge
8. The old house
LAUGHS
Laughs
A GUIDE
1. Crazy
2. Round
3. Like my Father
Page 1.
Characters not appearing
a. Beetle
b. The dream of horses
c. Blind Bird

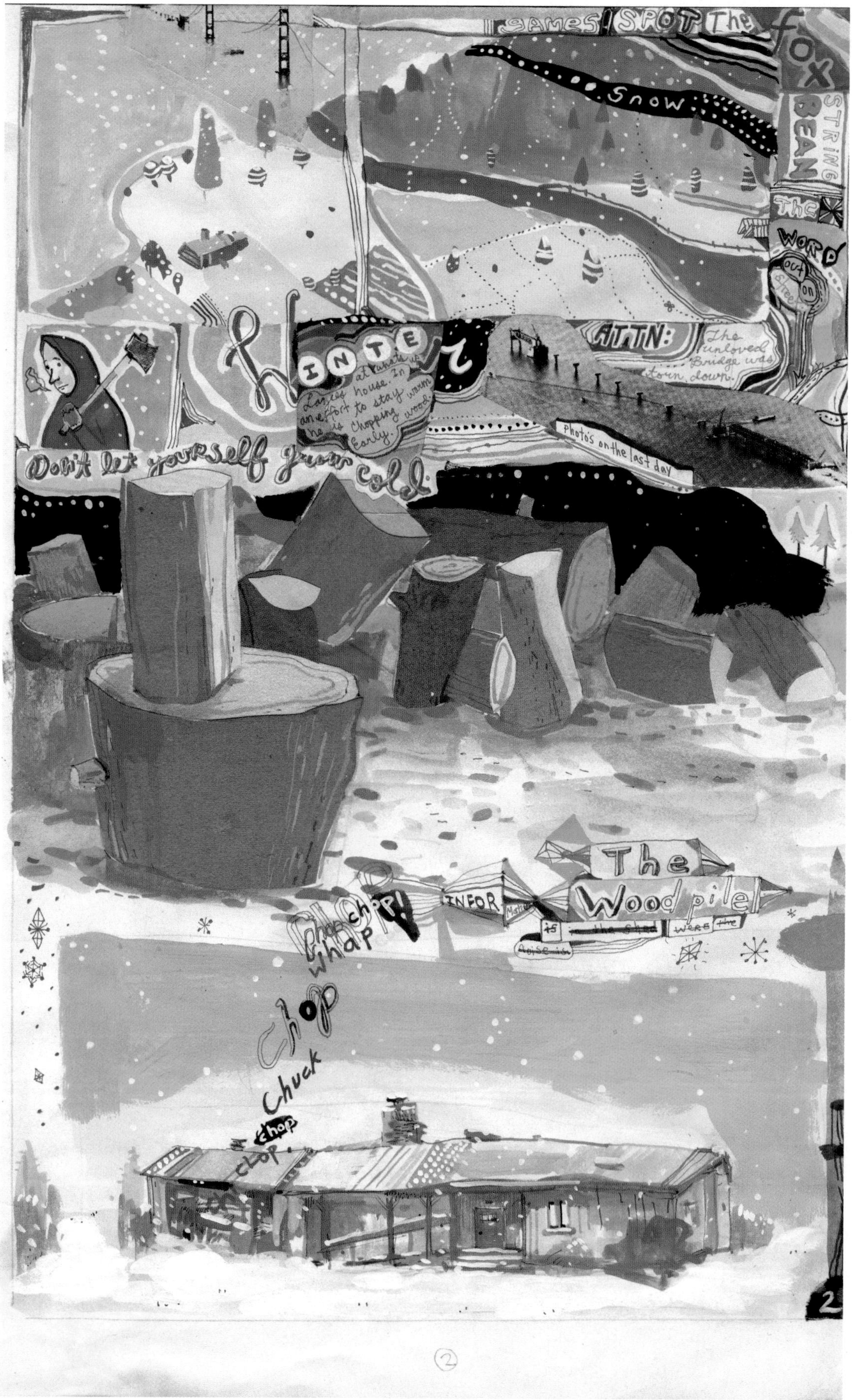

games SPOT The fox
STRING BEAN
The WORD
out on street
Snow
Winter
at what's up Lance's house. In an effort to stay warm he is Chopping wood. Early.
ATTN: The unloved Bridge was torn down.
Photo's on the last day
Don't let yourself grow cold.
The Woodpile
INFOR
chop chop!
whap
chop
chop
Chuck
chop
chop
2

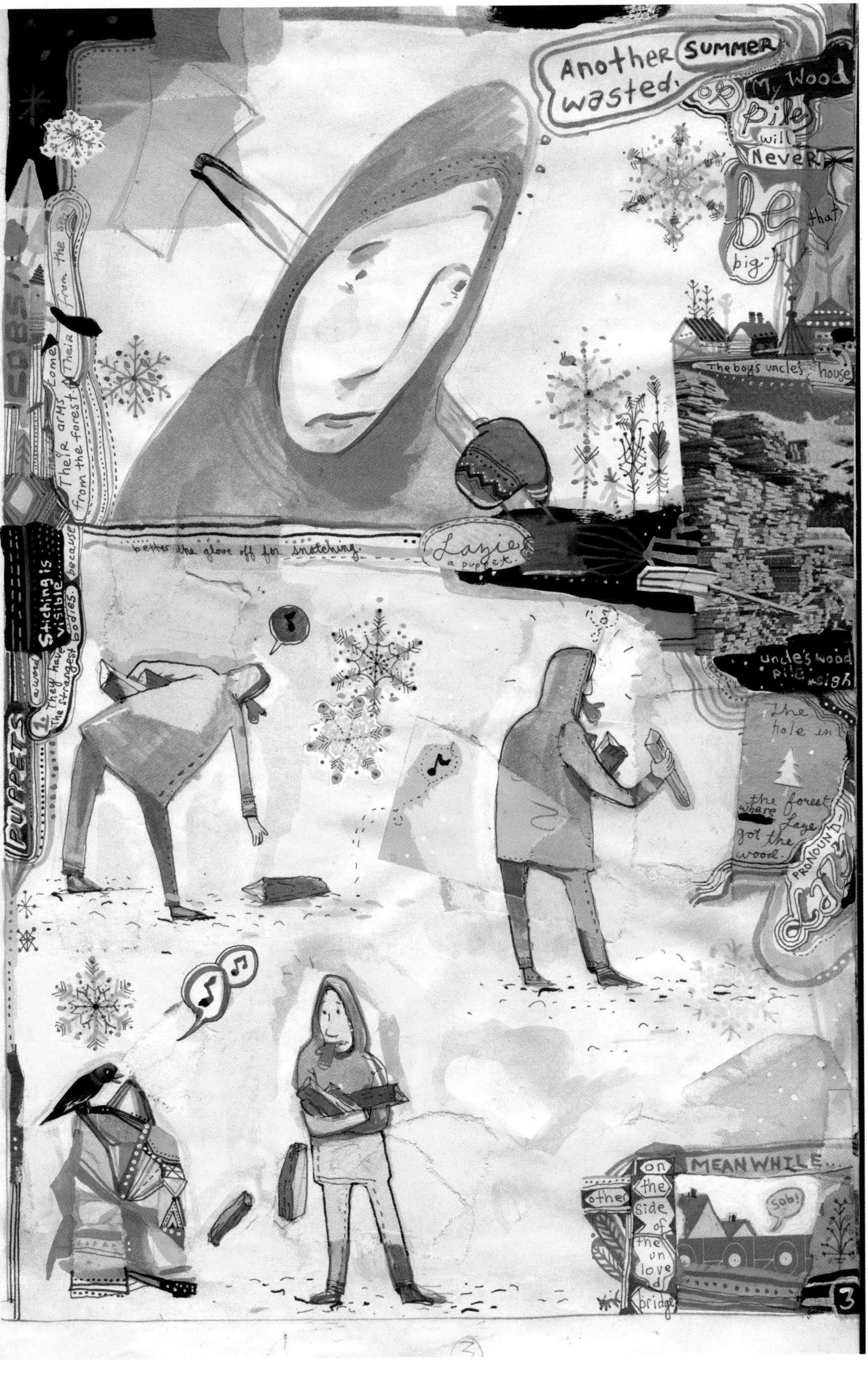
Another SUMMER wasted,
or My Wood pile will NeveR be that big"
Their arMS come from the forest Their from the
PUPPETS
1. a word They have The strangest bodies because Stiching is visible.....
bother the glove off for snatching.
Lazie a puppet.
The boys uncle's house
uncle's wood pile *sigh
The hole in the forest where Laze got the wood.
PRONOUN'D- Lazy
MEANWHILE...
on the other side of the un love d bridge
Sob!
3

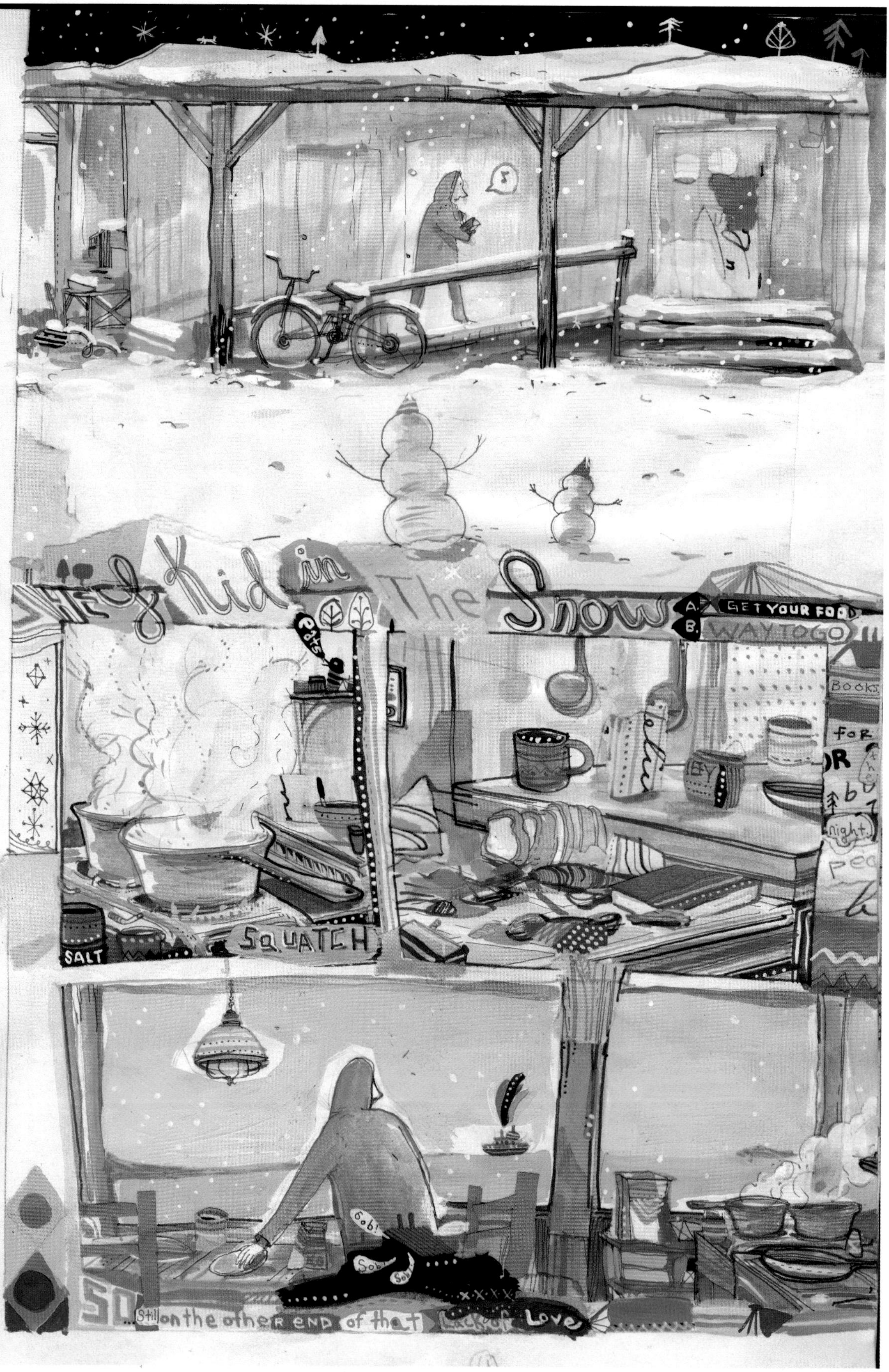
Kid in The Snow
eats
A. GET YOUR FOOD
B. WAY TO GO
BOOKS
SQUATCH
SALT
Gob!
Sob!
Sob!
SO... Still on the other end of that Lack of Love

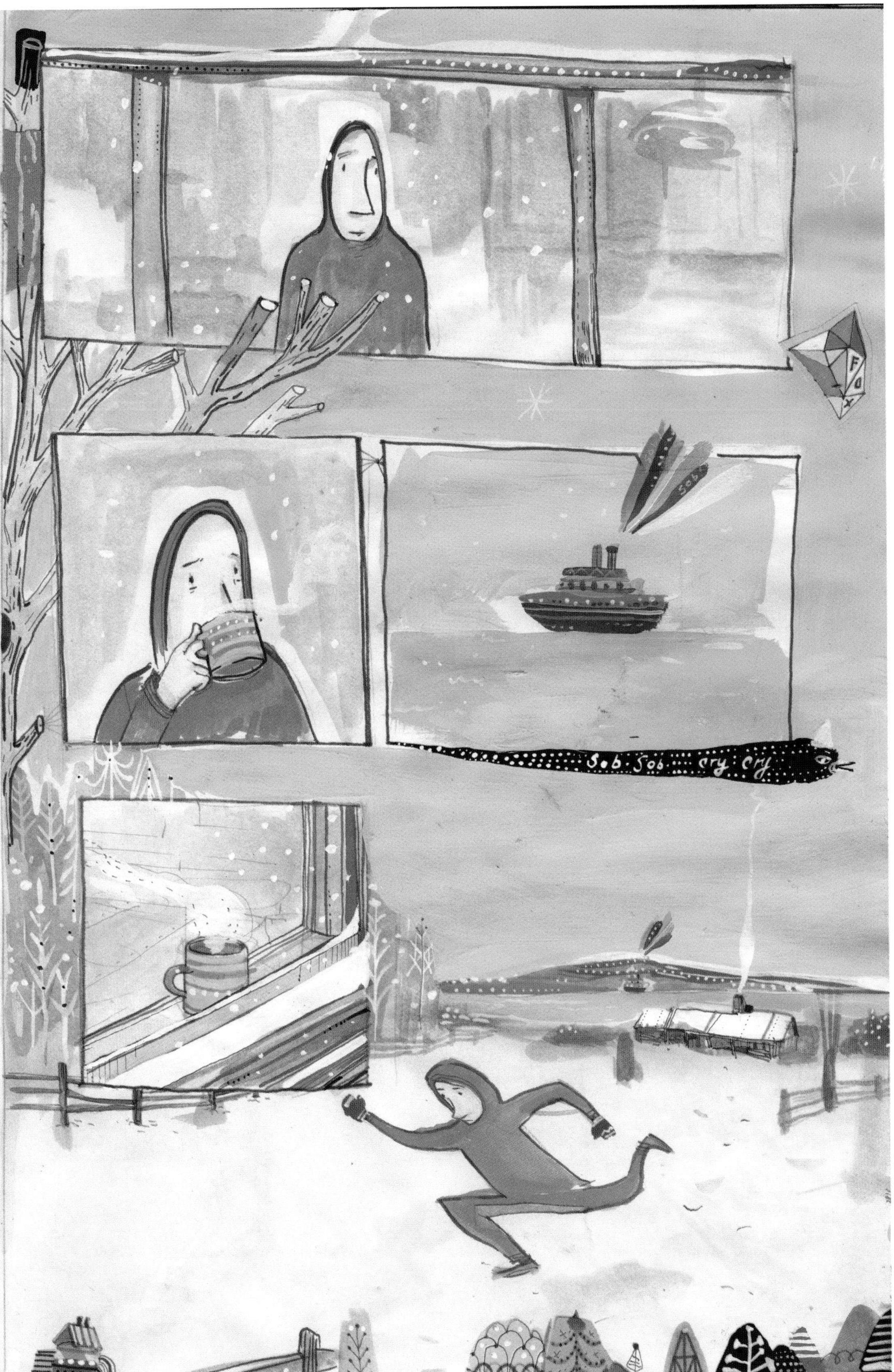
FOX
sob
Sob Sob cry cry

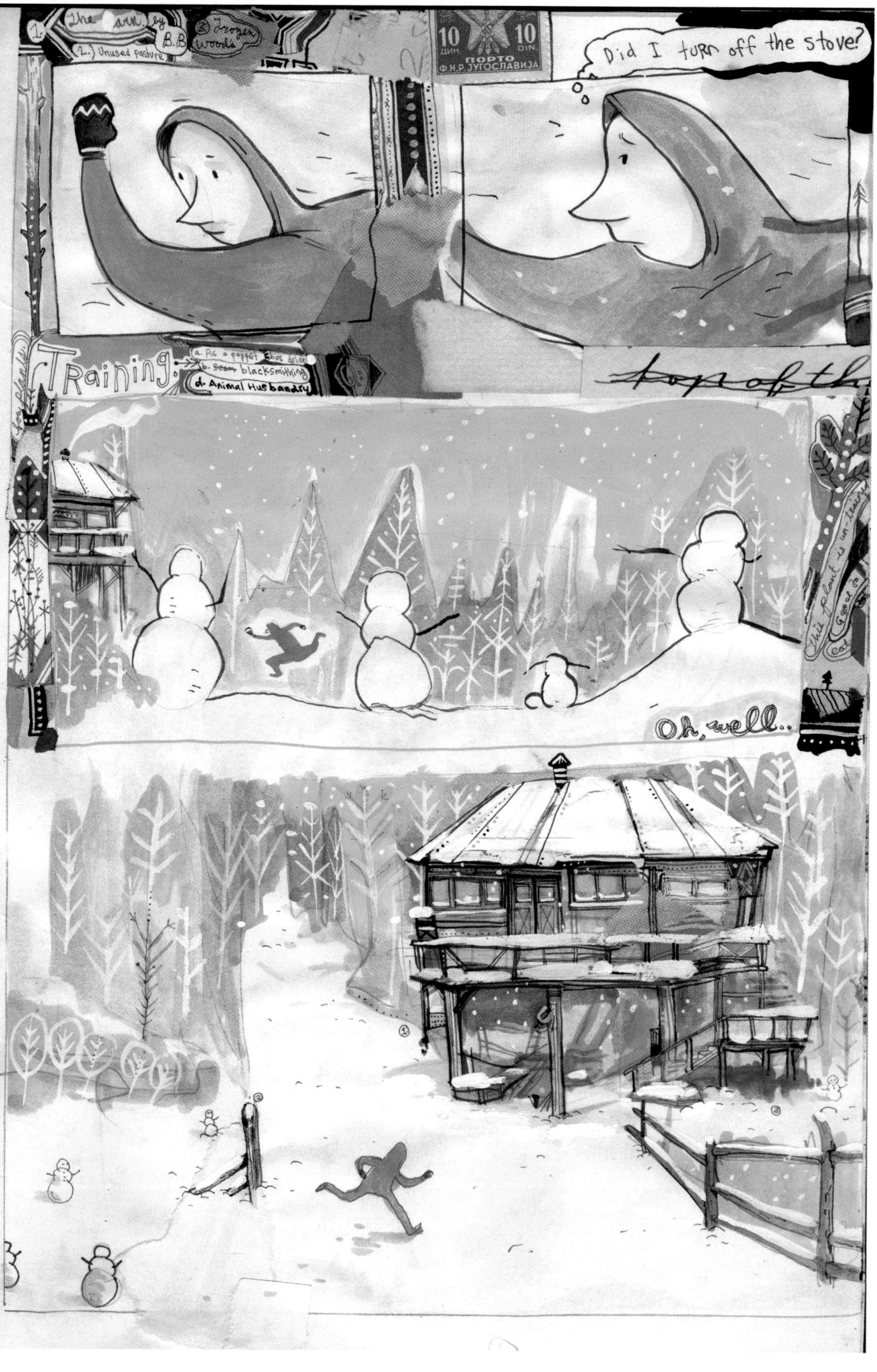
1. The arn. by B.B
2.) Unused pasture
3. Frozen woods
Did I turn off the stove?
Training.
a. As a puppet bus driver
b. seam blacksmithing
d. Animal Husbandry
Oh, well..

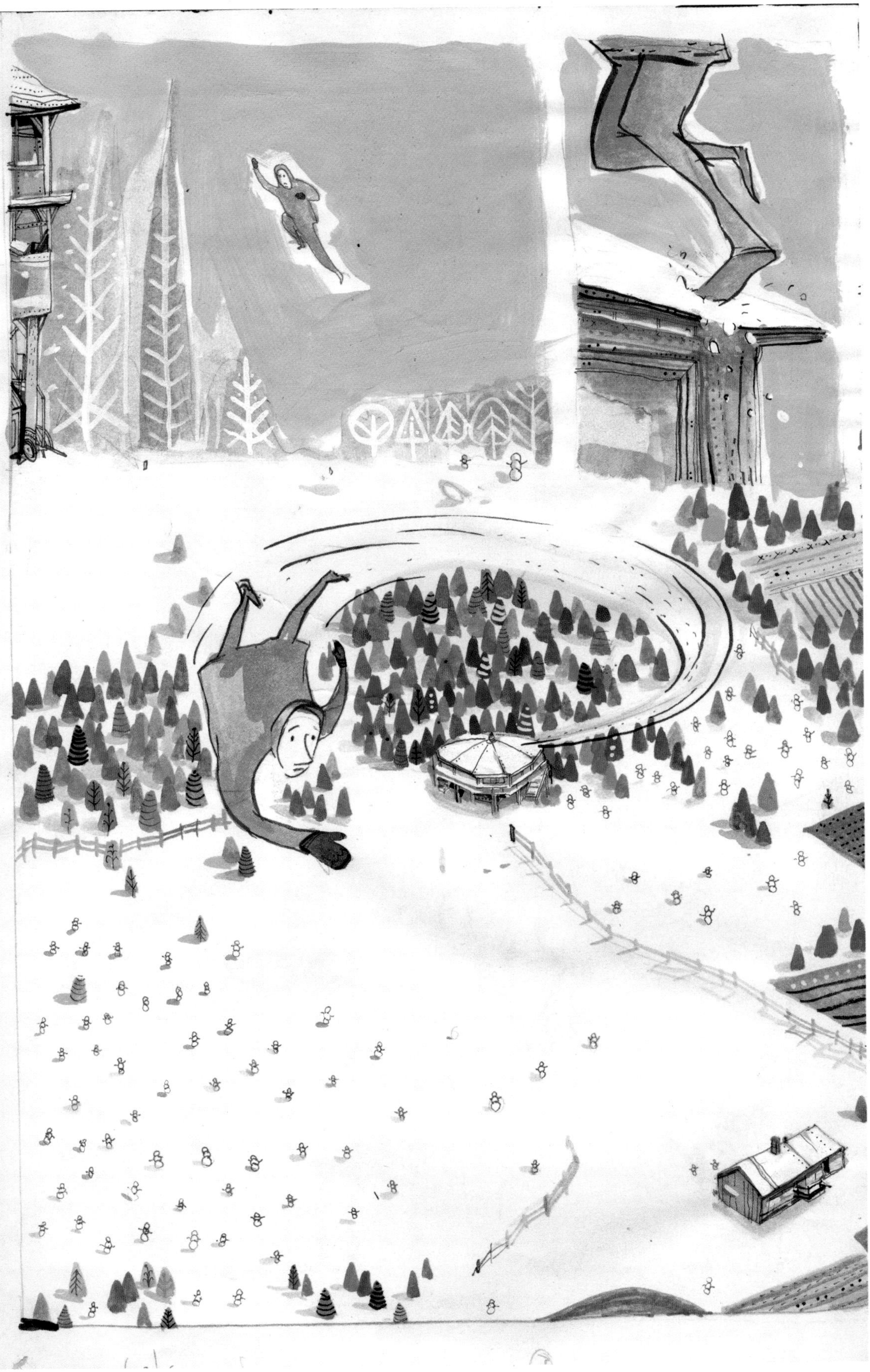

Get me away from here I'm dying

music by Belle & Sebastian
pictures by Catia Chien

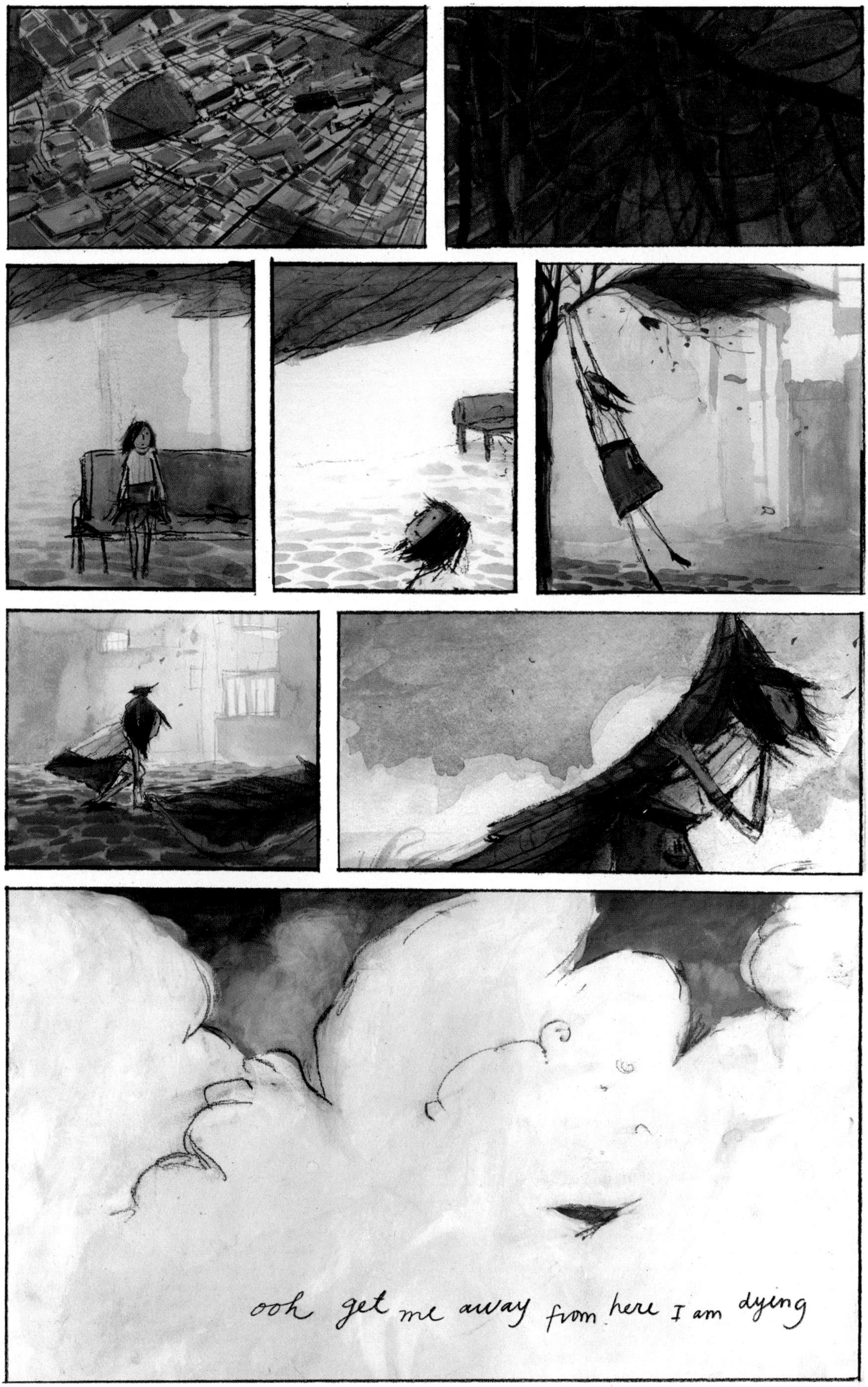
ooh get me away from here I am dying

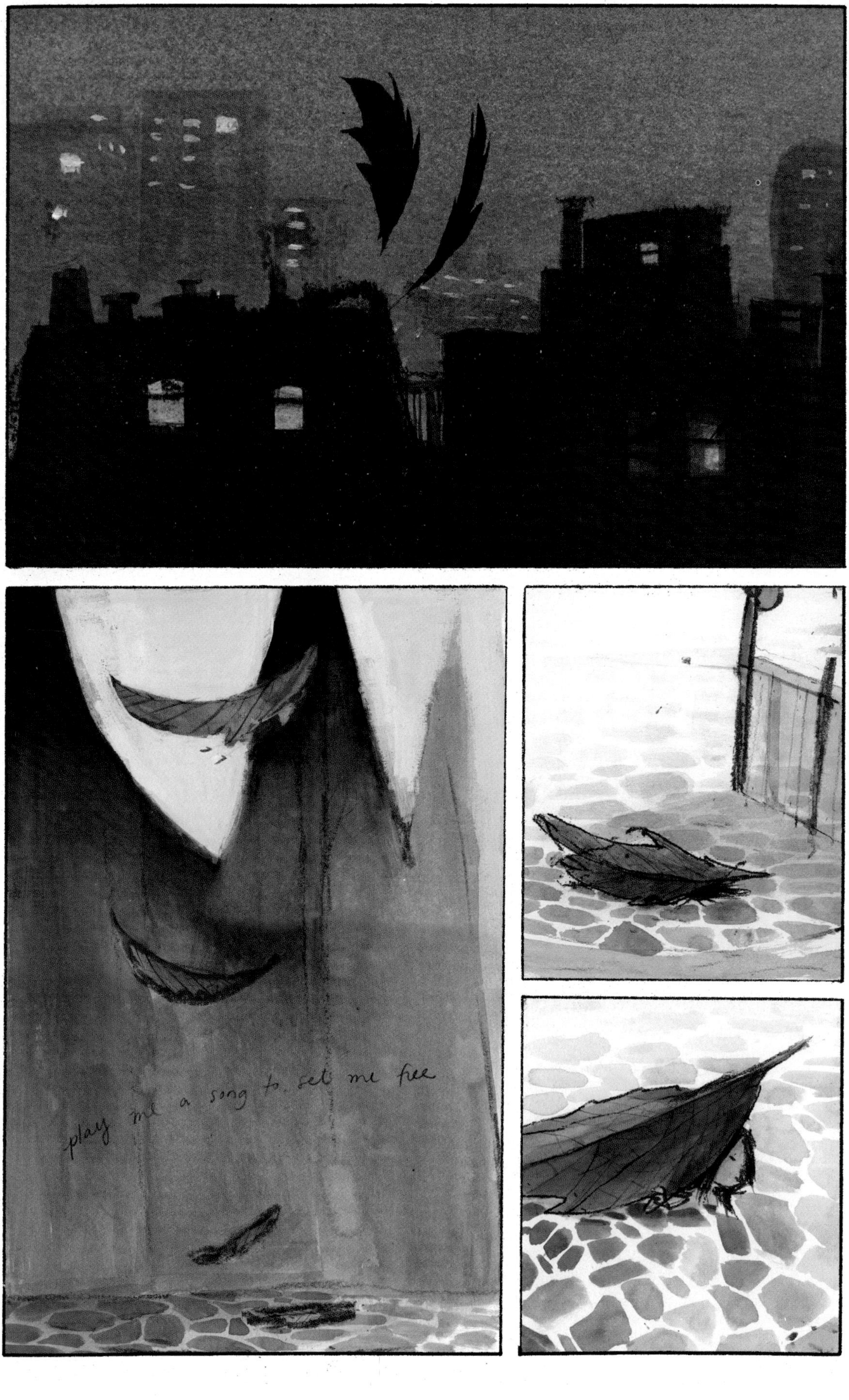
play me a song to set me free

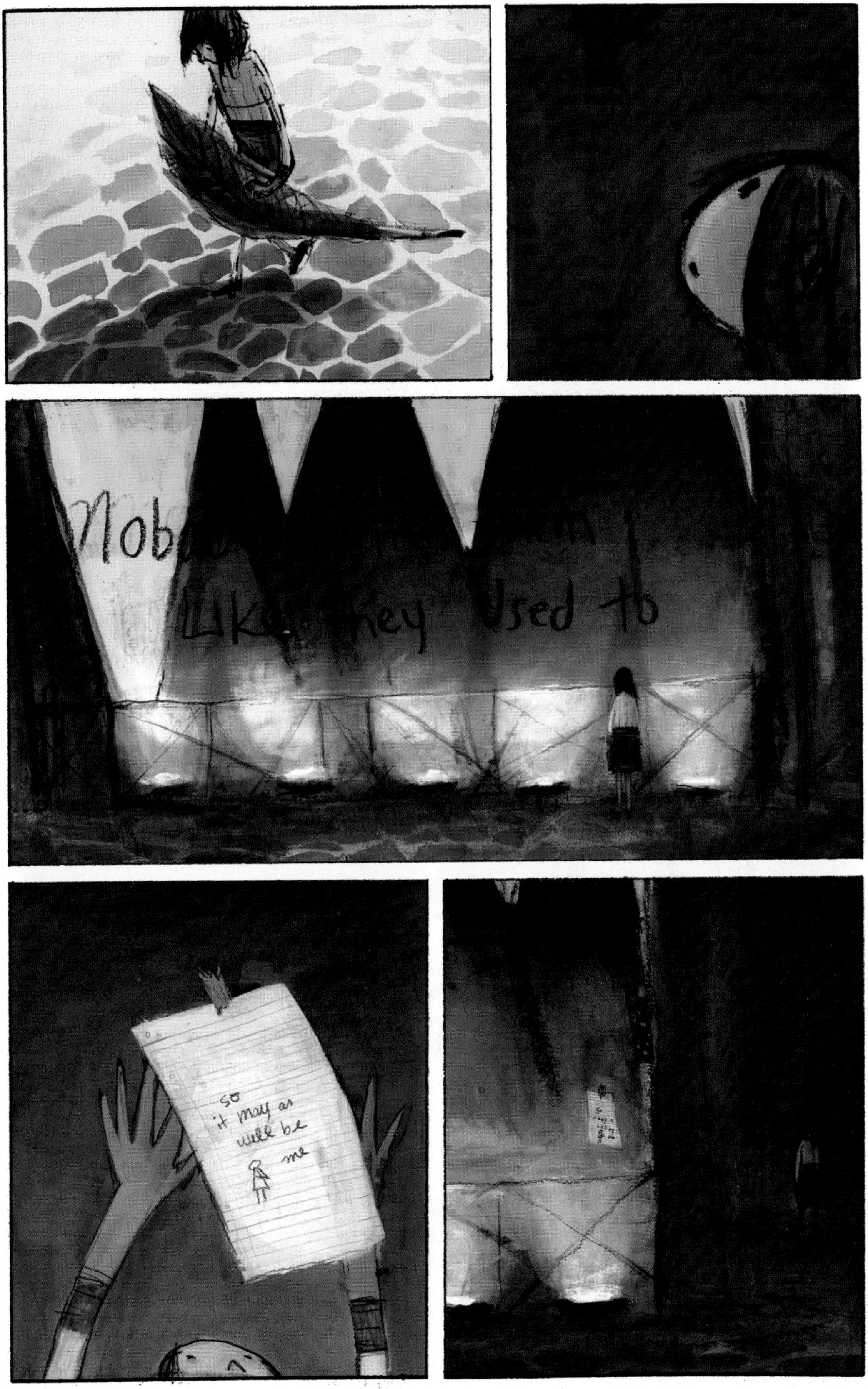
Nob
Like they Used to
so it may as well be me

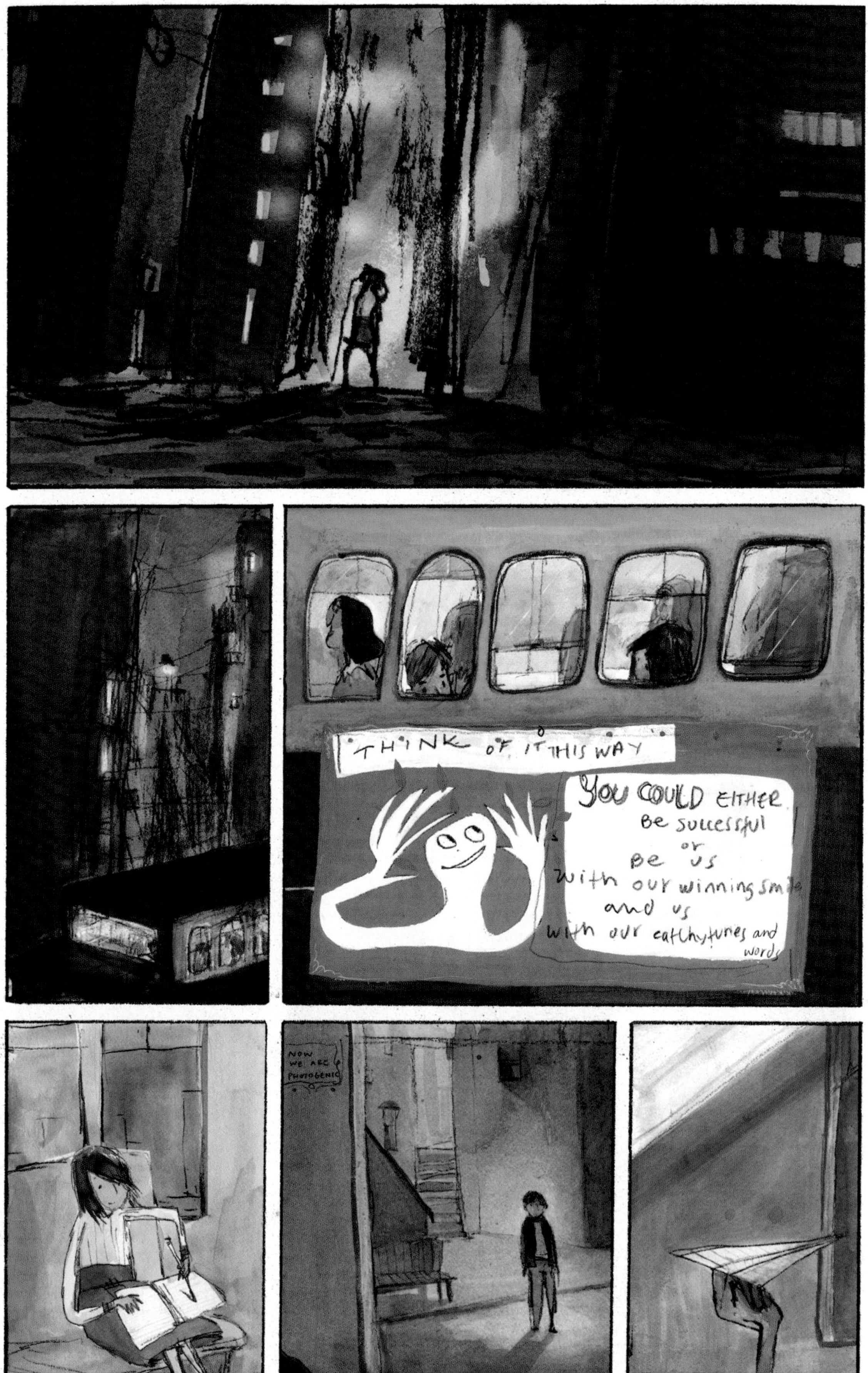
THINK OF IT THIS WAY
YOU COULD EITHER
be successful
or
be us
with our winning sm
and us
with our catlhytunes and words
NOW WE ARE PHOTOGENIC

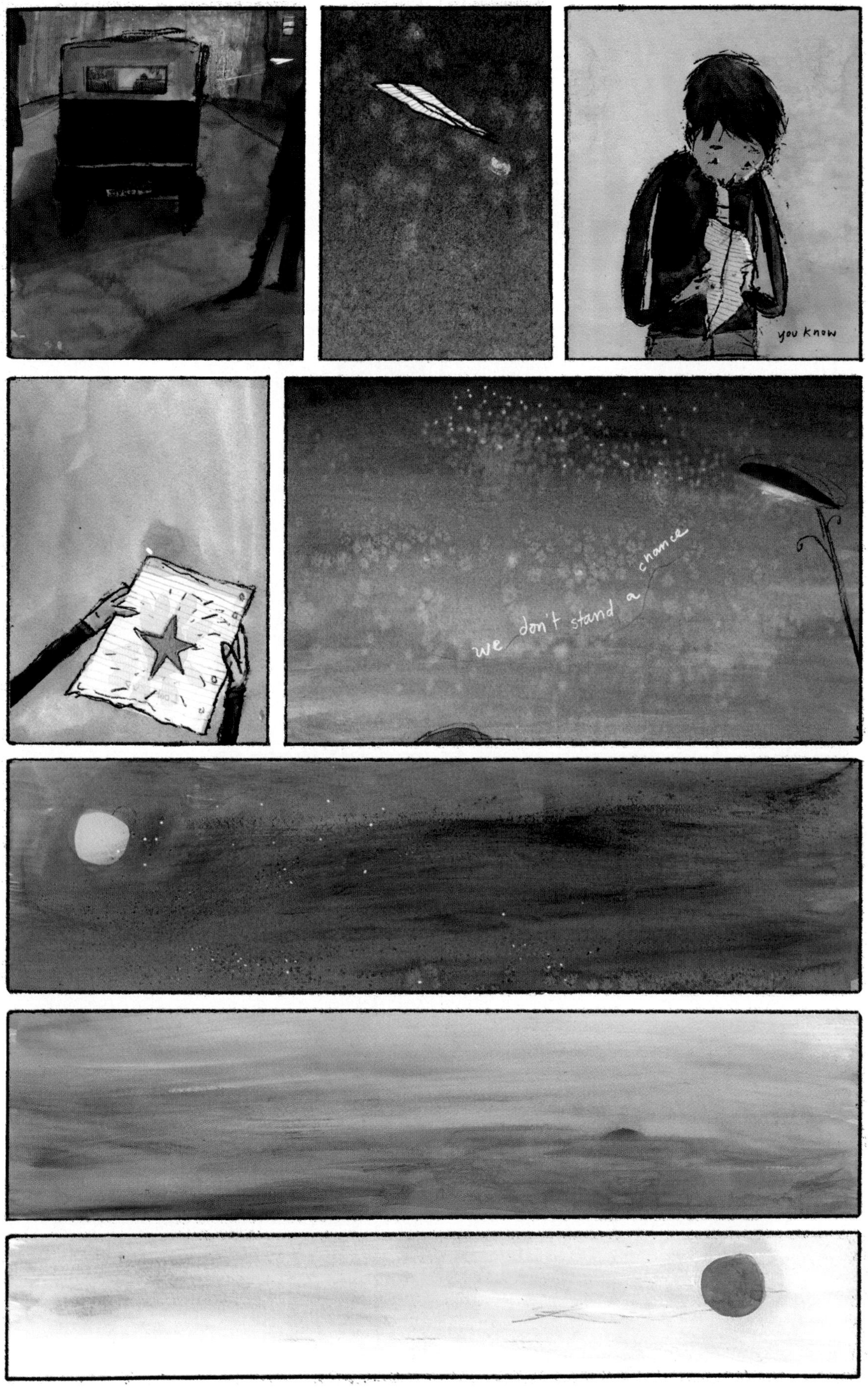
you know
we don't stand a chance

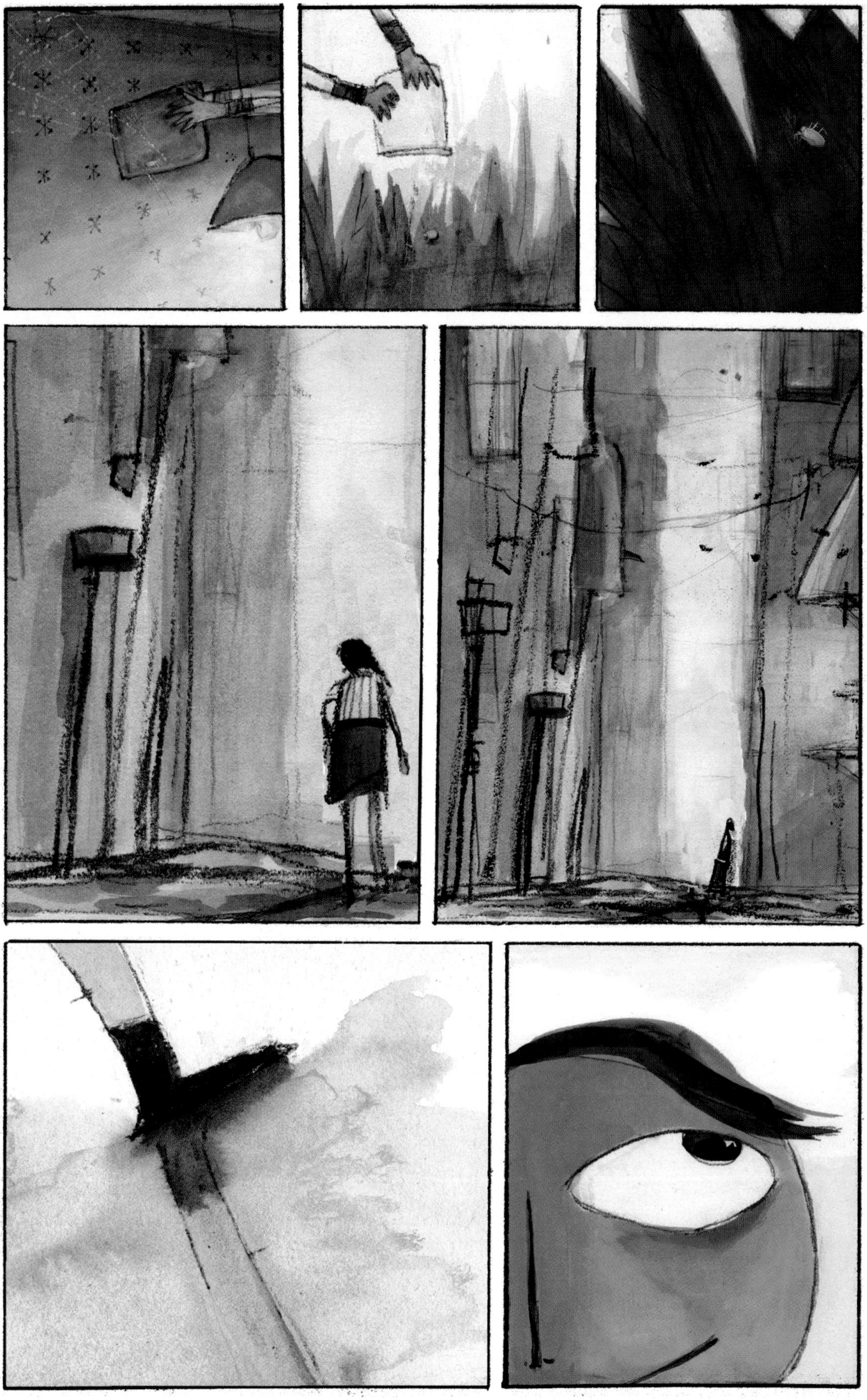

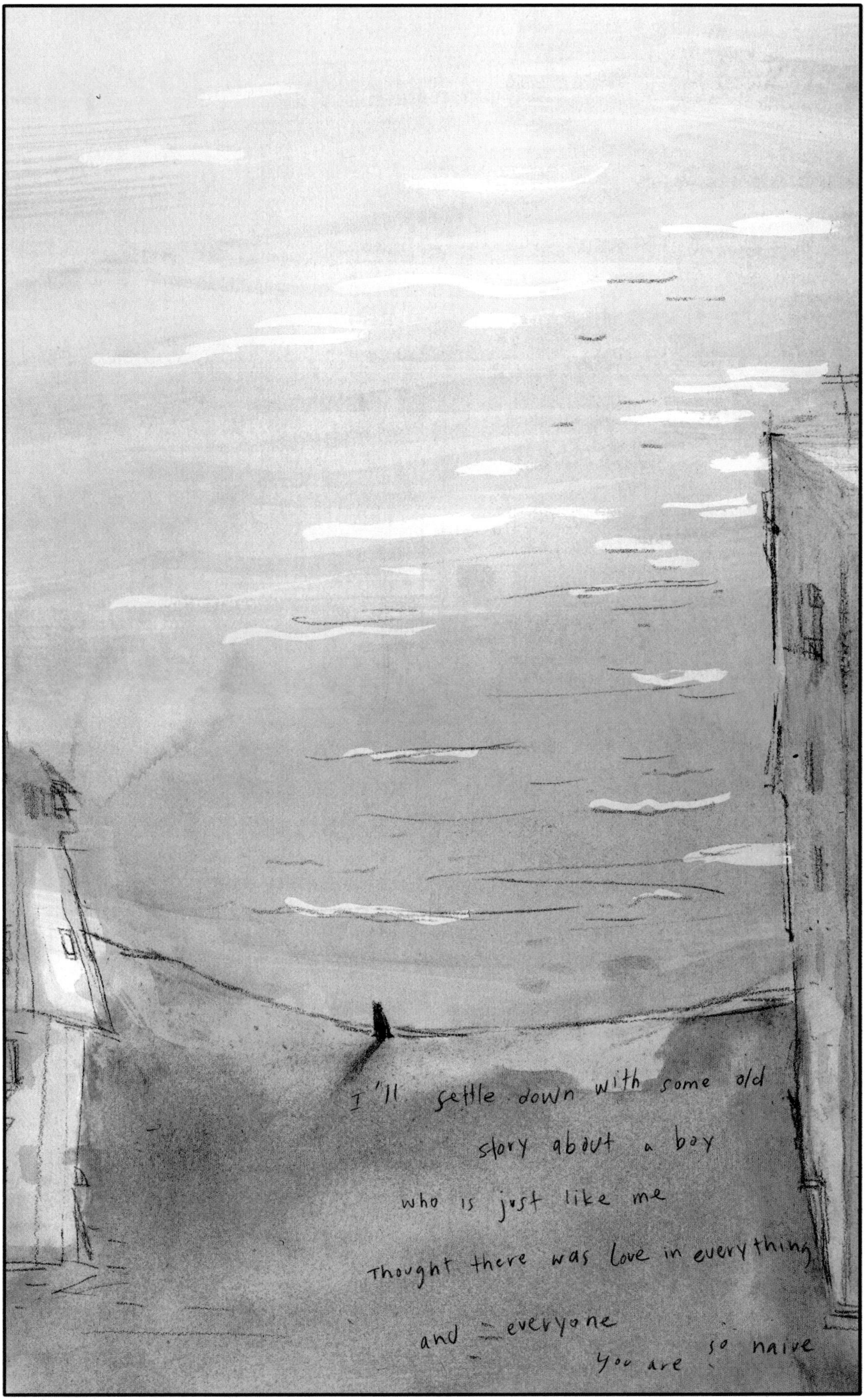
I'll settle down with some old
story about a boy
who is just like me
Thought there was love in everything
and everyone
You are so naive

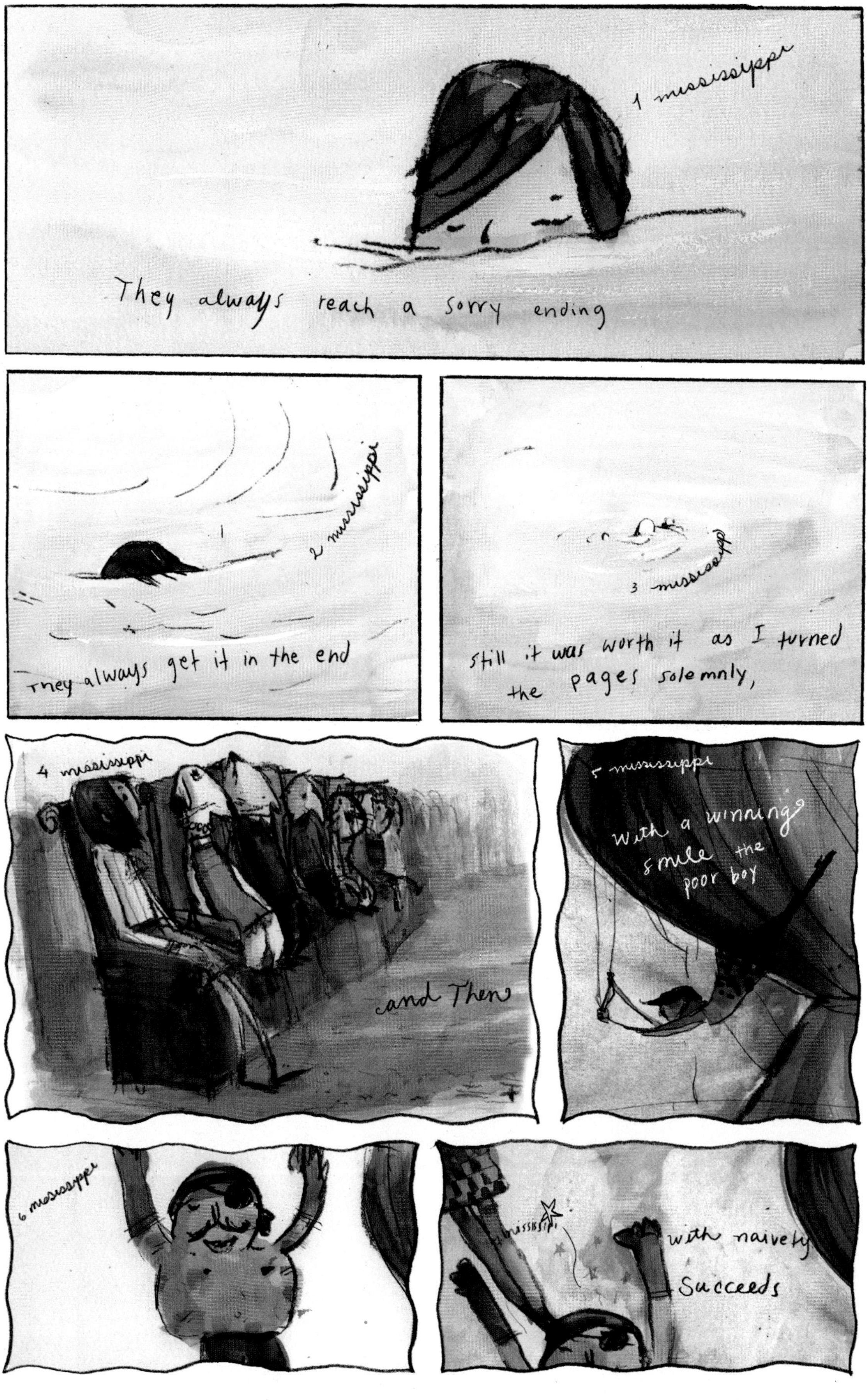
1 mississippi
They always reach a sorry ending
2 mississippi
They always get it in the end
3 mississippi
Still it was worth it as I turned the pages solemnly,
4 mississippi
and Then
5 mississippi
With a winning smile the poor boy
6 mississippi
7 mississipi
with naivety
Succeeds

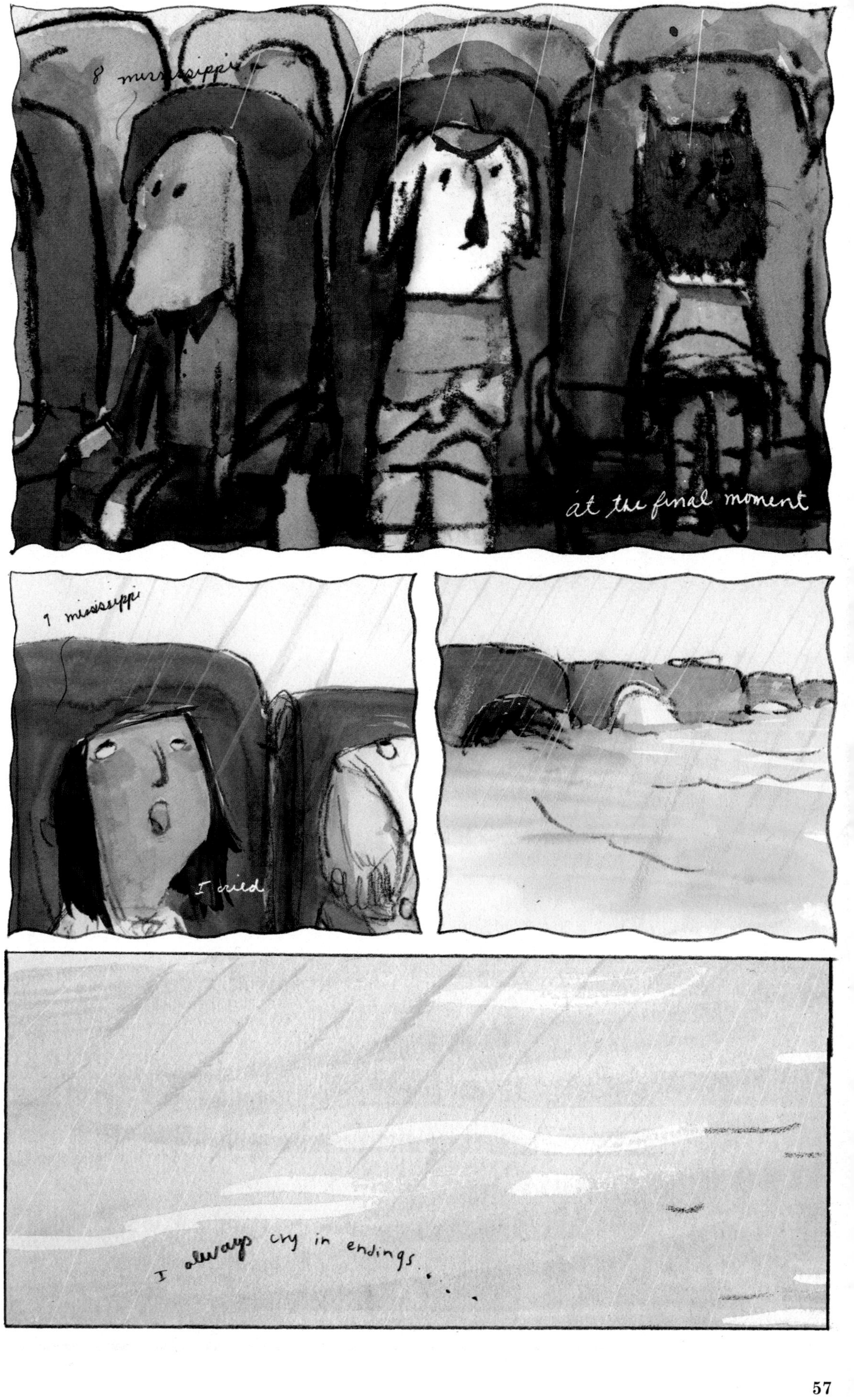

8 mississippi
at the final moment
9 mississippi
I cried
I always cry in endings...

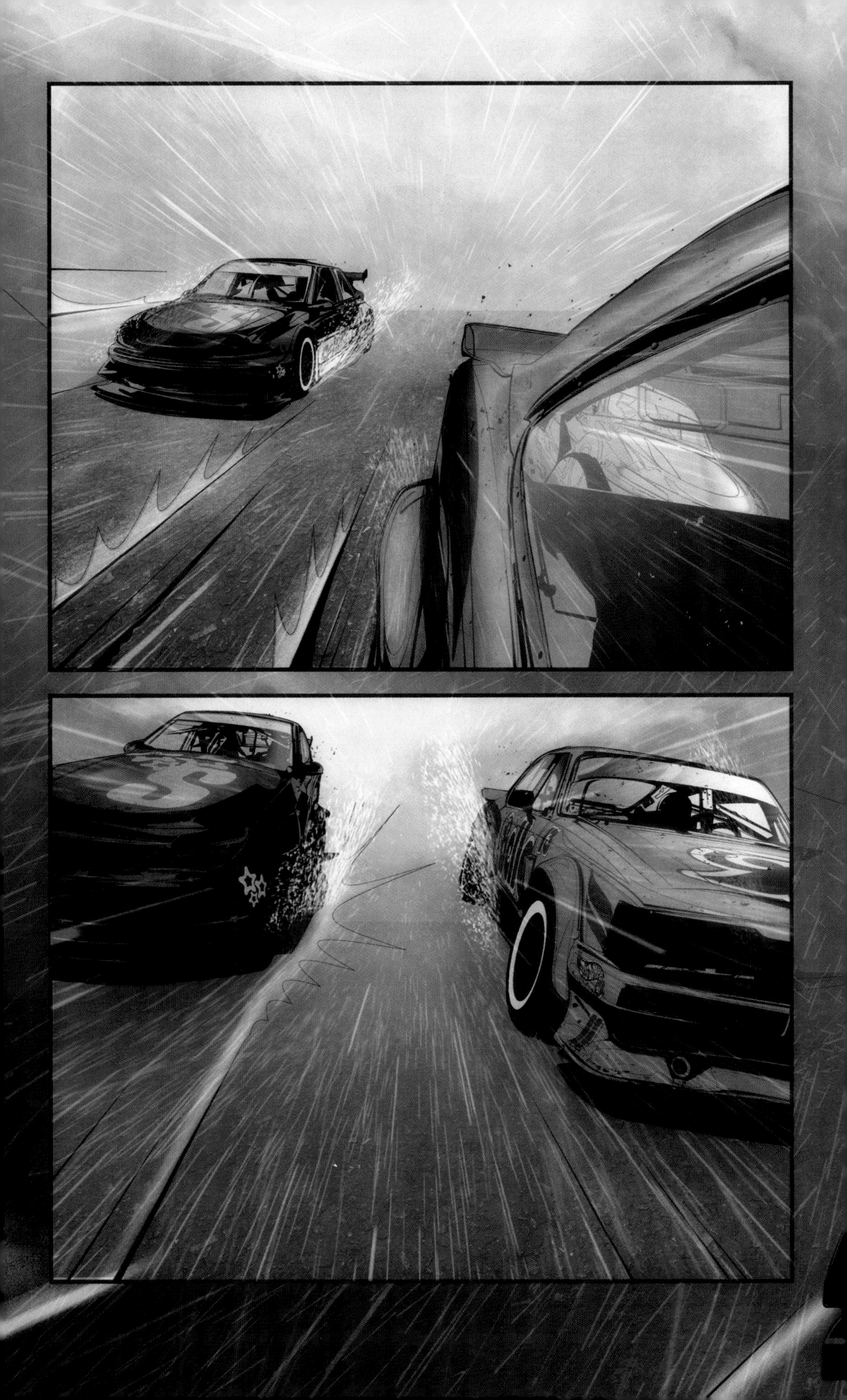

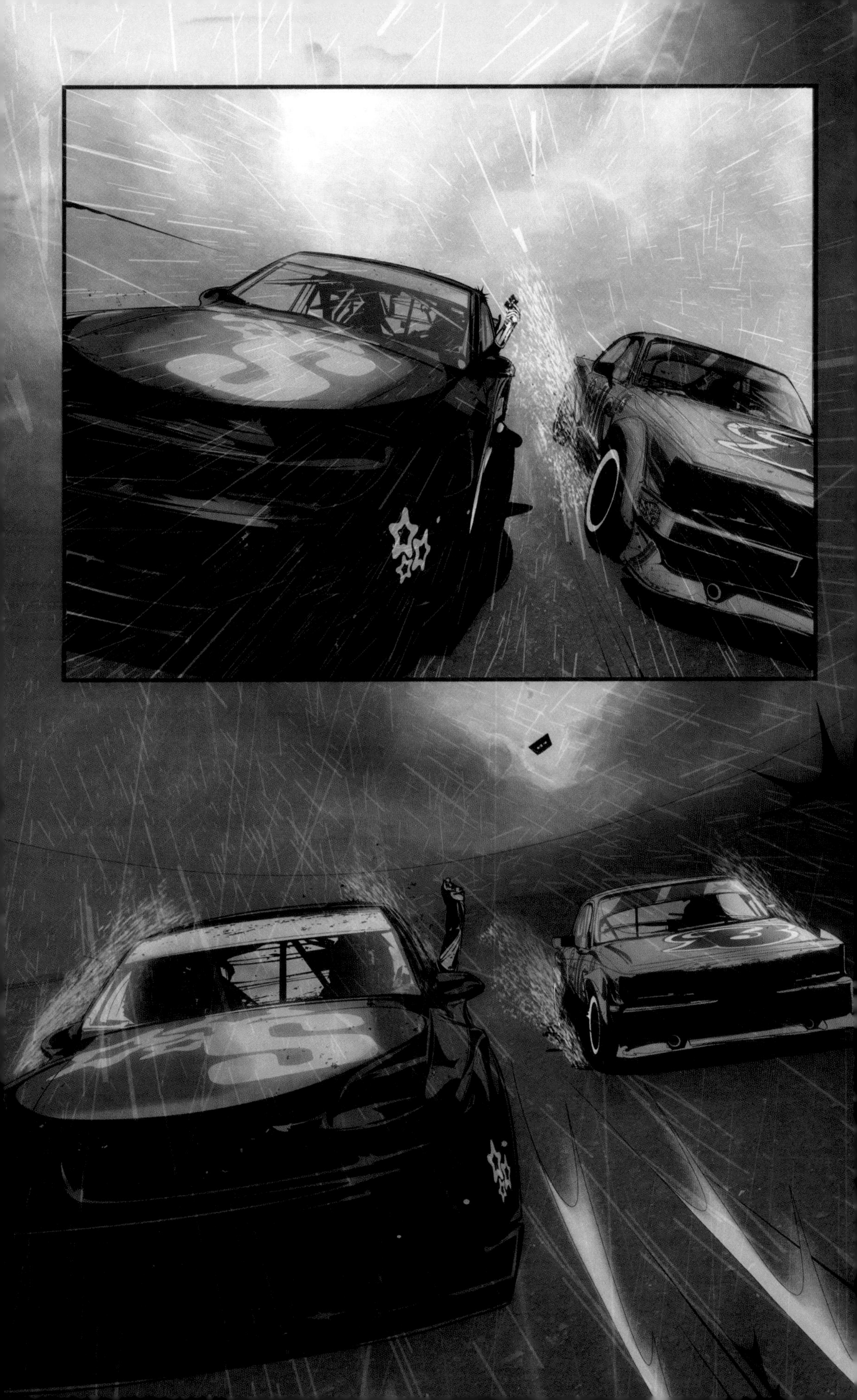

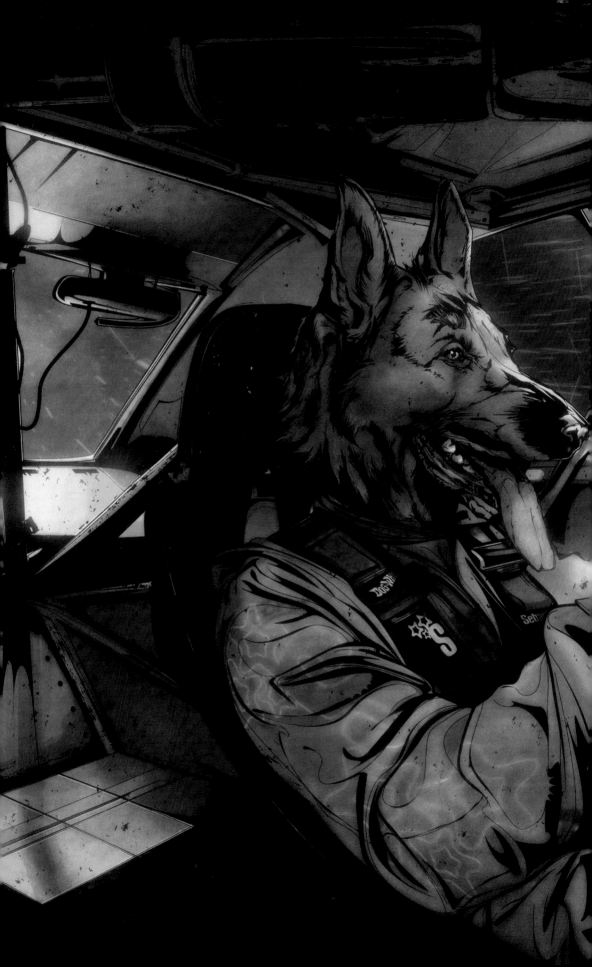

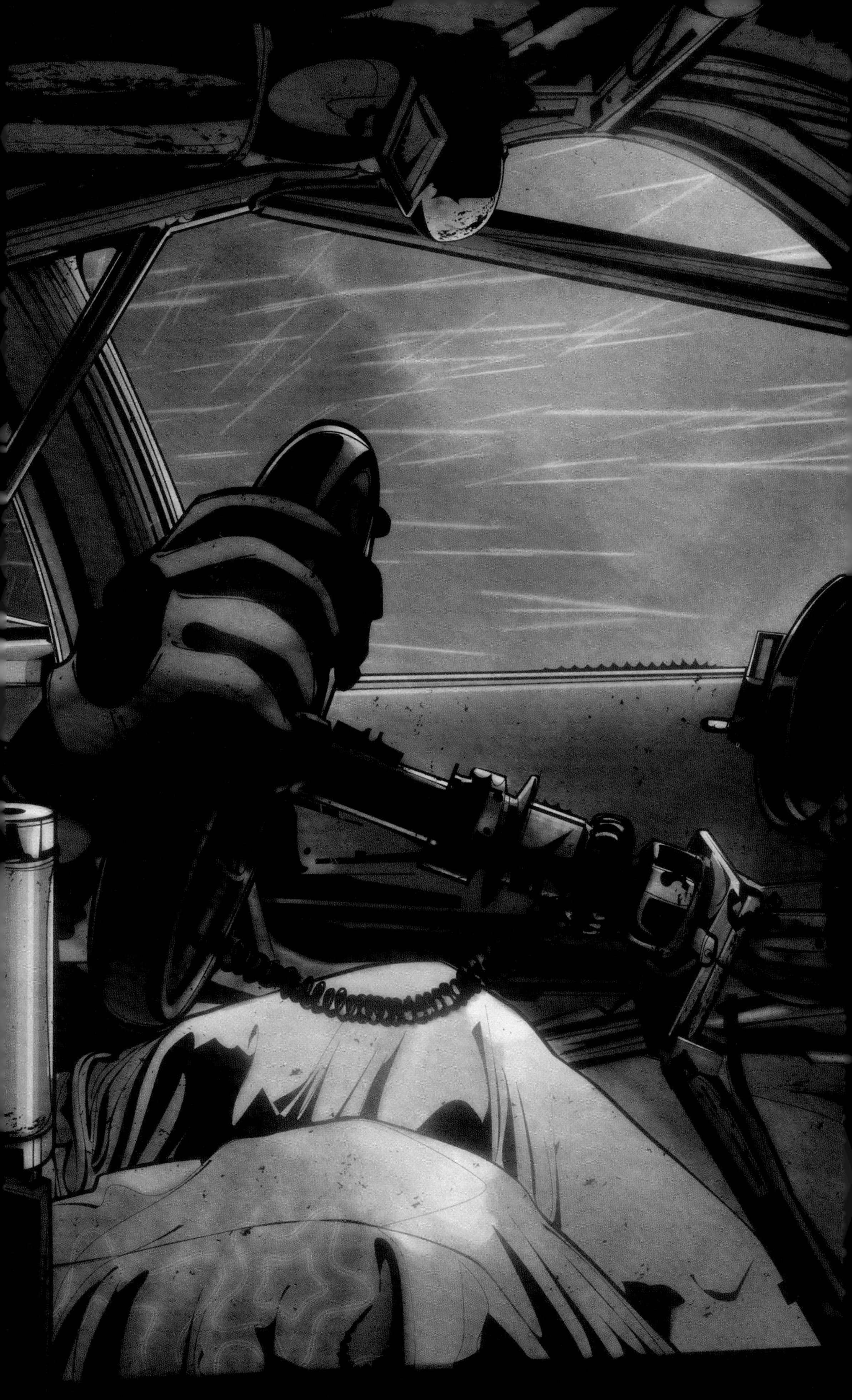

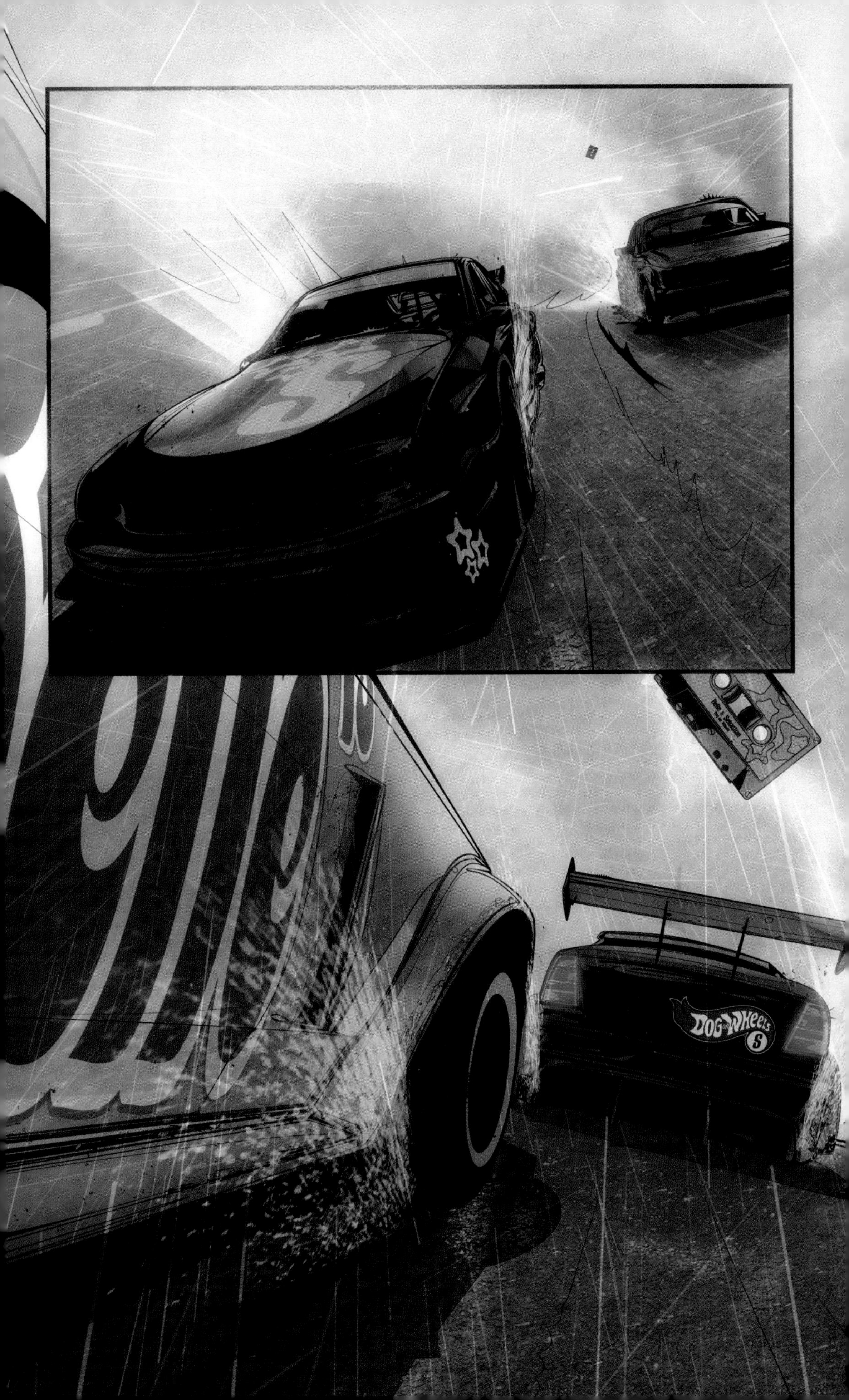
DOG WHEELS

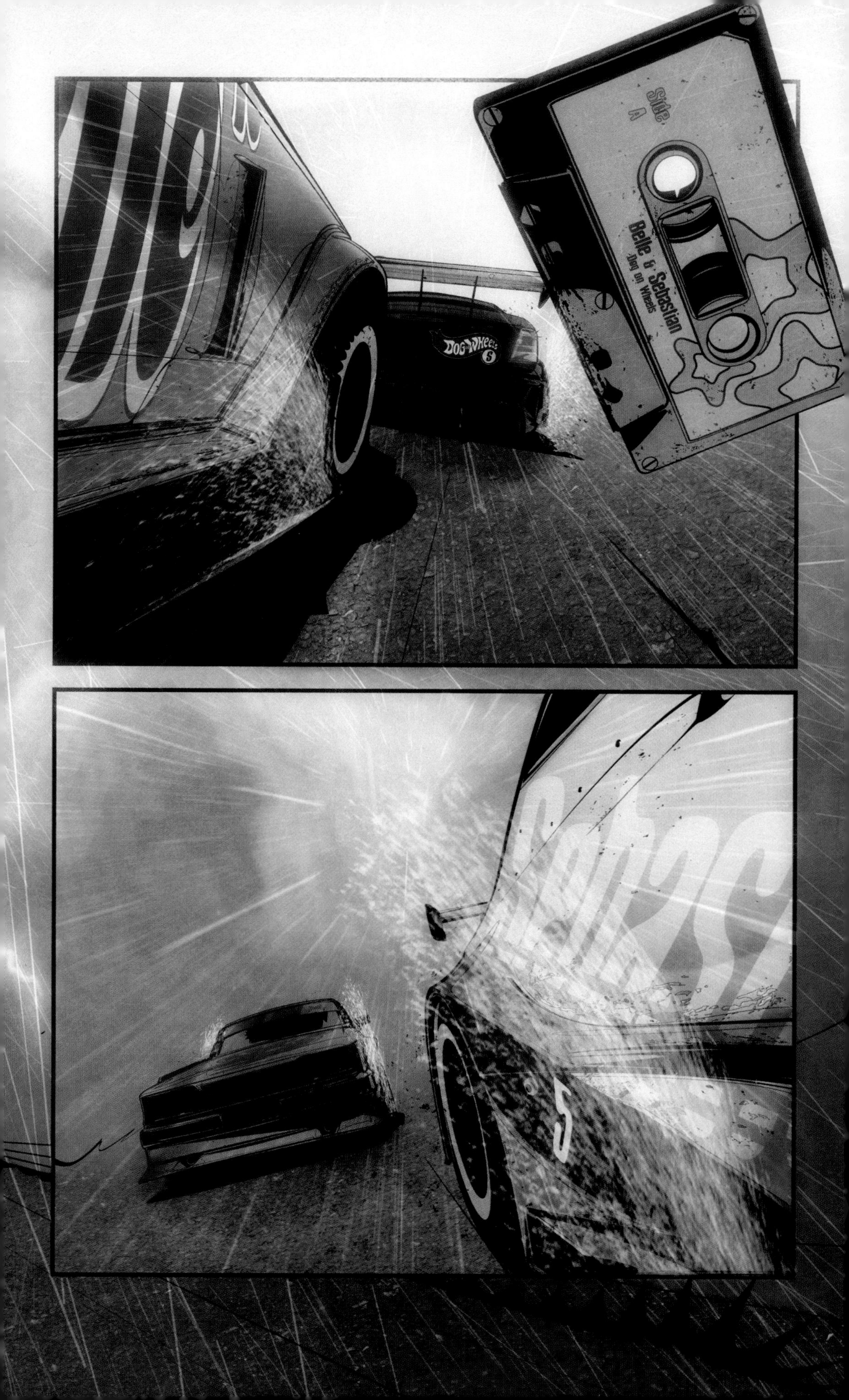
Side A
Belle & Sebastian
Dog on Wheels
Dog Wheels
5

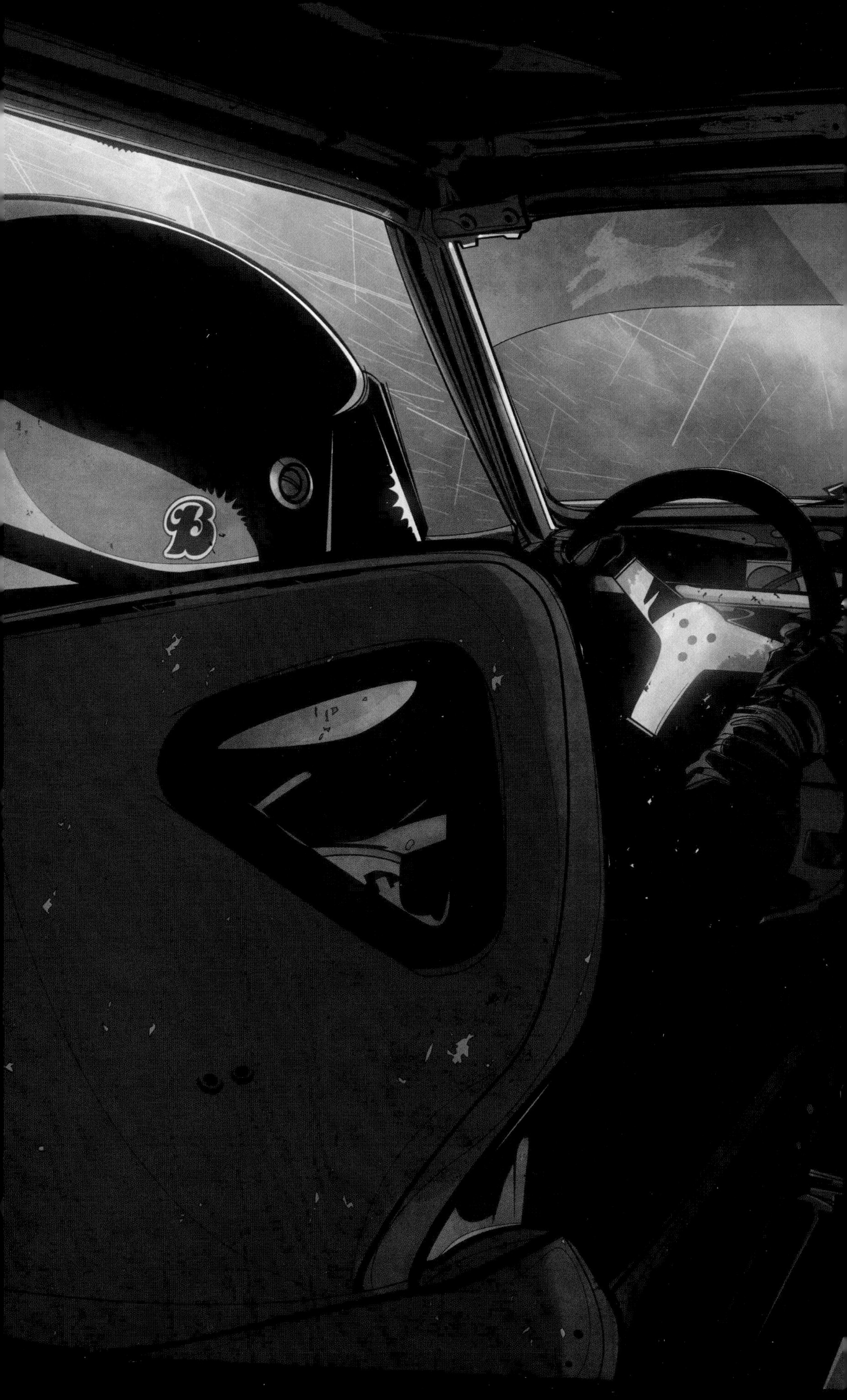

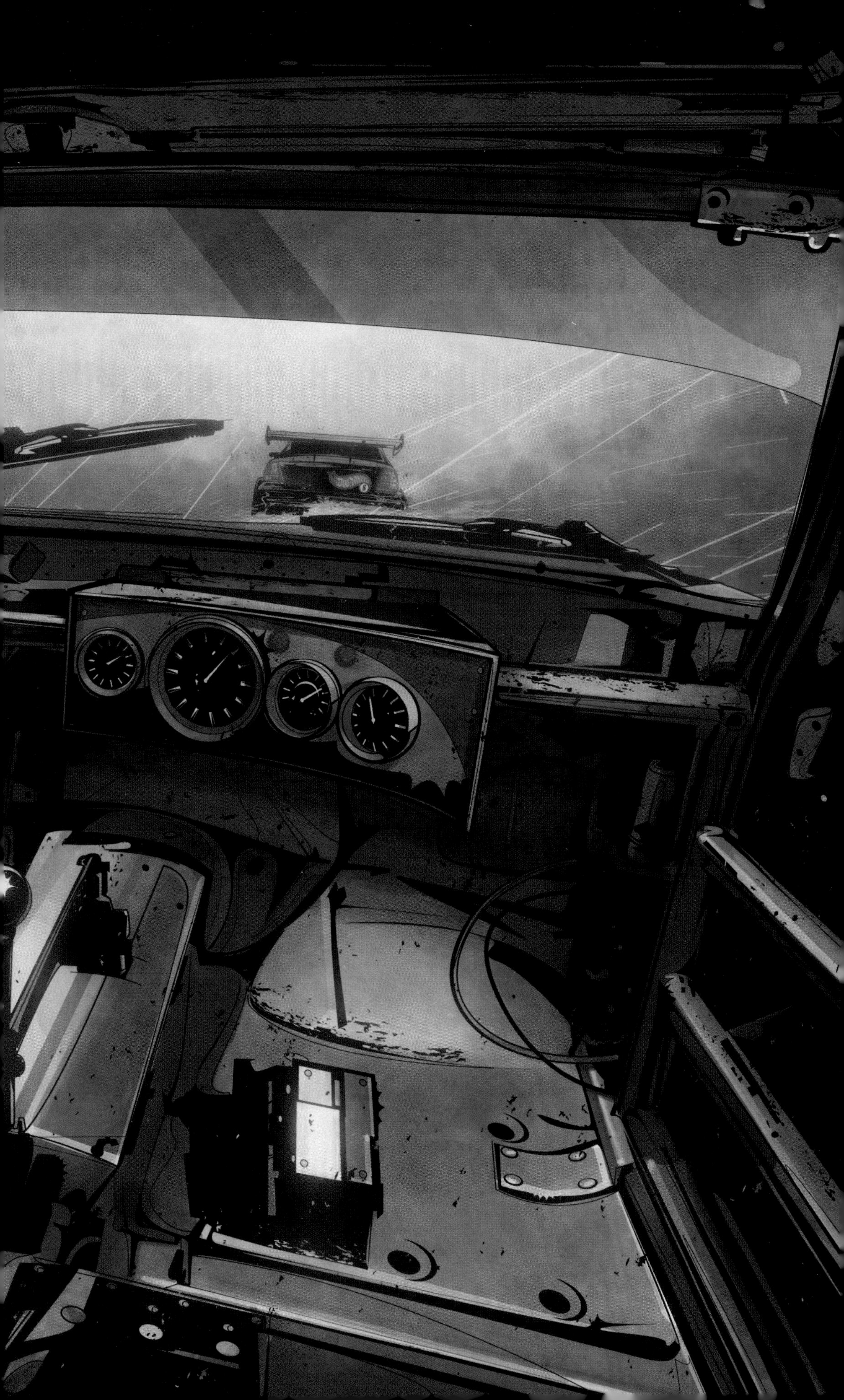

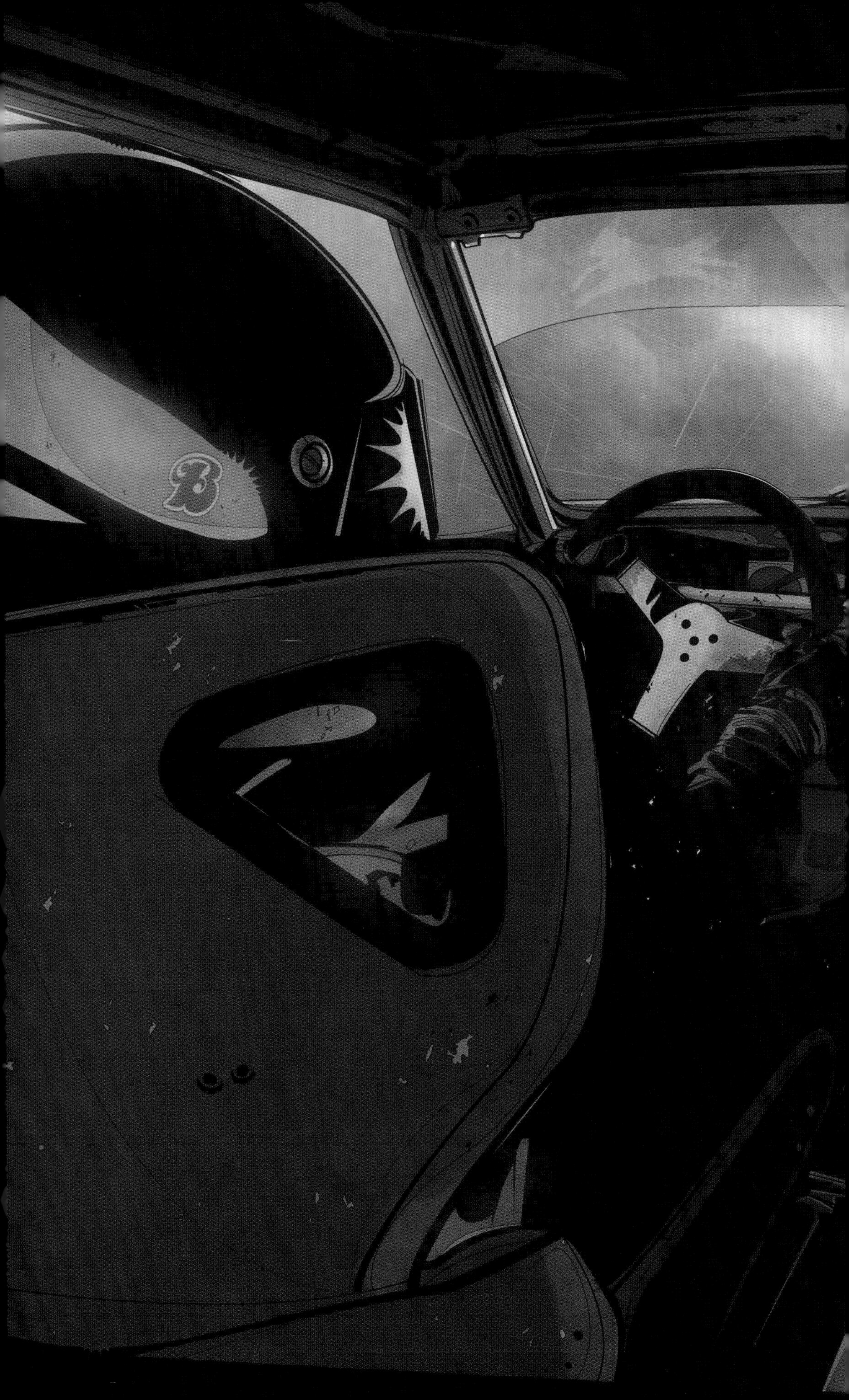

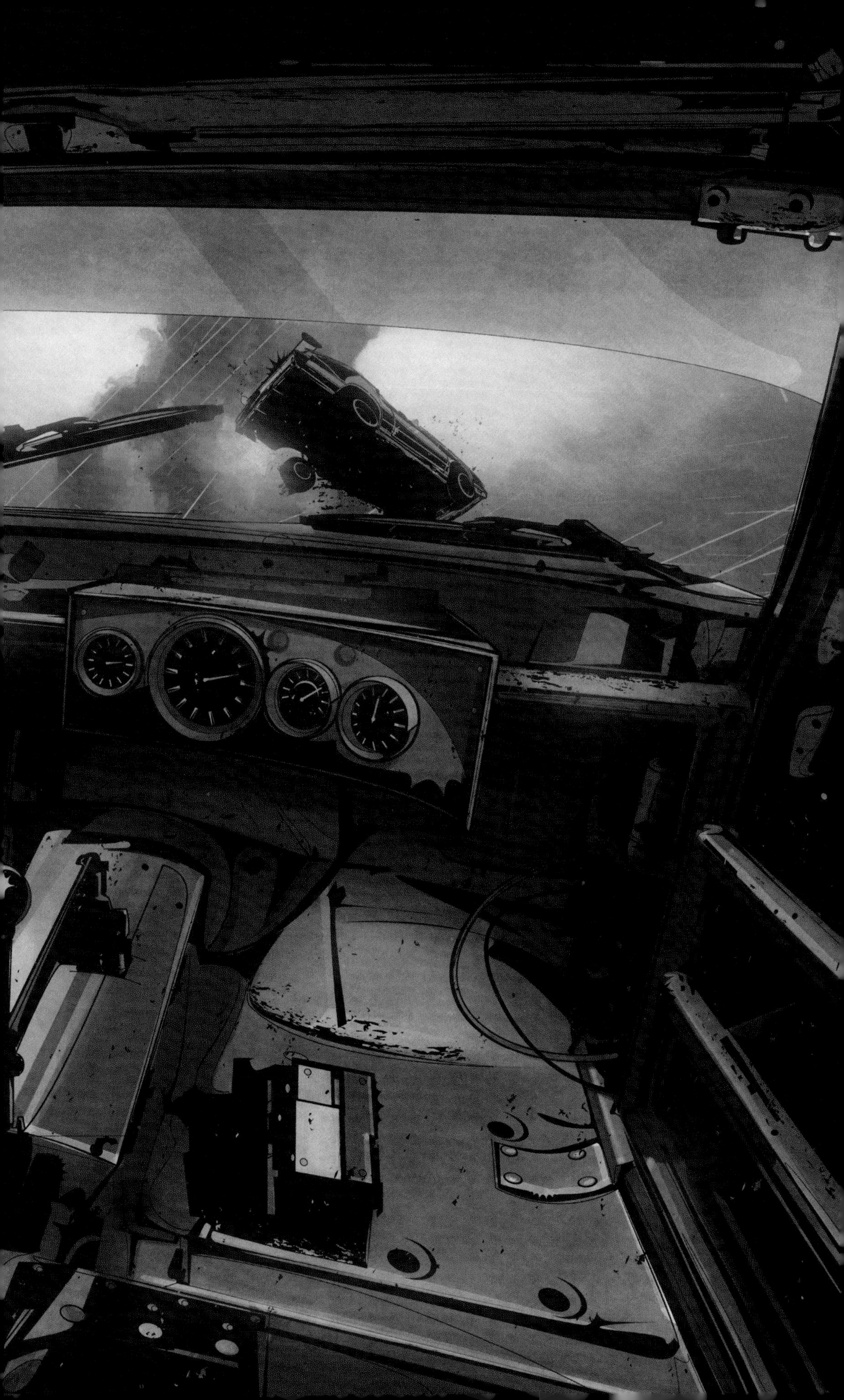

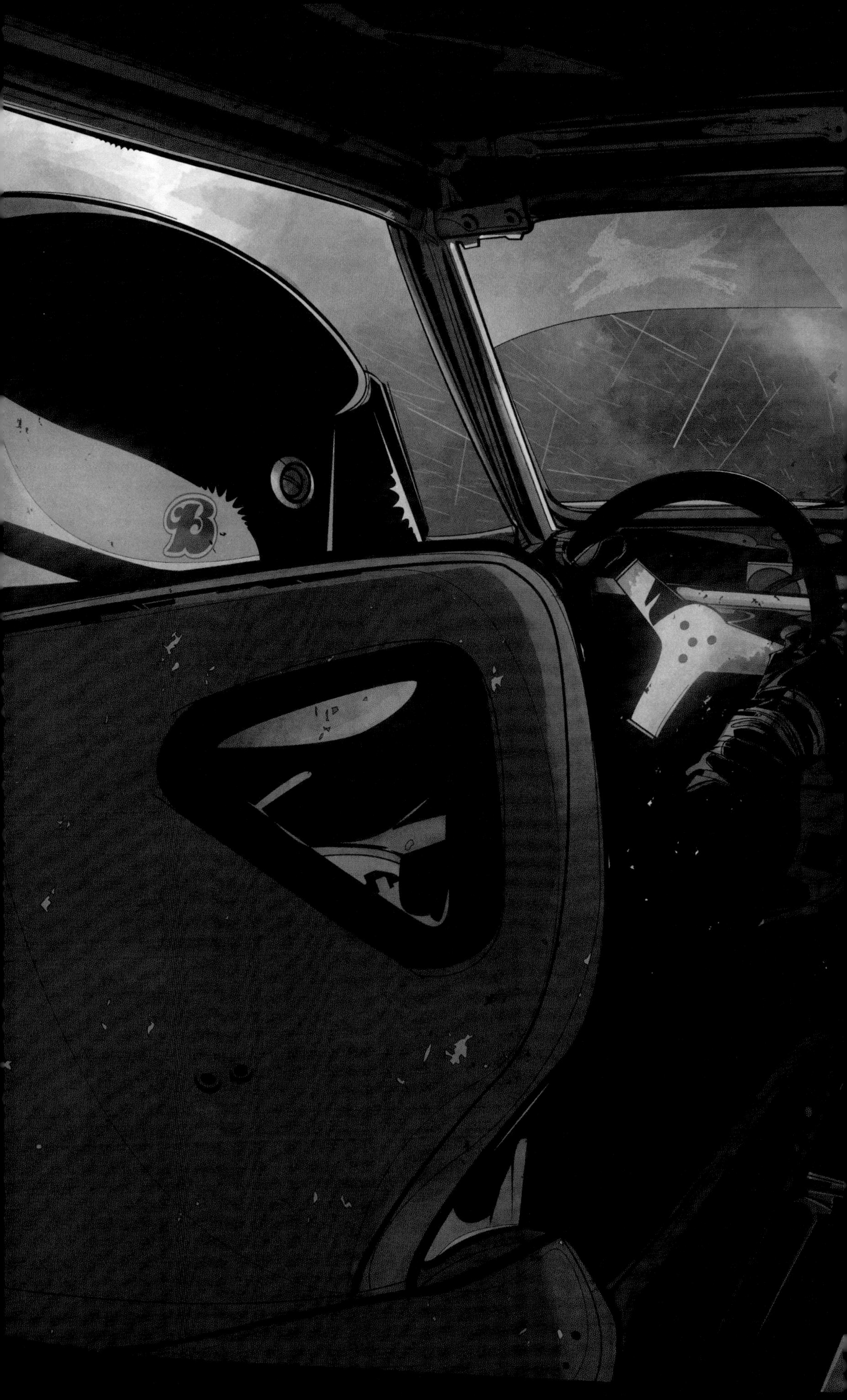

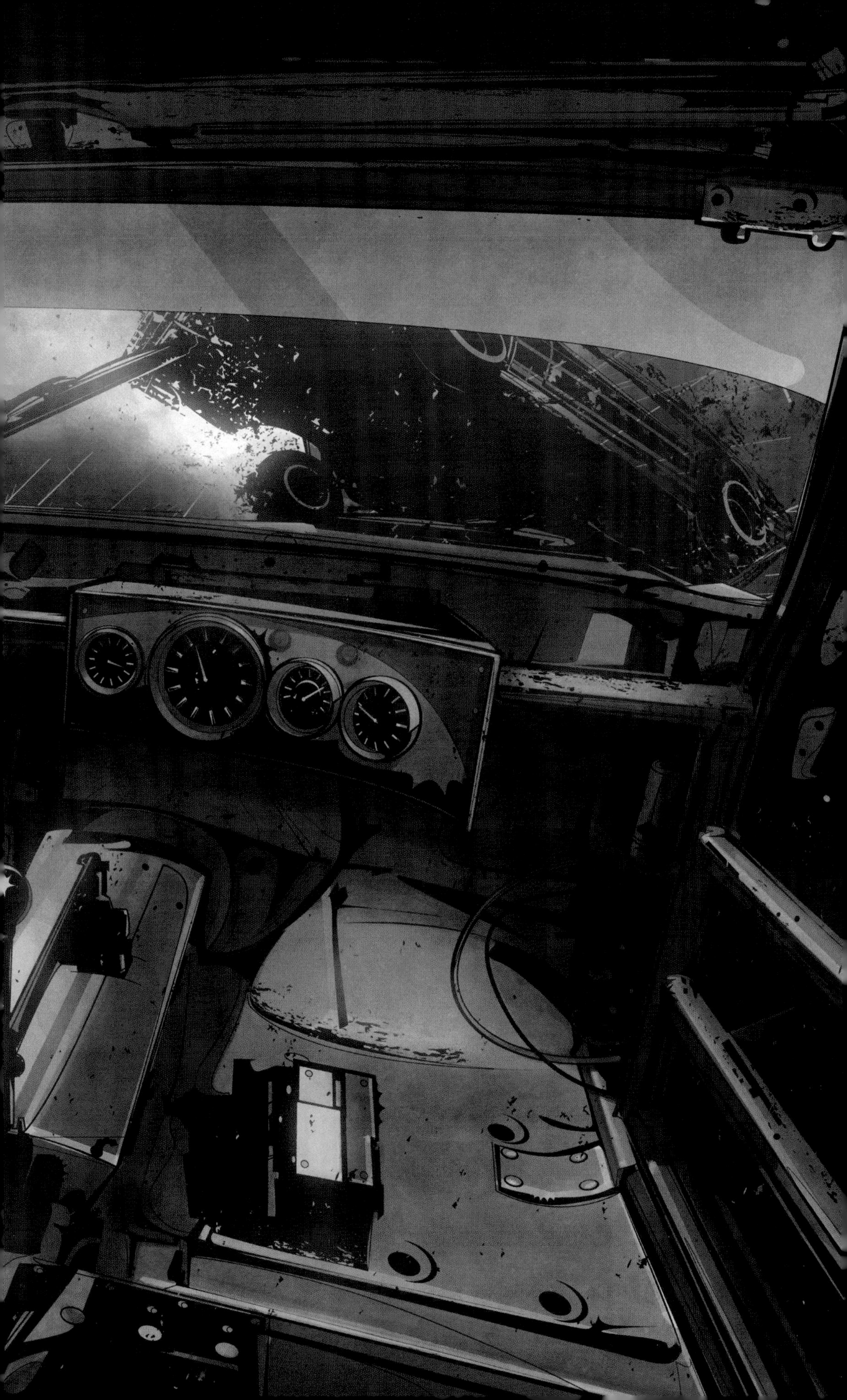

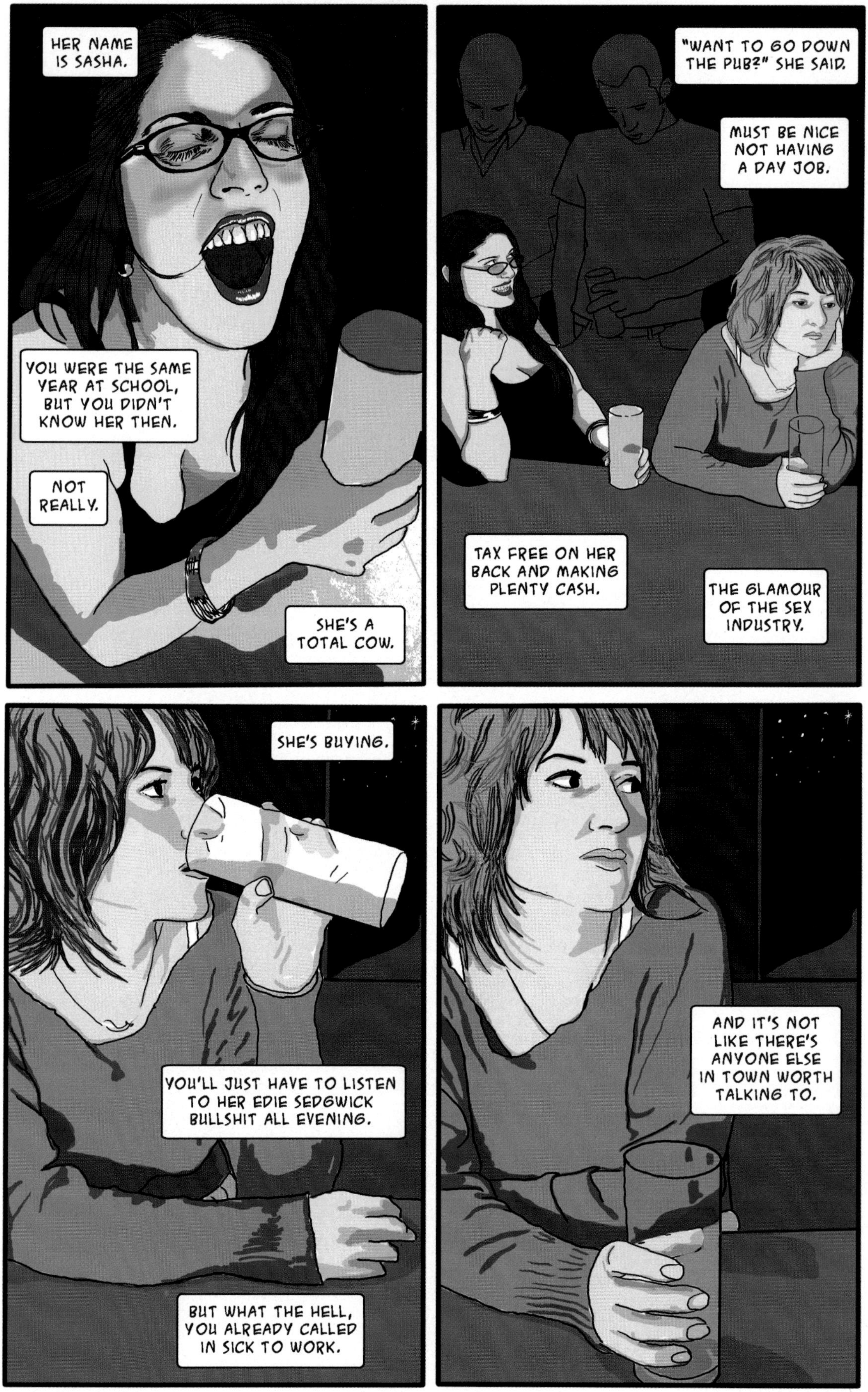
HER NAME IS SASHA.
YOU WERE THE SAME YEAR AT SCHOOL, BUT YOU DIDN'T KNOW HER THEN.
NOT REALLY.
SHE'S A TOTAL COW.
"WANT TO GO DOWN THE PUB?" SHE SAID.
MUST BE NICE NOT HAVING A DAY JOB.
TAX FREE ON HER BACK AND MAKING PLENTY CASH.
THE GLAMOUR OF THE SEX INDUSTRY.
SHE'S BUYING.
YOU'LL JUST HAVE TO LISTEN TO HER EDIE SEDGWICK BULLSHIT ALL EVENING.
BUT WHAT THE HELL, YOU ALREADY CALLED IN SICK TO WORK.
AND IT'S NOT LIKE THERE'S ANYONE ELSE IN TOWN WORTH TALKING TO.

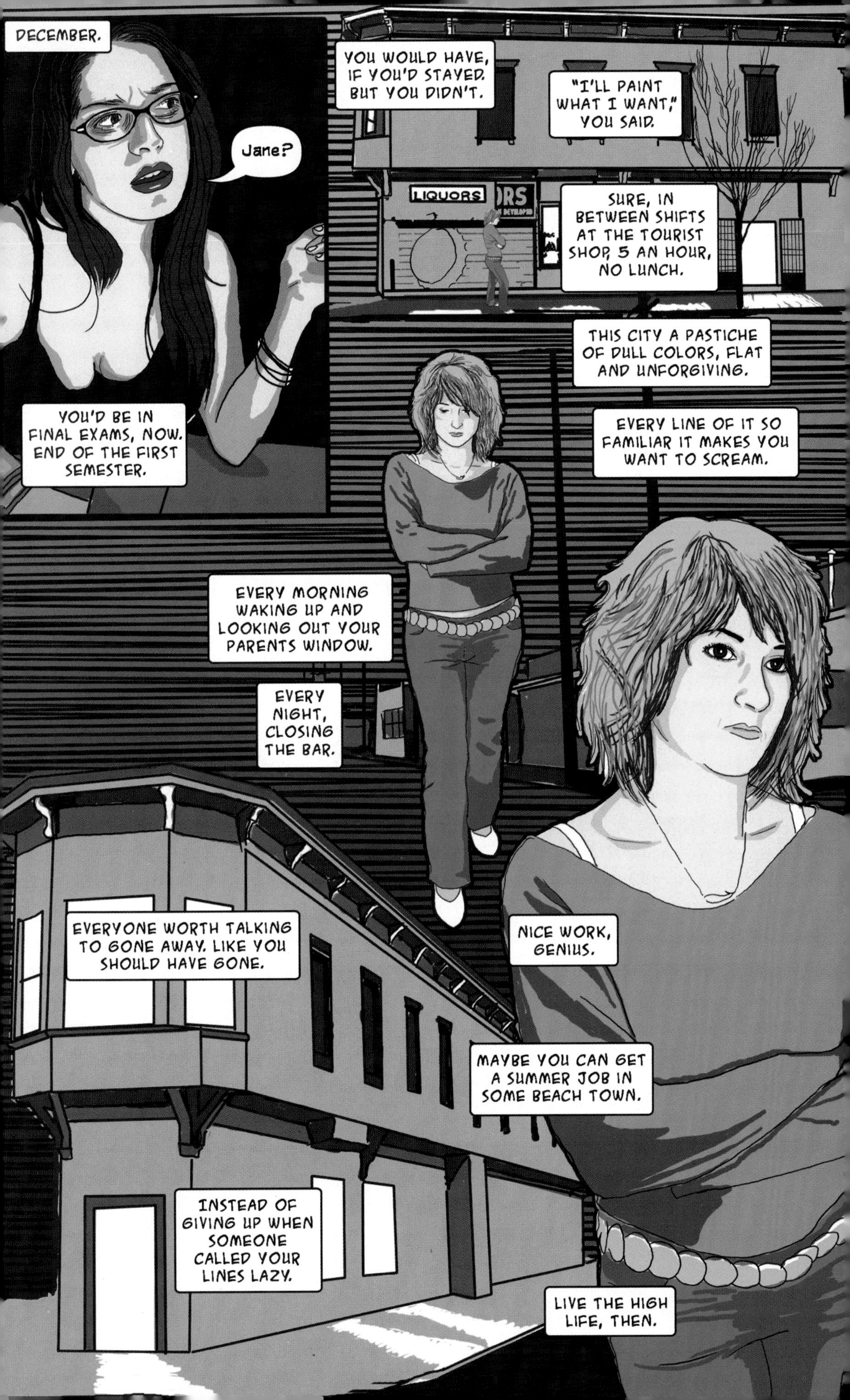
DECEMBER.
Jane?
YOU'D BE IN FINAL EXAMS, NOW. END OF THE FIRST SEMESTER.
YOU WOULD HAVE, IF YOU'D STAYED. BUT YOU DIDN'T.
"I'LL PAINT WHAT I WANT," YOU SAID.
LIQUORS
SURE, IN BETWEEN SHIFTS AT THE TOURIST SHOP, 5 AN HOUR, NO LUNCH.
THIS CITY A PASTICHE OF DULL COLORS, FLAT AND UNFORGIVING.
EVERY LINE OF IT SO FAMILIAR IT MAKES YOU WANT TO SCREAM.
EVERY MORNING WAKING UP AND LOOKING OUT YOUR PARENTS WINDOW.
EVERY NIGHT, CLOSING THE BAR.
EVERYONE WORTH TALKING TO GONE AWAY. LIKE YOU SHOULD HAVE GONE.
NICE WORK, GENIUS.
MAYBE YOU CAN GET A SUMMER JOB IN SOME BEACH TOWN.
INSTEAD OF GIVING UP WHEN SOMEONE CALLED YOUR LINES LAZY.
LIVE THE HIGH LIFE, THEN.

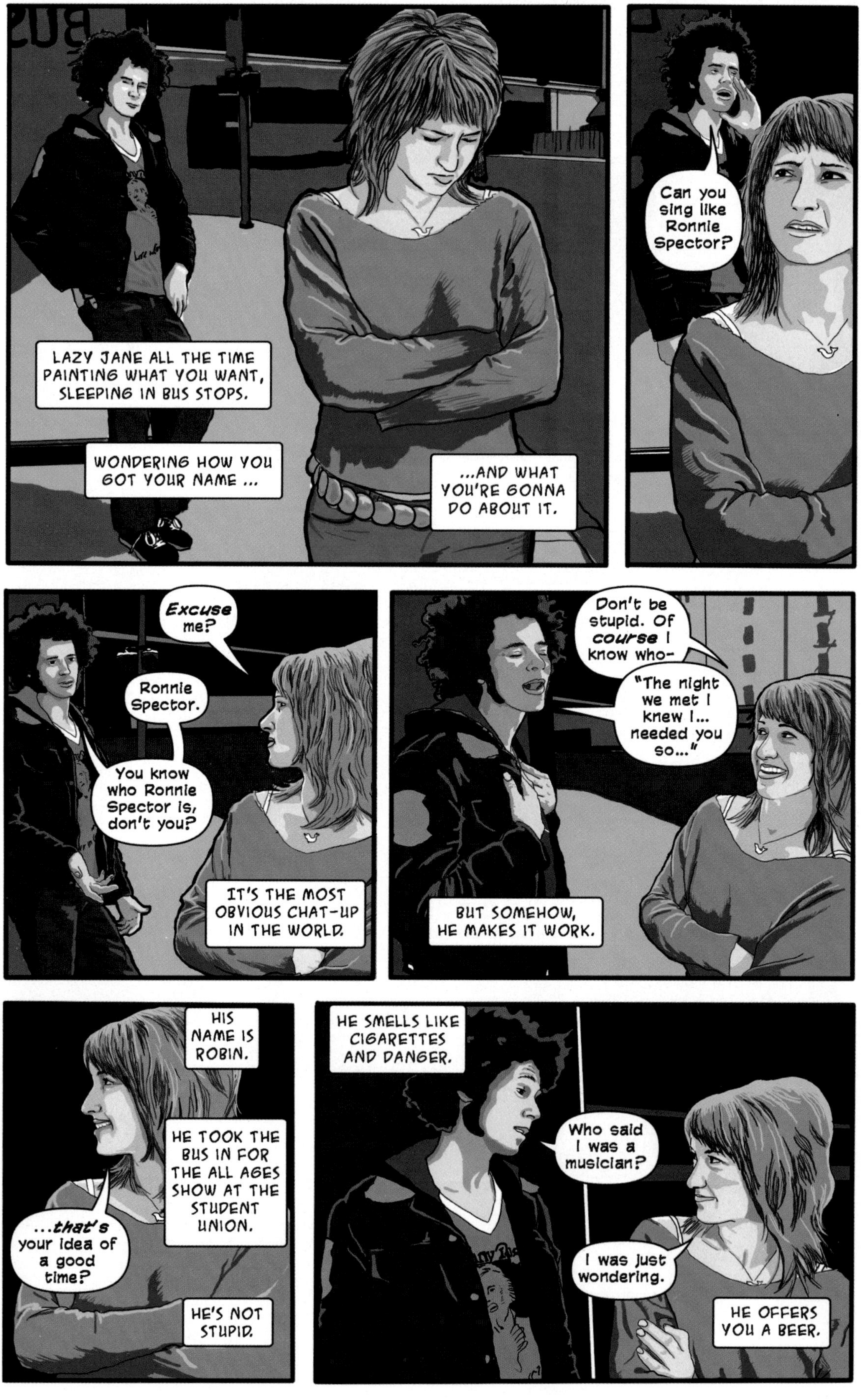
LAZY JANE ALL THE TIME PAINTING WHAT YOU WANT, SLEEPING IN BUS STOPS.
WONDERING HOW YOU GOT YOUR NAME ...
...AND WHAT YOU'RE GONNA DO ABOUT IT.
Can you sing like Ronnie Spector?
Excuse me?
Ronnie Spector.
You know who Ronnie Spector is, don't you?
IT'S THE MOST OBVIOUS CHAT-UP IN THE WORLD.
Don't be stupid. Of course I know who-
"The night we met I knew I... needed you so..."
BUT SOMEHOW, HE MAKES IT WORK.
HIS NAME IS ROBIN.
HE TOOK THE BUS IN FOR THE ALL AGES SHOW AT THE STUDENT UNION.
...that's your idea of a good time?
HE'S NOT STUPID.
HE SMELLS LIKE CIGARETTES AND DANGER.
Who said I was a musician?
I was just wondering.
HE OFFERS YOU A BEER.

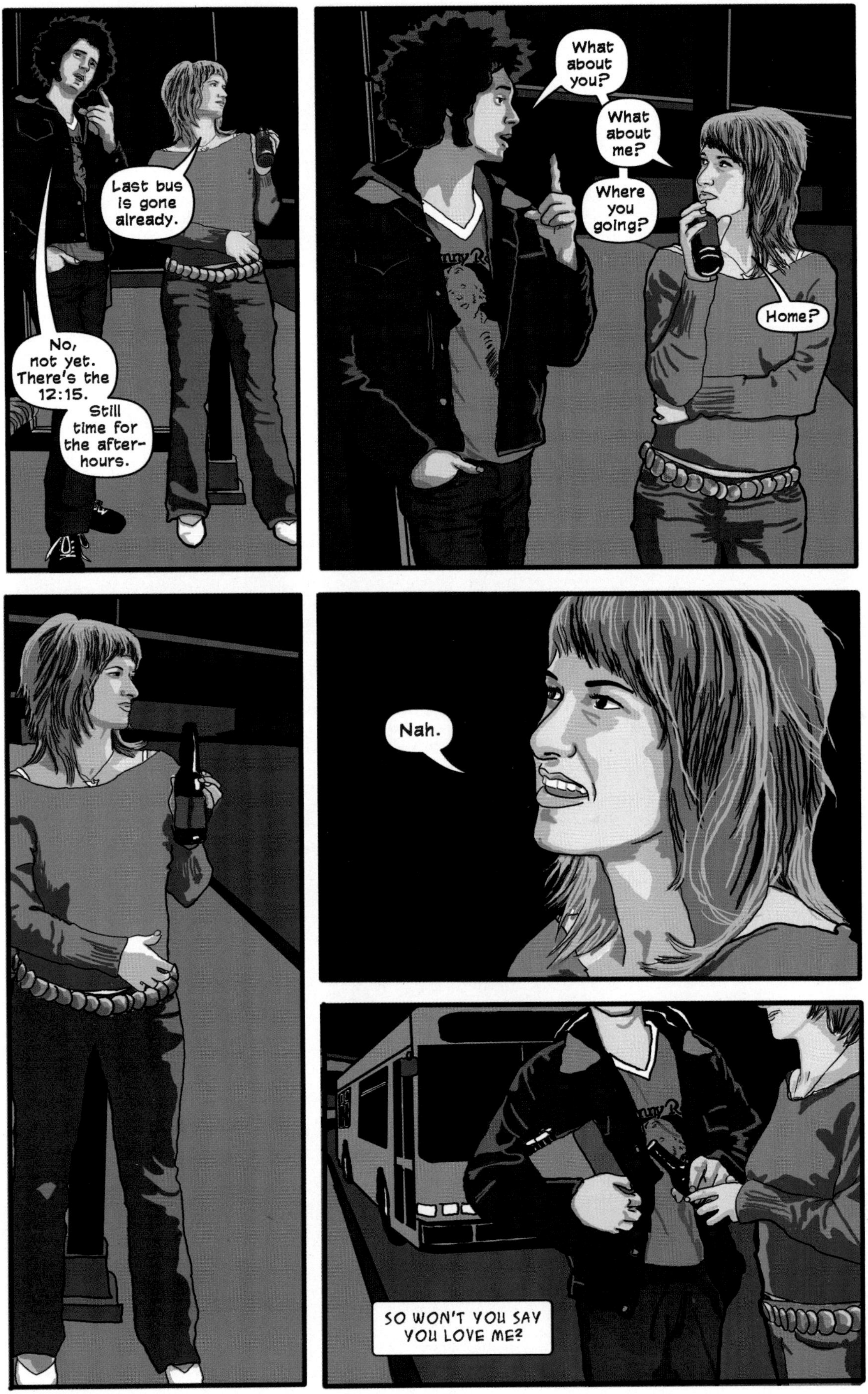
Last bus is gone already.
No, not yet. There's the 12:15.
Still time for the after-hours.
What about you?
What about me?
Where you going?
Home?
Nah.
SO WON'T YOU SAY YOU LOVE ME?

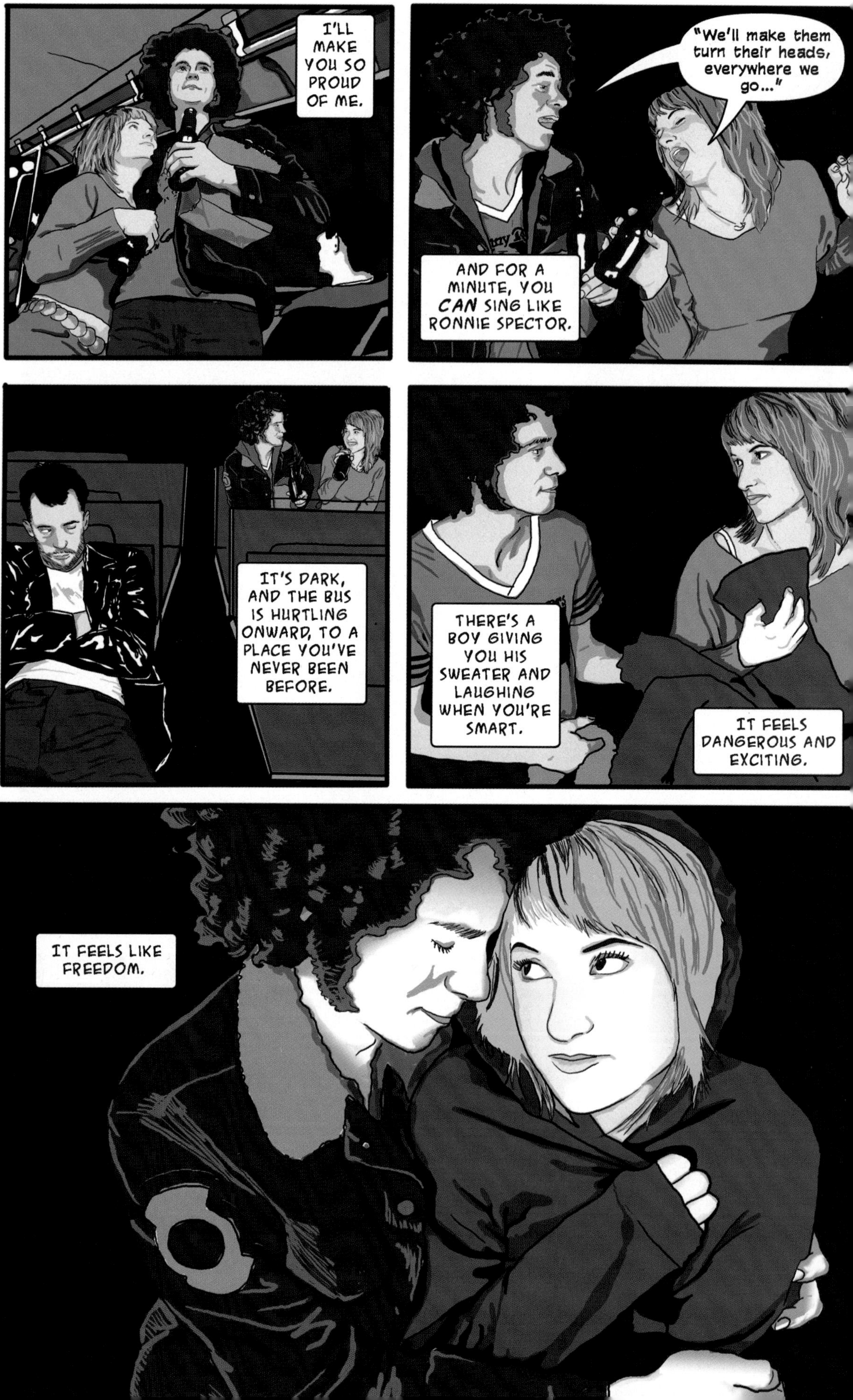
I'LL MAKE YOU SO PROUD OF ME.
"We'll make them turn their heads, everywhere we go..."
AND FOR A MINUTE, YOU CAN SING LIKE RONNIE SPECTOR.
IT'S DARK, AND THE BUS IS HURTLING ONWARD, TO A PLACE YOU'VE NEVER BEEN BEFORE.
THERE'S A BOY GIVING YOU HIS SWEATER AND LAUGHING WHEN YOU'RE SMART.
IT FEELS DANGEROUS AND EXCITING.
IT FEELS LIKE FREEDOM.

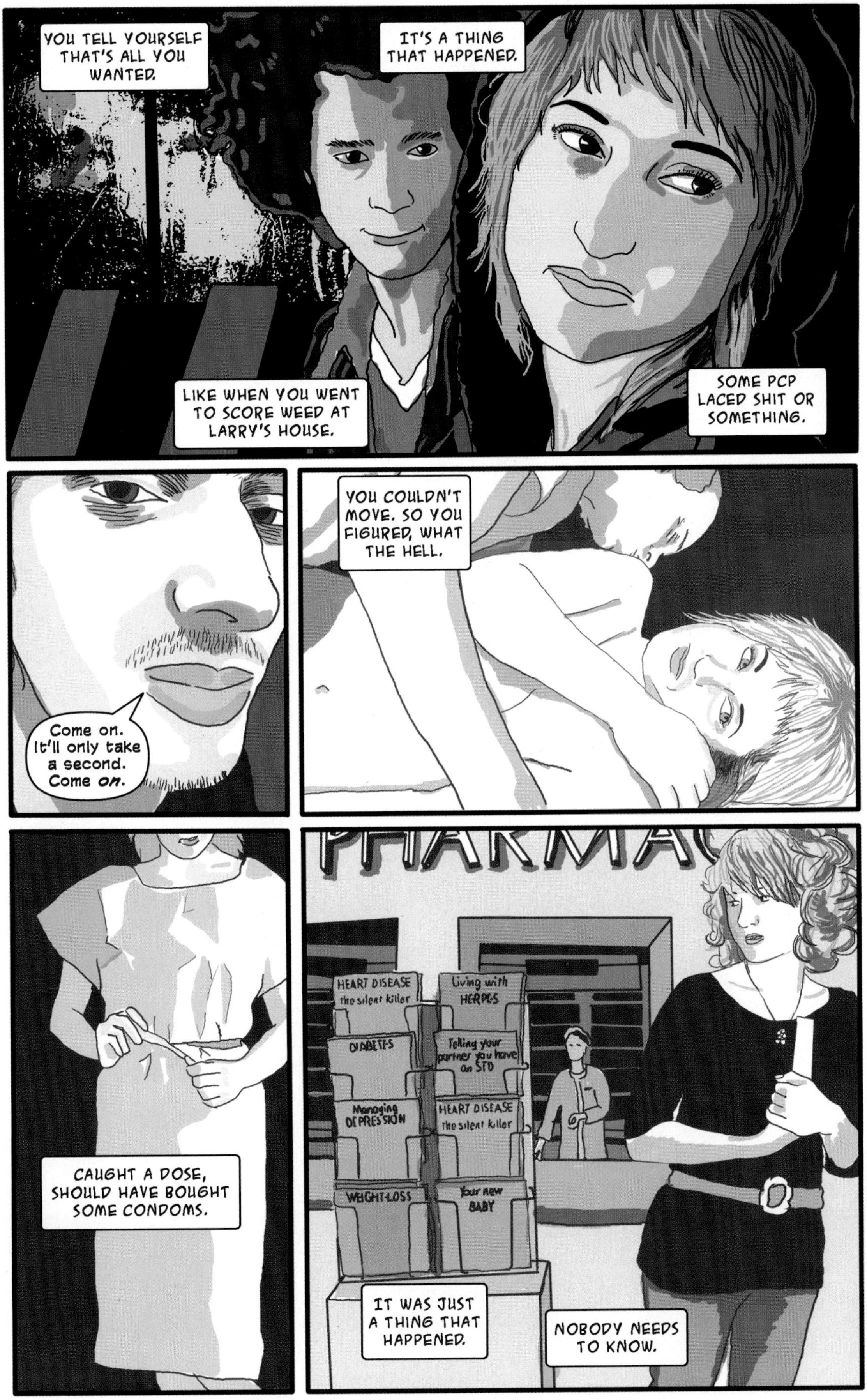
YOU TELL YOURSELF THAT'S ALL YOU WANTED.
IT'S A THING THAT HAPPENED.
LIKE WHEN YOU WENT TO SCORE WEED AT LARRY'S HOUSE.
SOME PCP LACED SHIT OR SOMETHING.
Come on. It'll only take a second. Come *on*.
YOU COULDN'T MOVE. SO YOU FIGURED, WHAT THE HELL.
CAUGHT A DOSE, SHOULD HAVE BOUGHT SOME CONDOMS.
PHARMAC
HEART DISEASE the silent killer
Living with HERPES
DIABETES
Telling your partner you have an STD
Managing DEPRESSION
HEART DISEASE the silent killer
WEIGHT-LOSS
Your new BABY
IT WAS JUST A THING THAT HAPPENED.
NOBODY NEEDS TO KNOW.

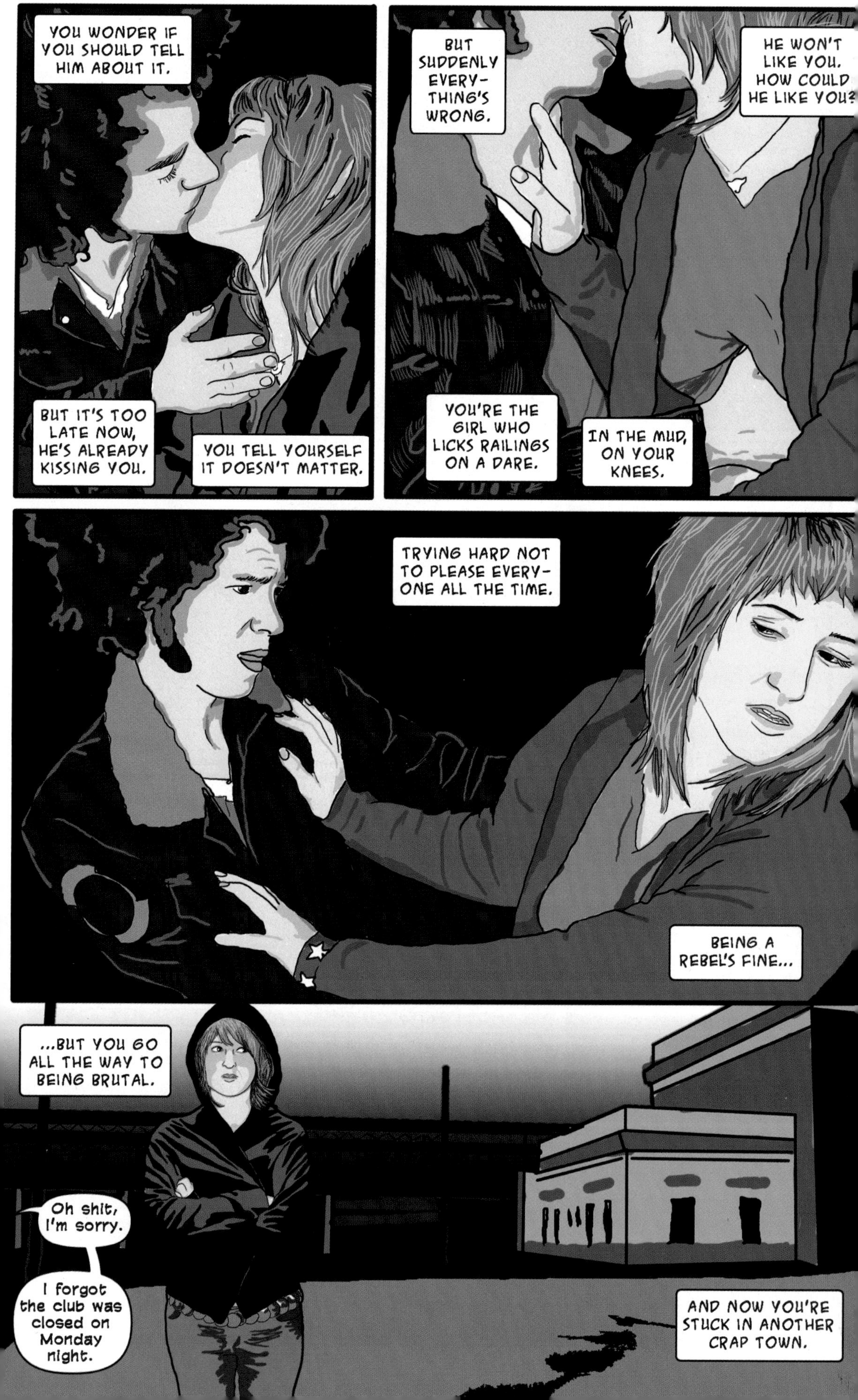

YOU WONDER IF YOU SHOULD TELL HIM ABOUT IT.
BUT IT'S TOO LATE NOW, HE'S ALREADY KISSING YOU.
YOU TELL YOURSELF IT DOESN'T MATTER.
BUT SUDDENLY EVERY-THING'S WRONG.
HE WON'T LIKE YOU. HOW COULD HE LIKE YOU?
YOU'RE THE GIRL WHO LICKS RAILINGS ON A DARE.
IN THE MUD, ON YOUR KNEES.
TRYING HARD NOT TO PLEASE EVERY-ONE ALL THE TIME.
BEING A REBEL'S FINE...
...BUT YOU GO ALL THE WAY TO BEING BRUTAL.
Oh shit, I'm sorry.
I forgot the club was closed on Monday night.
AND NOW YOU'RE STUCK IN ANOTHER CRAP TOWN.

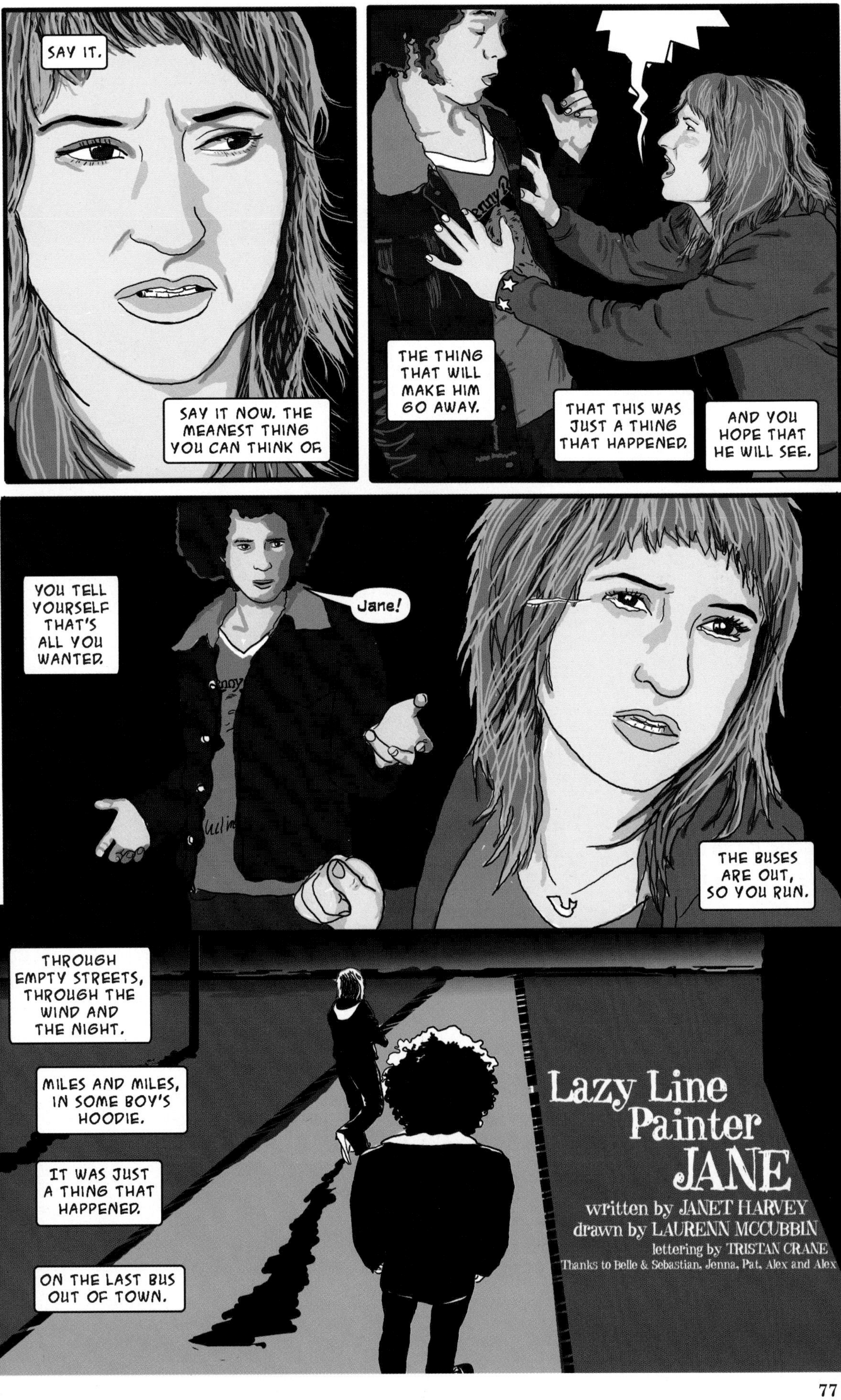
SAY IT.
SAY IT NOW. THE MEANEST THING YOU CAN THINK OF.
THE THING THAT WILL MAKE HIM GO AWAY.
THAT THIS WAS JUST A THING THAT HAPPENED.
AND YOU HOPE THAT HE WILL SEE.
YOU TELL YOURSELF THAT'S ALL YOU WANTED.
Jane!
THE BUSES ARE OUT, SO YOU RUN.
THROUGH EMPTY STREETS, THROUGH THE WIND AND THE NIGHT.
MILES AND MILES, IN SOME BOY'S HOODIE.
IT WAS JUST A THING THAT HAPPENED.
ON THE LAST BUS OUT OF TOWN.
Lazy Line Painter JANE
written by JANET HARVEY
drawn by LAURENN MCCUBBIN
lettering by TRISTAN CRANE
Thanks to Belle & Sebastian, Jenna, Pat, Alex and Alex

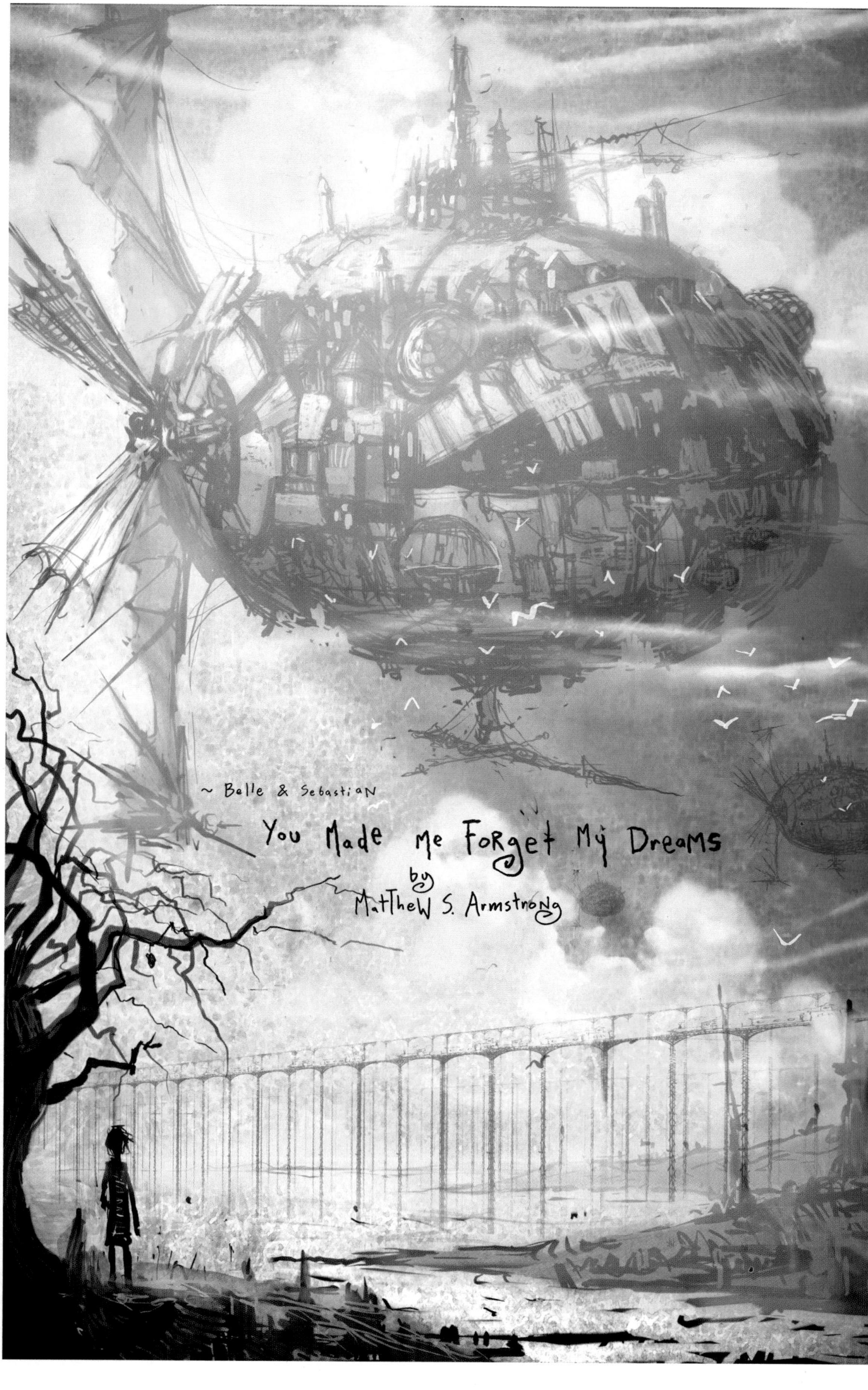
~ Belle & Sebastian
You Made me Forget My Dreams
by
Matthew S. Armstrong

You made me forget my Dreams

When I woke up to you sleeping

We had peace for a night at least

But the trouble starts today

This morning you'll say

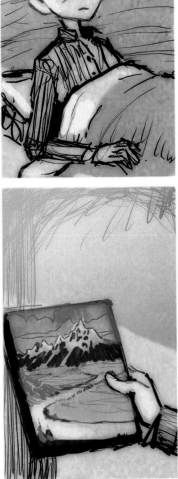

I'll see you sometime,

maybe and I

Fall back to uneasy sleep

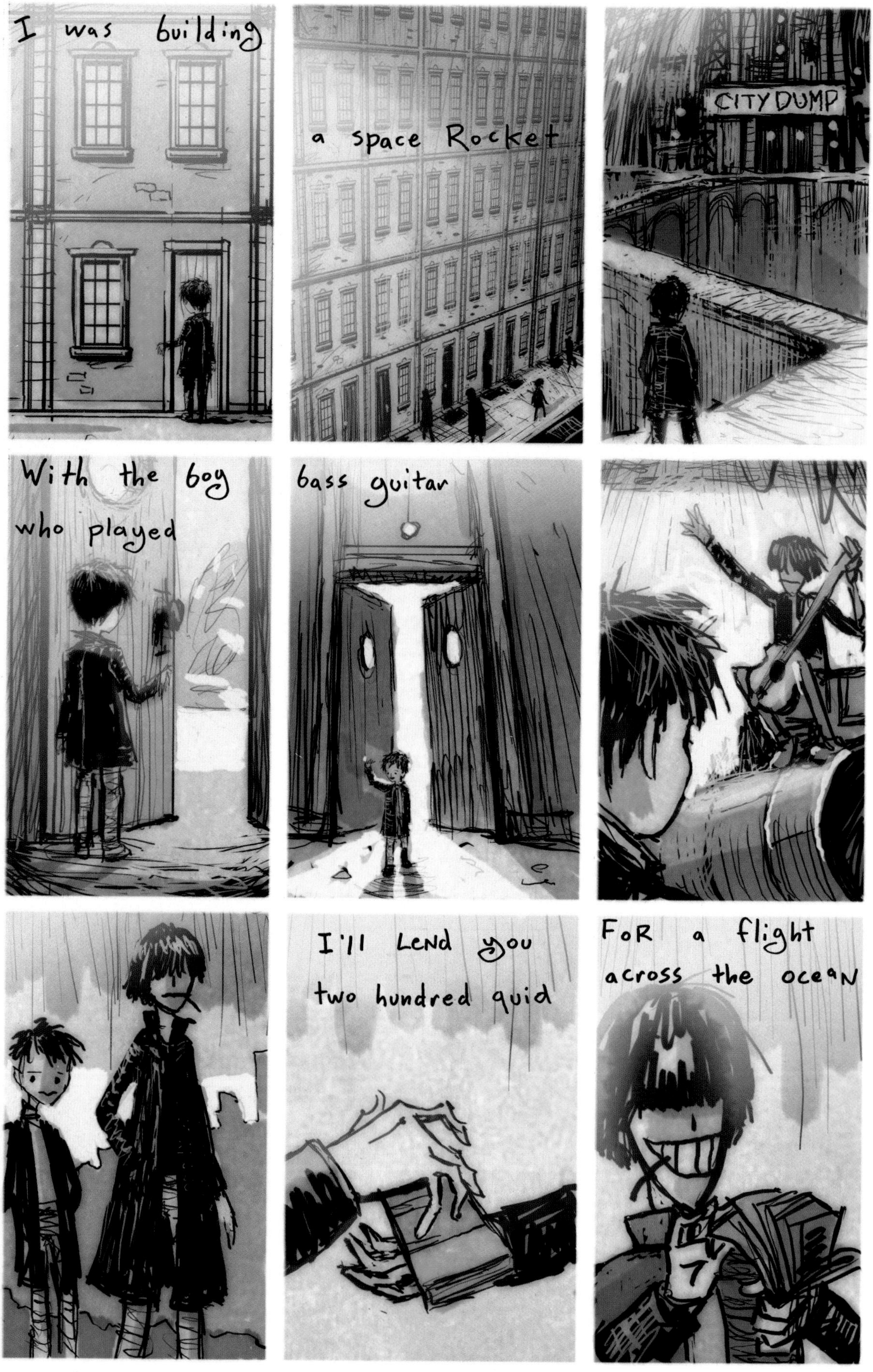
I was building
a space Rocket
CITY DUMP
With the boy who played
bass guitar
I'll Lend you two hundred quid
FoR a flight across the ocean

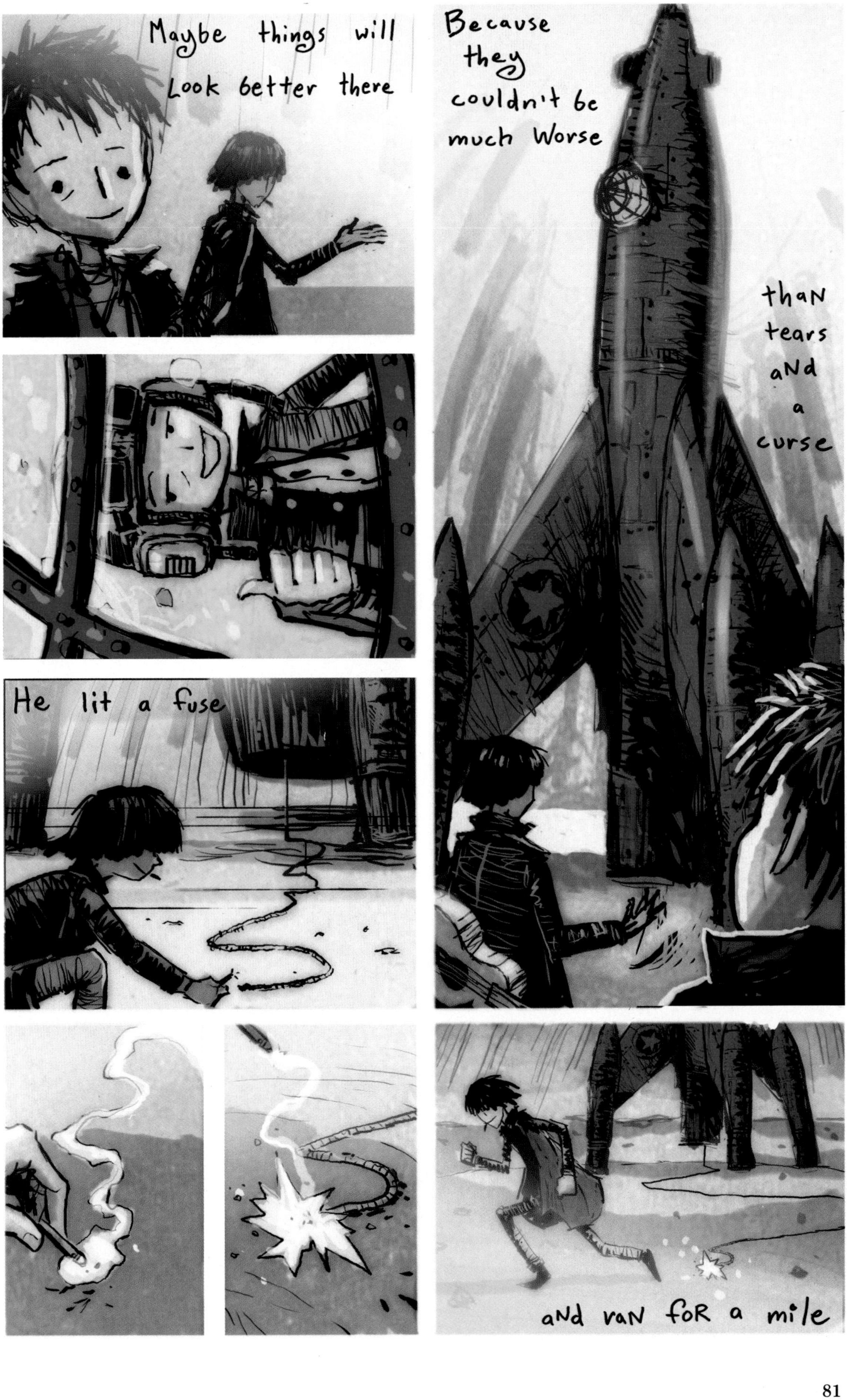
Maybe things will Look better there
Because they couldn't be much Worse
than tears and a curse
He lit a fuse
and ran for a mile

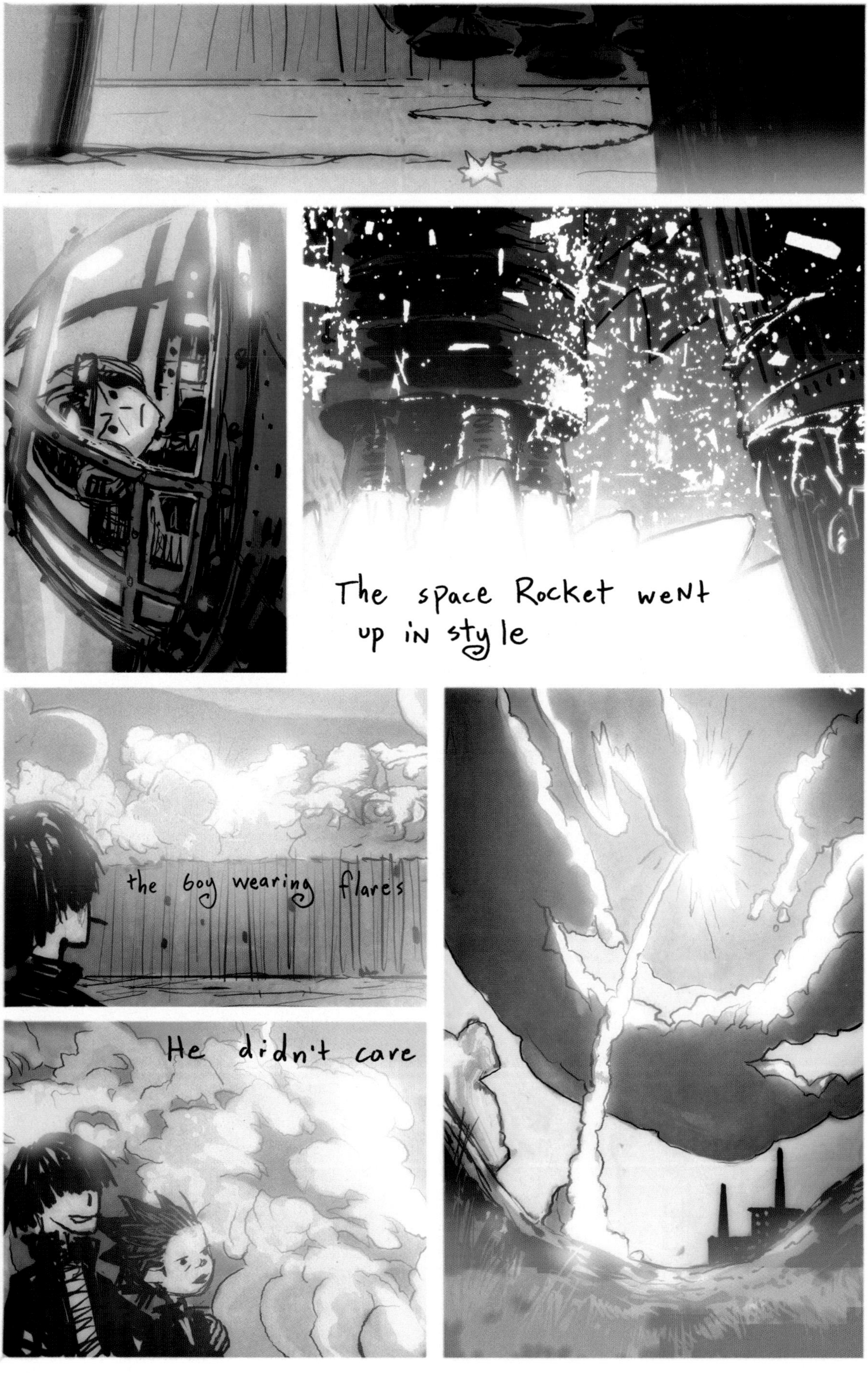
The space Rocket went up in style
the boy wearing flares
He didn't care

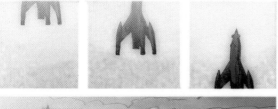

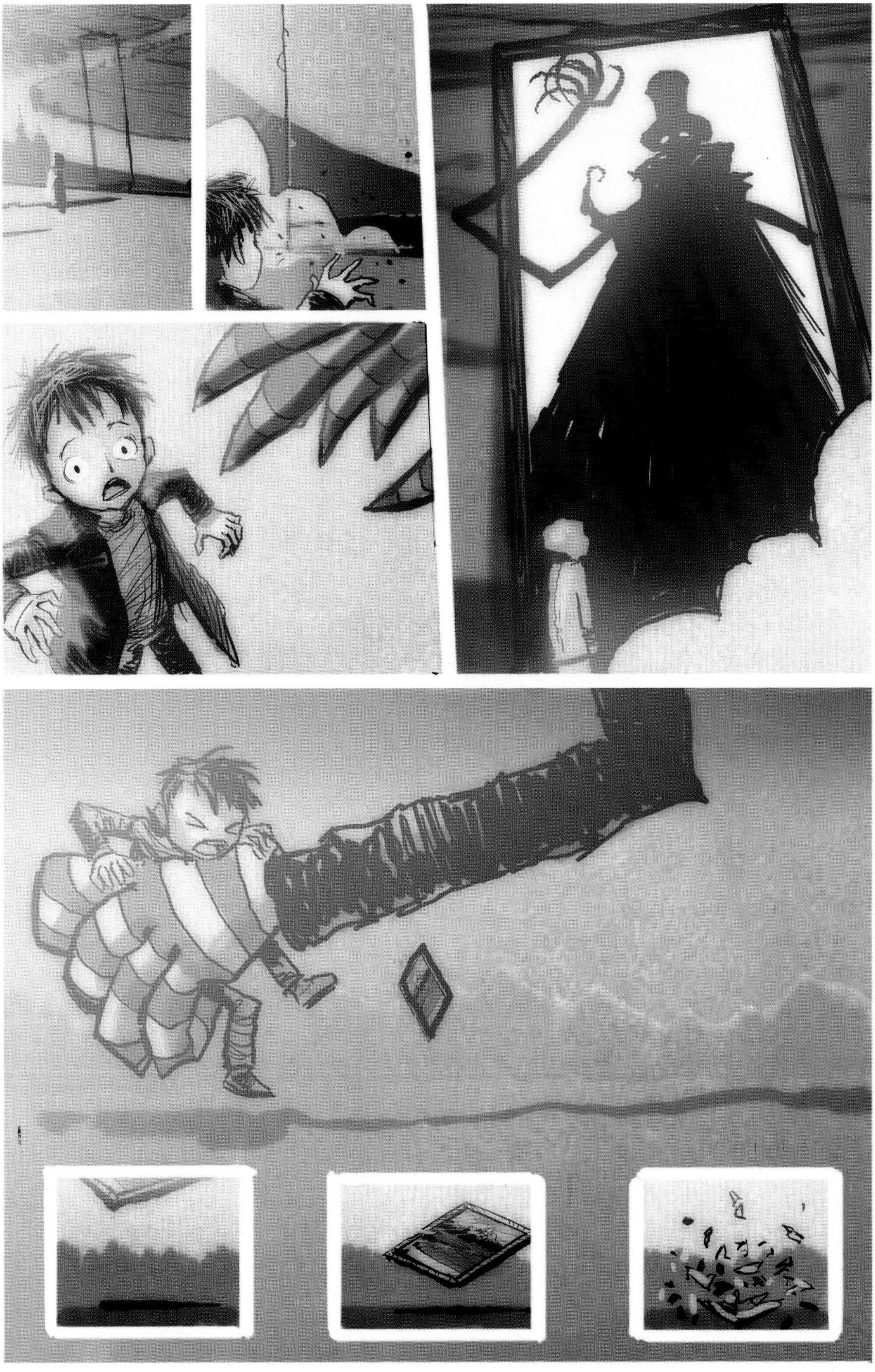

For Men
with guns,
Maturing
in age

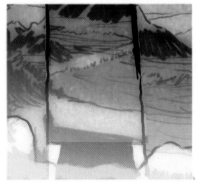
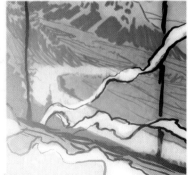

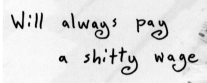

Will always pay
a shitty wage

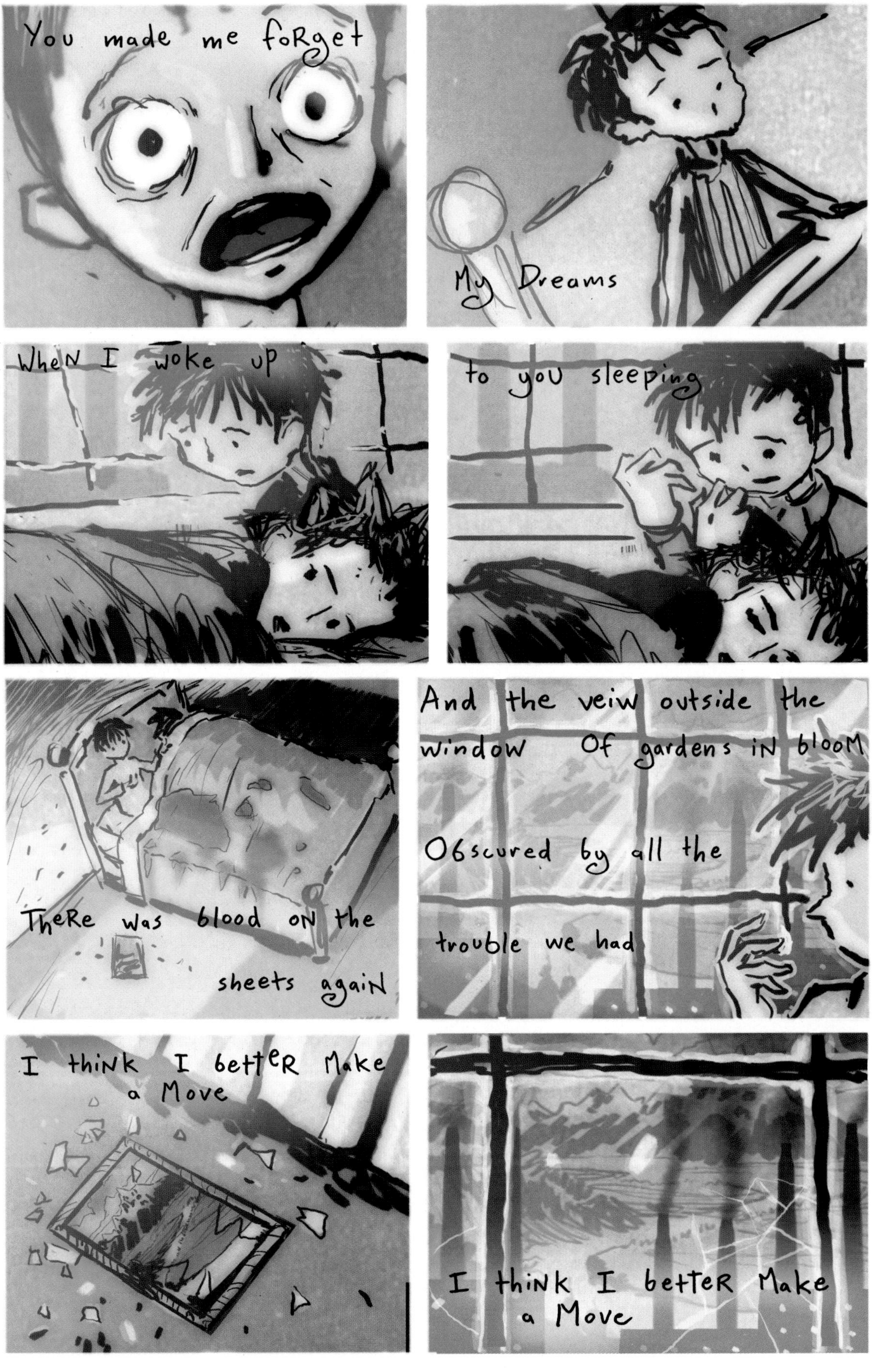
You made me forget
My Dreams
When I woke up
to you sleeping
There was blood on the sheets again
And the veiw outside the window Of gardens in bloom
Obscured by all the
trouble we had
I think I better make a move
I think I better make a move

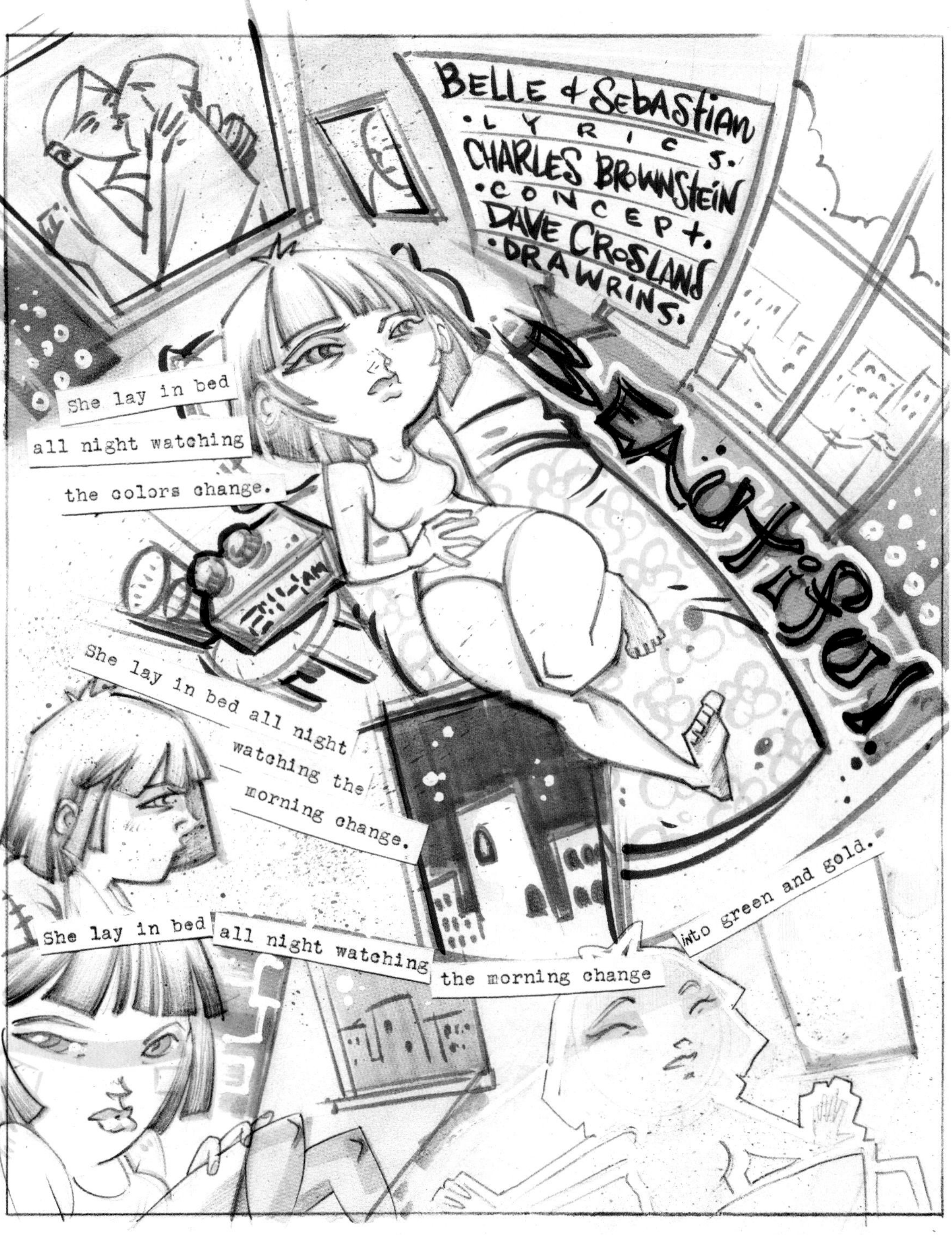
BELLE & SEBASTIAN
·LYRICS.
CHARLES BROWNSTEIN
·CONCEPT.
DAVE CROSLAND
·DRAWRINS.
BEAUTIFUL!
She lay in bed
all night watching
the colors change.
She lay in bed all night
watching the
morning change.
She lay in bed
all night watching
the morning change
into green and gold.

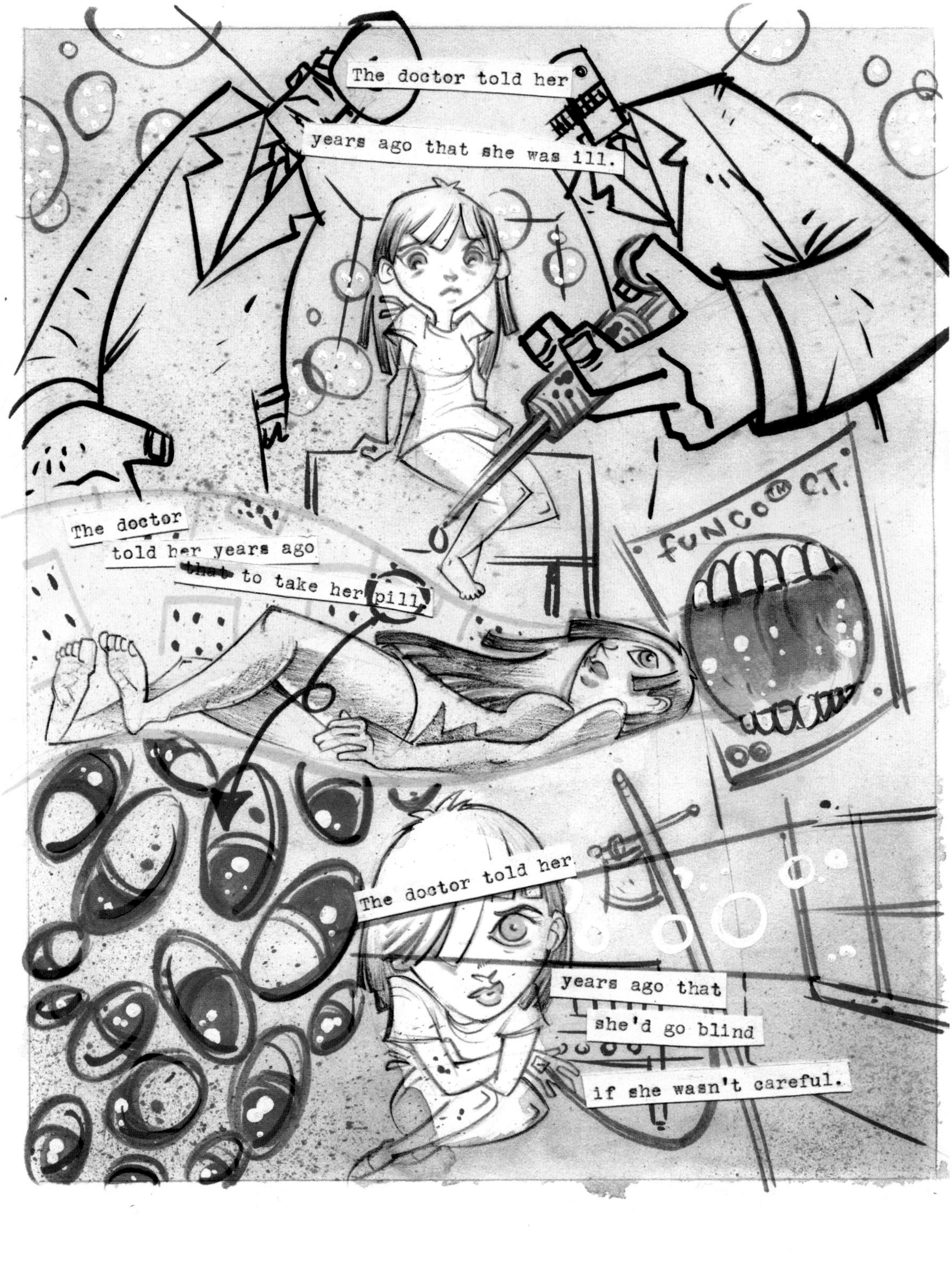
The doctor told her
years ago that she was ill.
The doctor
told her years ago
that to take her pill.
FUNCO™ C.T.
The doctor told her
years ago that
she'd go blind
if she wasn't careful.

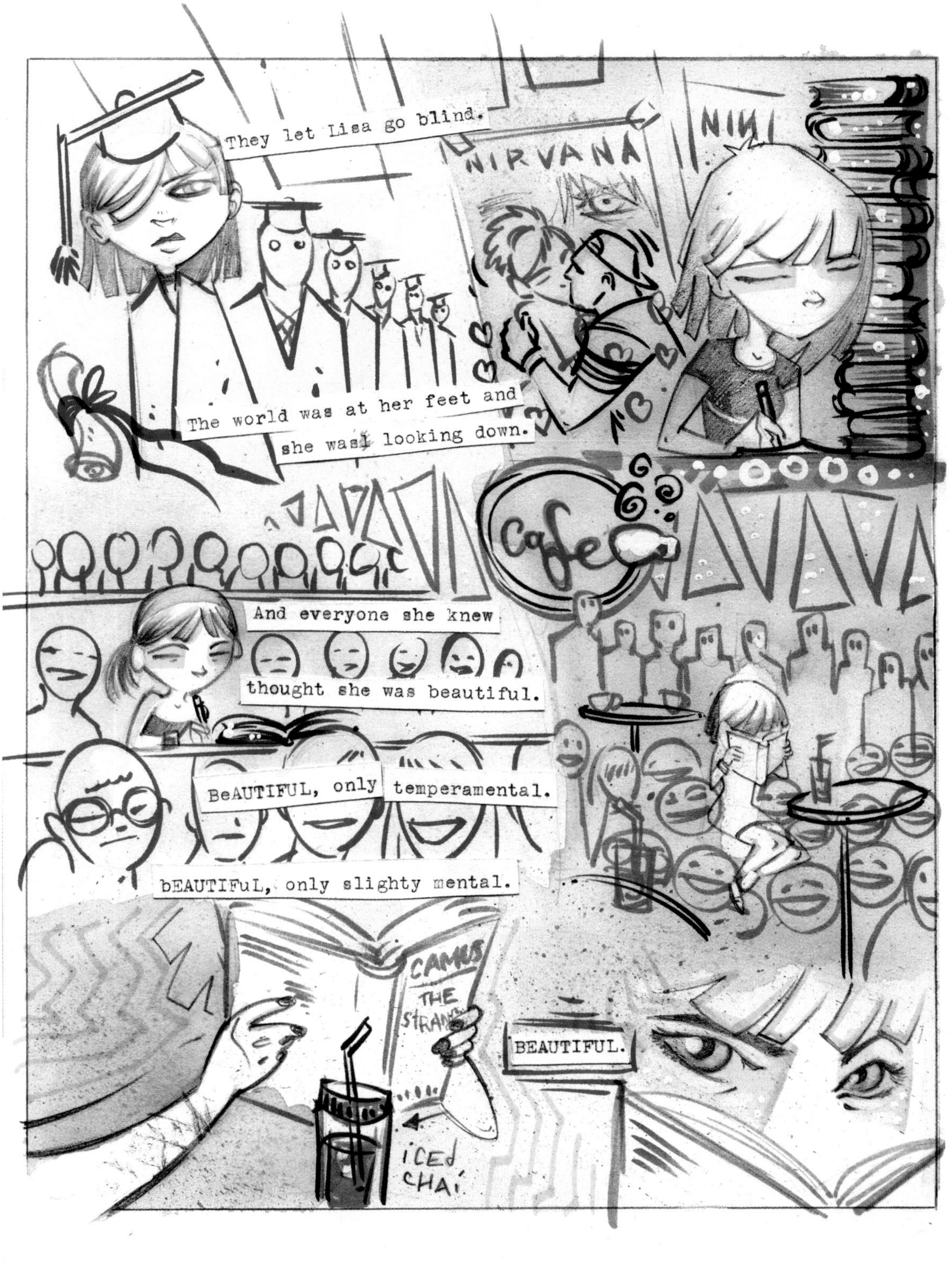
They let Lisa go blind.
NIRVANA
The world was at her feet and
she was looking down.
Cafe
And everyone she knew
thought she was beautiful.
BeAUTIFUL, only temperamental.
bEAUTIFuL, only slighty mental.
CAMUS
THE STRAN
BEAUTIFUL.
iCEd CHAi

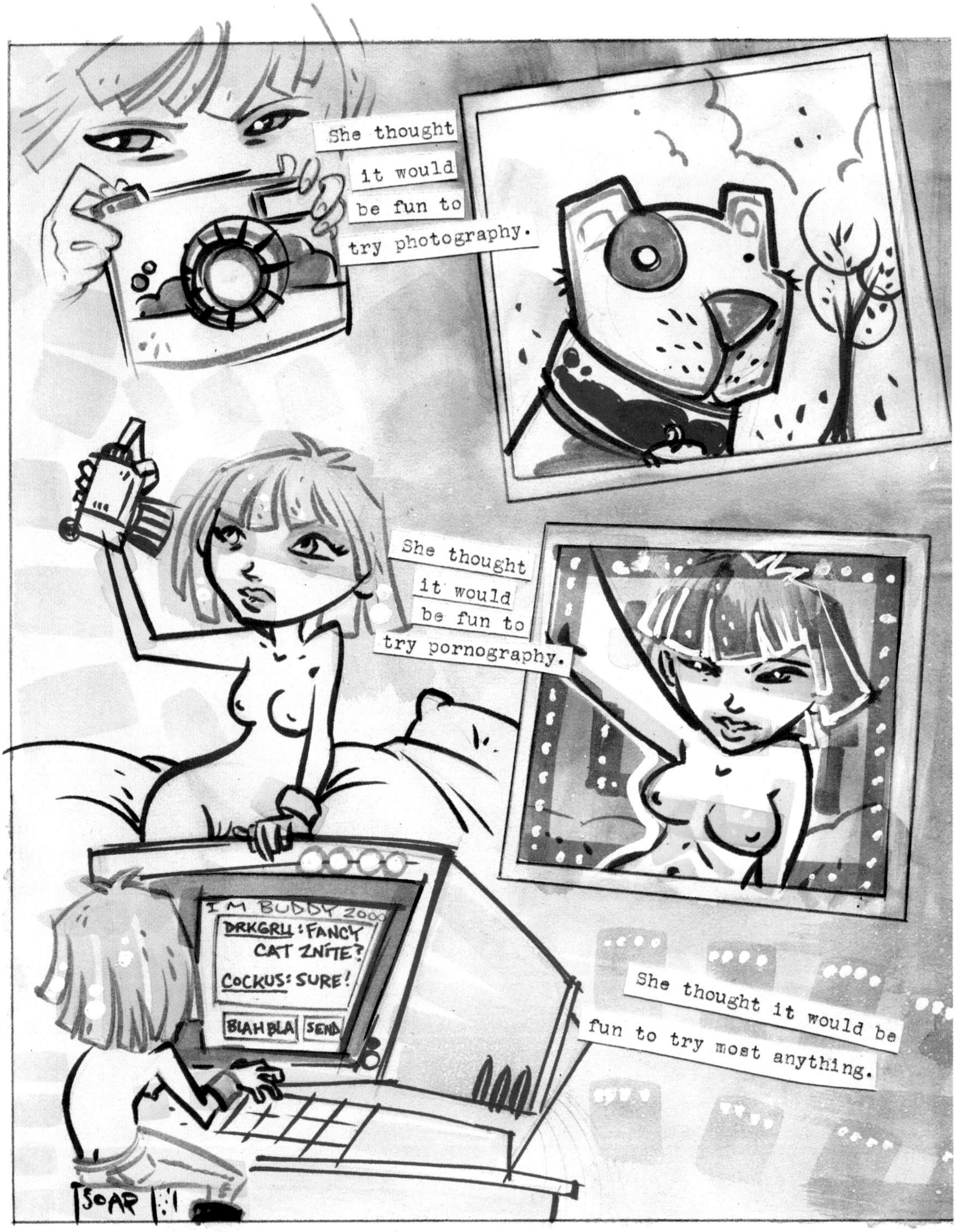
She thought it would be fun to try photography.
She thought it would be fun to try pornography.
I M BUDDY 2000
DRKGRL: FANCY CAT 2NITE?
COCKUS: SURE!
BLAH BLA
SEND
She thought it would be fun to try most anything.
TSOAP

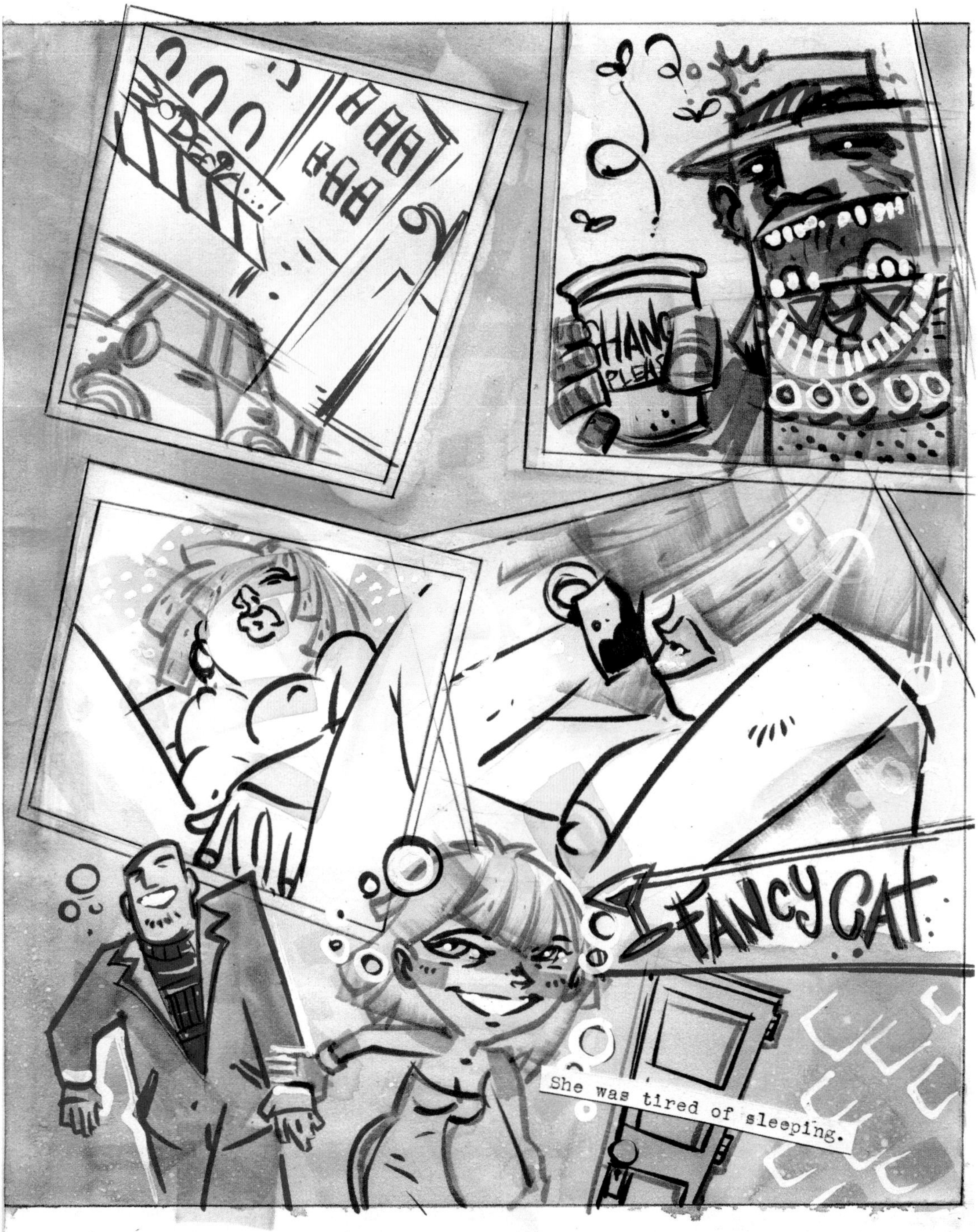
BODEGA
CHANG
PLEAS
FANCY CAT
She was tired of sleeping.

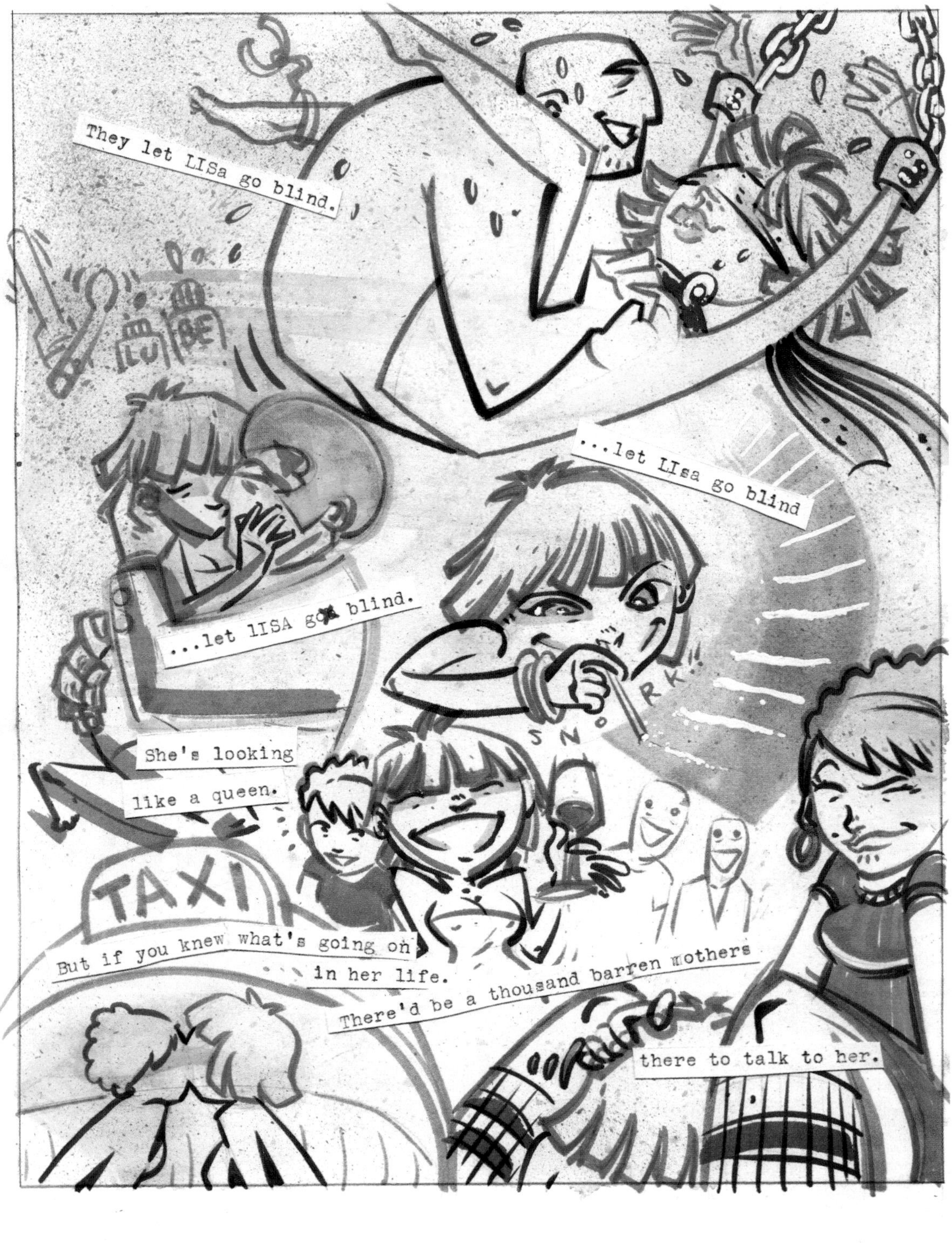
They let LISa go blind.
LUBE
...let LIsa go blind
...let lISA go blind.
SNORK!!
She's looking
like a queen.
TAXI
But if you knew what's going on
in her life.
There'd be a thousand barren mothers
there to talk to her.

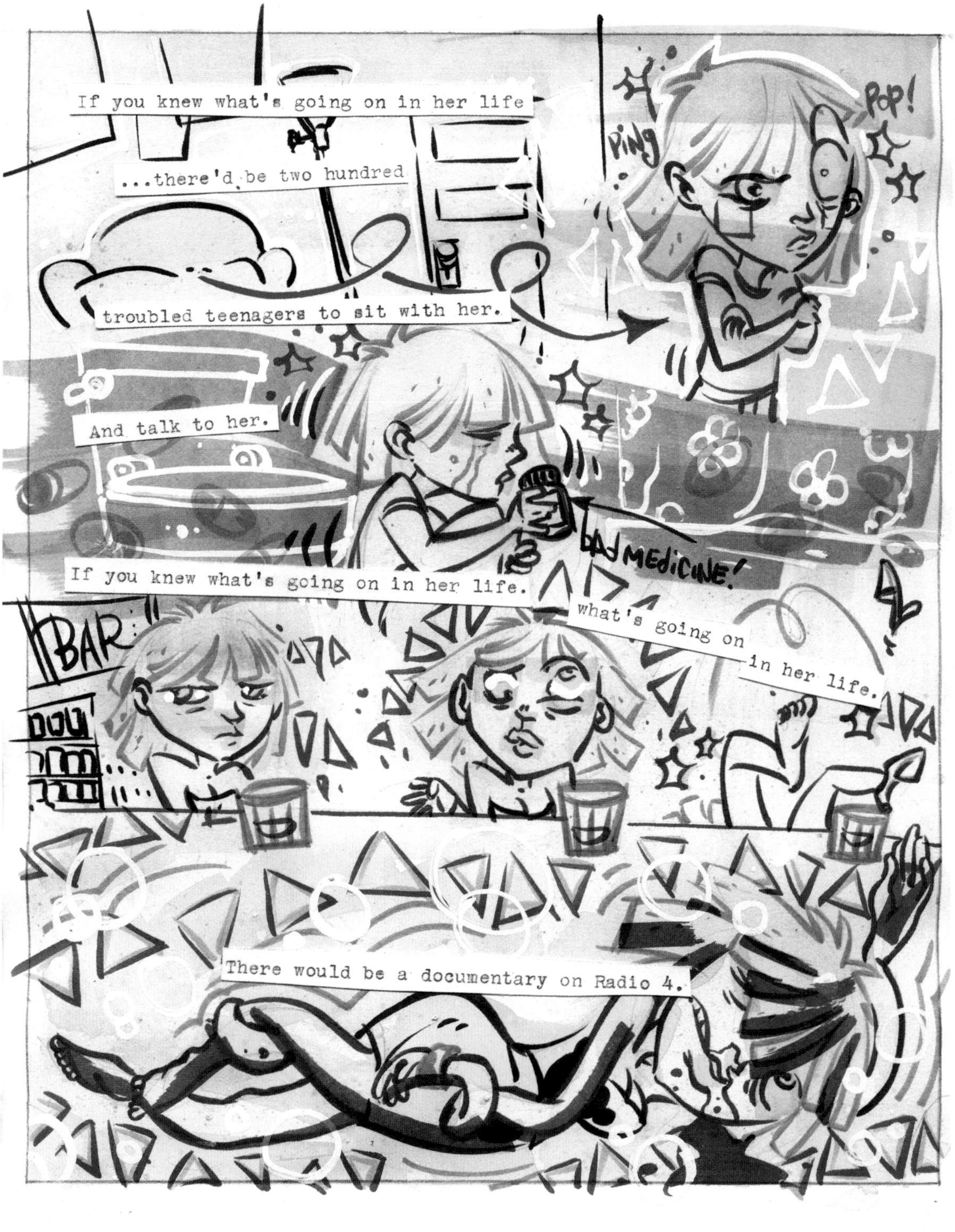
If you knew what's going on in her life
...there'd be two hundred
PING
POP!
troubled teenagers to sit with her.
And talk to her.
BAD MEDICINE!
If you knew what's going on in her life.
BAR
what's going on
in her life.
There would be a documentary on Radio 4.

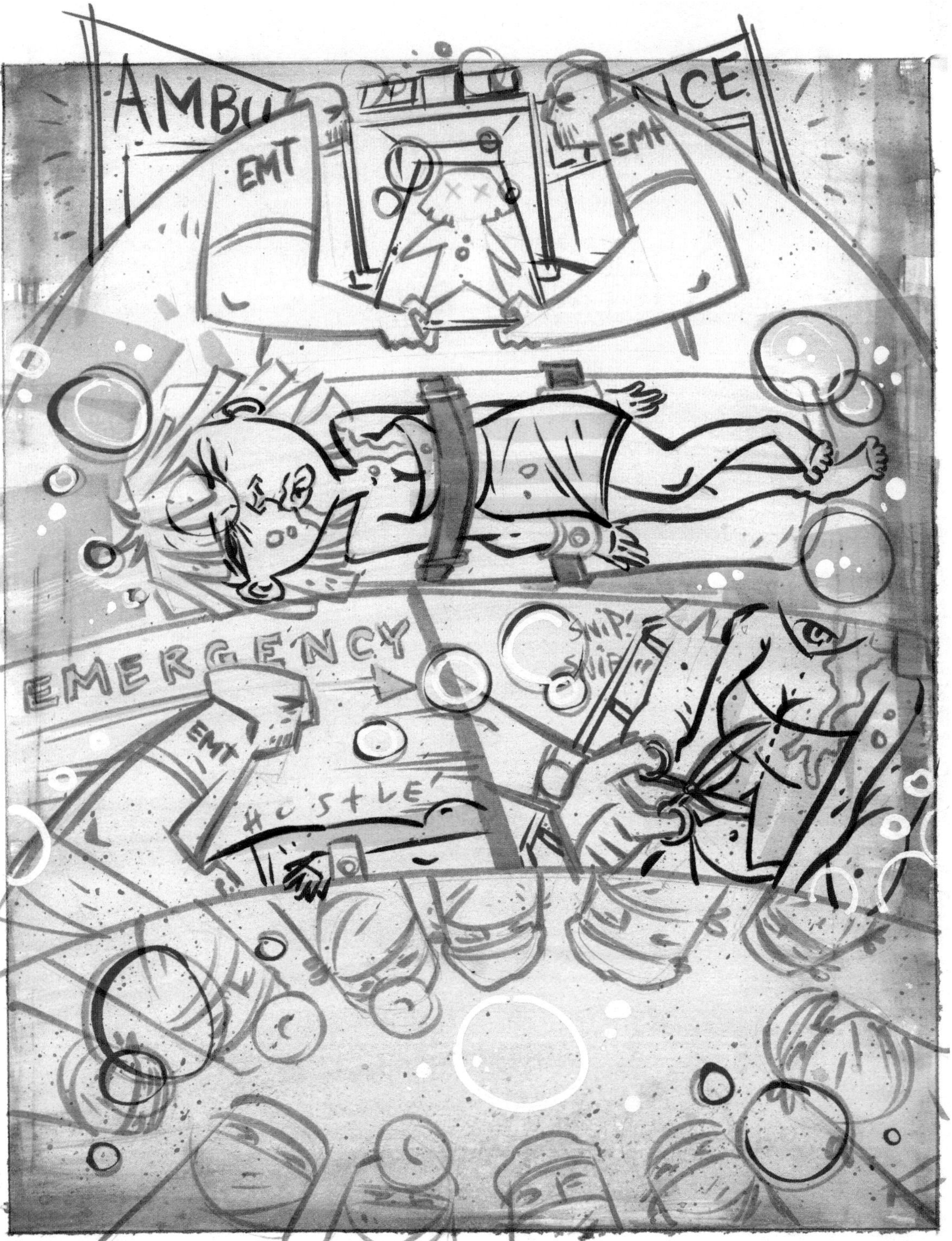
AMBU
NCE
EMT
EMT
EMERGENCY
SNIP!
EMT
HUSTLE

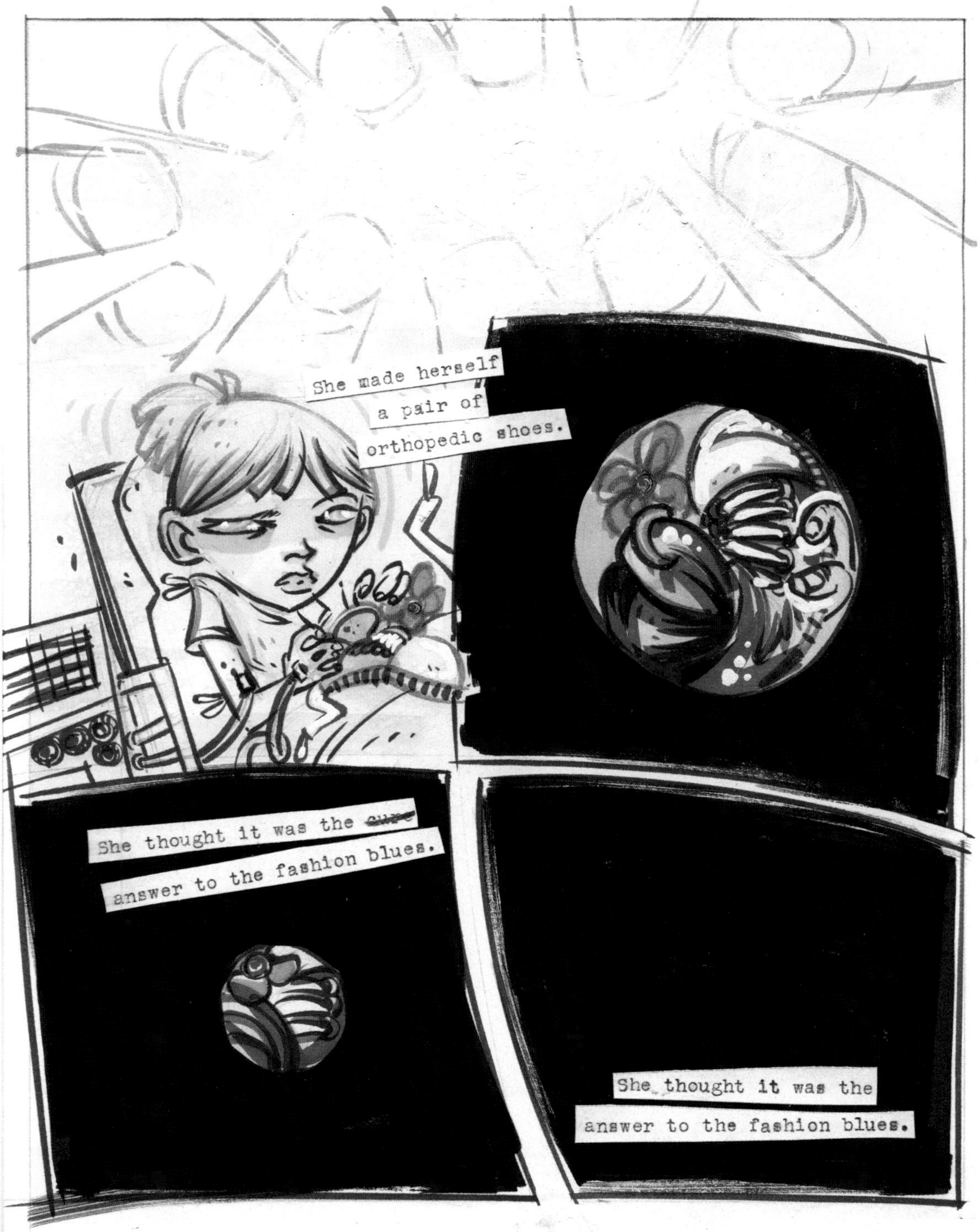
She made herself a pair of orthopedic shoes.
She thought it was the ~~cure~~ answer to the fashion blues.
She thought it was the answer to the fashion blues.

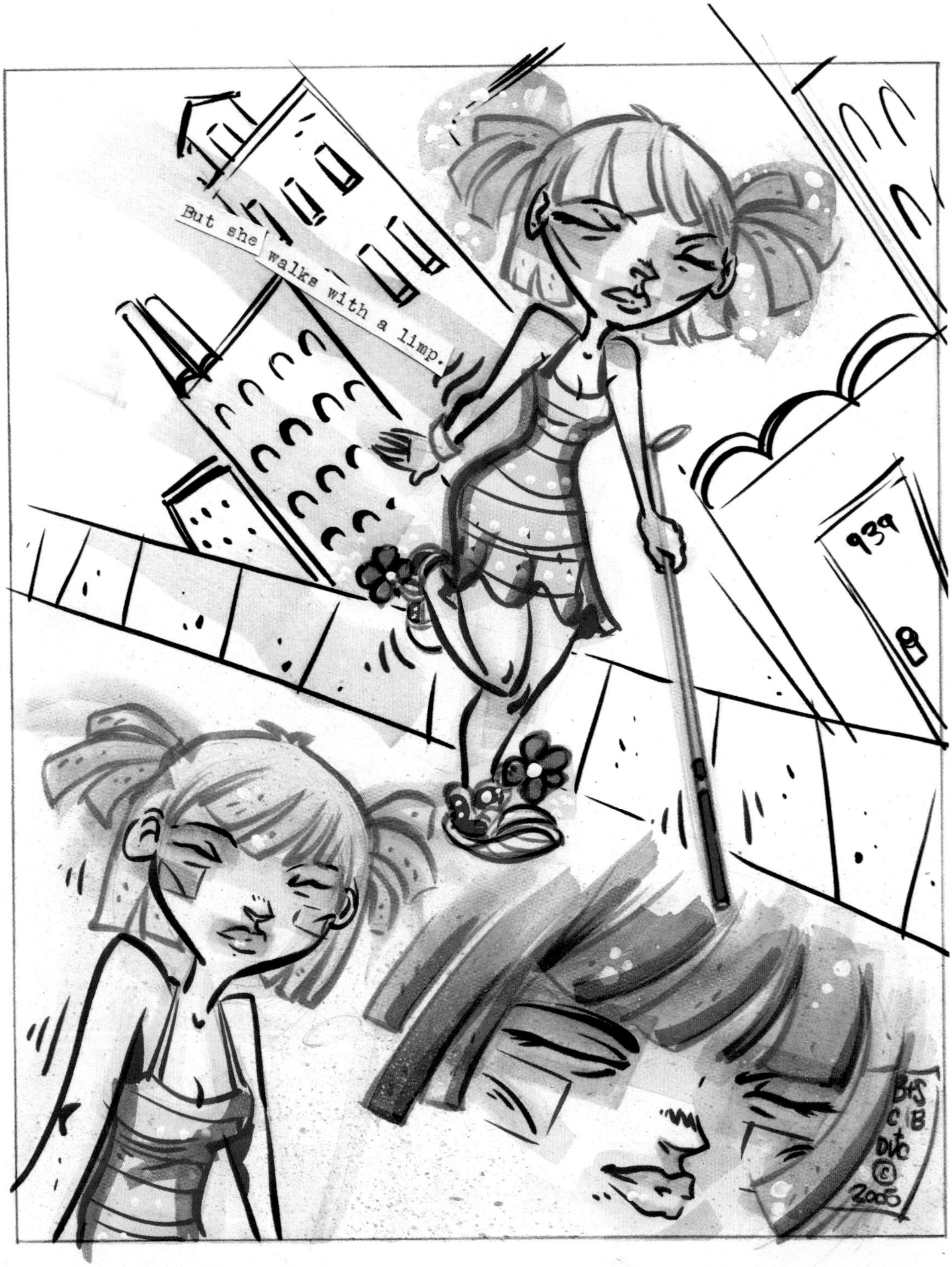
But she walks with a limp.
939
B+S
C B
+
DVC
©
2005

EASE YOU'RE FEET OFF IN THE SEA

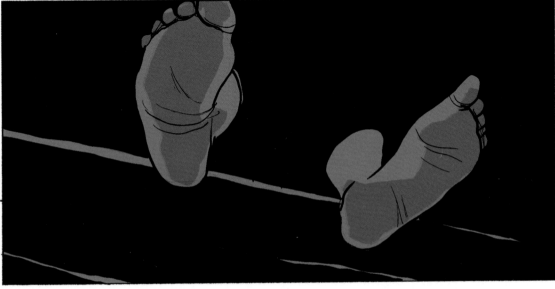

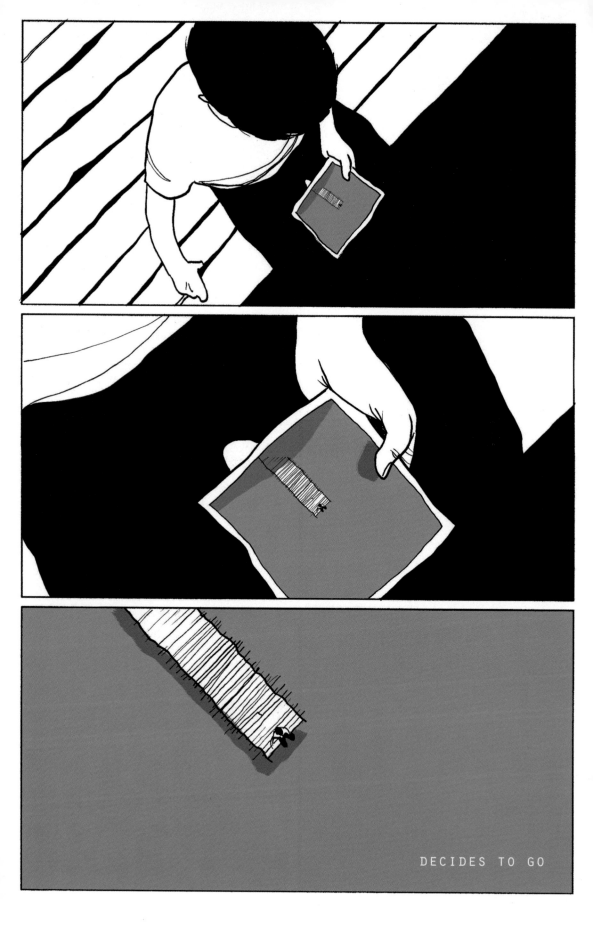

DECIDES TO GO

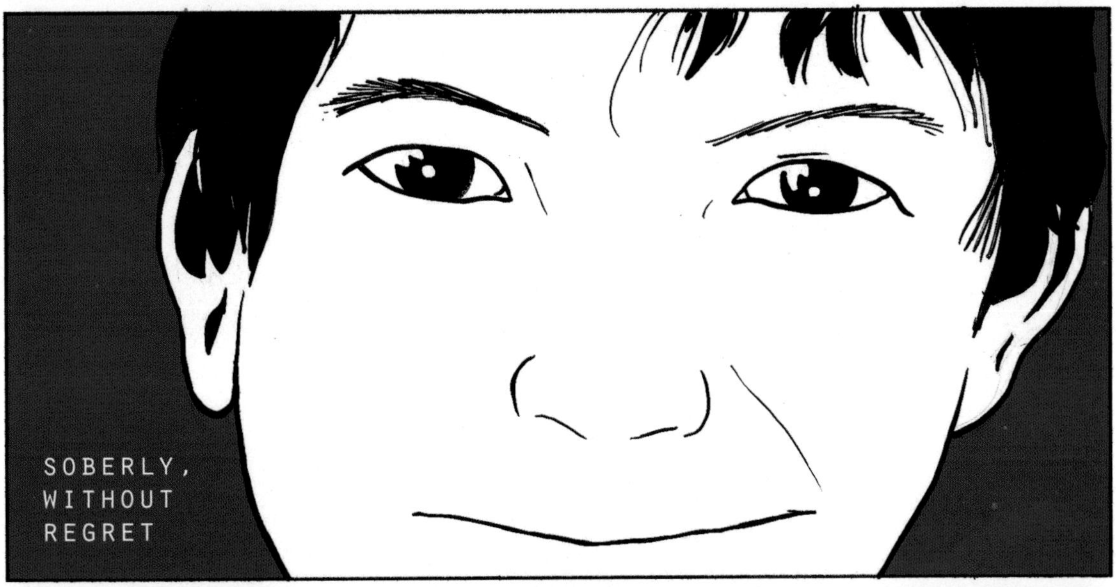
SOBERLY,
WITHOUT
REGRET

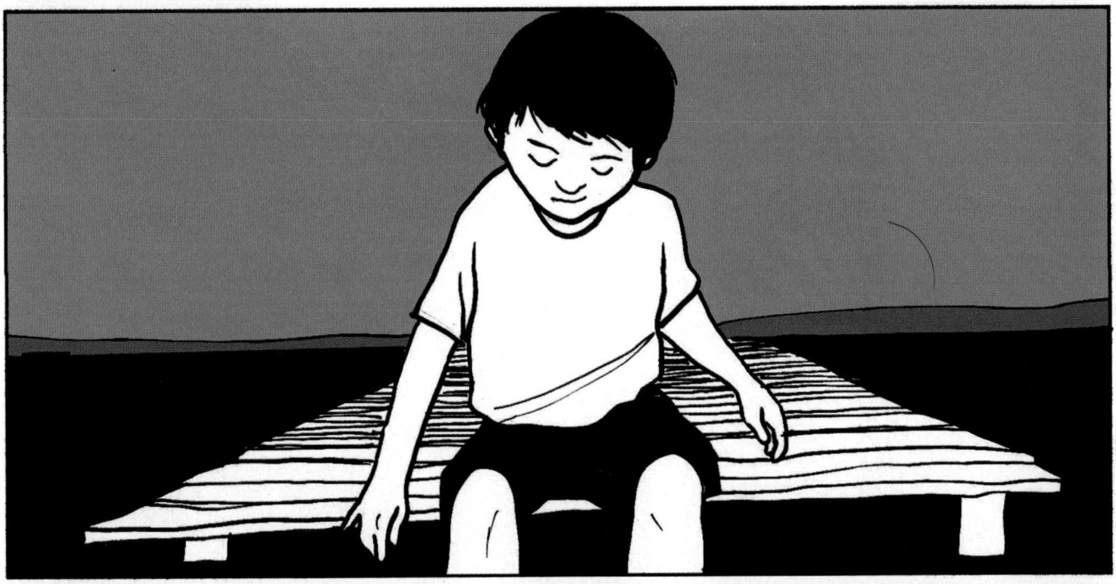

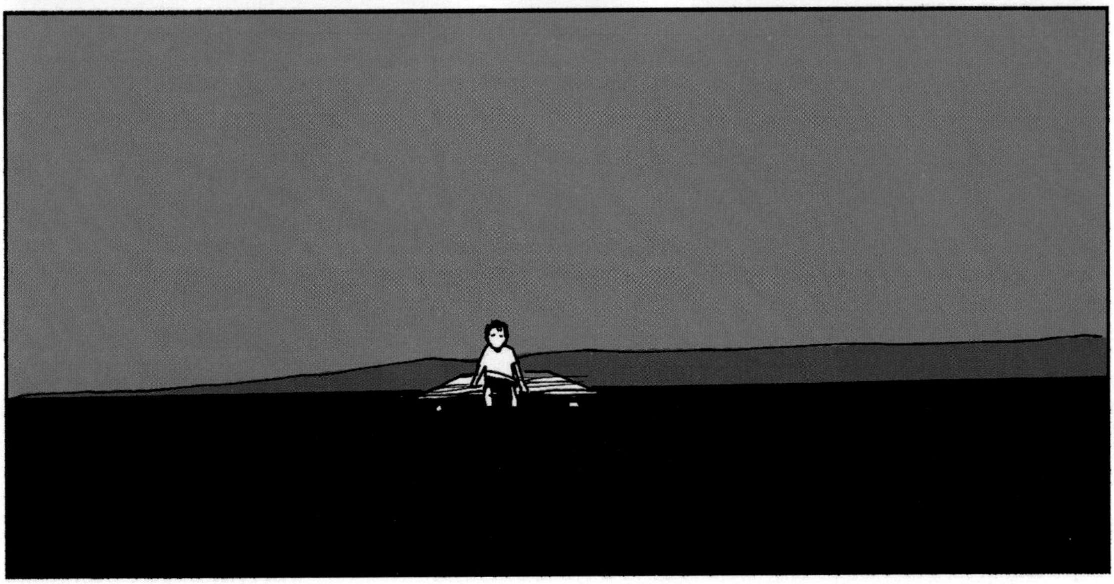

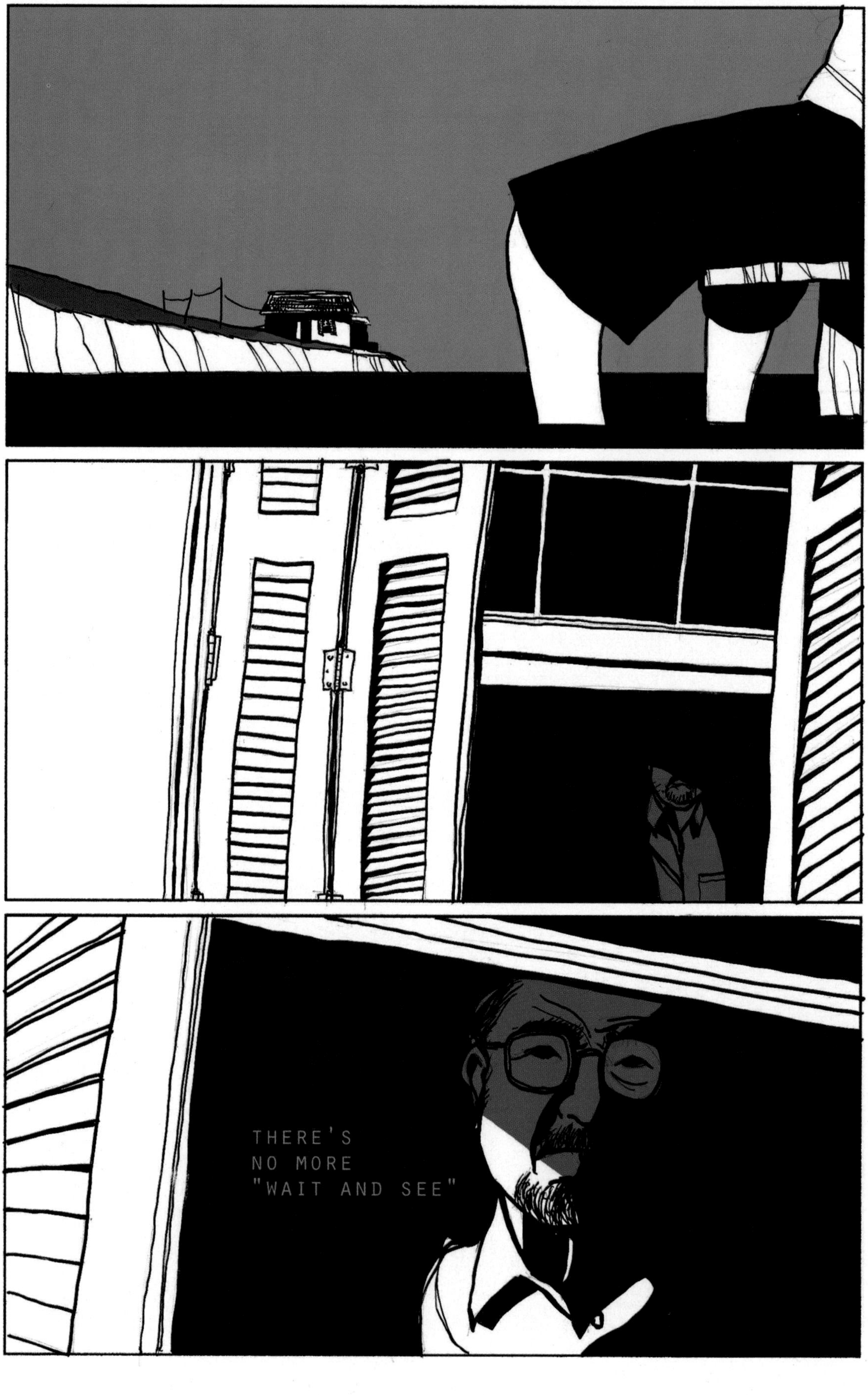
THERE'S
NO MORE
"WAIT AND SEE"

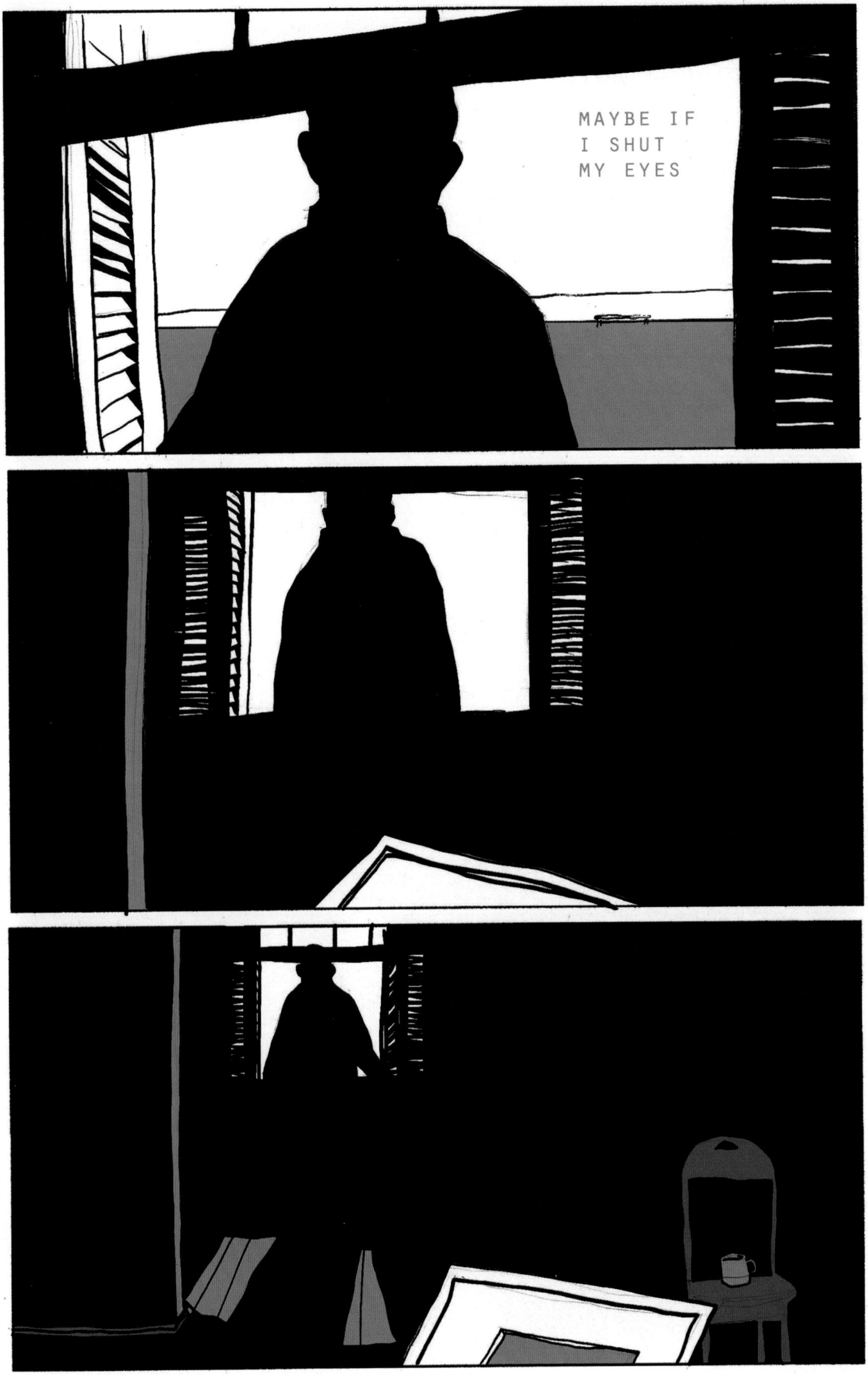
MAYBE IF I SHUT MY EYES

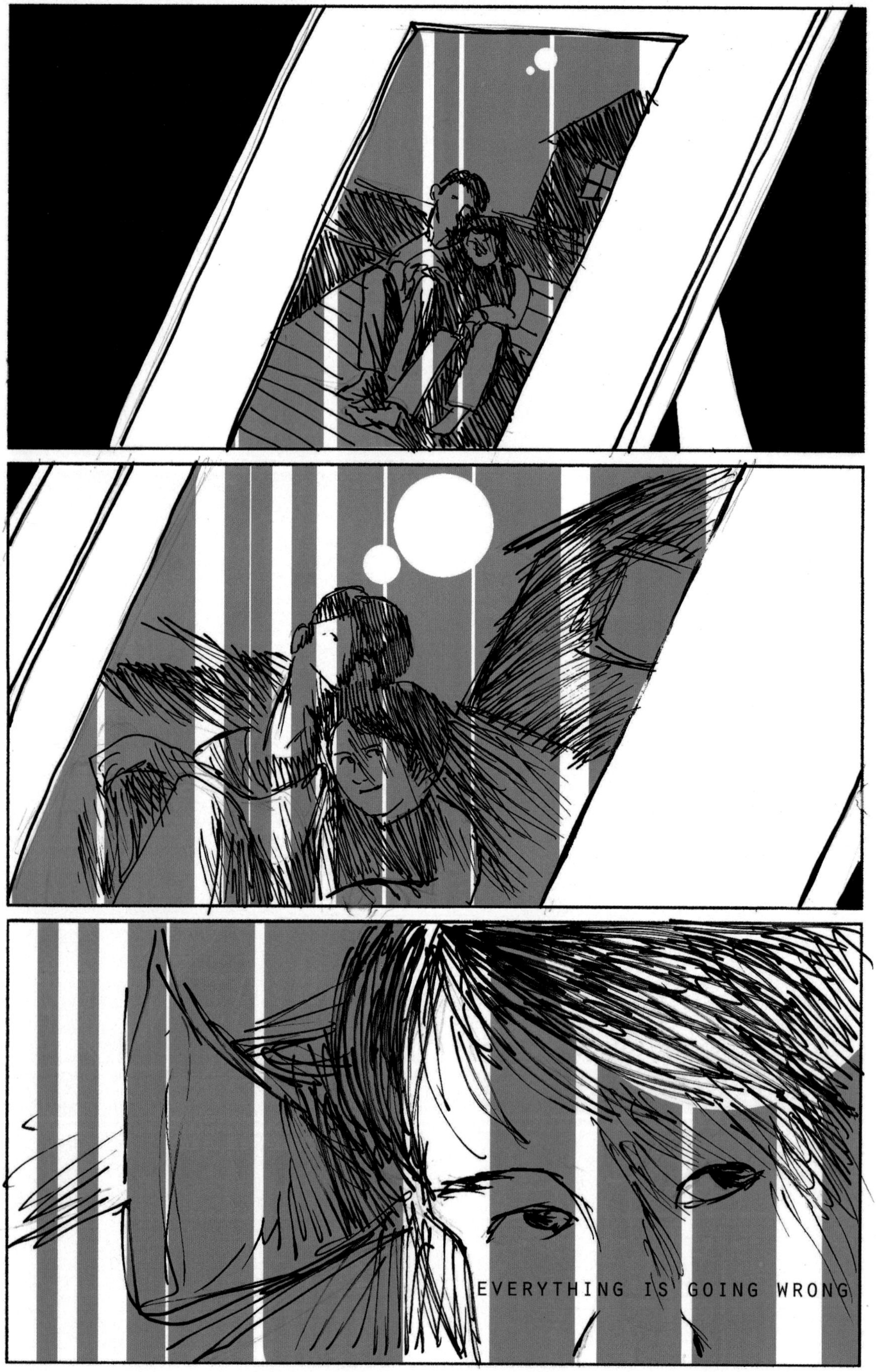
EVERYTHING IS GOING WRONG

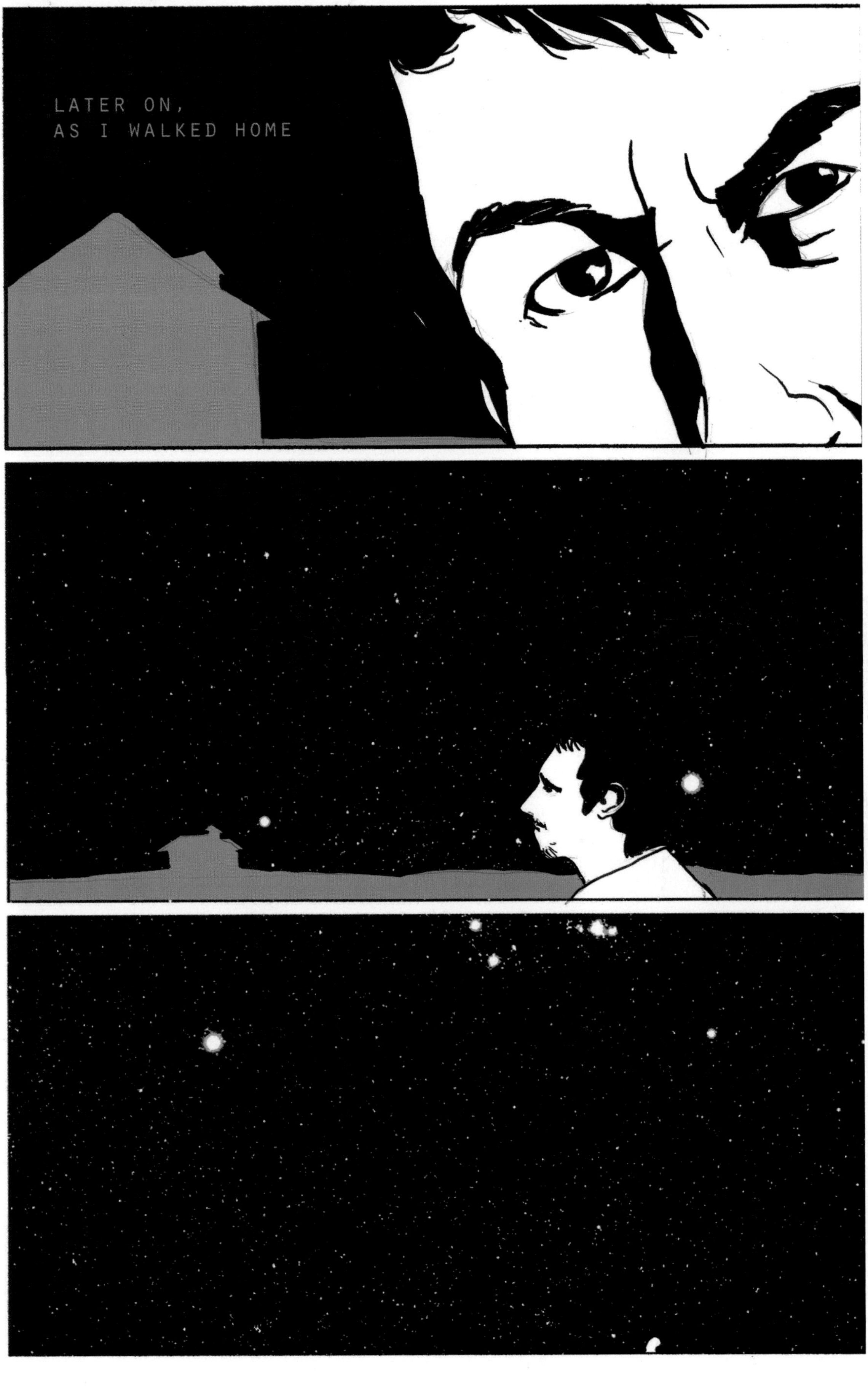
LATER ON,
AS I WALKED HOME

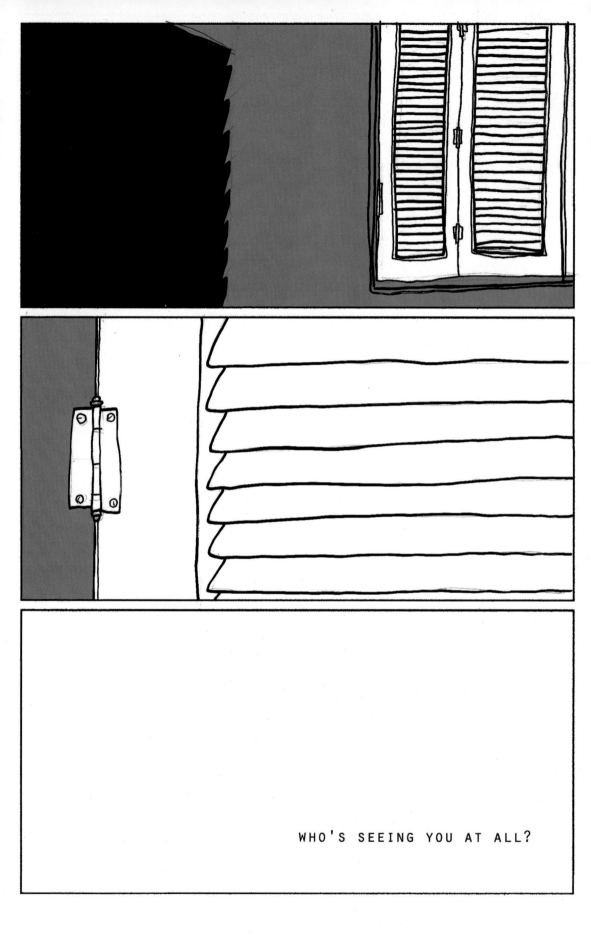

WHO'S SEEING YOU AT ALL?

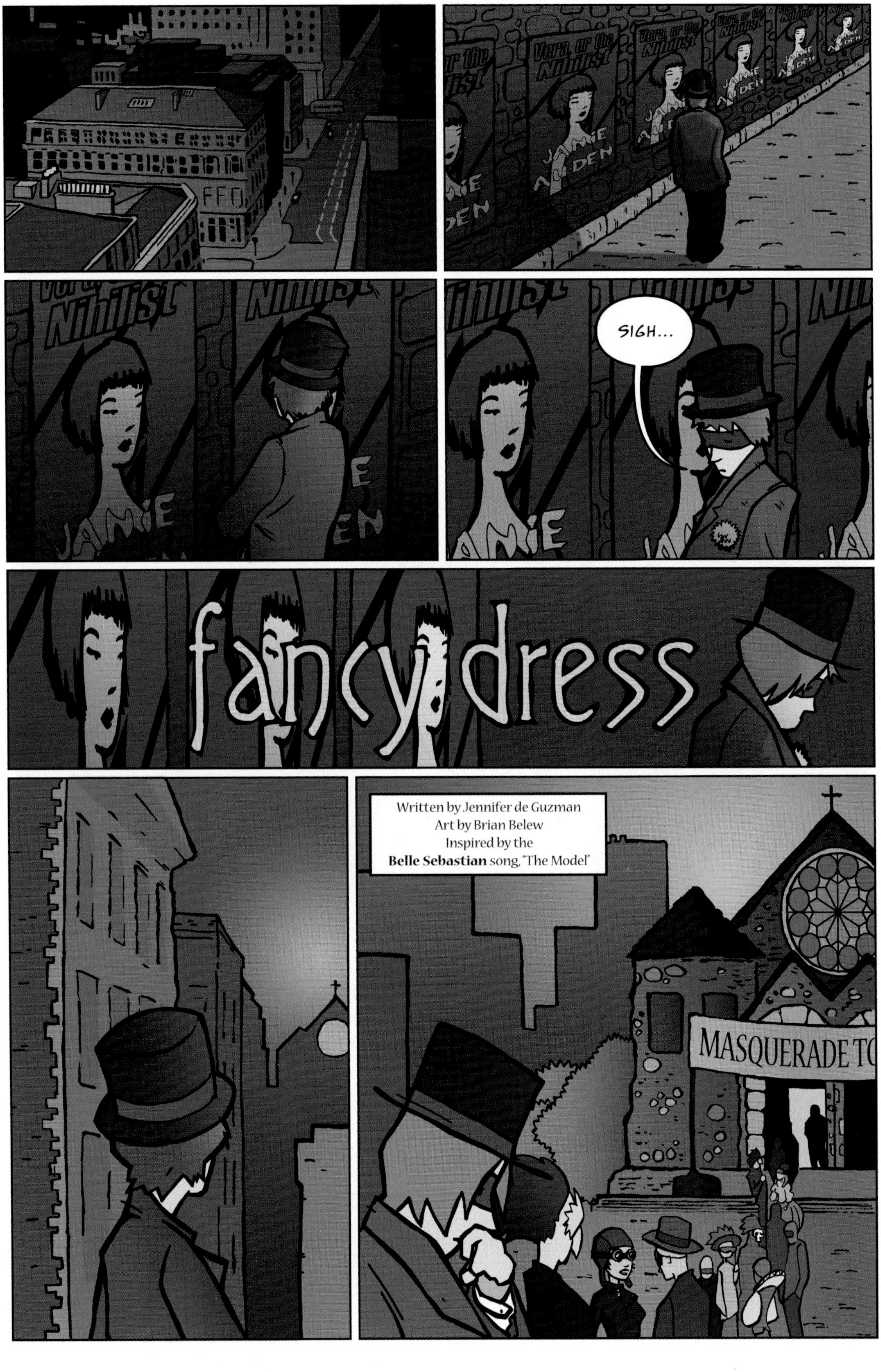
Vera, or the Nihilist
JAMIE AUDEN
SIGH...
fancy dress
Written by Jennifer de Guzman
Art by Brian Belew
Inspired by the
Belle Sebastian song, "The Model"
MASQUERADE TO

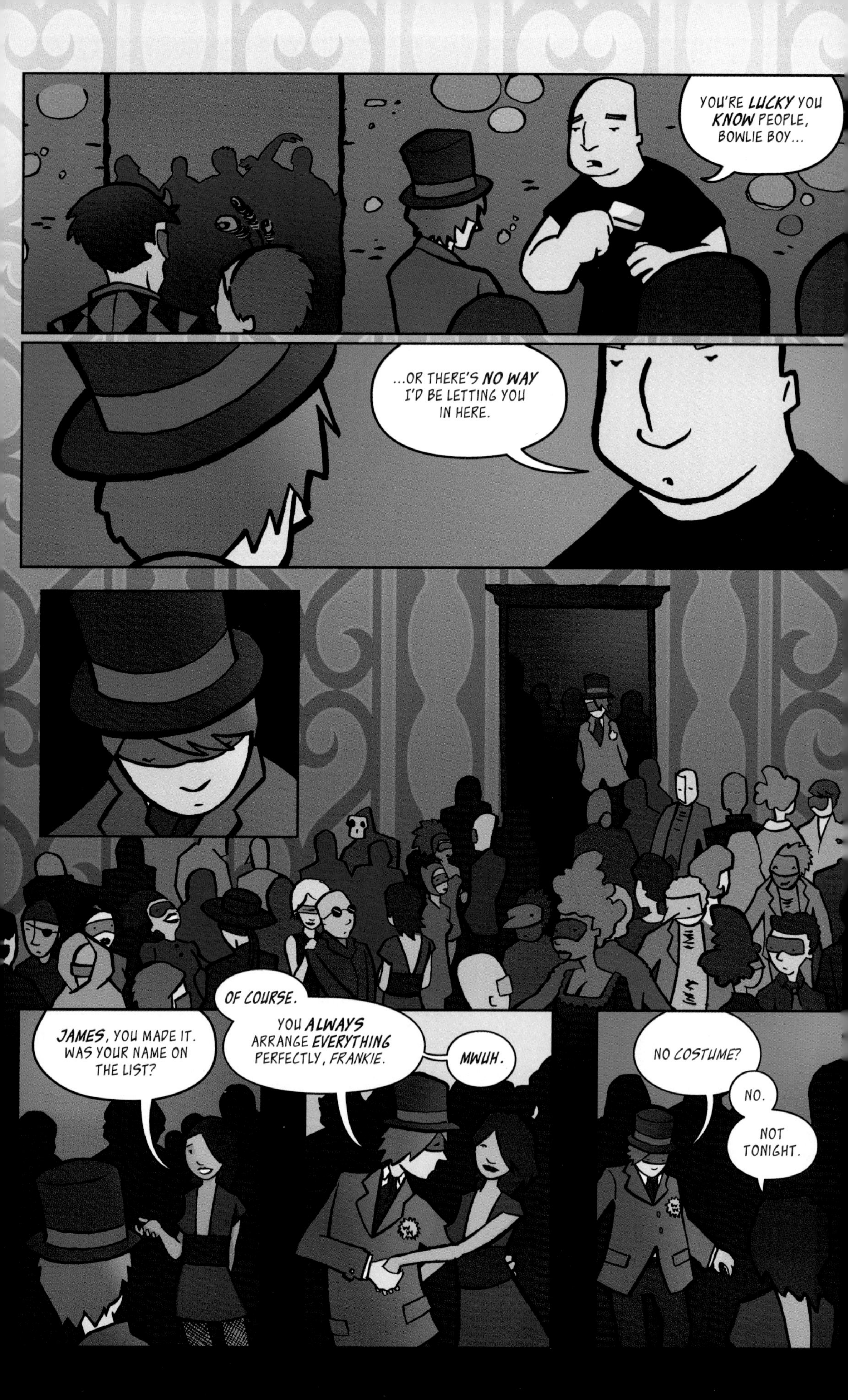
YOU'RE LUCKY YOU KNOW PEOPLE, BOWLIE BOY...
...OR THERE'S NO WAY I'D BE LETTING YOU IN HERE.
JAMES, YOU MADE IT. WAS YOUR NAME ON THE LIST?
OF COURSE.
YOU ALWAYS ARRANGE EVERYTHING PERFECTLY, FRANKIE.
MWUH.
NO COSTUME?
NO.
NOT TONIGHT.

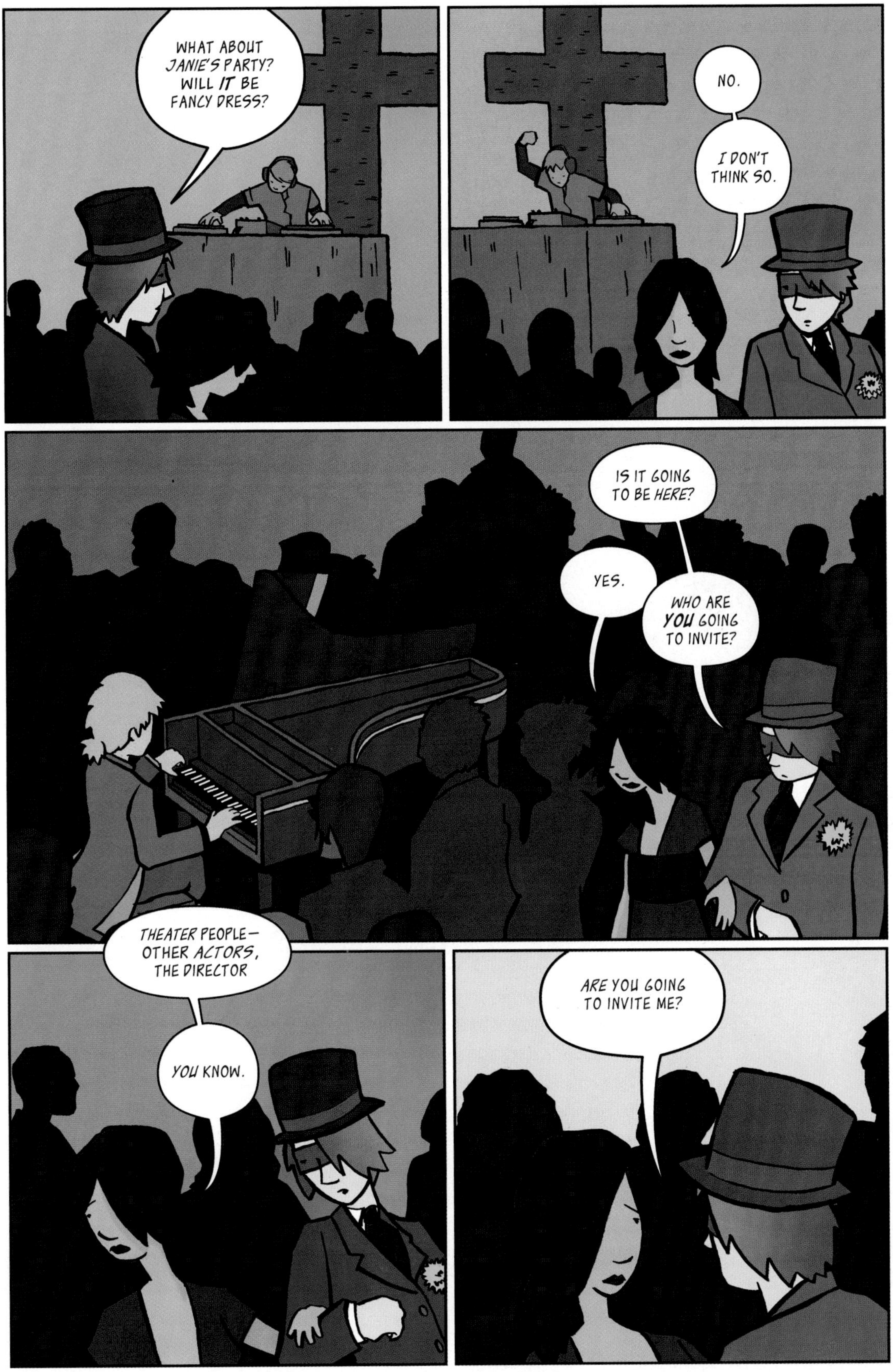
WHAT ABOUT JANIE'S PARTY? WILL IT BE FANCY DRESS?
NO.
I DON'T THINK SO.
IS IT GOING TO BE HERE?
YES.
WHO ARE YOU GOING TO INVITE?
THEATER PEOPLE— OTHER ACTORS, THE DIRECTOR
YOU KNOW.
ARE YOU GOING TO INVITE ME?

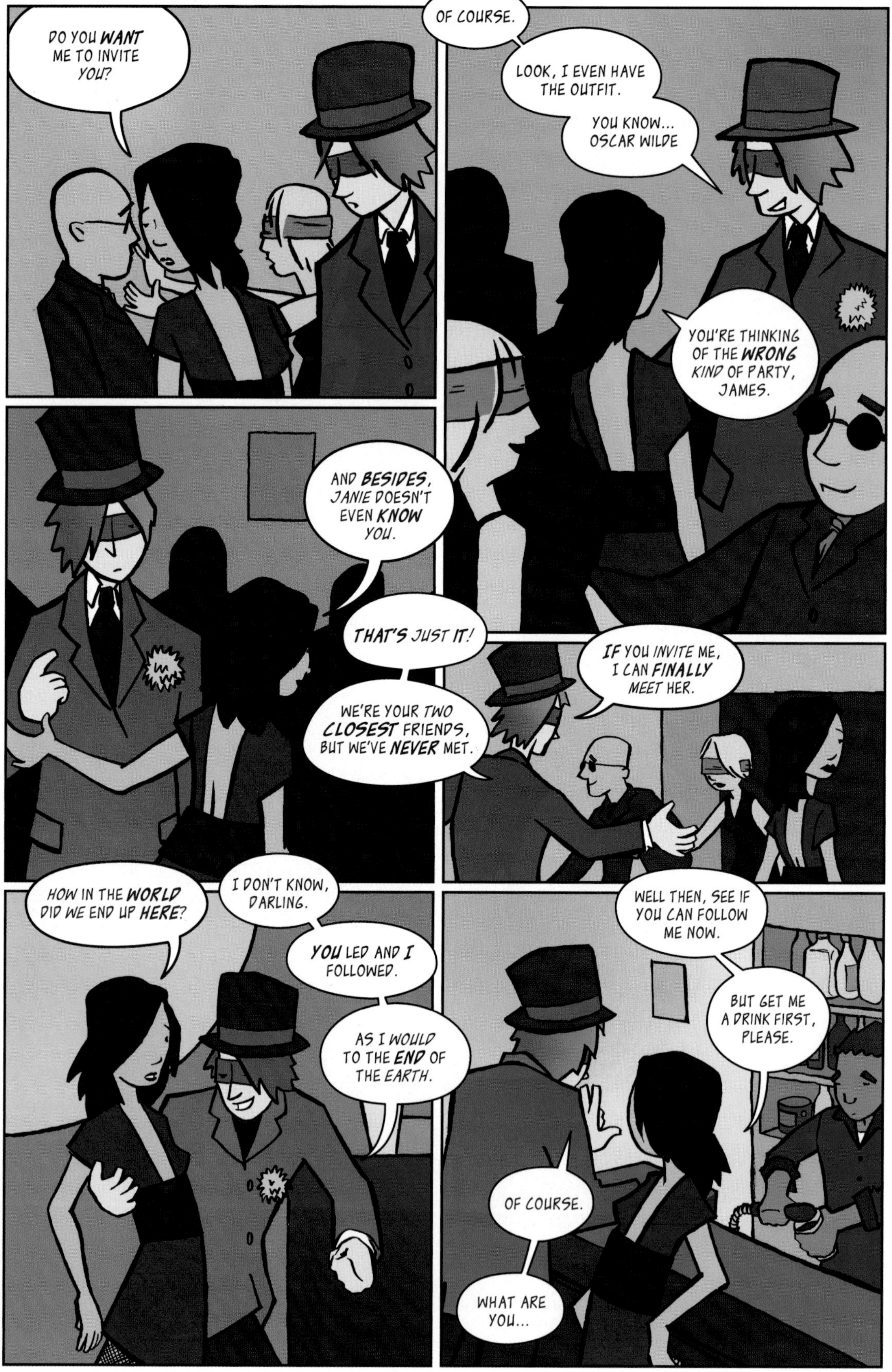
DO YOU WANT ME TO INVITE YOU?
OF COURSE.
LOOK, I EVEN HAVE THE OUTFIT.
YOU KNOW... OSCAR WILDE
YOU'RE THINKING OF THE WRONG KIND OF PARTY, JAMES.
AND BESIDES, JANIE DOESN'T EVEN KNOW YOU.
THAT'S JUST IT!
WE'RE YOUR TWO CLOSEST FRIENDS, BUT WE'VE NEVER MET.
IF YOU INVITE ME, I CAN FINALLY MEET HER.
HOW IN THE WORLD DID WE END UP HERE?
I DON'T KNOW, DARLING.
YOU LED AND I FOLLOWED.
AS I WOULD TO THE END OF THE EARTH.
WELL THEN, SEE IF YOU CAN FOLLOW ME NOW.
BUT GET ME A DRINK FIRST, PLEASE.
OF COURSE.
WHAT ARE YOU...

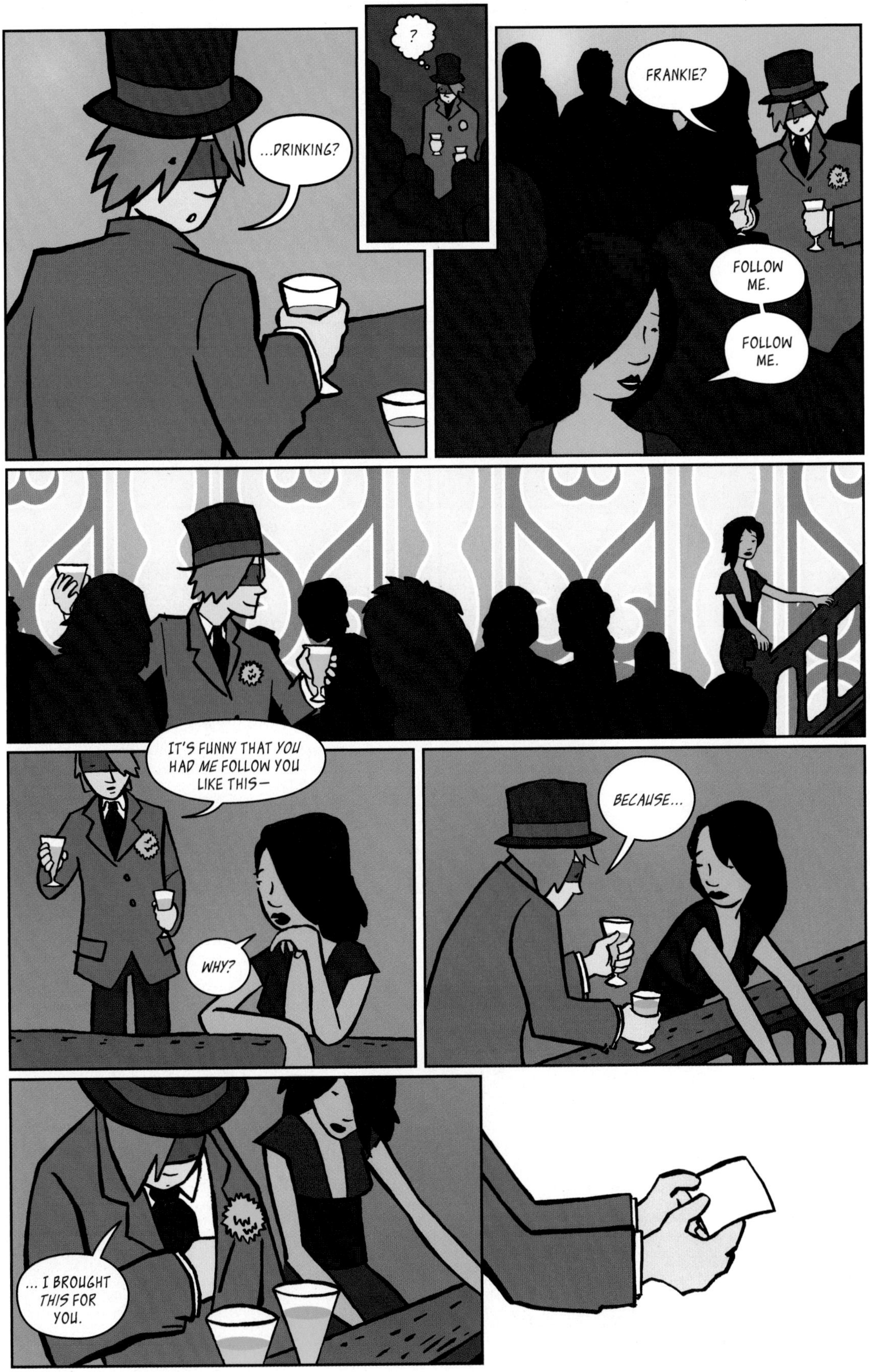
...DRINKING?
?
FRANKIE?
FOLLOW ME.
FOLLOW ME.
IT'S FUNNY THAT YOU HAD ME FOLLOW YOU LIKE THIS—
WHY?
BECAUSE...
... I BROUGHT THIS FOR YOU.

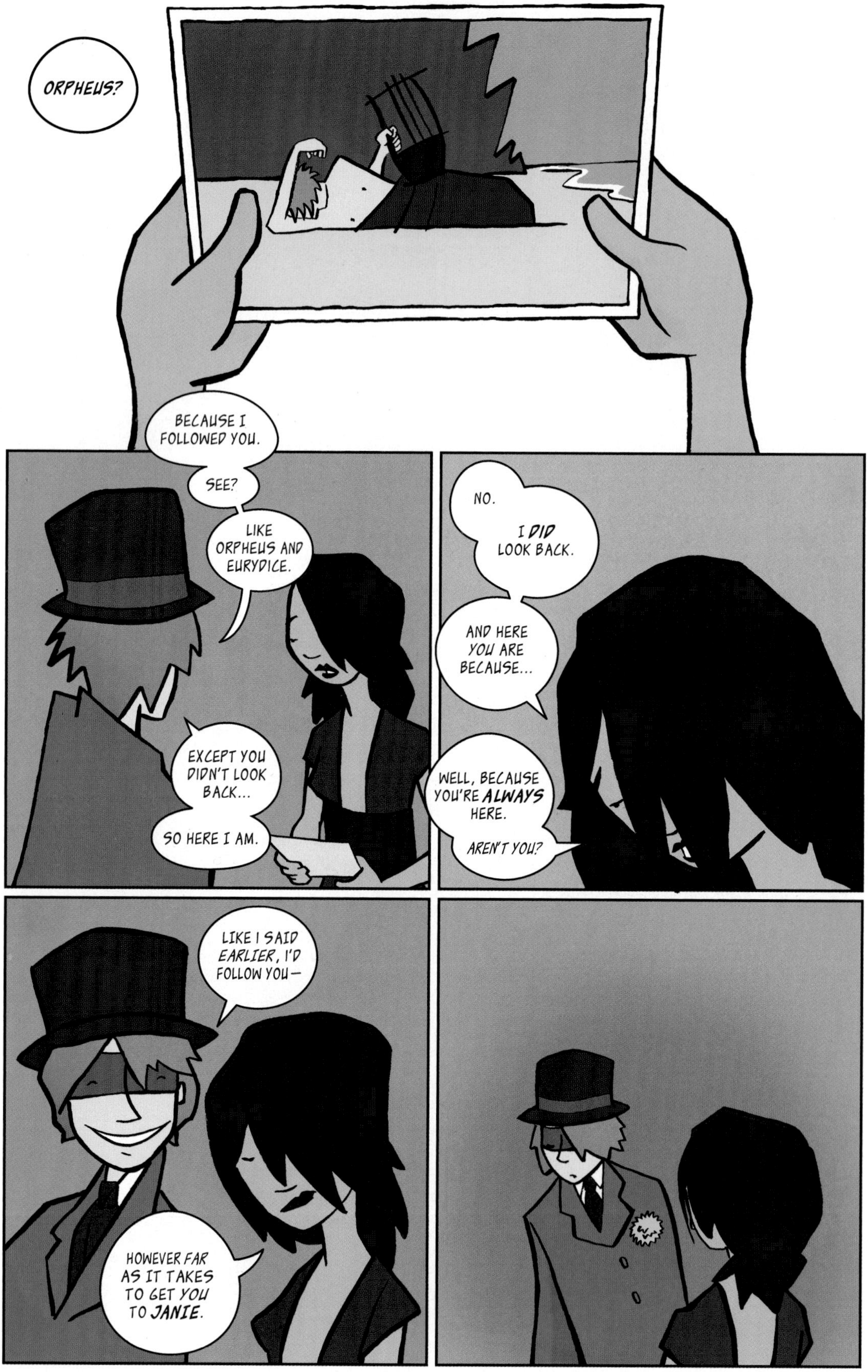

ORPHEUS?
BECAUSE I FOLLOWED YOU.
SEE?
LIKE ORPHEUS AND EURYDICE.
EXCEPT YOU DIDN'T LOOK BACK...
SO HERE I AM.
NO.
I DID LOOK BACK.
AND HERE YOU ARE BECAUSE...
WELL, BECAUSE YOU'RE ALWAYS HERE.
AREN'T YOU?
LIKE I SAID EARLIER, I'D FOLLOW YOU—
HOWEVER FAR AS IT TAKES TO GET YOU TO JANIE.

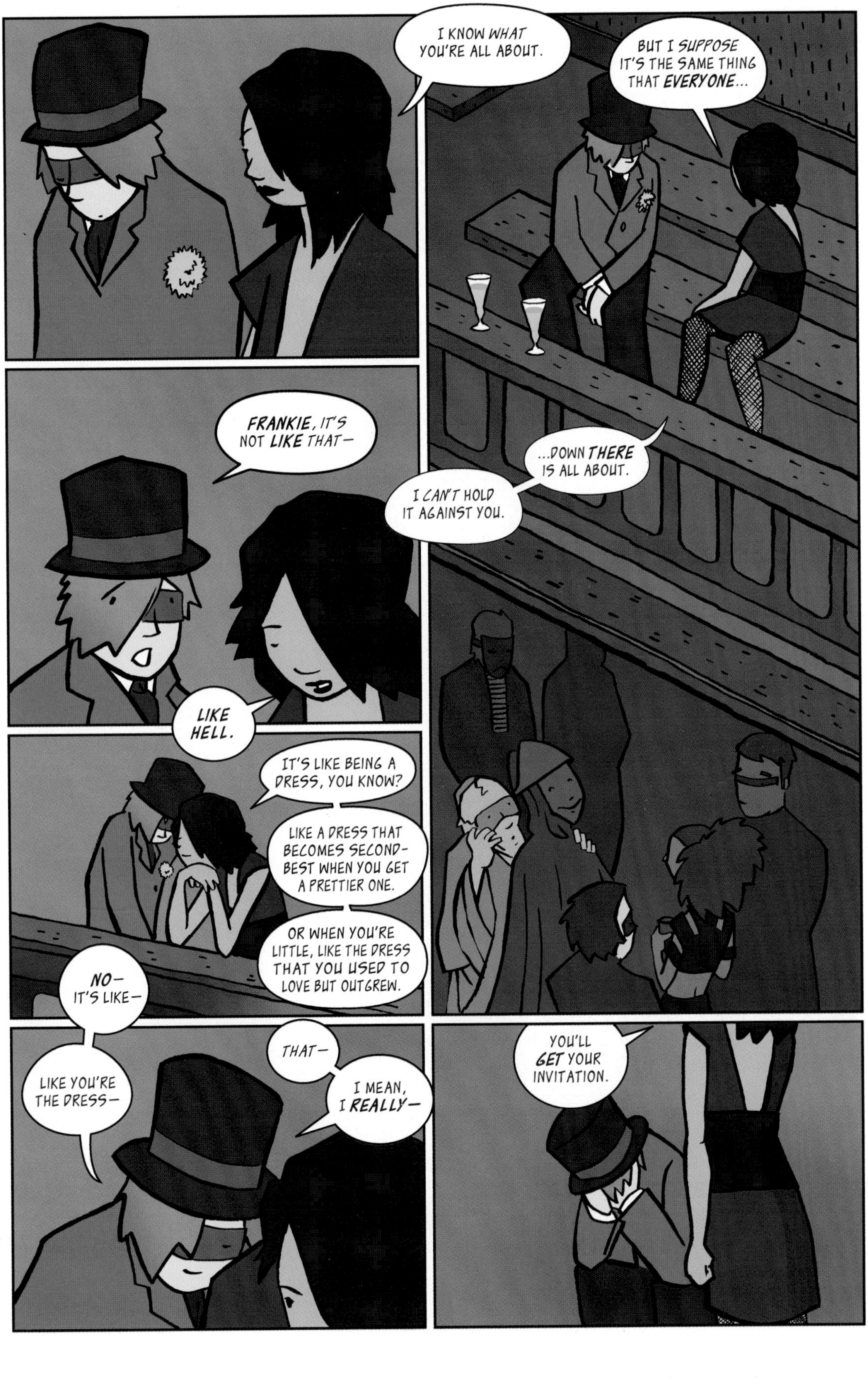
I KNOW WHAT YOU'RE ALL ABOUT.
BUT I SUPPOSE IT'S THE SAME THING THAT EVERYONE...
...DOWN THERE IS ALL ABOUT.
I CAN'T HOLD IT AGAINST YOU.
FRANKIE, IT'S NOT LIKE THAT—
LIKE HELL.
IT'S LIKE BEING A DRESS, YOU KNOW?
LIKE A DRESS THAT BECOMES SECOND-BEST WHEN YOU GET A PRETTIER ONE.
OR WHEN YOU'RE LITTLE, LIKE THE DRESS THAT YOU USED TO LOVE BUT OUTGREW.
NO— IT'S LIKE—
LIKE YOU'RE THE DRESS—
THAT—
I MEAN, I REALLY—
YOU'LL GET YOUR INVITATION.

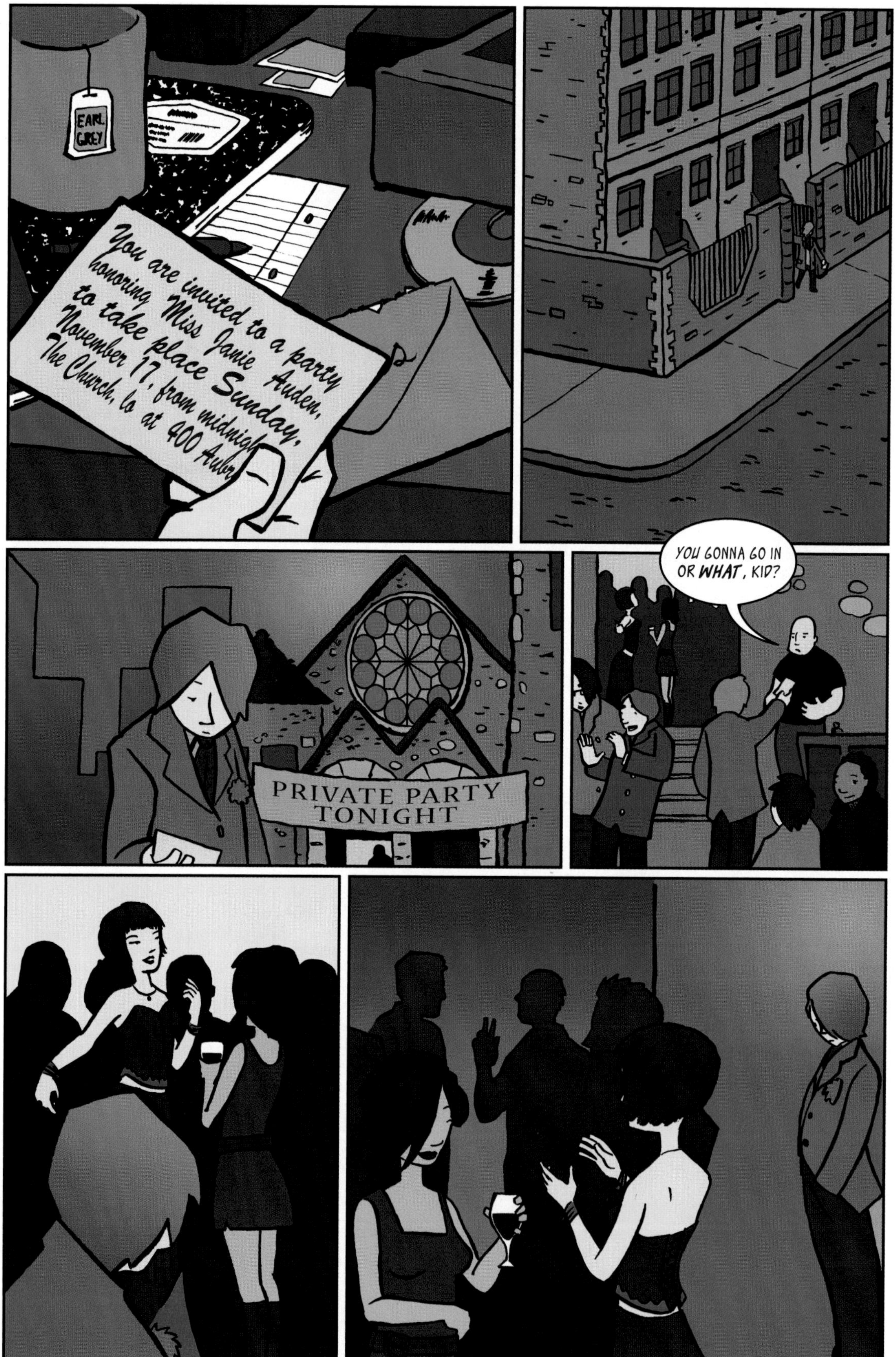
EARL GREY
You are invited to a party
honoring Miss Jamie Auden,
to take place Sunday,
November 17, from midnigh
The Church, lo at 400 Aub
PRIVATE PARTY TONIGHT
YOU GONNA GO IN OR WHAT, KID?

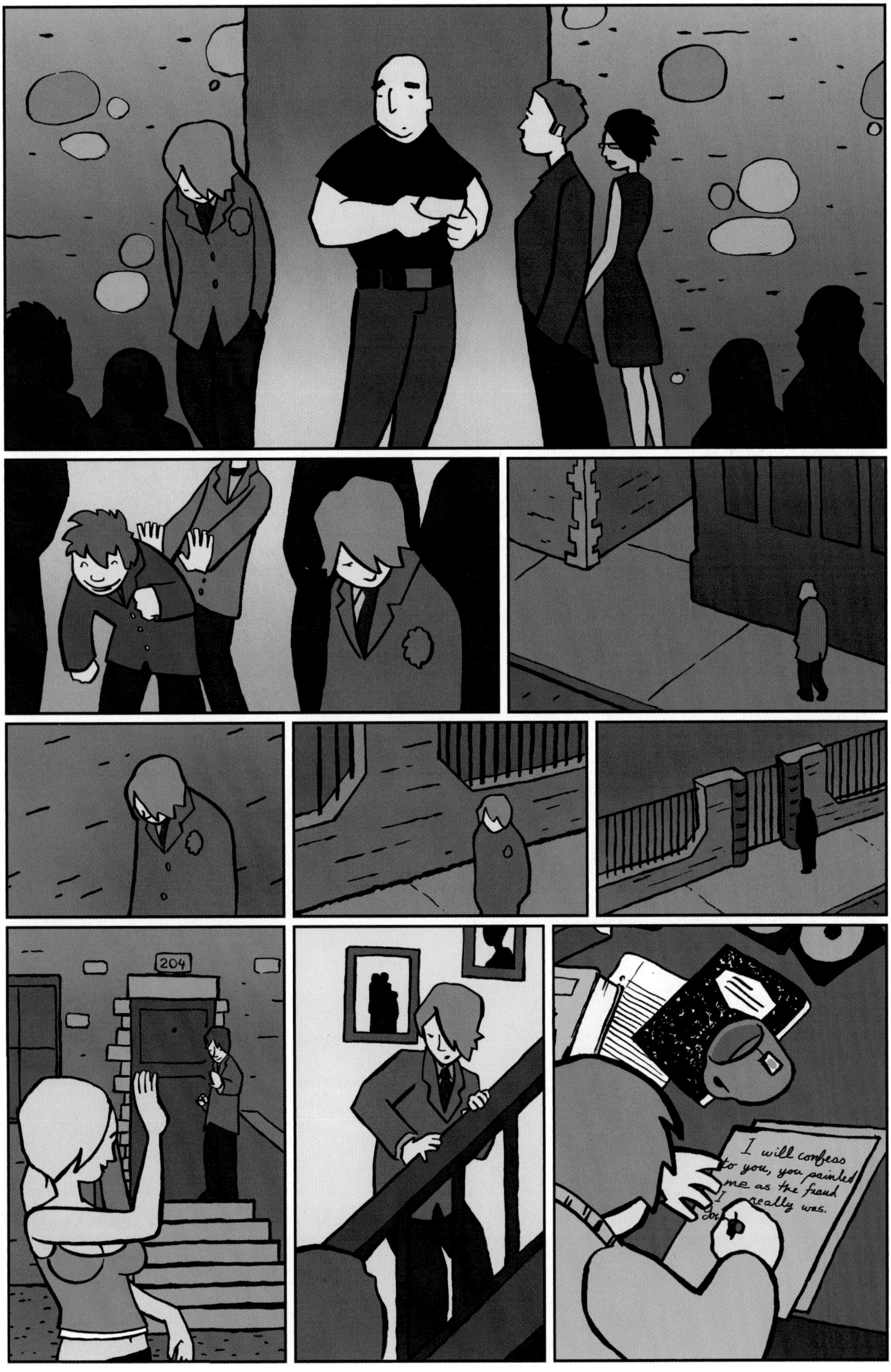
204
I will confess
to you, you painted
me as the fraud
I really was.

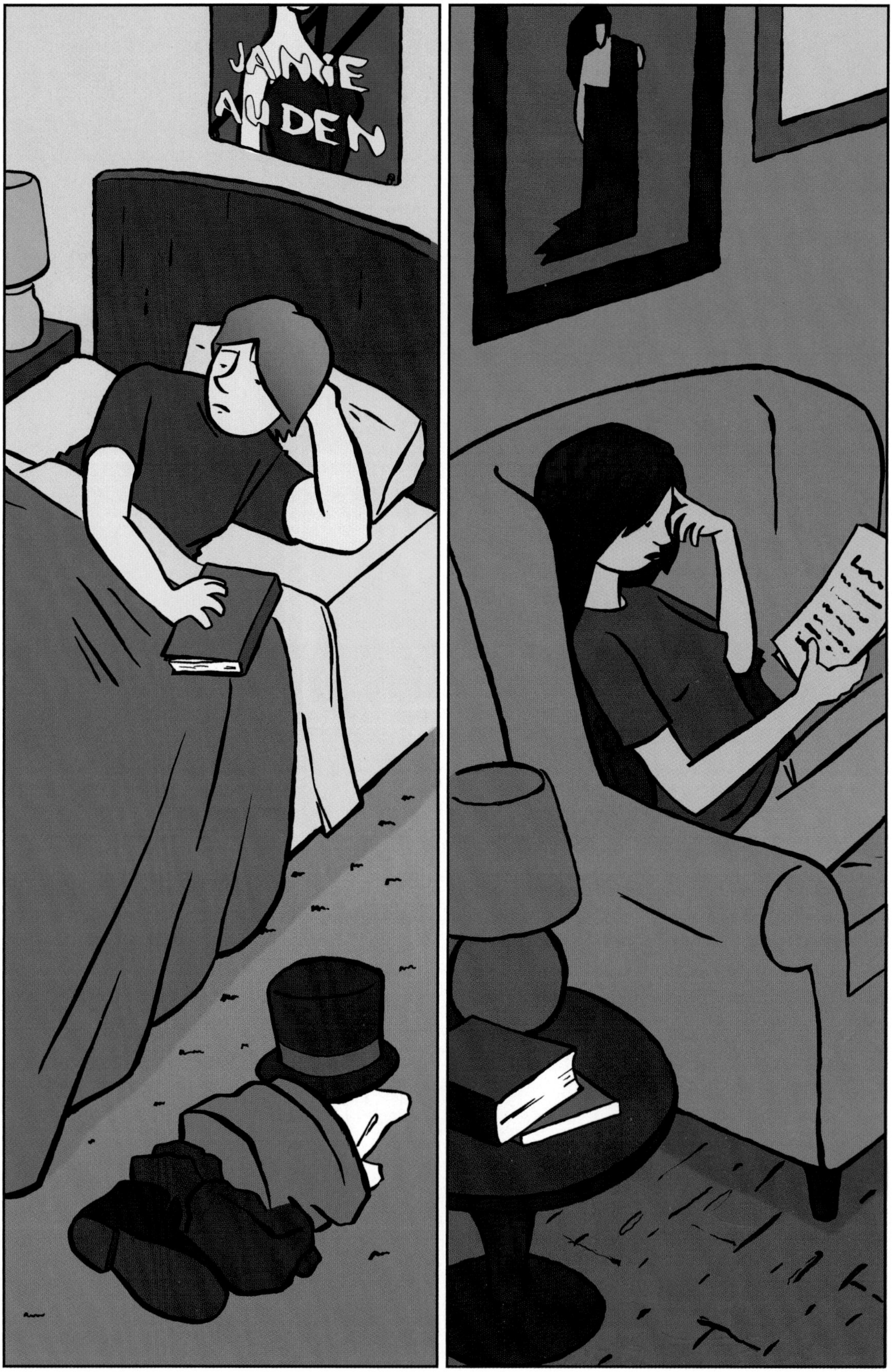
JAMIE
AUDEN

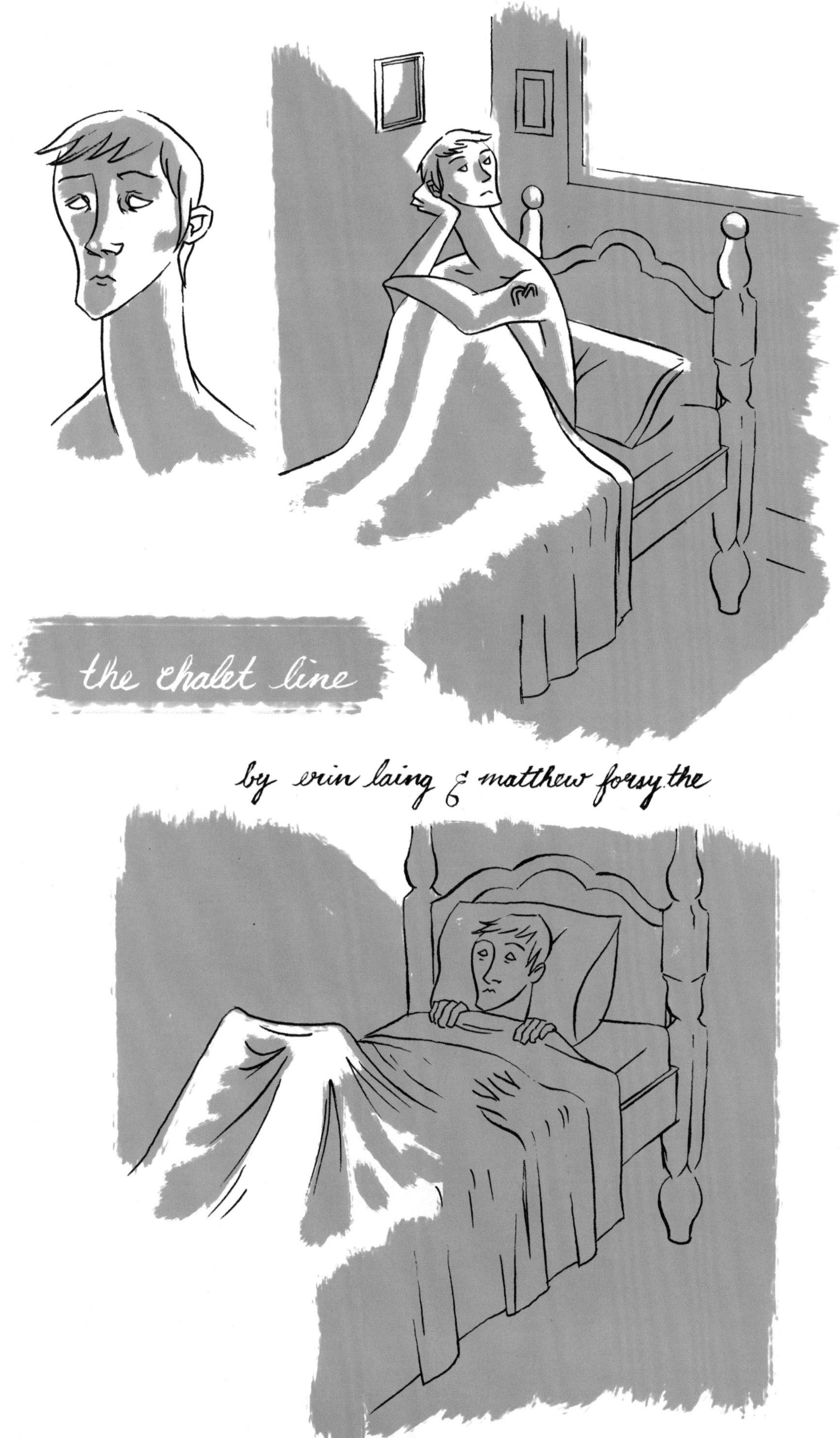
the chalet line
by erin laing & matthew forsythe

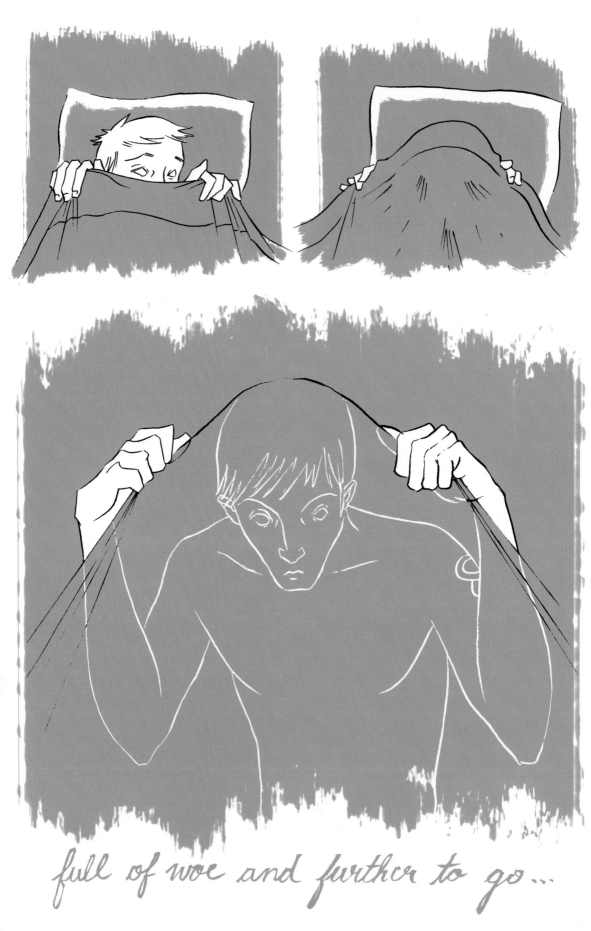

full of woe and further to go...

a mate of mine

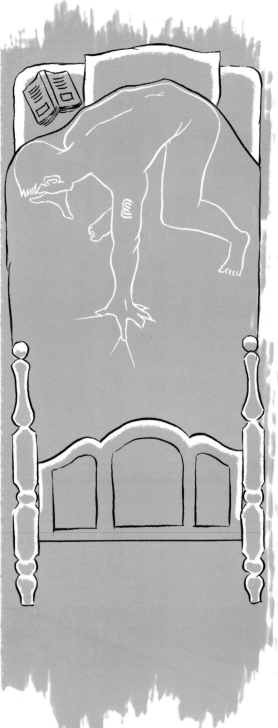

to london there is

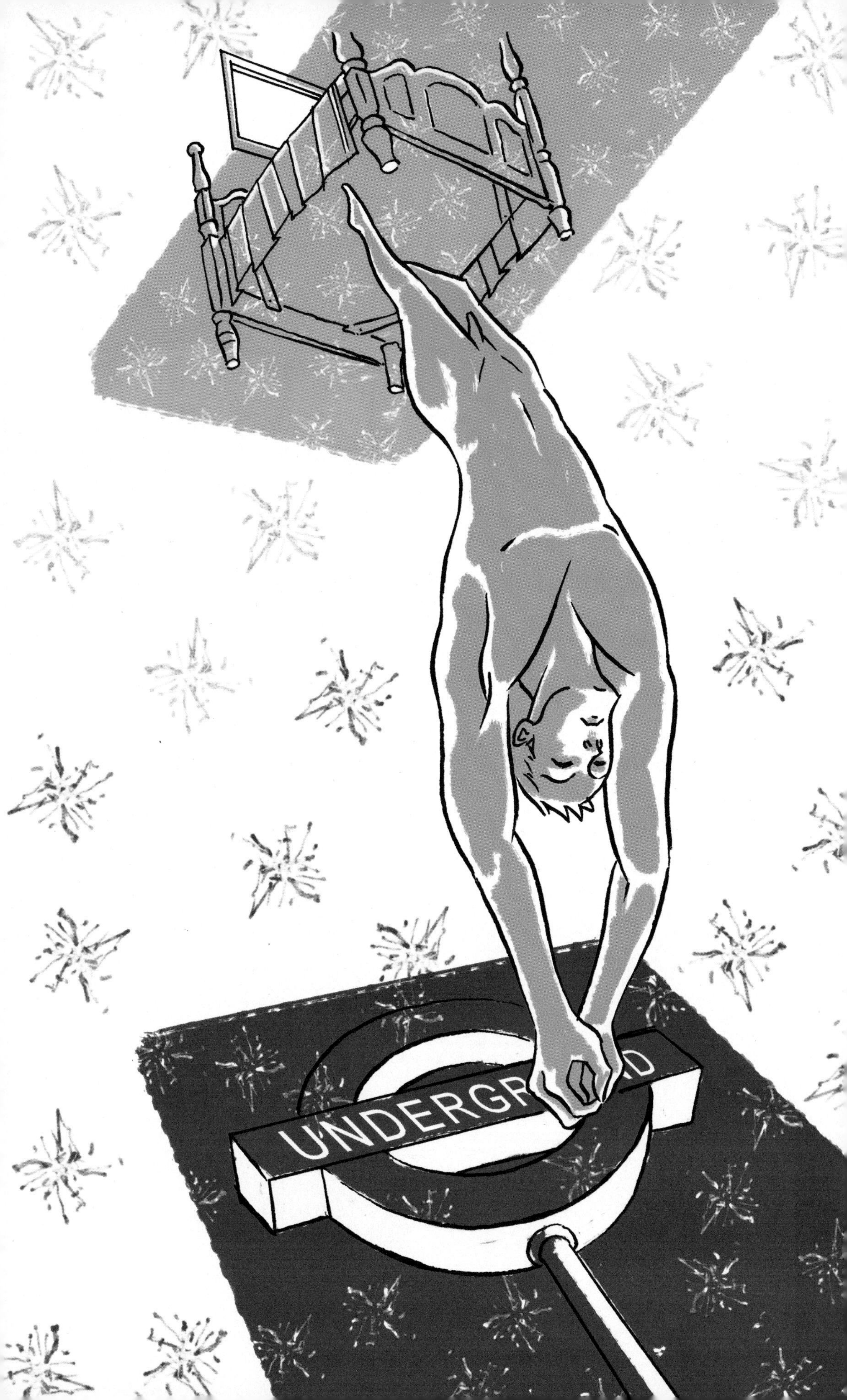
UNDERGR D

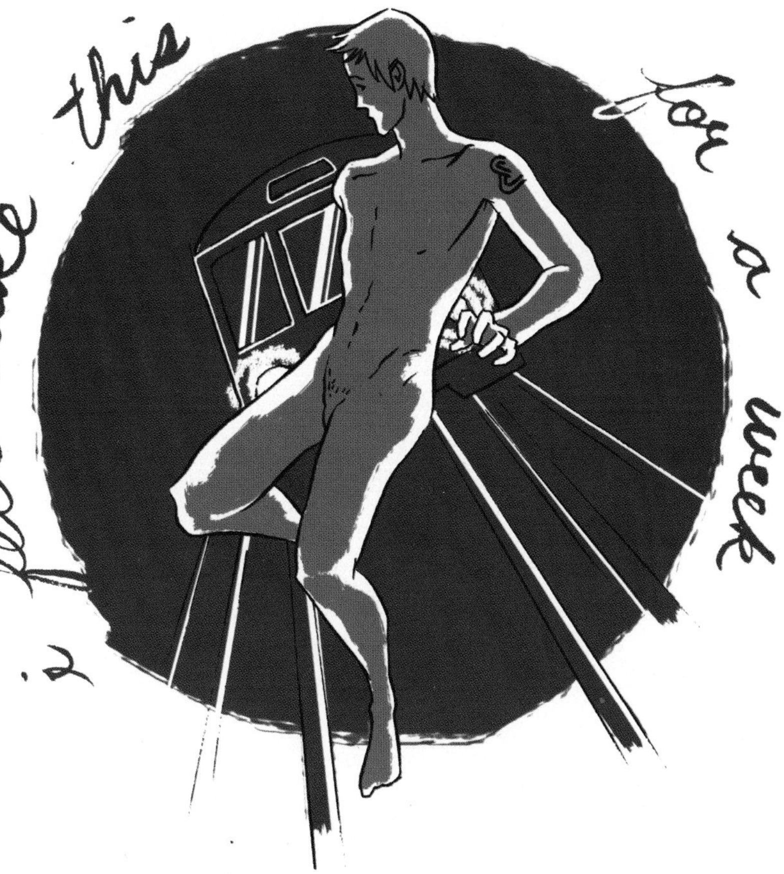
i felt like this for a week

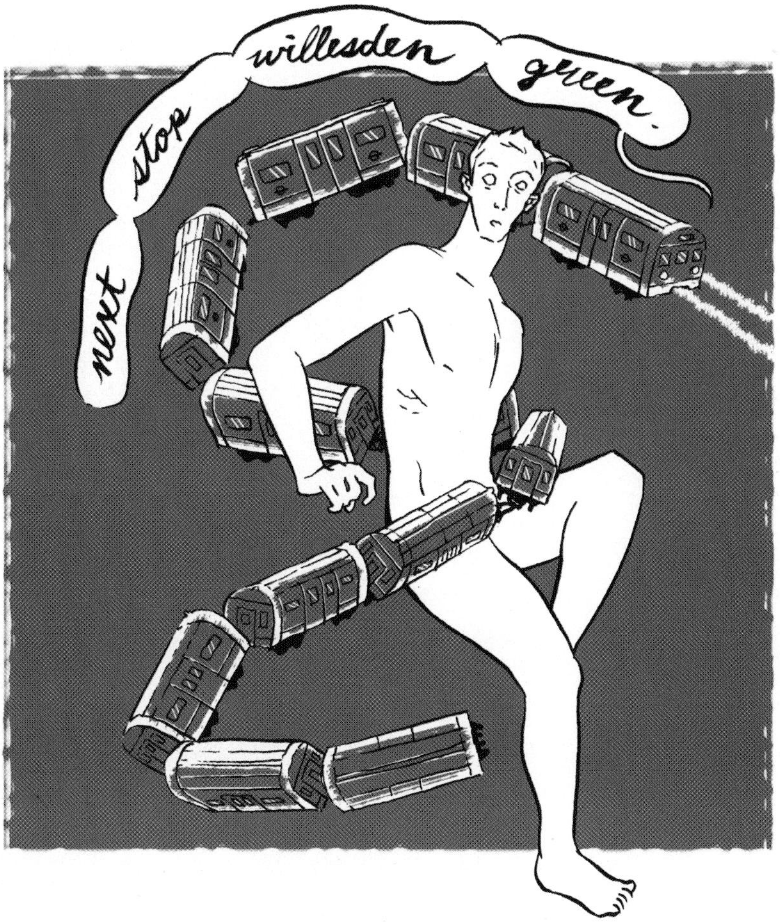
next stop willesden green.

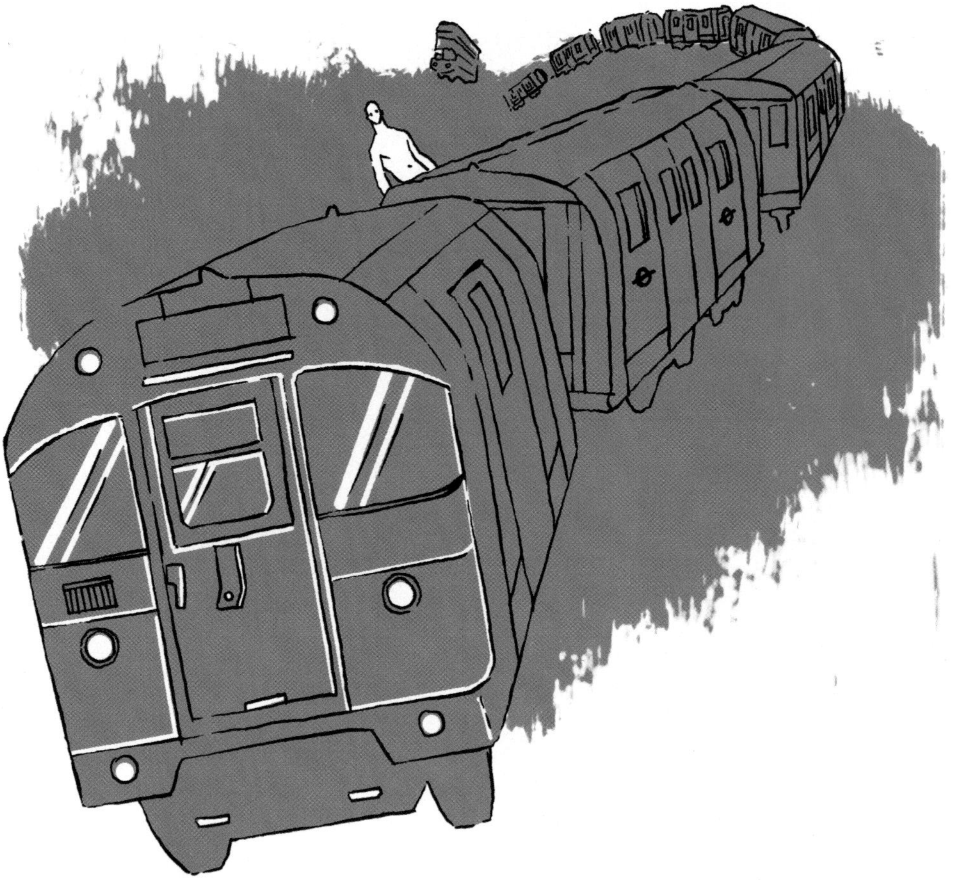

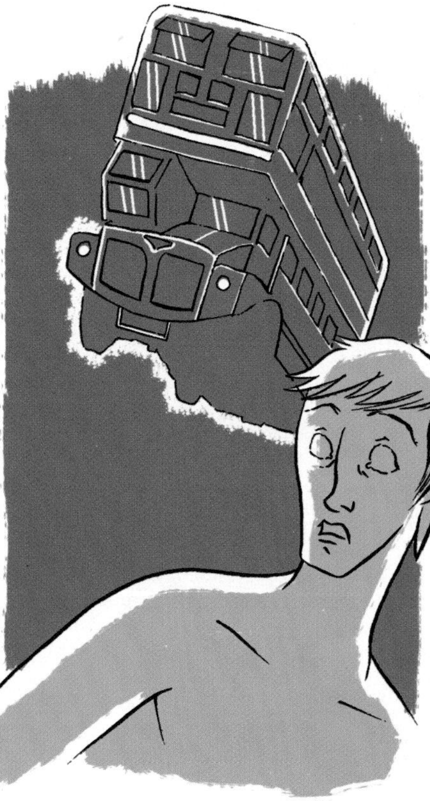

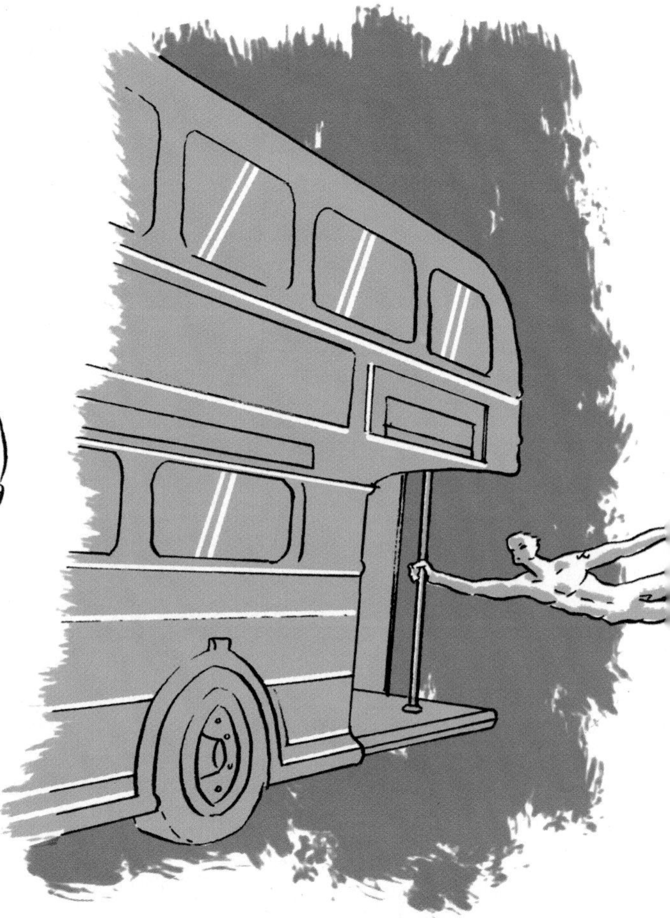

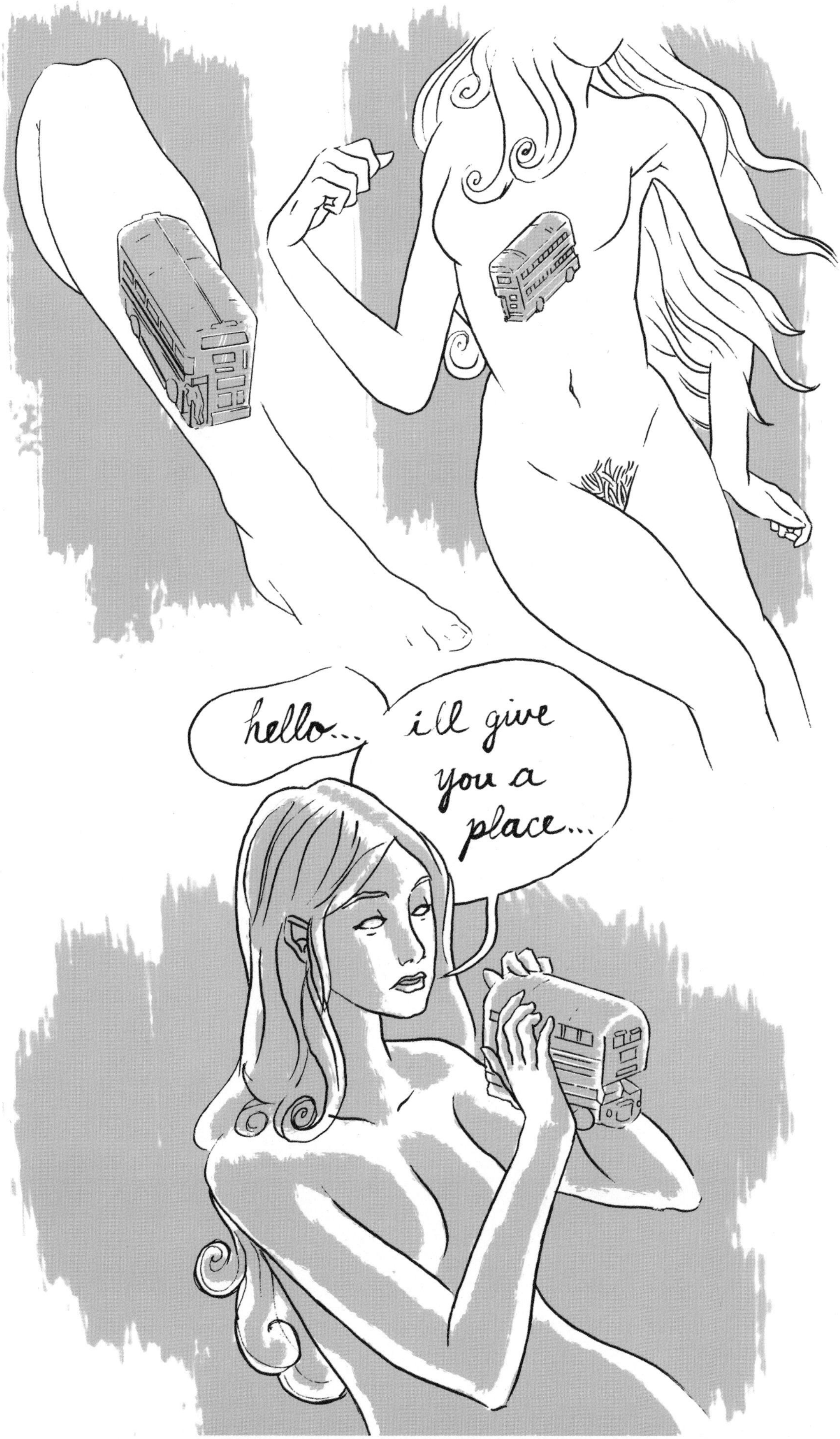
hello...
ill give you a place...

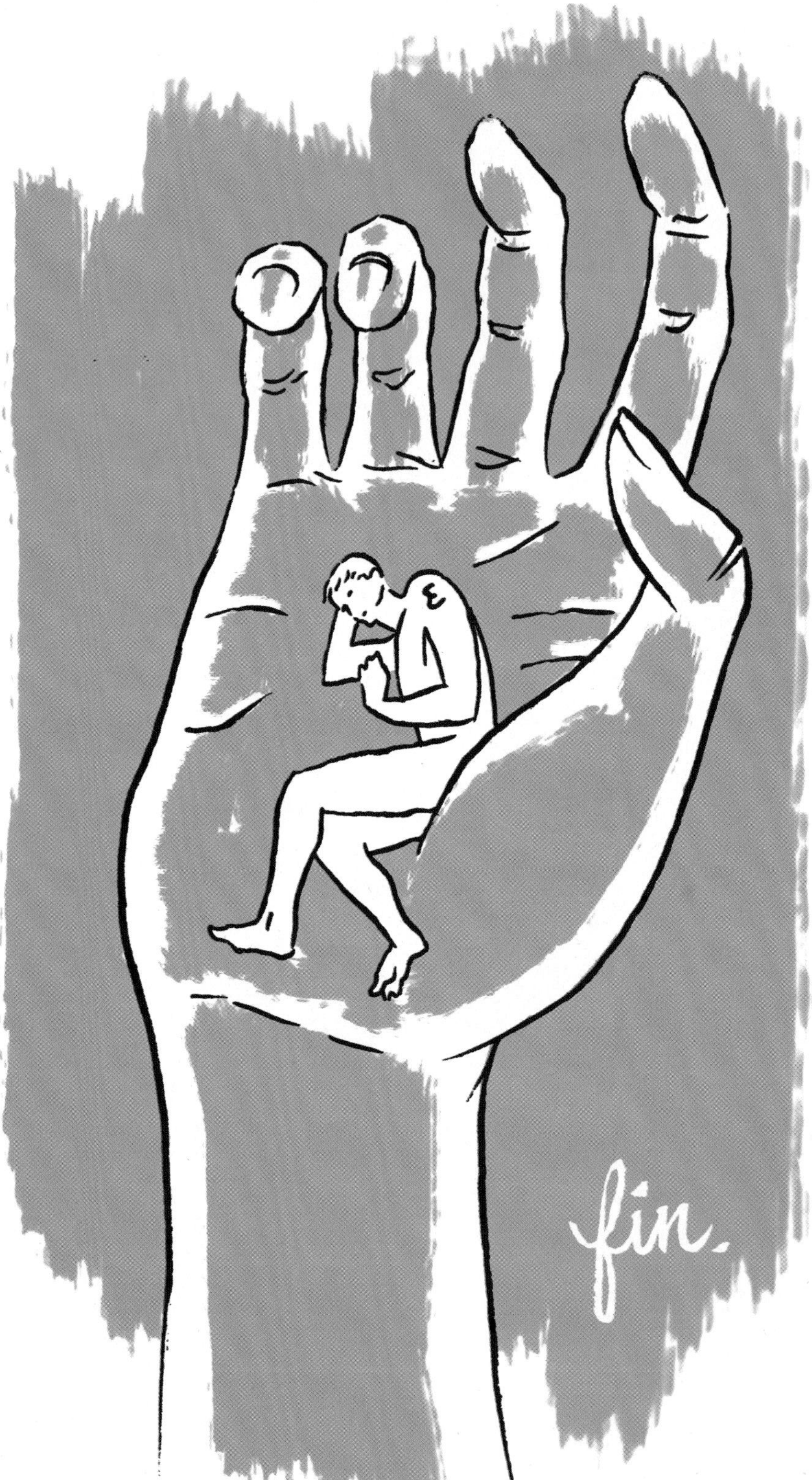
fin.

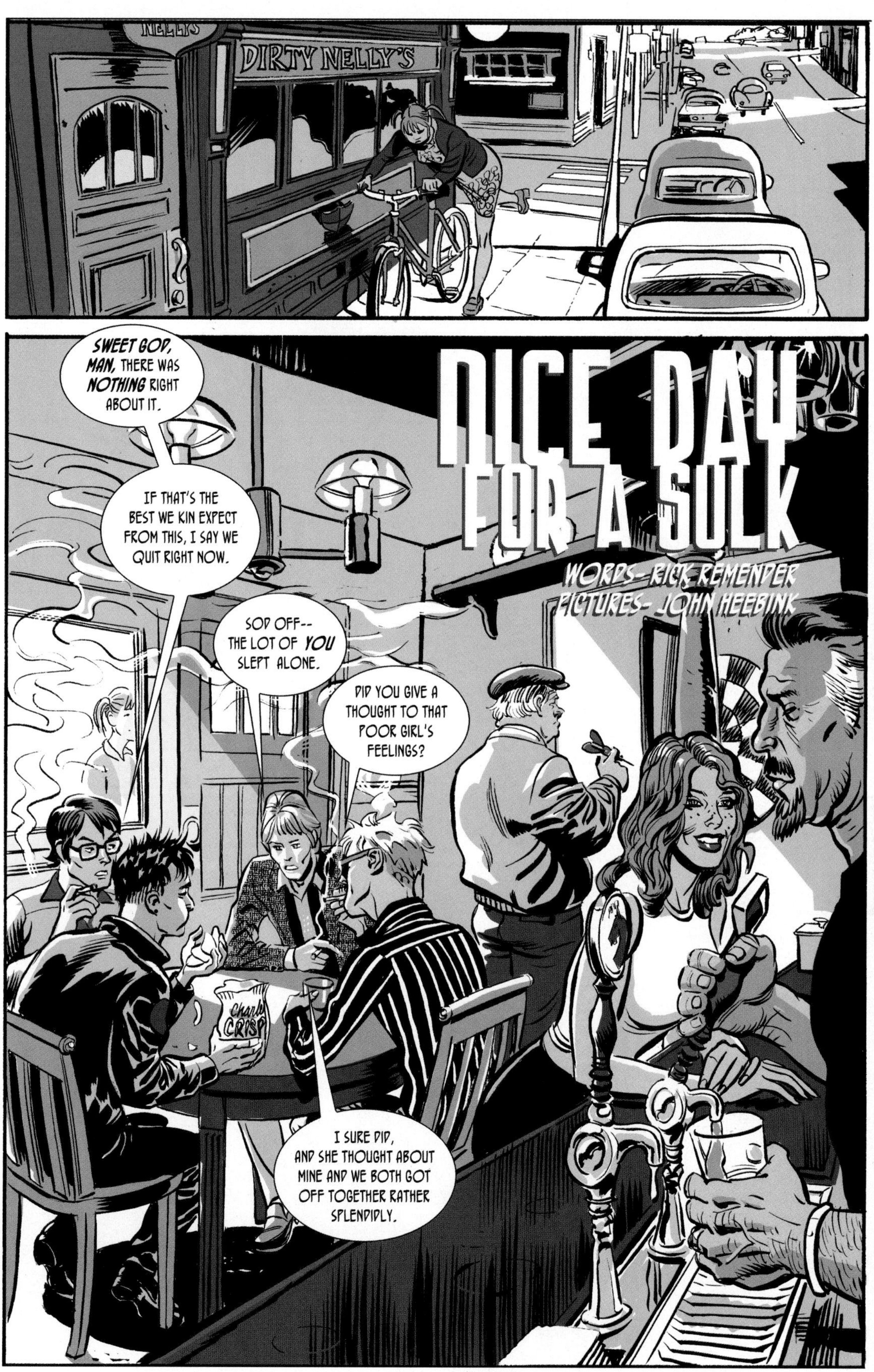
NELLY'S
DIRTY NELLY'S
NICE DAY FOR A SULK
WORDS- RICK REMENDER
PICTURES- JOHN HEEBINK
SWEET GOD, MAN, THERE WAS NOTHING RIGHT ABOUT IT.
IF THAT'S THE BEST WE KIN EXPECT FROM THIS, I SAY WE QUIT RIGHT NOW.
SOD OFF-- THE LOT OF YOU SLEPT ALONE.
DID YOU GIVE A THOUGHT TO THAT POOR GIRL'S FEELINGS?
I SURE DID, AND SHE THOUGHT ABOUT MINE AND WE BOTH GOT OFF TOGETHER RATHER SPLENDIDLY.

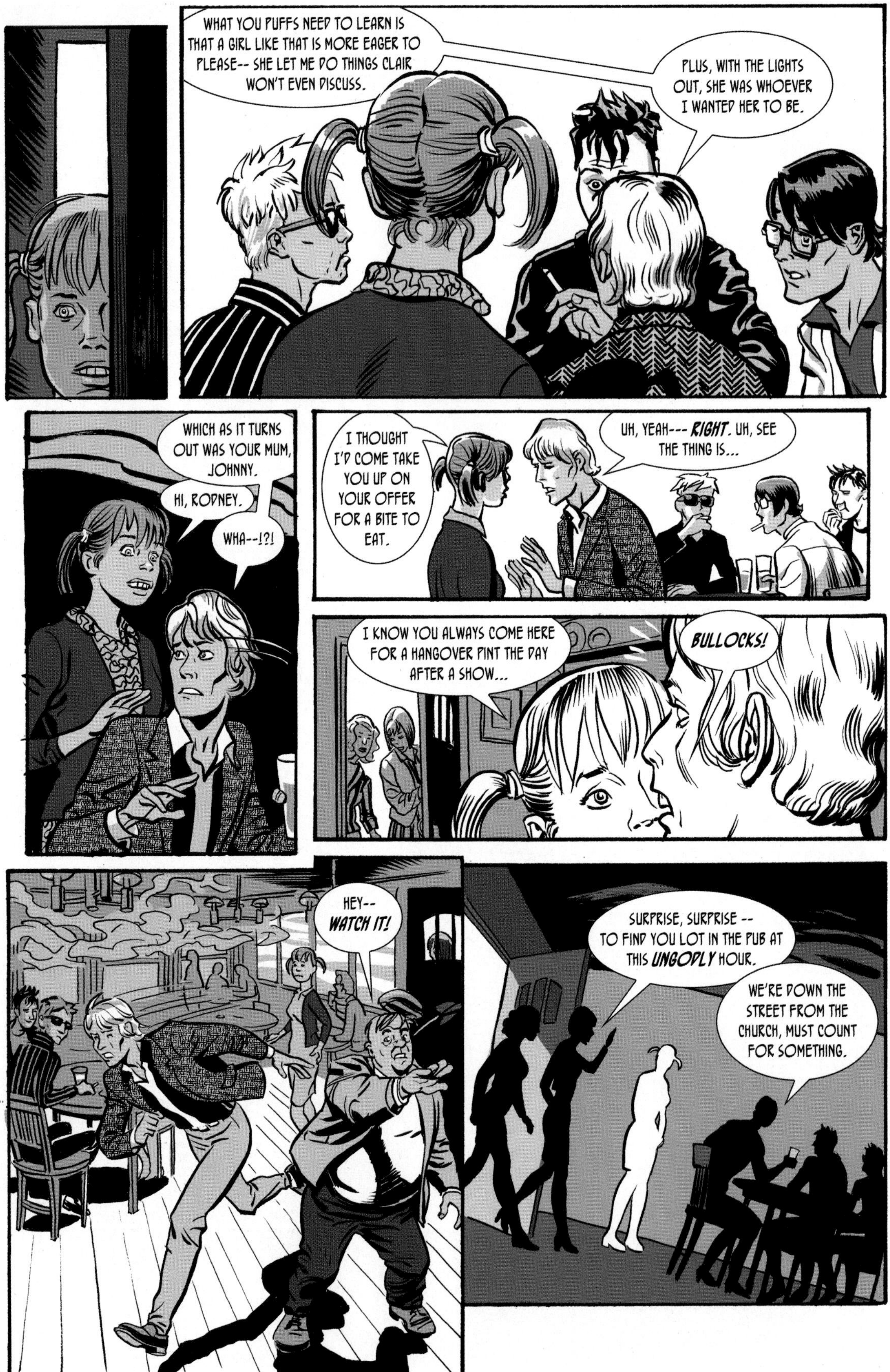
WHAT YOU PUFFS NEED TO LEARN IS THAT A GIRL LIKE THAT IS MORE EAGER TO PLEASE-- SHE LET ME DO THINGS CLAIR WON'T EVEN DISCUSS.
PLUS, WITH THE LIGHTS OUT, SHE WAS WHOEVER I WANTED HER TO BE.
WHICH AS IT TURNS OUT WAS YOUR MUM, JOHNNY.
HI, RODNEY.
WHA--!?!
I THOUGHT I'D COME TAKE YOU UP ON YOUR OFFER FOR A BITE TO EAT.
UH, YEAH--- RIGHT. UH, SEE THE THING IS...
I KNOW YOU ALWAYS COME HERE FOR A HANGOVER PINT THE DAY AFTER A SHOW...
BULLOCKS!
HEY-- WATCH IT!
SURPRISE, SURPRISE -- TO FIND YOU LOT IN THE PUB AT THIS UNGODLY HOUR.
WE'RE DOWN THE STREET FROM THE CHURCH, MUST COUNT FOR SOMETHING.

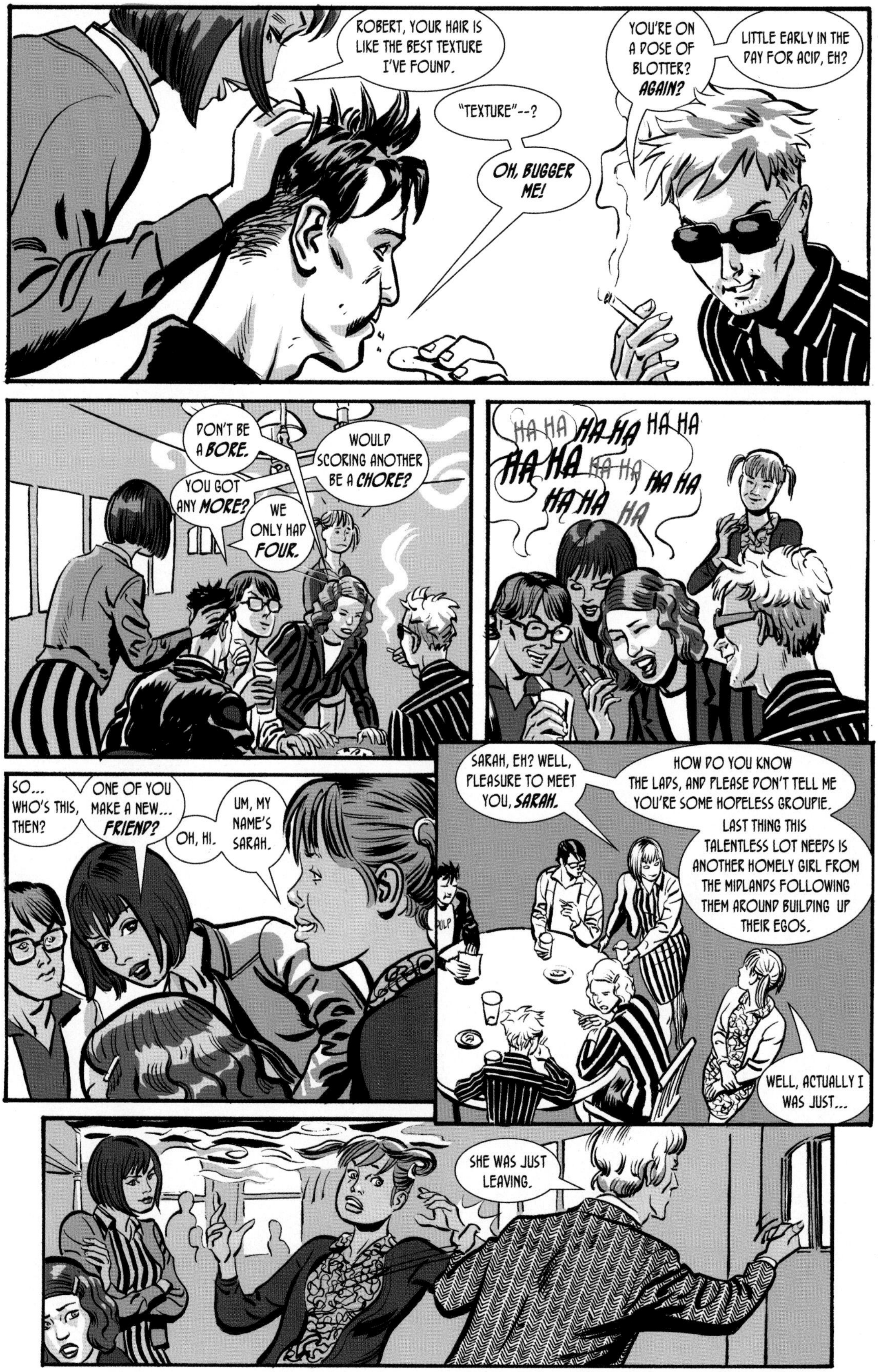
ROBERT, YOUR HAIR IS LIKE THE BEST TEXTURE I'VE FOUND.
"TEXTURE"--?
OH, BUGGER ME!
YOU'RE ON A DOSE OF BLOTTER? AGAIN?
LITTLE EARLY IN THE DAY FOR ACID, EH?
DON'T BE A BORE.
WOULD SCORING ANOTHER BE A CHORE?
YOU GOT ANY MORE?
WE ONLY HAD FOUR.
HA HA HA HA HA HA
HA HA HA HA HA HA
HA HA HA
SO... WHO'S THIS, THEN?
ONE OF YOU MAKE A NEW... FRIEND?
OH, HI.
UM, MY NAME'S SARAH.
SARAH, EH? WELL, PLEASURE TO MEET YOU, SARAH.
HOW DO YOU KNOW THE LADS, AND PLEASE DON'T TELL ME YOU'RE SOME HOPELESS GROUPIE.
LAST THING THIS TALENTLESS LOT NEEDS IS ANOTHER HOMELY GIRL FROM THE MIDLANDS FOLLOWING THEM AROUND BUILDING UP THEIR EGOS.
WELL, ACTUALLY I WAS JUST...
SHE WAS JUST LEAVING.

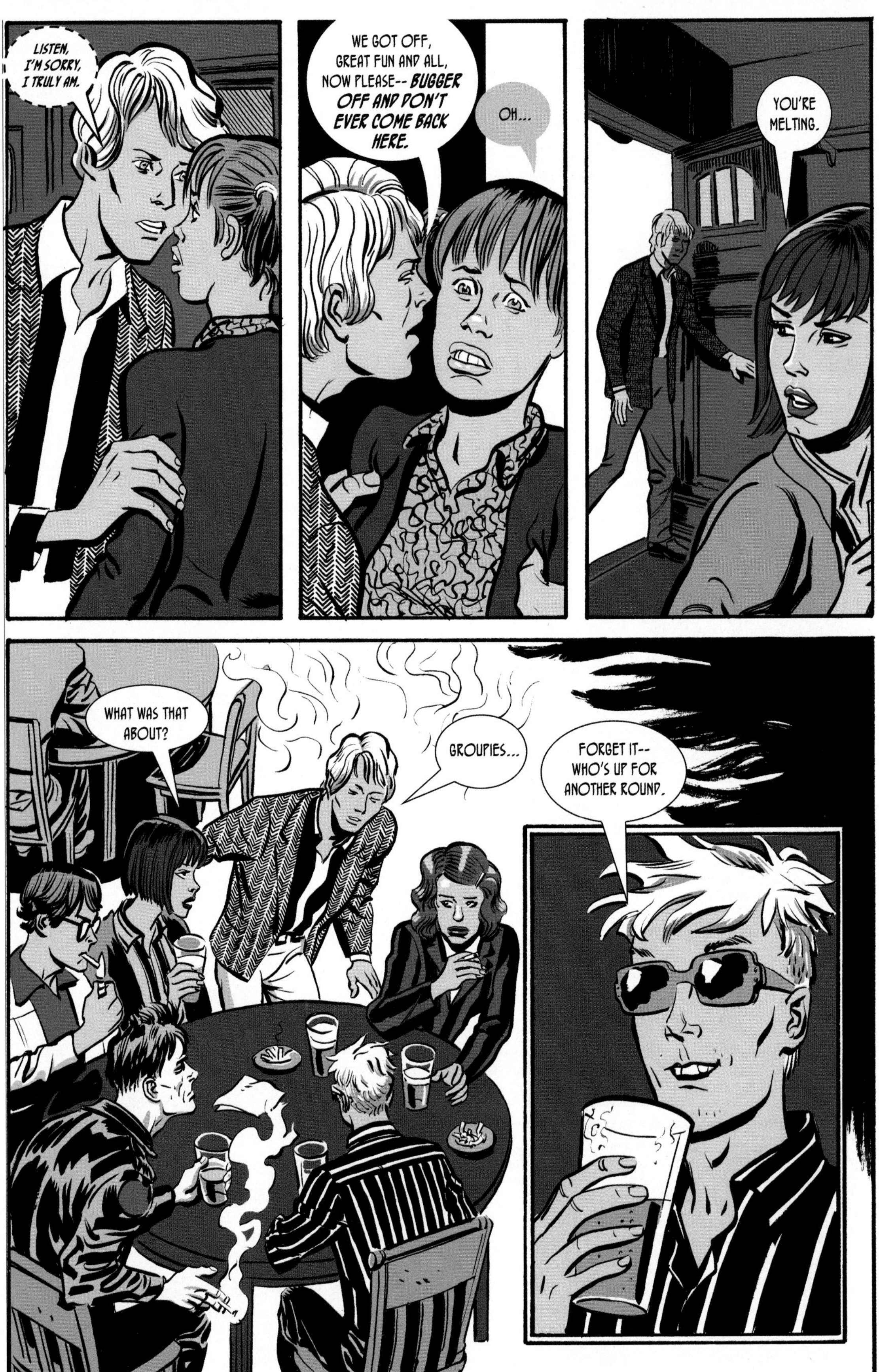
LISTEN, I'M SORRY, I TRULY AM.
WE GOT OFF, GREAT FUN AND ALL, NOW PLEASE-- BUGGER OFF AND DON'T EVER COME BACK HERE.
OH...
YOU'RE MELTING.
WHAT WAS THAT ABOUT?
GROUPIES...
FORGET IT-- WHO'S UP FOR ANOTHER ROUND.

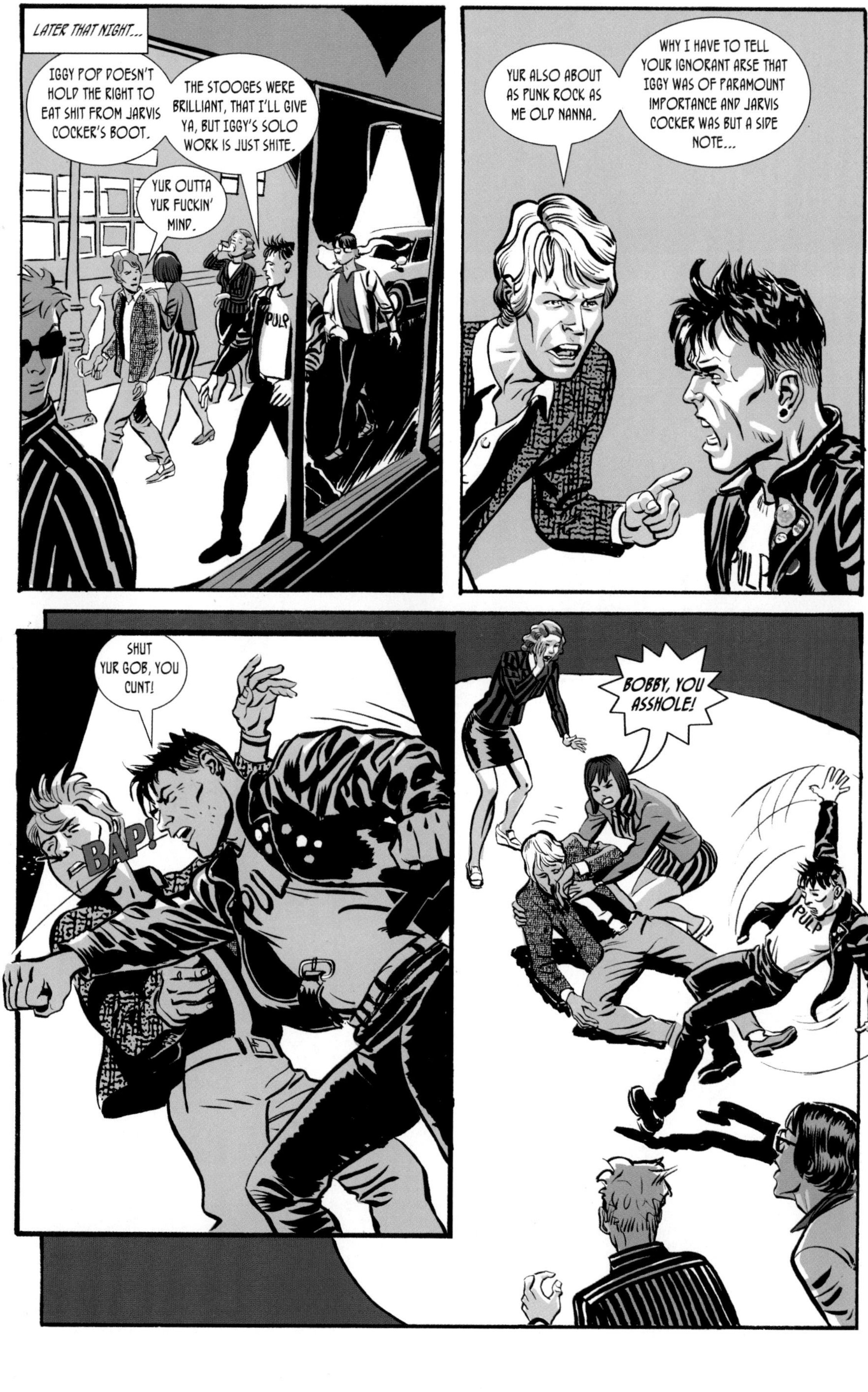

LATER THAT NIGHT...
IGGY POP DOESN'T HOLD THE RIGHT TO EAT SHIT FROM JARVIS COCKER'S BOOT.
THE STOOGES WERE BRILLIANT, THAT I'LL GIVE YA, BUT IGGY'S SOLO WORK IS JUST SHITE.
YUR OUTTA YUR FUCKIN' MIND.
PULP
YUR ALSO ABOUT AS PUNK ROCK AS ME OLD NANNA.
WHY I HAVE TO TELL YOUR IGNORANT ARSE THAT IGGY WAS OF PARAMOUNT IMPORTANCE AND JARVIS COCKER WAS BUT A SIDE NOTE...
PULP
SHUT YUR GOB, YOU CUNT!
BAP!
PUL
BOBBY, YOU ASSHOLE!
PULP

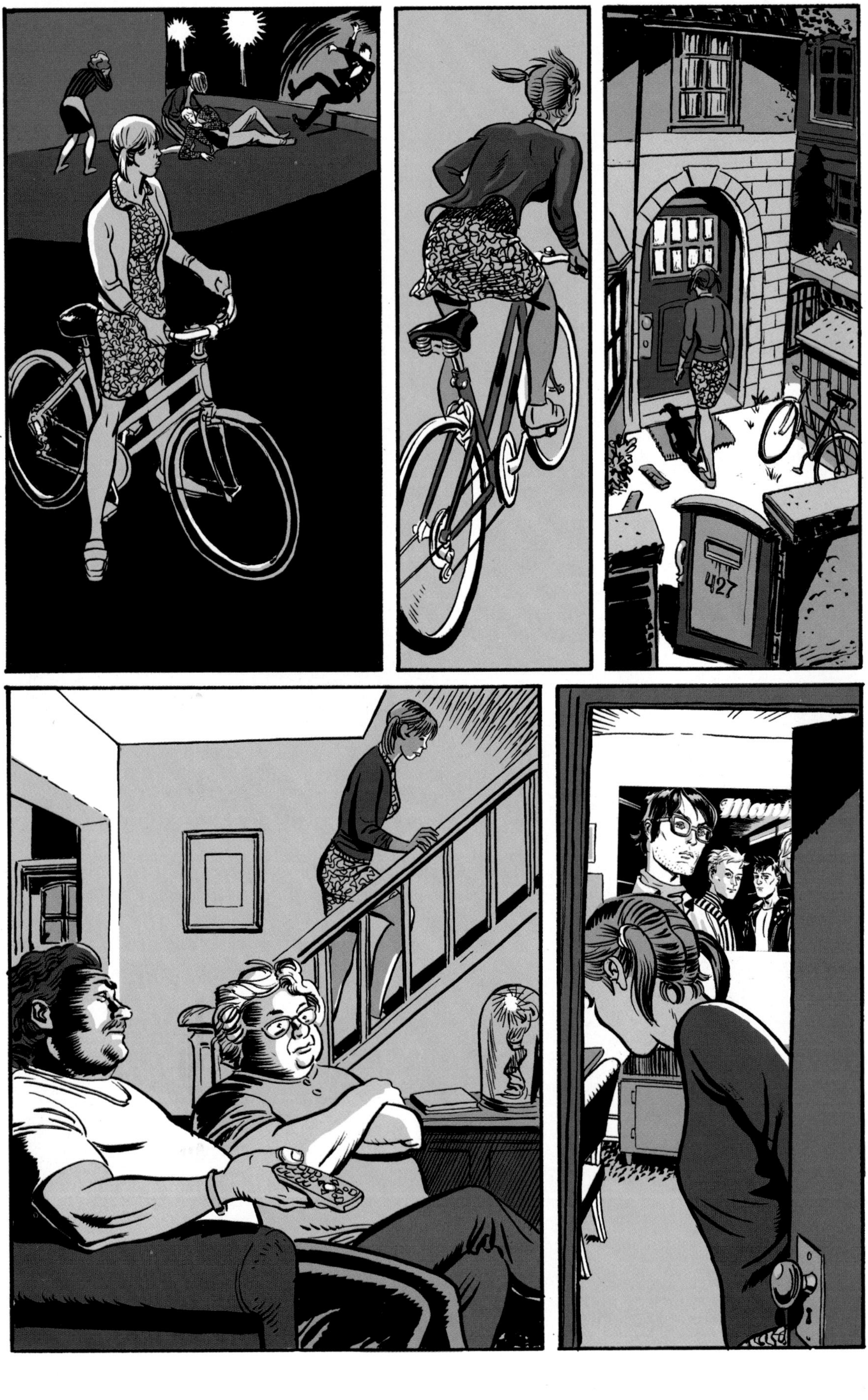
427

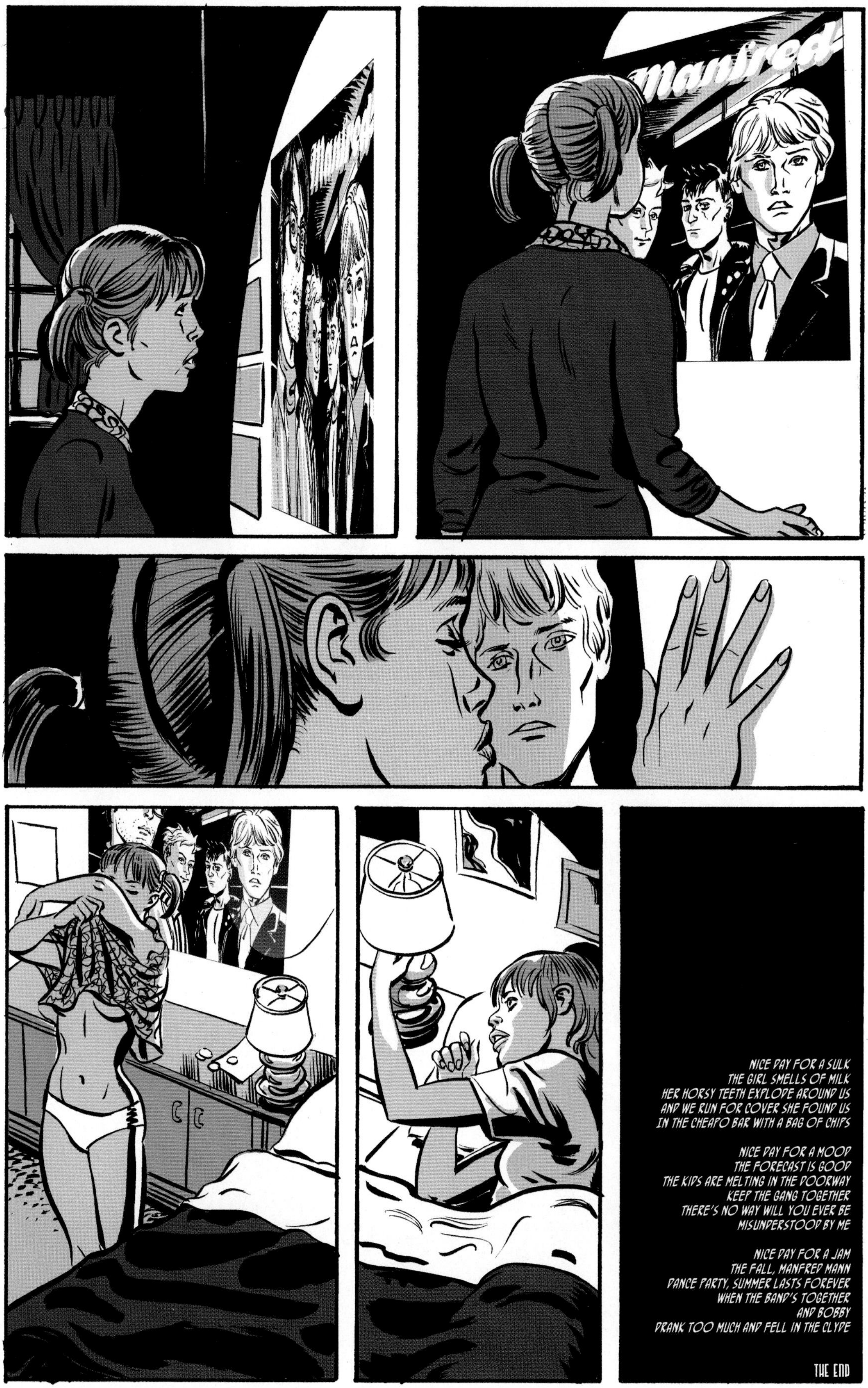
Manfred
NICE DAY FOR A SULK
THE GIRL SMELLS OF MILK
HER HORSY TEETH EXPLODE AROUND US
AND WE RUN FOR COVER SHE FOUND US
IN THE CHEAPO BAR WITH A BAG OF CHIPS
NICE DAY FOR A MOOD
THE FORECAST IS GOOD
THE KIDS ARE MELTING IN THE DOORWAY
KEEP THE GANG TOGETHER
THERE'S NO WAY WILL YOU EVER BE
MISUNDERSTOOD BY ME
NICE DAY FOR A JAM
THE FALL, MANFRED MANN
DANCE PARTY, SUMMER LASTS FOREVER
WHEN THE BAND'S TOGETHER
AND BOBBY
DRANK TOO MUCH AND FELL IN THE CLYDE
THE END

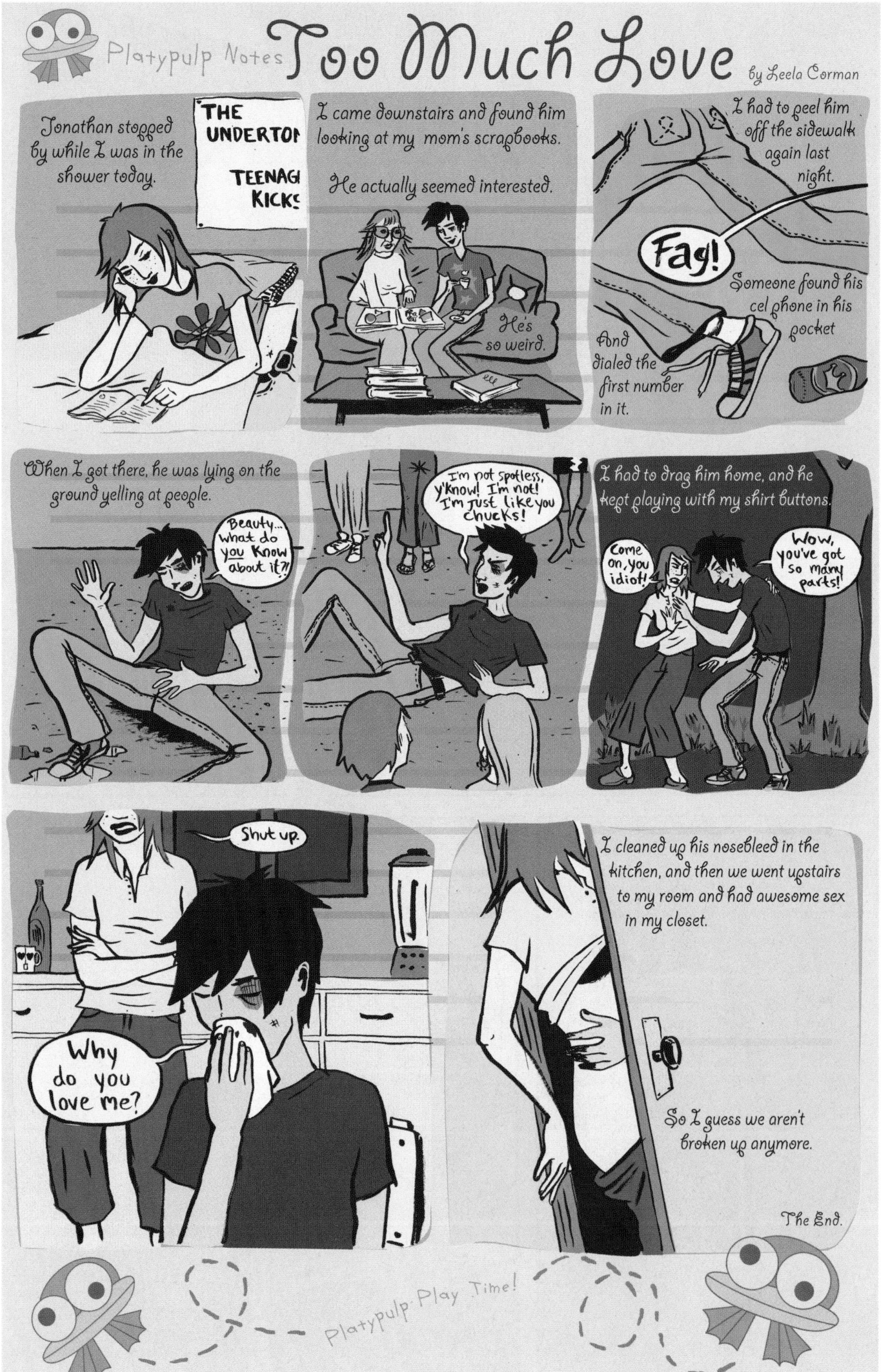
Platypulp Notes
Too Much Love
by Leela Corman
Jonathan stopped by while I was in the shower today.
THE UNDERTON
TEENAG KICKS
I came downstairs and found him looking at my mom's scrapbooks.
He actually seemed interested.
He's so weird.
I had to peel him off the sidewalk again last night.
Fag!
Someone found his cel phone in his pocket
And dialed the first number in it.
When I got there, he was lying on the ground yelling at people.
Beauty... what do you know about it?!
I'm not spotless, y'know! I'm not! I'm just like you chucks!
I had to drag him home, and he kept playing with my shirt buttons.
Come on, you idiot!
Wow, you've got so many parts!
Shut up.
Why do you love me?
I cleaned up his nosebleed in the kitchen, and then we went upstairs to my room and had awesome sex in my closet.
So I guess we aren't broken up anymore.
The End.
Platypulp Play Time!

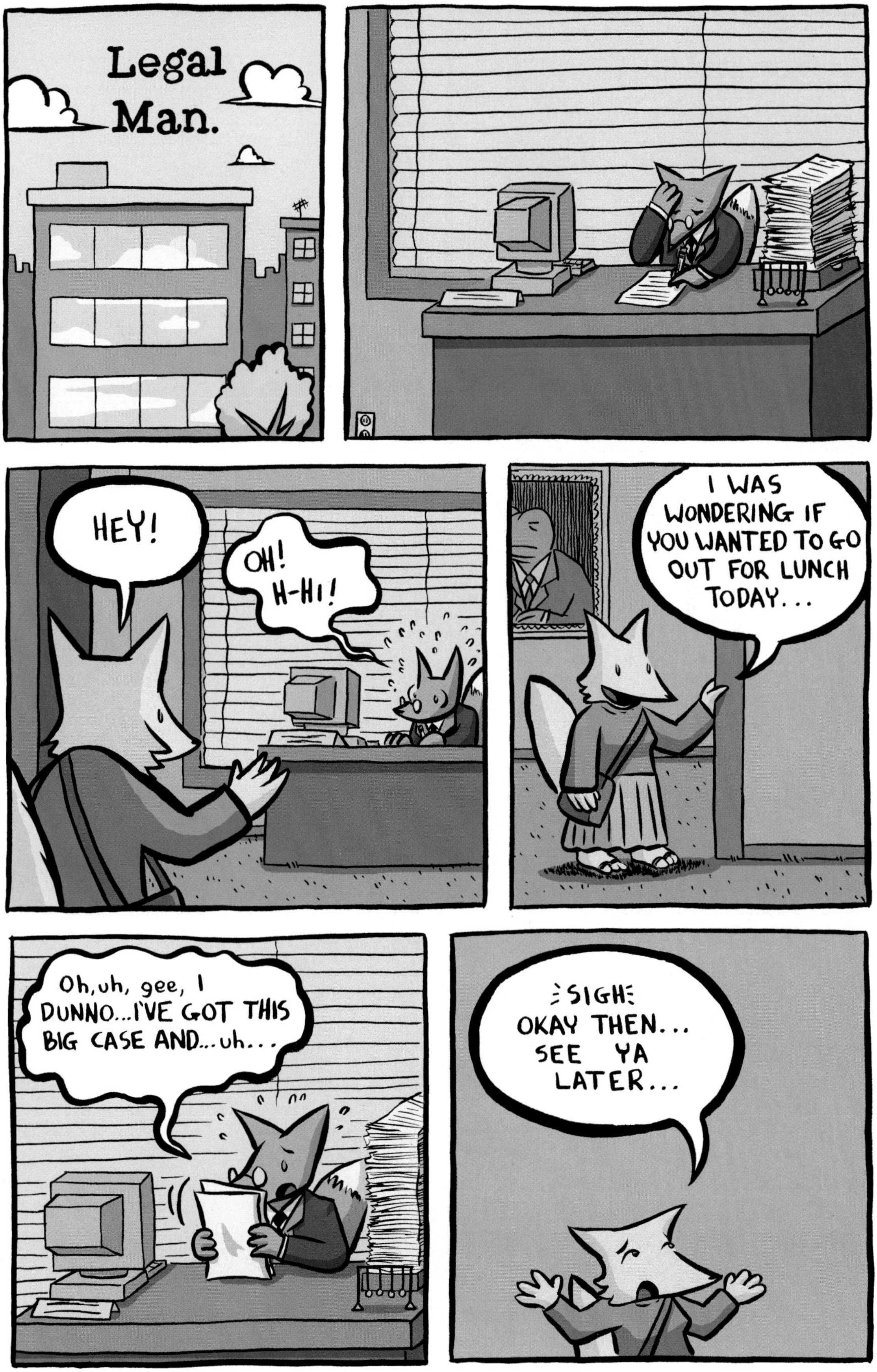
Legal Man.
HEY!
OH! H-HI!
I WAS WONDERING IF YOU WANTED TO GO OUT FOR LUNCH TODAY...
Oh, uh, gee, I DUNNO...I'VE GOT THIS BIG CASE AND...uh...
SIGH OKAY THEN... SEE YA LATER...

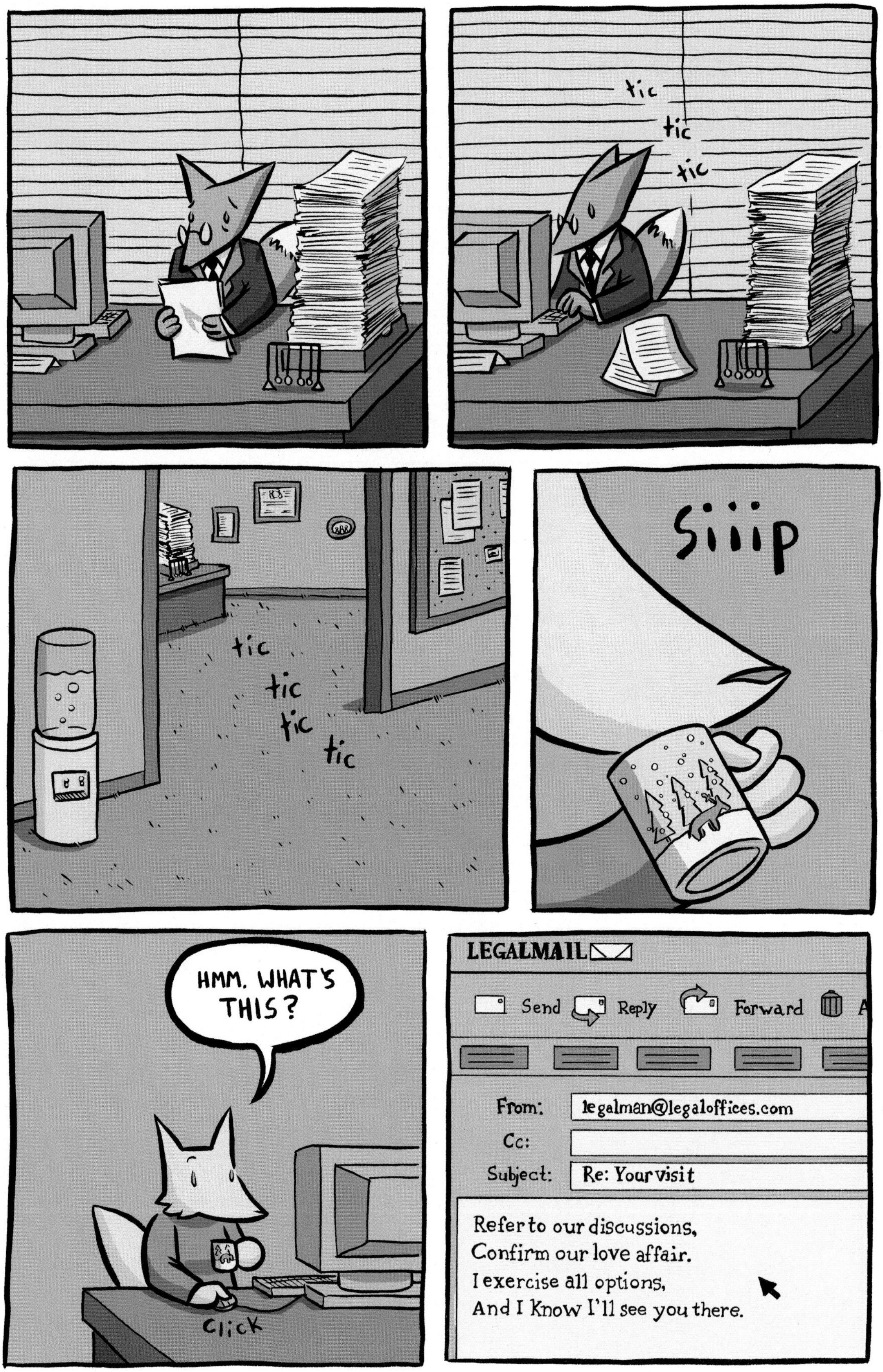
tic
tic
tic
tic
tic
tic
tic
Siiip
HMM. WHAT'S THIS?
Click
LEGALMAIL
Send
Reply
Forward
From:
legalman@legaloffices.com
Cc:
Subject:
Re: Your visit
Refer to our discussions,
Confirm our love affair.
I exercise all options,
And I Know I'll see you there.

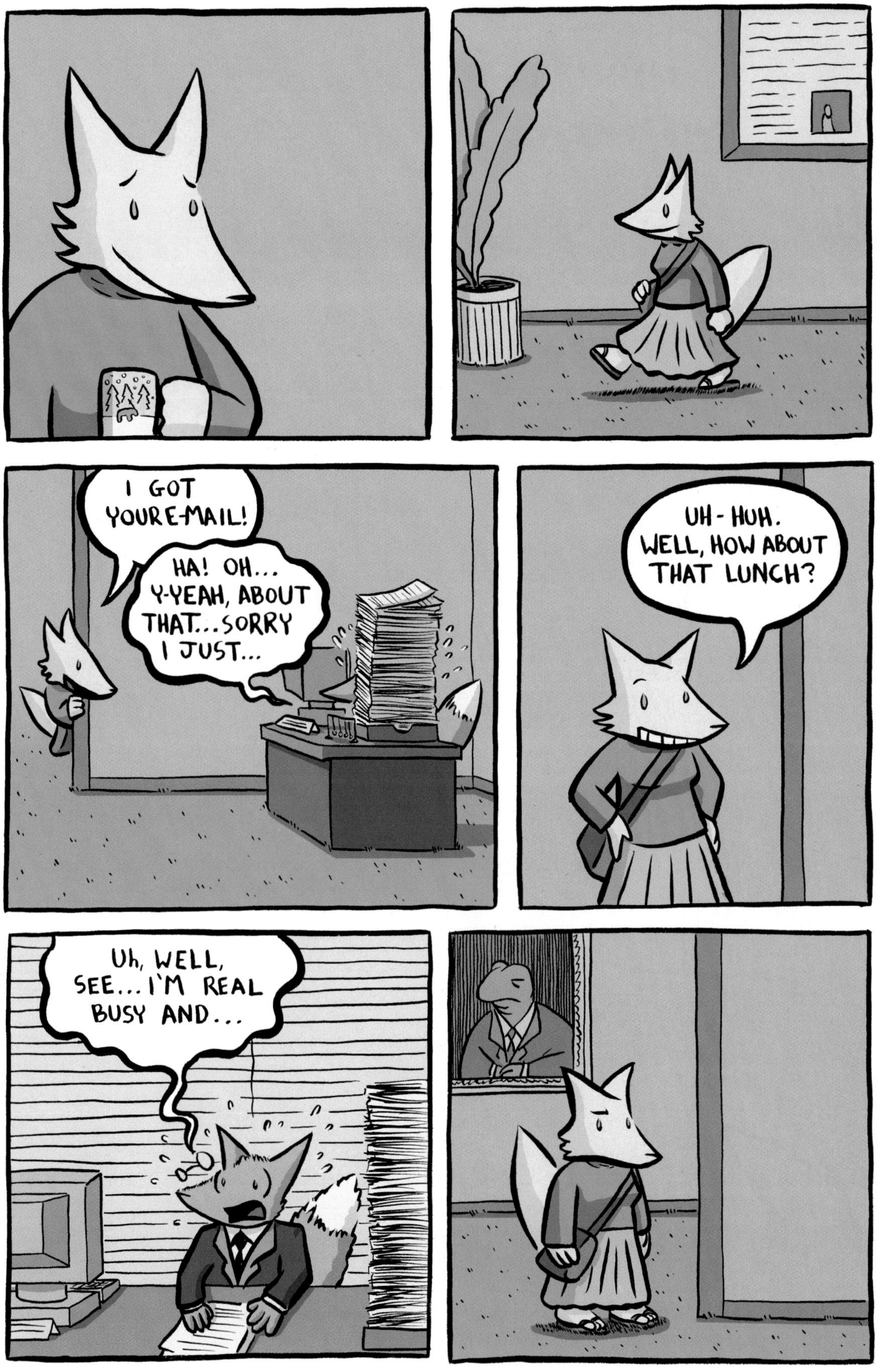
I GOT YOUR E-MAIL!
HA! OH... Y-YEAH, ABOUT THAT... SORRY I JUST...
UH-HUH. WELL, HOW ABOUT THAT LUNCH?
Uh, WELL, SEE... I'M REAL BUSY AND...

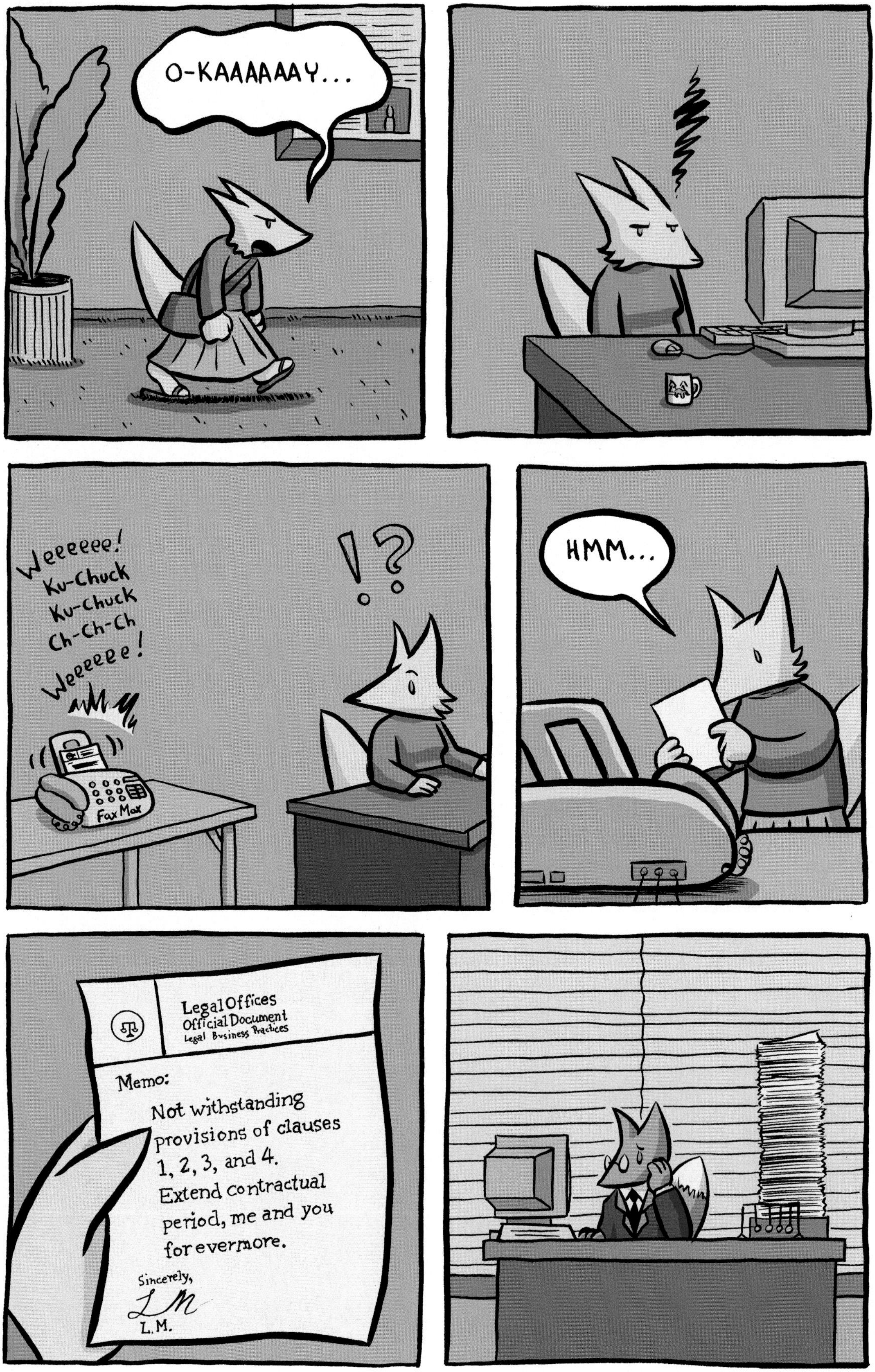
O-KAAAAAAY...
Weeeeee!
Ku-Chuck
Ku-Chuck
Ch-Ch-Ch
Weeeeee!
Fax Max
HMM...
Legal Offices
Official Document
Legal Business Practices
Memo:
Not withstanding provisions of clauses 1, 2, 3, and 4. Extend contractual period, me and you forevermore.
Sincerely,
L.M.

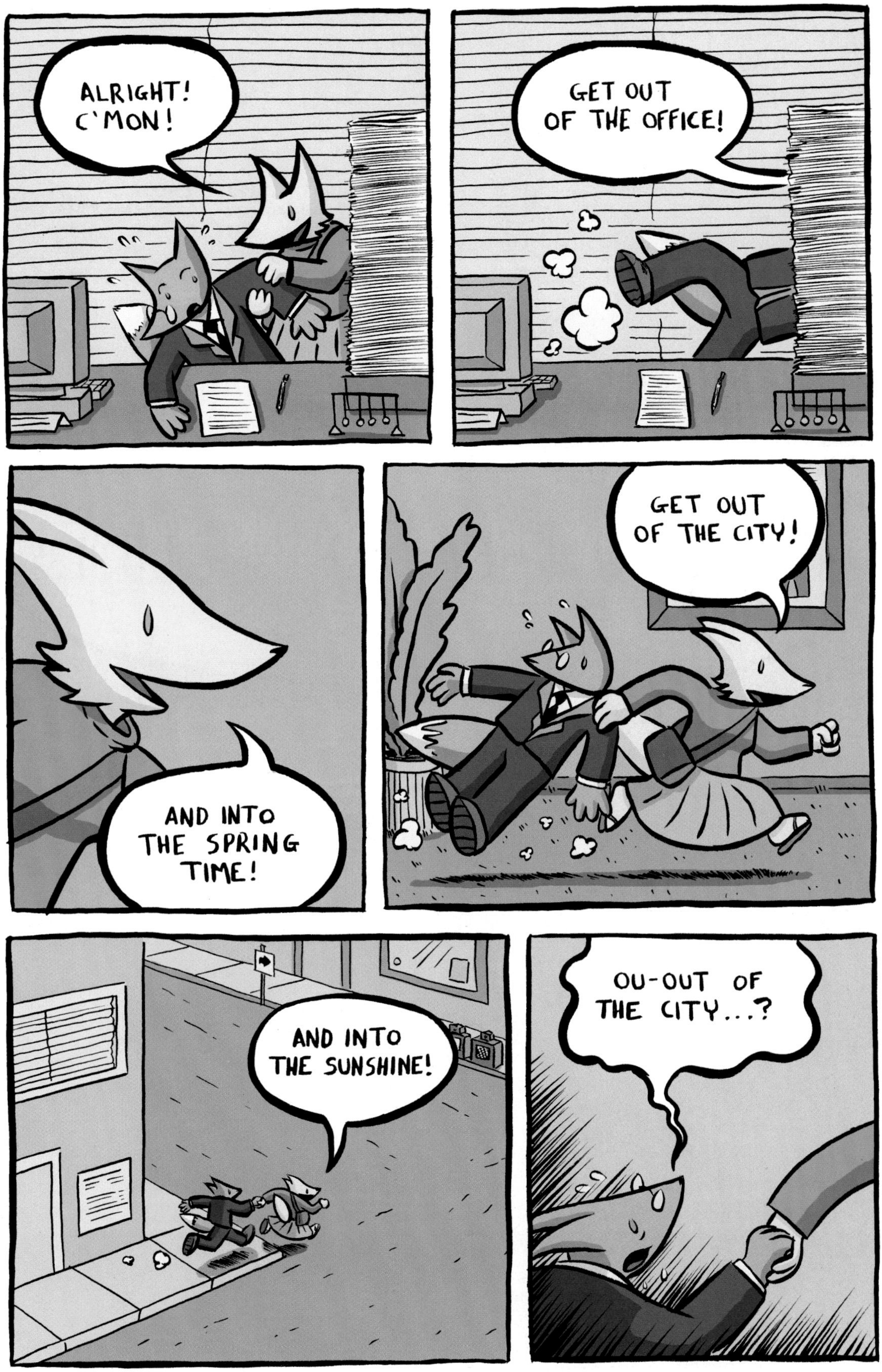
ALRIGHT! C'MON!
GET OUT OF THE OFFICE!
AND INTO THE SPRING TIME!
GET OUT OF THE CITY!
AND INTO THE SUNSHINE!
OU-OUT OF THE CITY...?

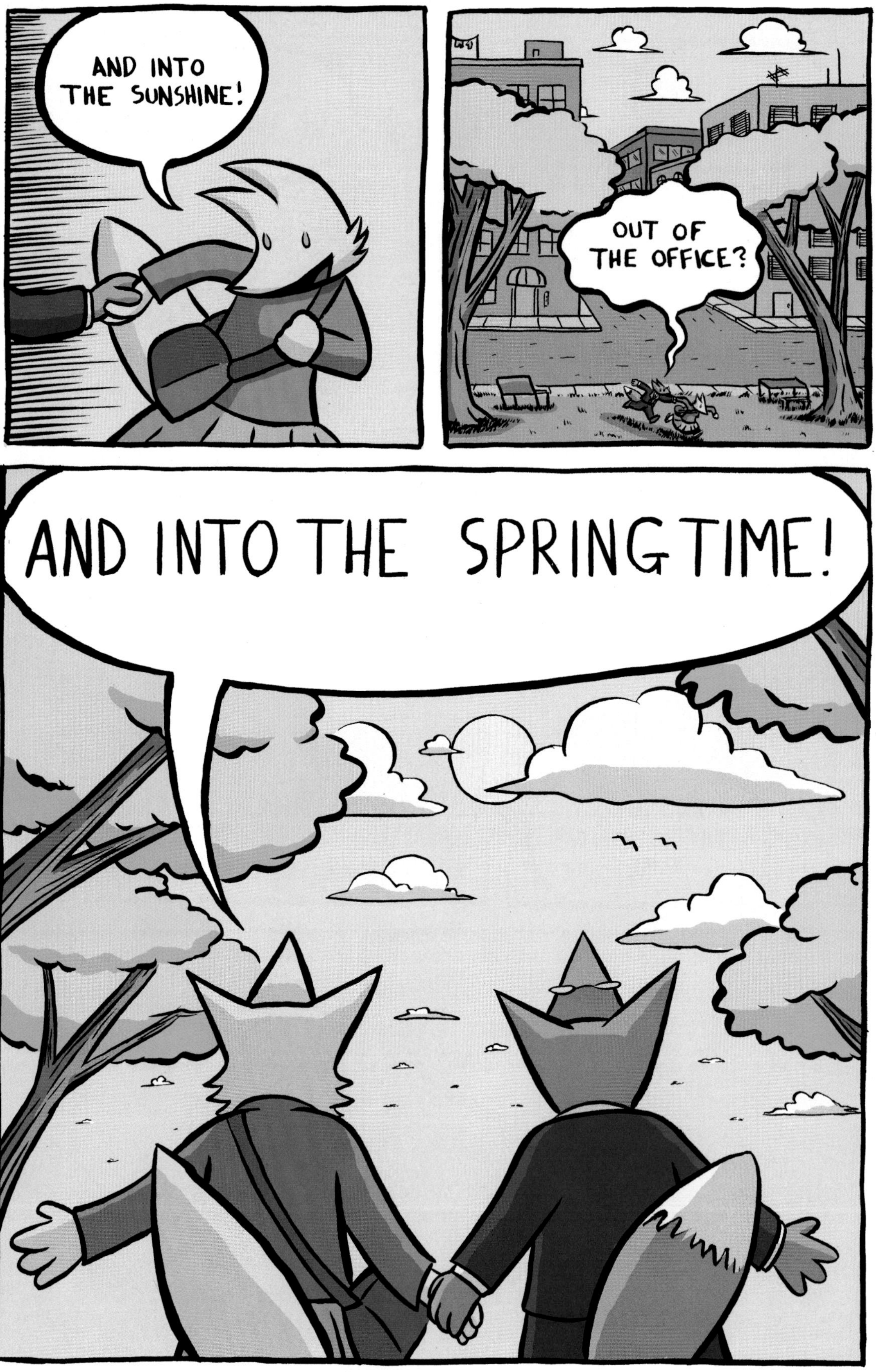
AND INTO THE SUNSHINE!
OUT OF THE OFFICE?
AND INTO THE SPRINGTIME!

MARX AND ENGELS

Adapted by Jamie S. Rich & Marc Ellerby

Special Thanks to Ian Carney

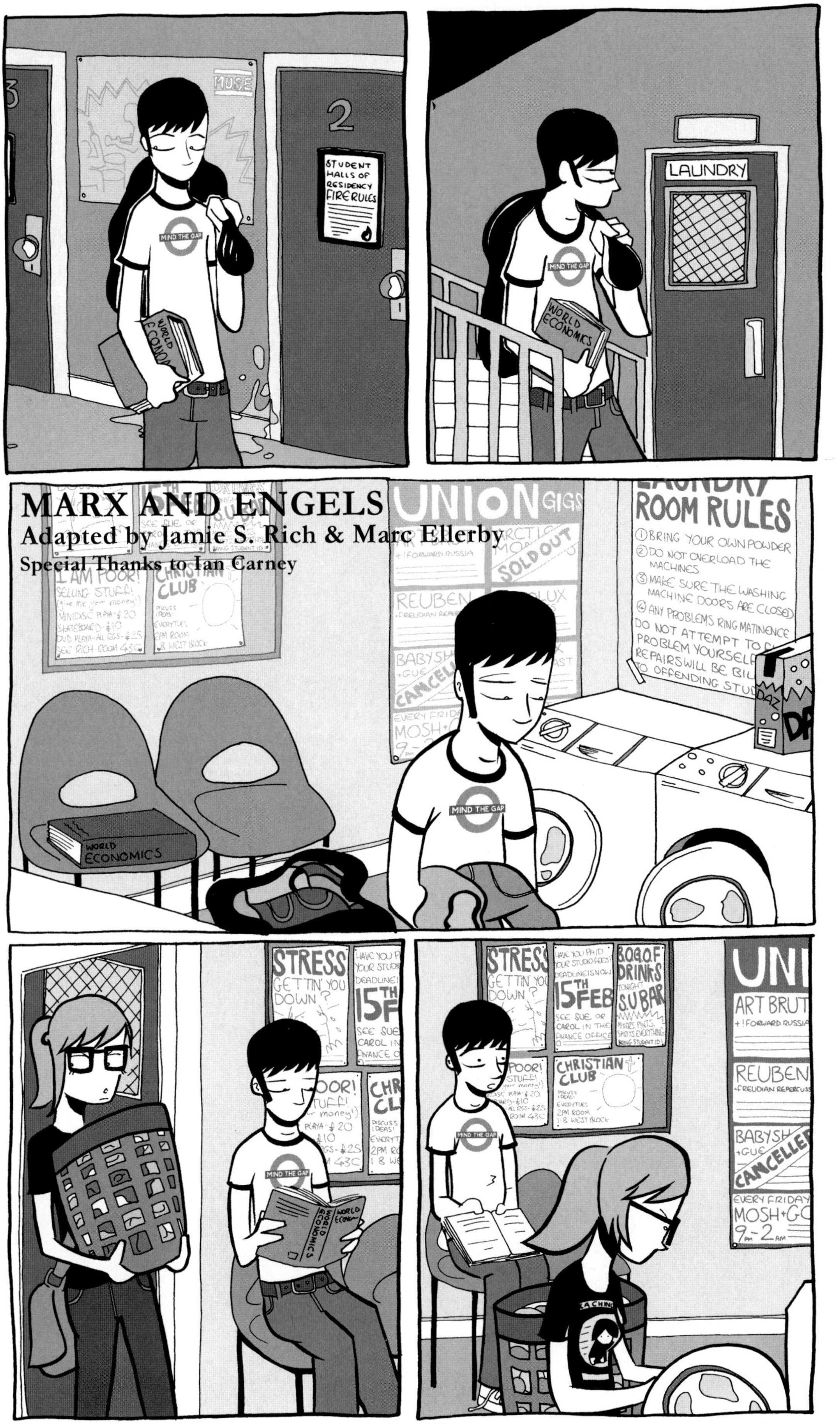

MUSE
2
STUDENT HALLS OF RESIDENCY FIRE RULES
MIND THE GAP
WORLD ECONOMICS
LAUNDRY
UNION GIGS
SOLD OUT
ROOM RULES
① BRING YOUR OWN POWDER
② DO NOT OVERLOAD THE MACHINES
③ MAKE SURE THE WASHING MACHINE DOORS ARE CLOSED
④ ANY PROBLEMS RING MATINENCE
I AM POOR! SELLING STUFF!
CHRISTIAN CLUB
REUBEN
CANCELLED
DAZ
STRESS GETTIN' YOU DOWN?
HAVE YOU PAID YOUR STUDIO FEES? DEADLINE IS NOW 15TH FEB
B.O.G.O.F DRINKS TONIGHT S.U. BAR
ART BRUT
EVERY FRIDAY MOSH+GO 9PM–2AM

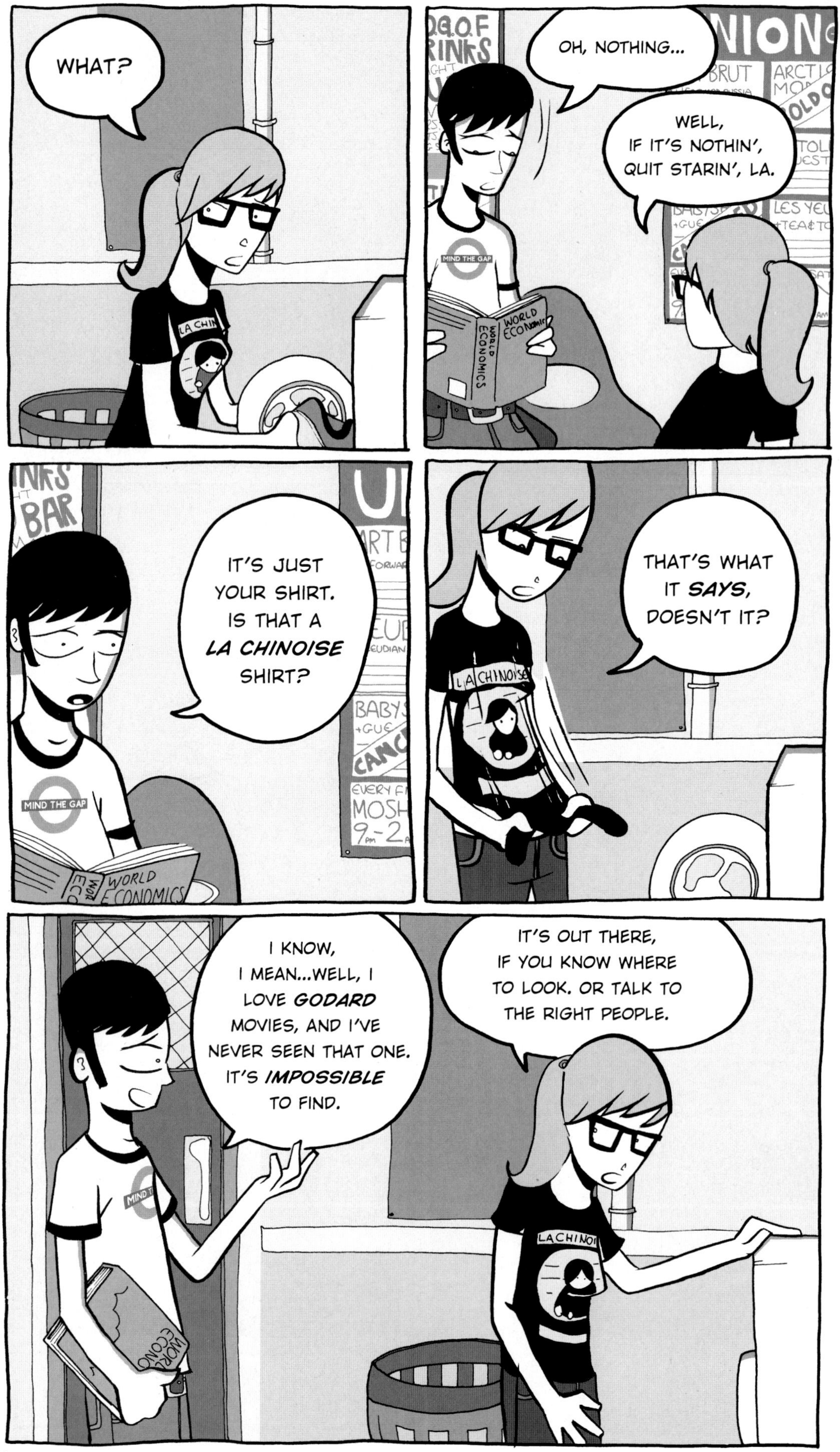
WHAT?
OH, NOTHING...
WELL, IF IT'S NOTHIN', QUIT STARIN', LA.
WORLD ECONOMICS
MIND THE GAP
IT'S JUST YOUR SHIRT. IS THAT A *LA CHINOISE* SHIRT?
THAT'S WHAT IT *SAYS,* DOESN'T IT?
LA CHINOISE
I KNOW, I MEAN...WELL, I LOVE *GODARD* MOVIES, AND I'VE NEVER SEEN THAT ONE. IT'S *IMPOSSIBLE* TO FIND.
IT'S OUT THERE, IF YOU KNOW WHERE TO LOOK. OR TALK TO THE RIGHT PEOPLE.

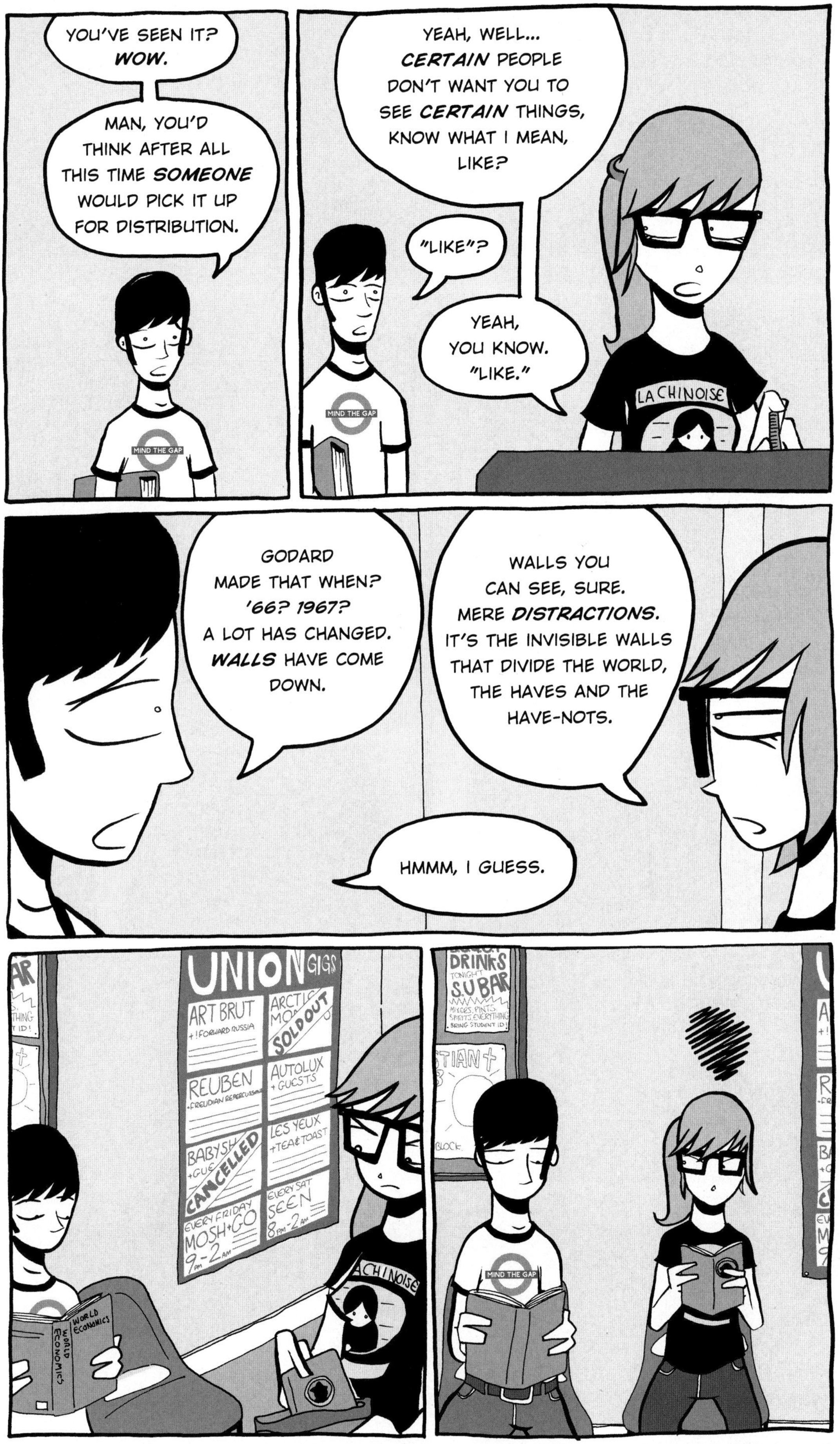
YOU'VE SEEN IT? WOW.
MAN, YOU'D THINK AFTER ALL THIS TIME SOMEONE WOULD PICK IT UP FOR DISTRIBUTION.
MIND THE GAP
YEAH, WELL... CERTAIN PEOPLE DON'T WANT YOU TO SEE CERTAIN THINGS, KNOW WHAT I MEAN, LIKE?
"LIKE"?
YEAH, YOU KNOW. "LIKE."
LA CHINOISE
GODARD MADE THAT WHEN? '66? 1967? A LOT HAS CHANGED. WALLS HAVE COME DOWN.
WALLS YOU CAN SEE, SURE. MERE DISTRACTIONS. IT'S THE INVISIBLE WALLS THAT DIVIDE THE WORLD, THE HAVES AND THE HAVE-NOTS.
HMMM, I GUESS.
UNION GIGS
ART BRUT +! FORWARD RUSSIA
ARCTIC MO SOLD OUT
REUBEN +FREUDIAN REPERCUSSIONS
AUTOLUX + GUESTS
BABYSH +GUE CANCELLED
LES YEUX +TEA & TOAST
EVERY FRIDAY MOSH+GO 9PM-2AM
EVERY SAT SEEN 8PM-2AM
WORLD ECONOMICS
DRINKS TONIGHT S.U BAR
MIXERS, PINTS, SPIRITS, EVERYTHING BRING STUDENT ID!
MIND THE GAP

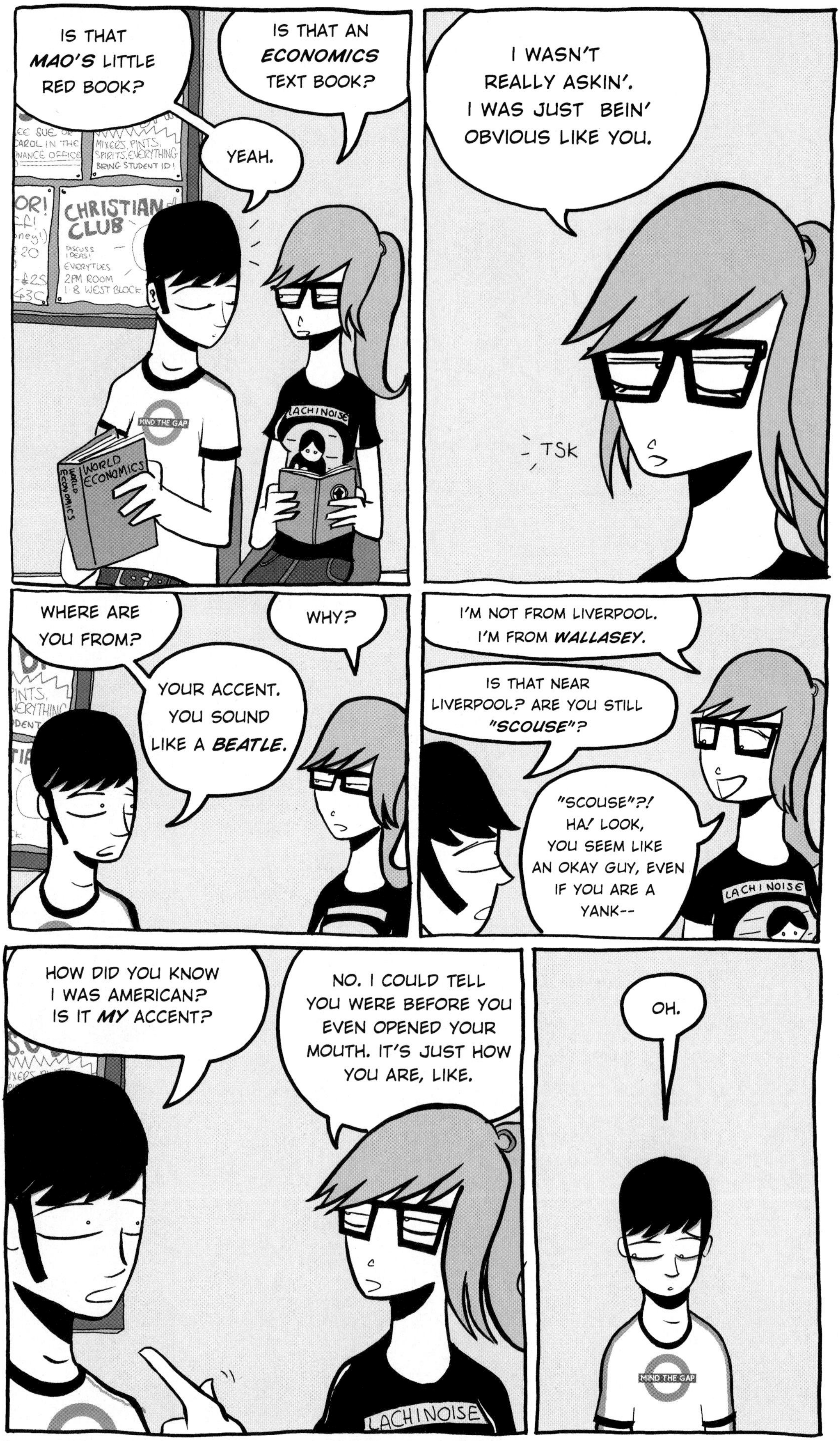
IS THAT MAO'S LITTLE RED BOOK?
IS THAT AN ECONOMICS TEXT BOOK?
YEAH.
MIXERS, PINTS, SPIRITS, EVERYTHING BRING STUDENT ID!
CHRISTIAN CLUB
DISCUSS IDEAS! EVERY TUES 2PM ROOM 1.8 WEST BLOCK
MIND THE GAP
WORLD ECONOMICS
LACHINOISE
I WASN'T REALLY ASKIN'. I WAS JUST BEIN' OBVIOUS LIKE YOU.
TSK
WHERE ARE YOU FROM?
WHY?
YOUR ACCENT. YOU SOUND LIKE A BEATLE.
I'M NOT FROM LIVERPOOL. I'M FROM WALLASEY.
IS THAT NEAR LIVERPOOL? ARE YOU STILL "SCOUSE"?
"SCOUSE"?! HA! LOOK, YOU SEEM LIKE AN OKAY GUY, EVEN IF YOU ARE A YANK--
LACHINOISE
HOW DID YOU KNOW I WAS AMERICAN? IS IT MY ACCENT?
NO. I COULD TELL YOU WERE BEFORE YOU EVEN OPENED YOUR MOUTH. IT'S JUST HOW YOU ARE, LIKE.
LACHINOISE
OH.
MIND THE GAP

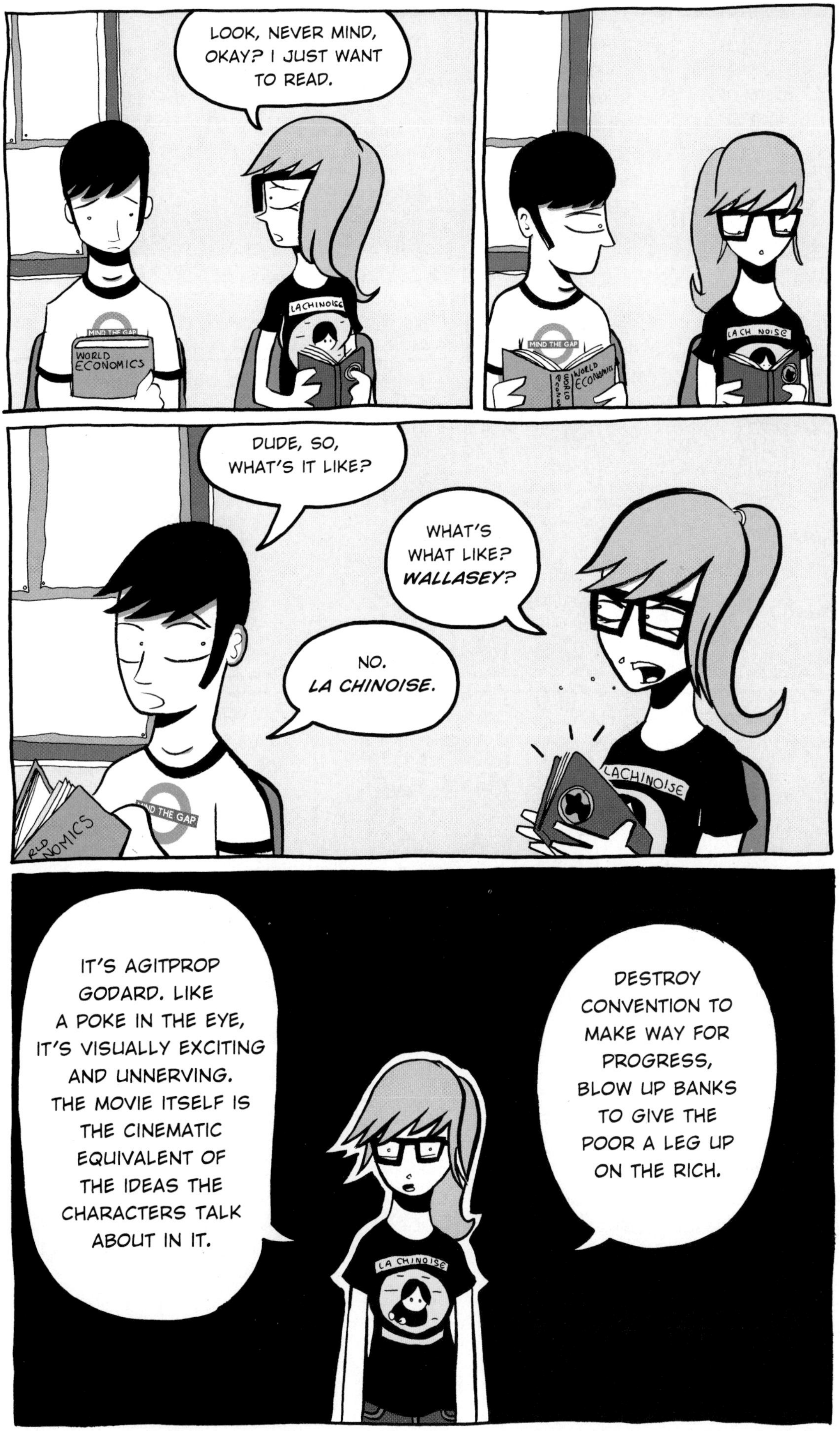
LOOK, NEVER MIND, OKAY? I JUST WANT TO READ.
MIND THE GAP
WORLD ECONOMICS
LA CHINOISE
DUDE, SO, WHAT'S IT LIKE?
WHAT'S WHAT LIKE? *WALLASEY?*
NO. *LA CHINOISE.*
IT'S AGITPROP GODARD. LIKE A POKE IN THE EYE, IT'S VISUALLY EXCITING AND UNNERVING. THE MOVIE ITSELF IS THE CINEMATIC EQUIVALENT OF THE IDEAS THE CHARACTERS TALK ABOUT IN IT.
DESTROY CONVENTION TO MAKE WAY FOR PROGRESS, BLOW UP BANKS TO GIVE THE POOR A LEG UP ON THE RICH.

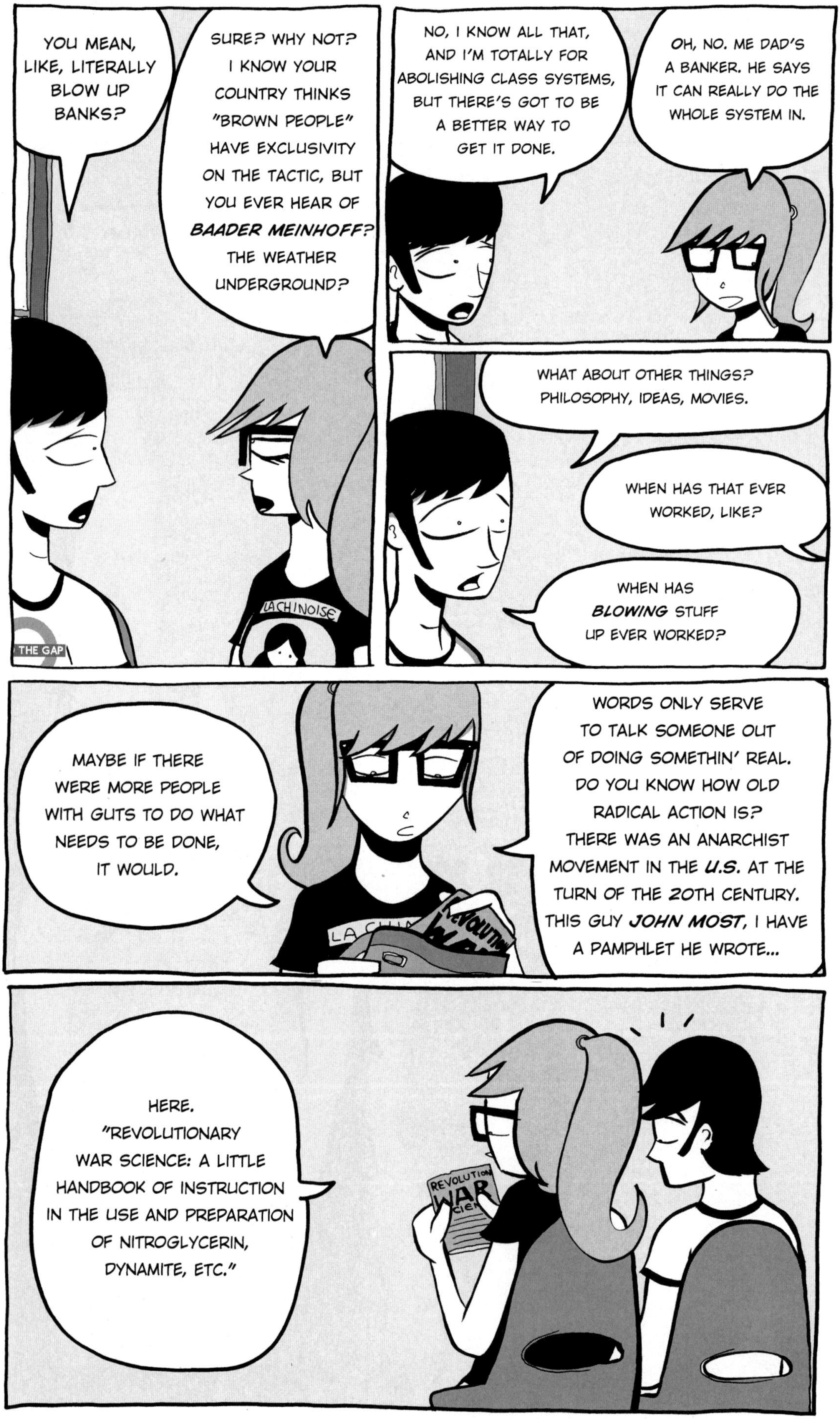
YOU MEAN, LIKE, LITERALLY BLOW UP BANKS?
SURE? WHY NOT? I KNOW YOUR COUNTRY THINKS "BROWN PEOPLE" HAVE EXCLUSIVITY ON THE TACTIC, BUT YOU EVER HEAR OF BAADER MEINHOFF? THE WEATHER UNDERGROUND?
LA CHINOISE
THE GAP
NO, I KNOW ALL THAT, AND I'M TOTALLY FOR ABOLISHING CLASS SYSTEMS, BUT THERE'S GOT TO BE A BETTER WAY TO GET IT DONE.
OH, NO. ME DAD'S A BANKER. HE SAYS IT CAN REALLY DO THE WHOLE SYSTEM IN.
WHAT ABOUT OTHER THINGS? PHILOSOPHY, IDEAS, MOVIES.
WHEN HAS THAT EVER WORKED, LIKE?
WHEN HAS BLOWING STUFF UP EVER WORKED?
MAYBE IF THERE WERE MORE PEOPLE WITH GUTS TO DO WHAT NEEDS TO BE DONE, IT WOULD.
WORDS ONLY SERVE TO TALK SOMEONE OUT OF DOING SOMETHIN' REAL. DO YOU KNOW HOW OLD RADICAL ACTION IS? THERE WAS AN ANARCHIST MOVEMENT IN THE U.S. AT THE TURN OF THE 20TH CENTURY. THIS GUY JOHN MOST, I HAVE A PAMPHLET HE WROTE...
HERE. "REVOLUTIONARY WAR SCIENCE: A LITTLE HANDBOOK OF INSTRUCTION IN THE USE AND PREPARATION OF NITROGLYCERIN, DYNAMITE, ETC."

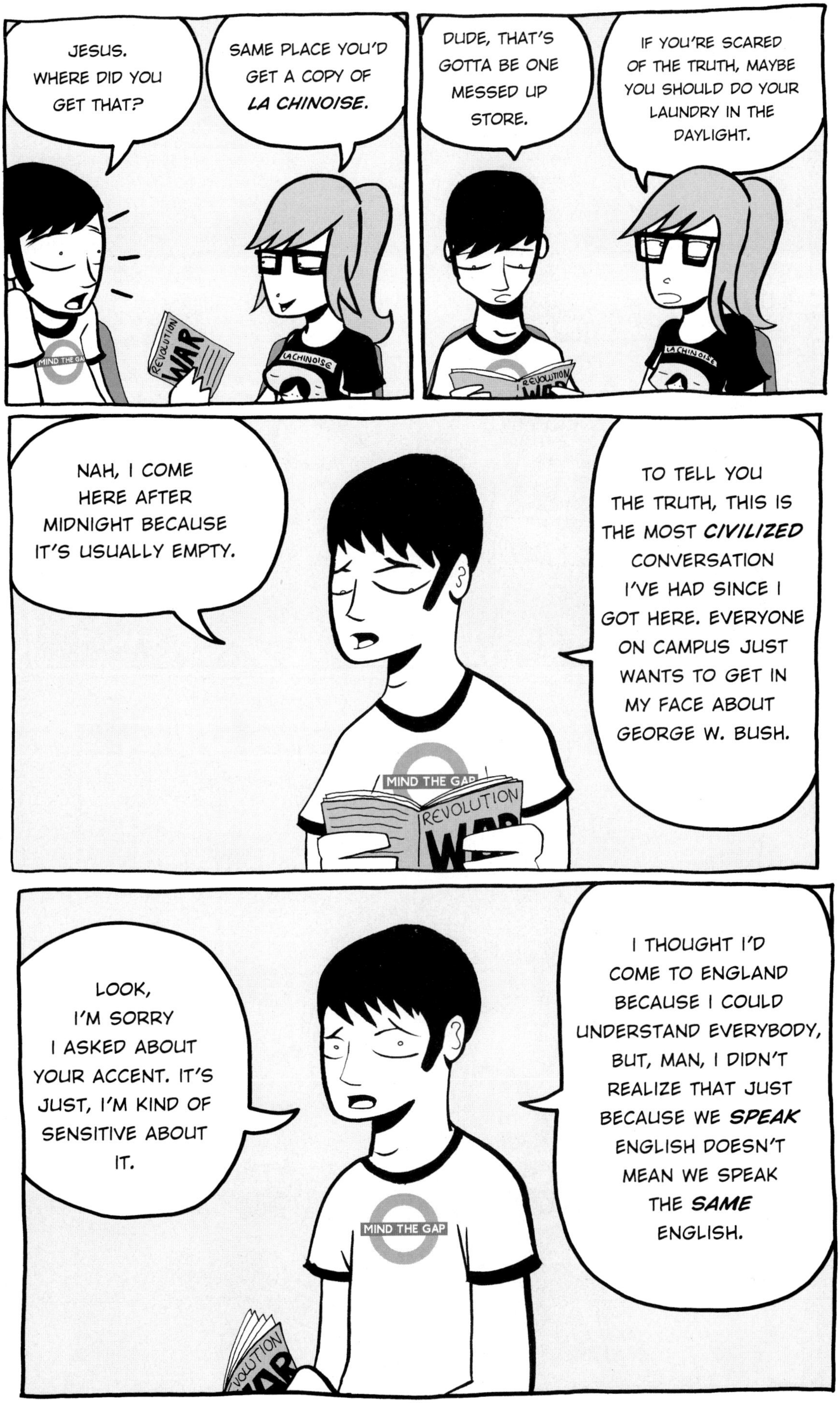
JESUS. WHERE DID YOU GET THAT?
SAME PLACE YOU'D GET A COPY OF *LA CHINOISE.*
MIND THE GAP
REVOLUTION WAR
LA CHINOISE
DUDE, THAT'S GOTTA BE ONE MESSED UP STORE.
IF YOU'RE SCARED OF THE TRUTH, MAYBE YOU SHOULD DO YOUR LAUNDRY IN THE DAYLIGHT.
NAH, I COME HERE AFTER MIDNIGHT BECAUSE IT'S USUALLY EMPTY.
TO TELL YOU THE TRUTH, THIS IS THE MOST *CIVILIZED* CONVERSATION I'VE HAD SINCE I GOT HERE. EVERYONE ON CAMPUS JUST WANTS TO GET IN MY FACE ABOUT GEORGE W. BUSH.
MIND THE GAP
REVOLUTION
LOOK, I'M SORRY I ASKED ABOUT YOUR ACCENT. IT'S JUST, I'M KIND OF SENSITIVE ABOUT IT.
I THOUGHT I'D COME TO ENGLAND BECAUSE I COULD UNDERSTAND EVERYBODY, BUT, MAN, I DIDN'T REALIZE THAT JUST BECAUSE WE *SPEAK* ENGLISH DOESN'T MEAN WE SPEAK THE *SAME* ENGLISH.
MIND THE GAP

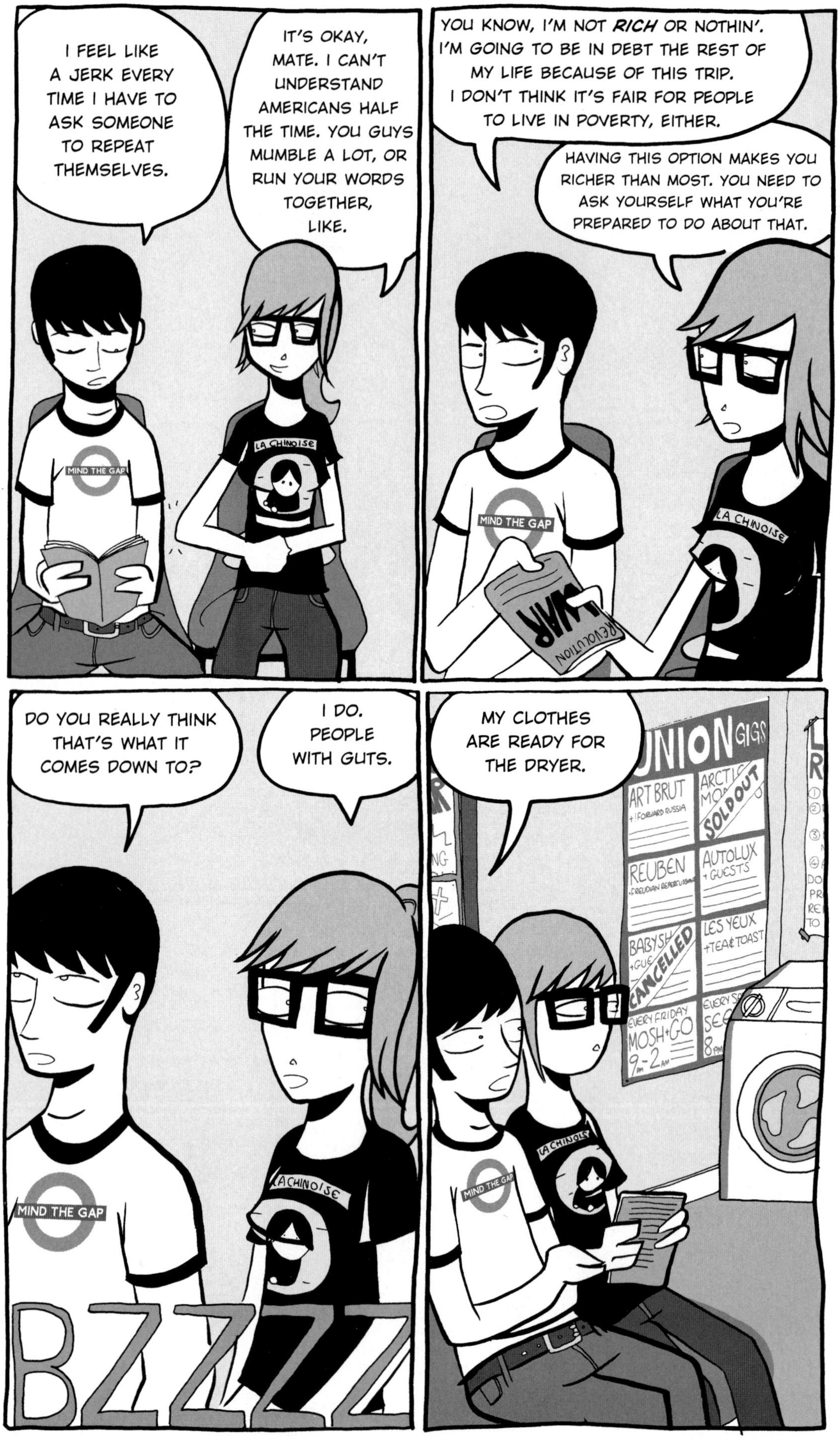
I FEEL LIKE A JERK EVERY TIME I HAVE TO ASK SOMEONE TO REPEAT THEMSELVES.
IT'S OKAY, MATE. I CAN'T UNDERSTAND AMERICANS HALF THE TIME. YOU GUYS MUMBLE A LOT, OR RUN YOUR WORDS TOGETHER, LIKE.
MIND THE GAP
LA CHINOISE
YOU KNOW, I'M NOT ***RICH*** OR NOTHIN'. I'M GOING TO BE IN DEBT THE REST OF MY LIFE BECAUSE OF THIS TRIP. I DON'T THINK IT'S FAIR FOR PEOPLE TO LIVE IN POVERTY, EITHER.
HAVING THIS OPTION MAKES YOU RICHER THAN MOST. YOU NEED TO ASK YOURSELF WHAT YOU'RE PREPARED TO DO ABOUT THAT.
DO YOU REALLY THINK THAT'S WHAT IT COMES DOWN TO?
I DO. PEOPLE WITH GUTS.
BZZZZ
MY CLOTHES ARE READY FOR THE DRYER.
UNION GIGS
ART BRUT
+ I FORWARD RUSSIA
SOLD OUT
REUBEN
AUTOLUX
+ GUESTS
LES YEUX
+ TEA & TOAST
CANCELLED
EVERY FRIDAY
MOSH + GO
9PM-2AM

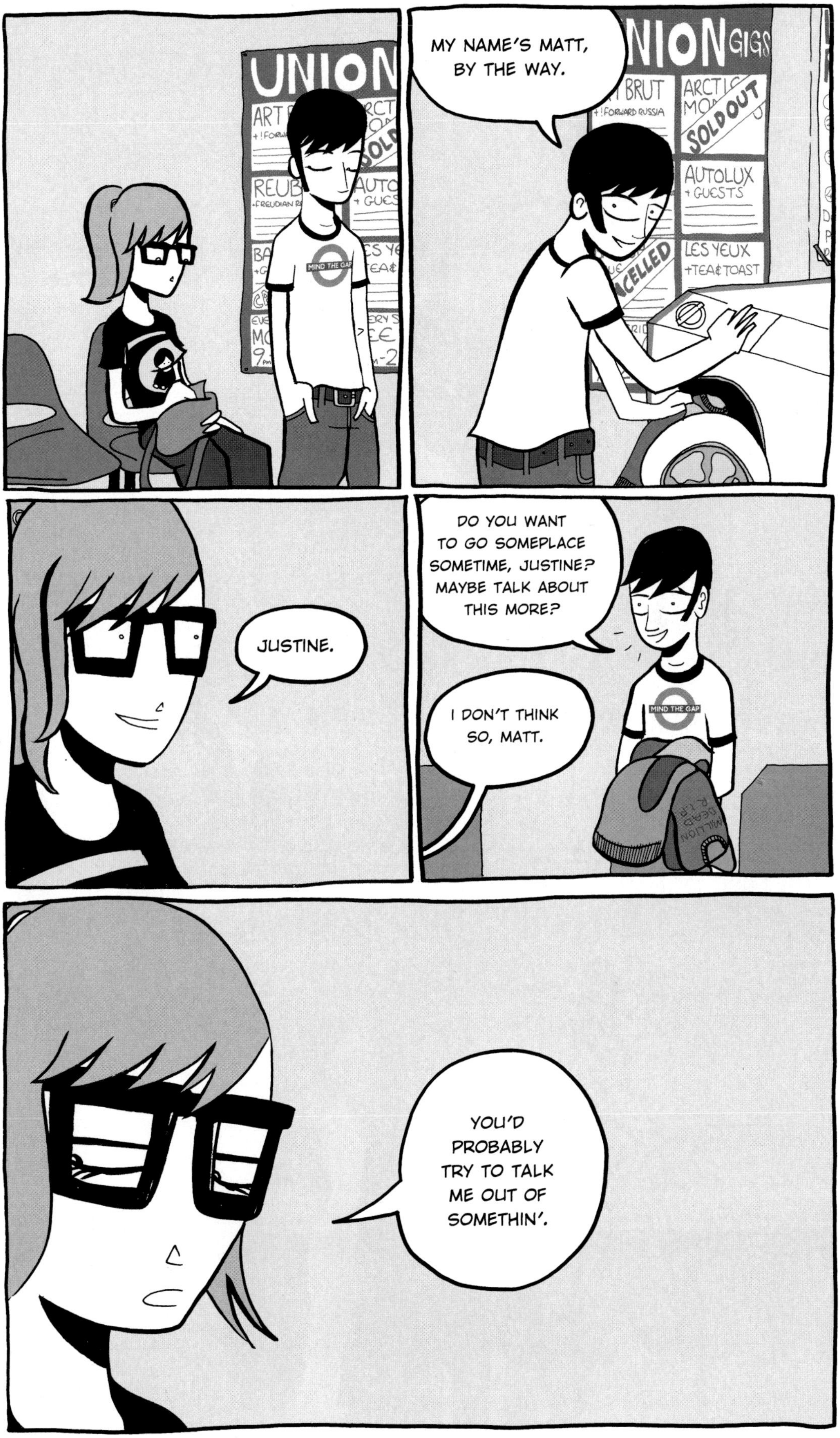
UNION
MIND THE GAP
MY NAME'S MATT, BY THE WAY.
UNION GIGS
ART BRUT
+! FORWARD RUSSIA
SOLD OUT
AUTOLUX
+ GUESTS
LES YEUX
+TEA&TOAST
JUSTINE.
DO YOU WANT TO GO SOMEPLACE SOMETIME, JUSTINE? MAYBE TALK ABOUT THIS MORE?
I DON'T THINK SO, MATT.
MIND THE GAP
MILLION DEAD R.I.P
YOU'D PROBABLY TRY TO TALK ME OUT OF SOMETHIN'.

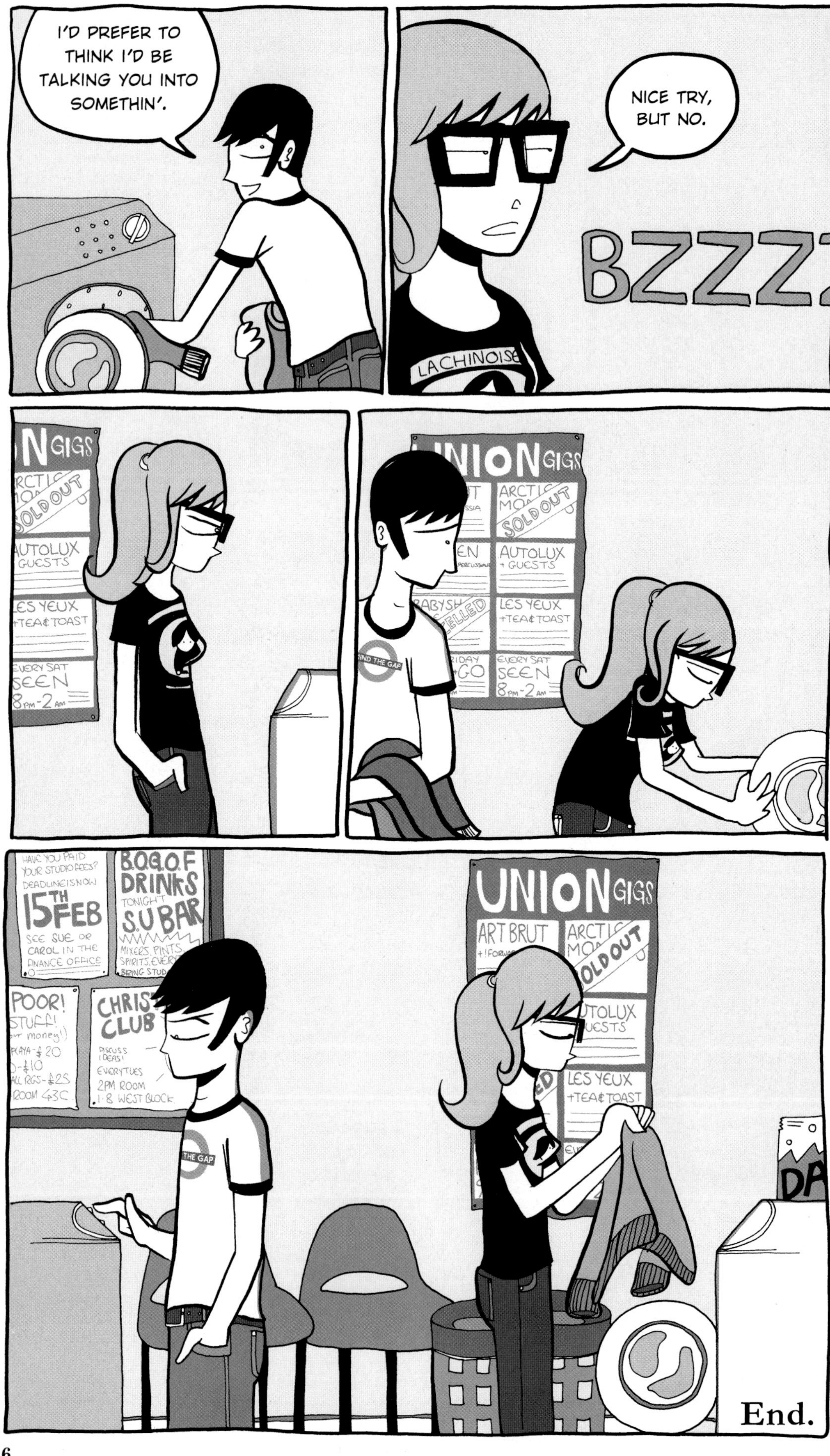
I'D PREFER TO THINK I'D BE TALKING YOU INTO SOMETHIN'.
NICE TRY, BUT NO.
BZZZ
LACHINOISE
UNION GIGS
SOLD OUT
AUTOLUX + GUESTS
LES YEUX +TEA & TOAST
EVERY SAT SEEN 8PM-2AM
HAVE YOU PAID YOUR STUDIO FEES? DEADLINE IS NOW 15TH FEB SEE SUE OR CAROL IN THE FINANCE OFFICE
B.O.G.O.F DRINKS TONIGHT S.U BAR
ART BRUT
End.

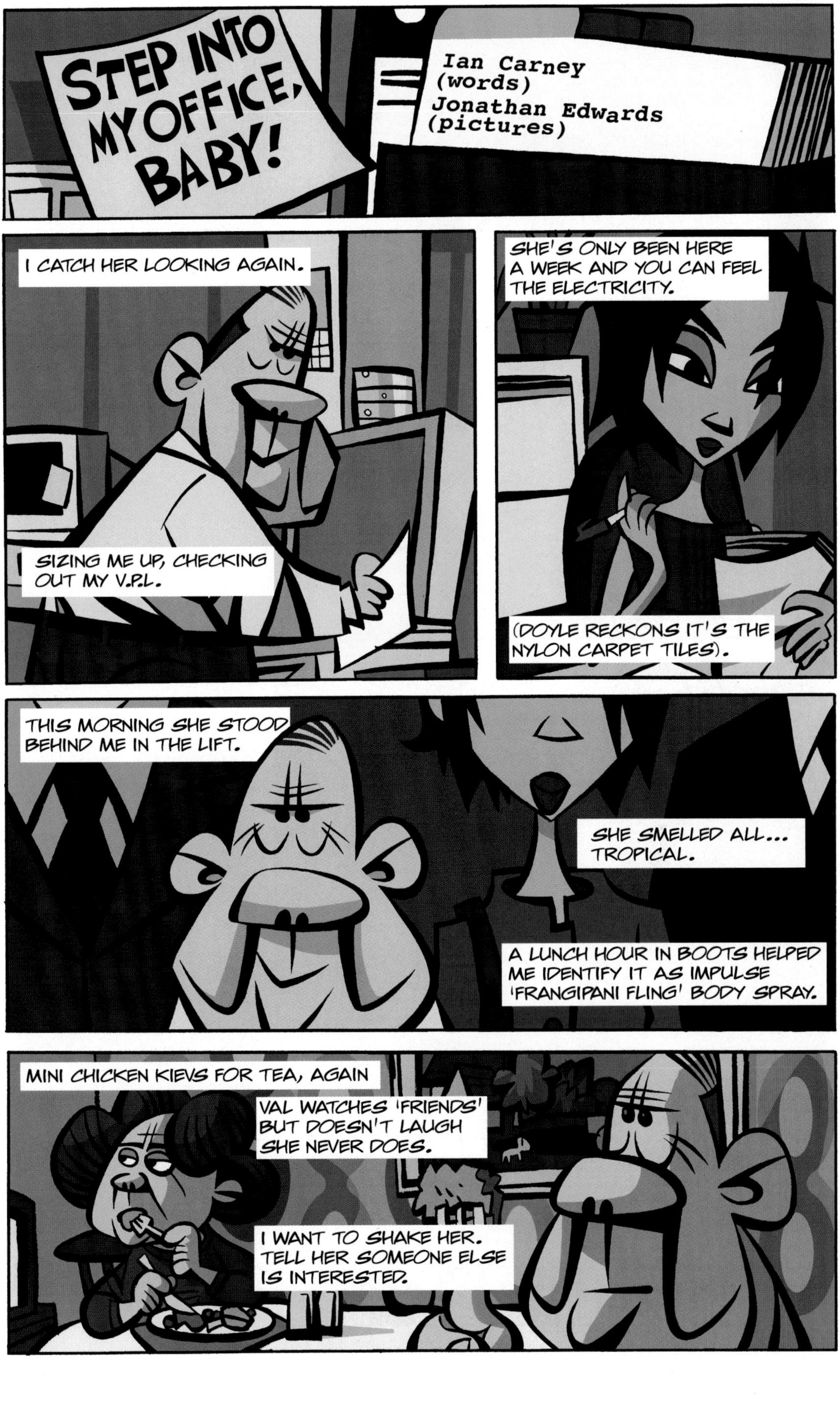
STEP INTO MY OFFICE, BABY!
Ian Carney (words)
Jonathan Edwards (pictures)
I CATCH HER LOOKING AGAIN.
SIZING ME UP, CHECKING OUT MY V.P.L.
SHE'S ONLY BEEN HERE A WEEK AND YOU CAN FEEL THE ELECTRICITY.
(DOYLE RECKONS IT'S THE NYLON CARPET TILES).
THIS MORNING SHE STOOD BEHIND ME IN THE LIFT.
SHE SMELLED ALL... TROPICAL.
A LUNCH HOUR IN BOOTS HELPED ME IDENTIFY IT AS IMPULSE 'FRANGIPANI FLING' BODY SPRAY.
MINI CHICKEN KIEVS FOR TEA, AGAIN
VAL WATCHES 'FRIENDS' BUT DOESN'T LAUGH SHE NEVER DOES.
I WANT TO SHAKE HER. TELL HER SOMEONE ELSE IS INTERESTED.

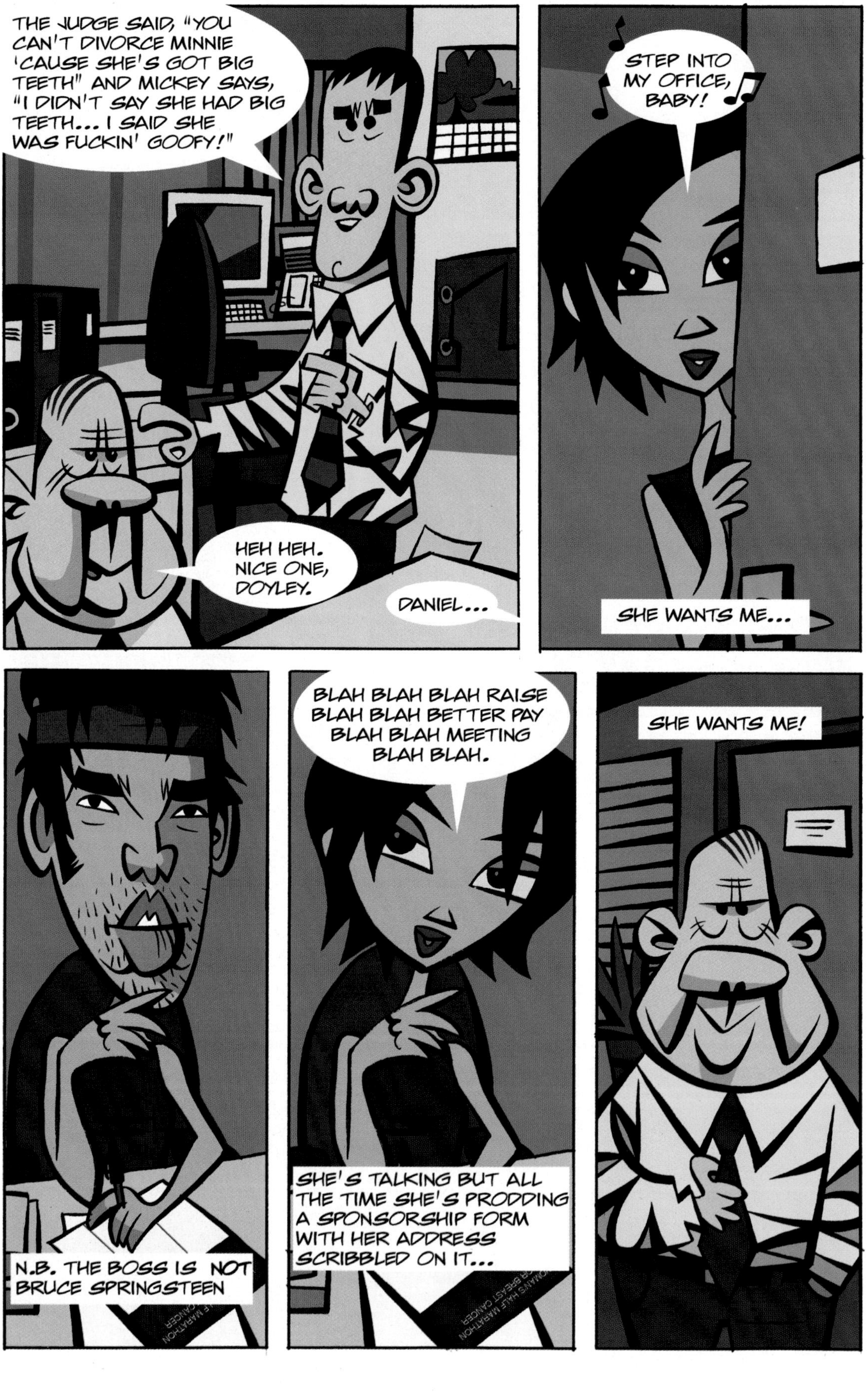
THE JUDGE SAID, "YOU CAN'T DIVORCE MINNIE 'CAUSE SHE'S GOT BIG TEETH" AND MICKEY SAYS, "I DIDN'T SAY SHE HAD BIG TEETH... I SAID SHE WAS FUCKIN' GOOFY!"
HEH HEH. NICE ONE, DOYLEY.
DANIEL...
STEP INTO MY OFFICE, BABY!
SHE WANTS ME...
N.B. THE BOSS IS NOT BRUCE SPRINGSTEEN
BLAH BLAH BLAH RAISE BLAH BLAH BETTER PAY BLAH BLAH MEETING BLAH BLAH.
SHE'S TALKING BUT ALL THE TIME SHE'S PRODDING A SPONSORSHIP FORM WITH HER ADDRESS SCRIBBLED ON IT...
SHE WANTS ME!

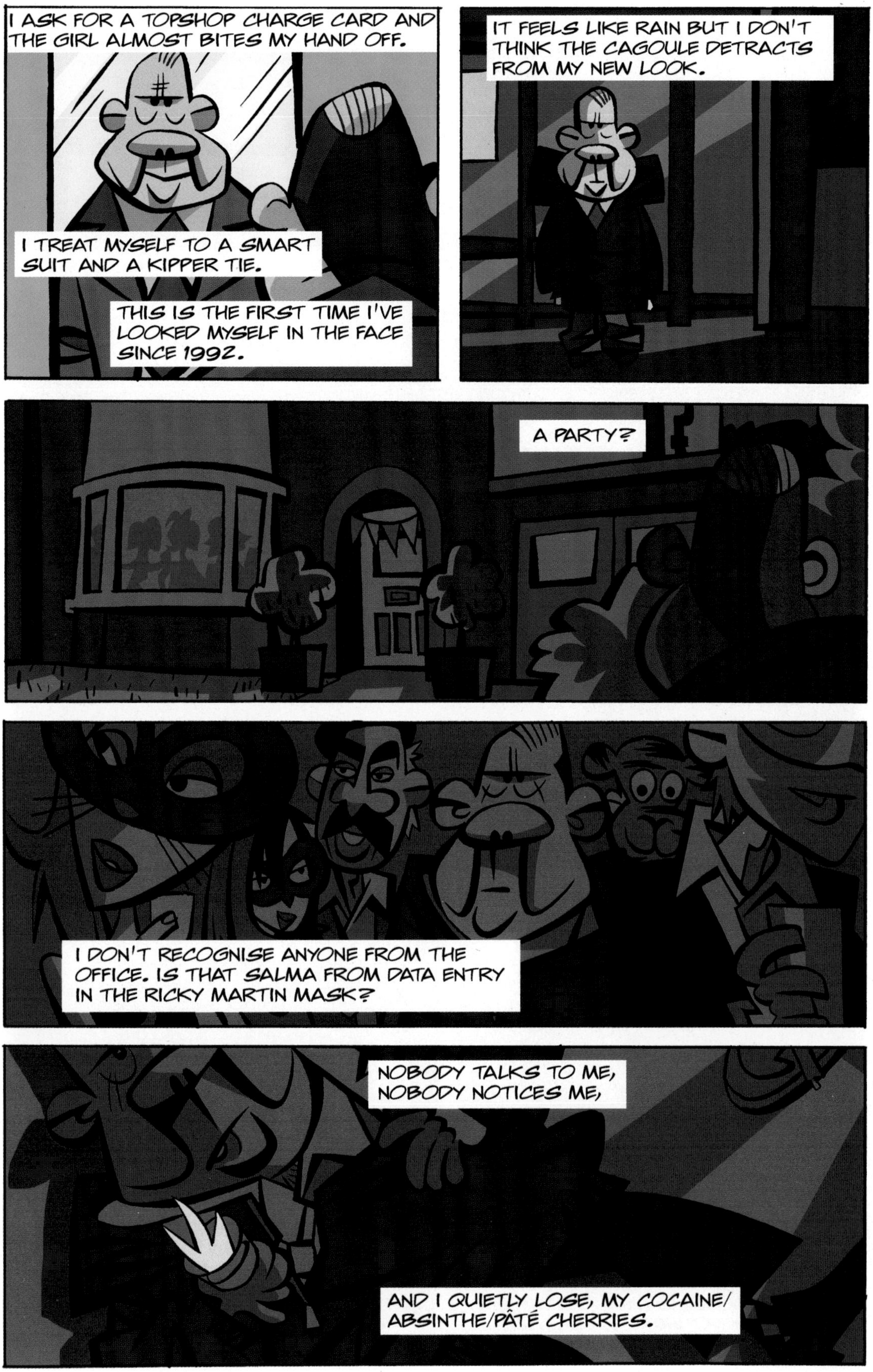
I ASK FOR A TOPSHOP CHARGE CARD AND THE GIRL ALMOST BITES MY HAND OFF.
I TREAT MYSELF TO A SMART SUIT AND A KIPPER TIE.
THIS IS THE FIRST TIME I'VE LOOKED MYSELF IN THE FACE SINCE 1992.
IT FEELS LIKE RAIN BUT I DON'T THINK THE CAGOULE DETRACTS FROM MY NEW LOOK.
A PARTY?
I DON'T RECOGNISE ANYONE FROM THE OFFICE. IS THAT SALMA FROM DATA ENTRY IN THE RICKY MARTIN MASK?
NOBODY TALKS TO ME, NOBODY NOTICES ME,
AND I QUIETLY LOSE, MY COCAINE/ ABSINTHE/PÂTÉ CHERRIES.

THEN I SEE HER, ALL DRESSED UP IN A LITTLE RED DRESS AND, COINCIDENTALLY, A SPRINGSTEEN MASK.

STEP INTO MY OFFICE, BABY.

UH.. THE COAT'S NOT REALLY PART OF THE OUTFIT... I'M GOING ON THE ATKINS... NEXT WEEK... I'M... uh... SORRY... DID I SCRATCH YOU?

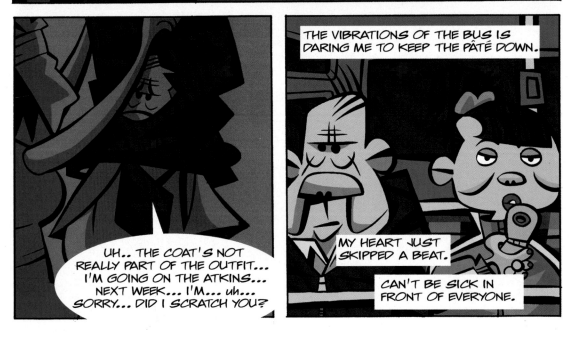

THE VIBRATIONS OF THE BUS IS DARING ME TO KEEP THE PÂTÉ DOWN.

MY HEART JUST SKIPPED A BEAT.

CAN'T BE SICK IN FRONT OF EVERYONE.

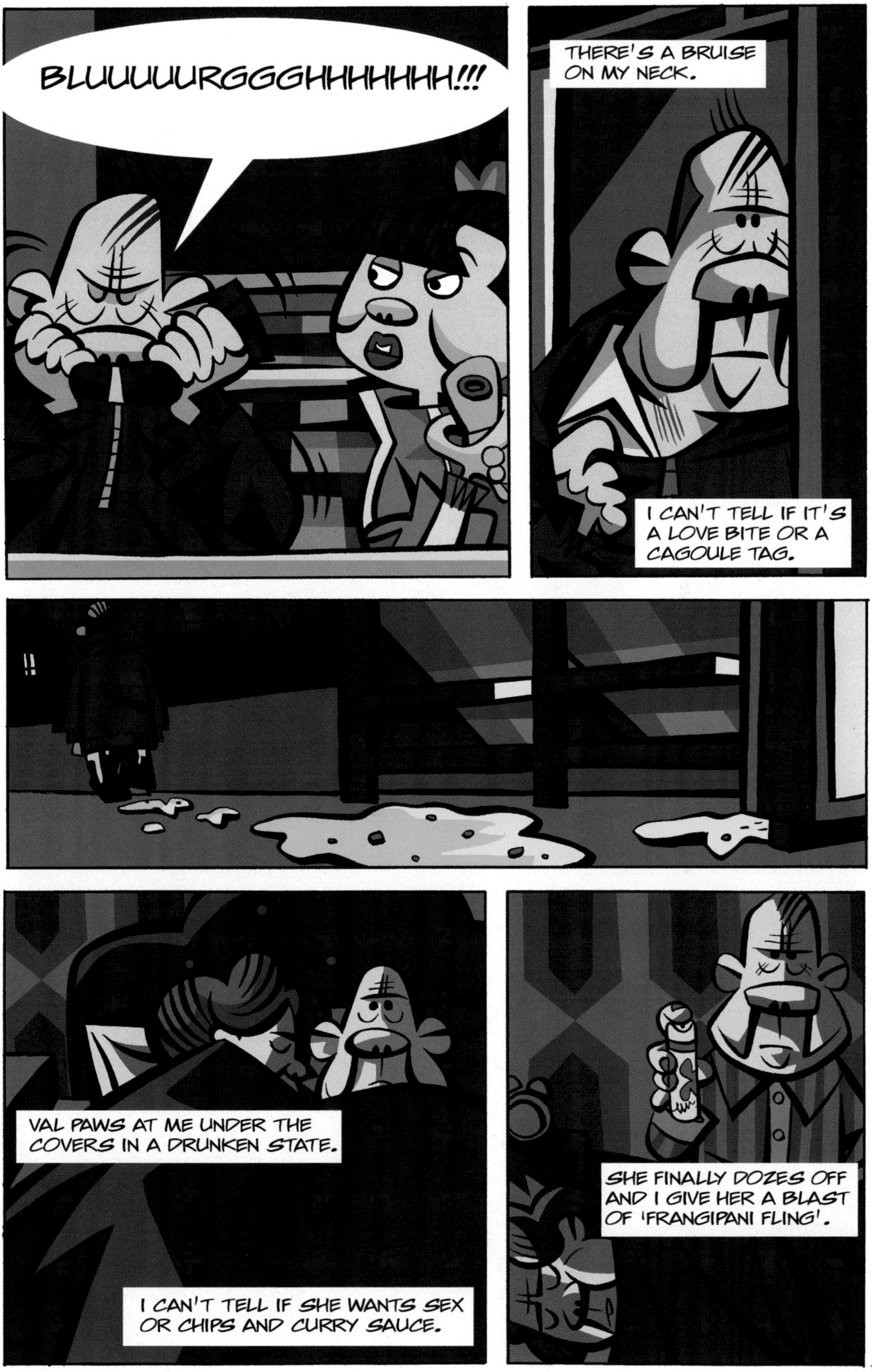
BLUUUUURGGGHHHHHH!!!
THERE'S A BRUISE ON MY NECK.
I CAN'T TELL IF IT'S A LOVE BITE OR A CAGOULE TAG.
VAL PAWS AT ME UNDER THE COVERS IN A DRUNKEN STATE.
I CAN'T TELL IF SHE WANTS SEX OR CHIPS AND CURRY SAUCE.
SHE FINALLY DOZES OFF AND I GIVE HER A BLAST OF 'FRANGIPANI FLING'.

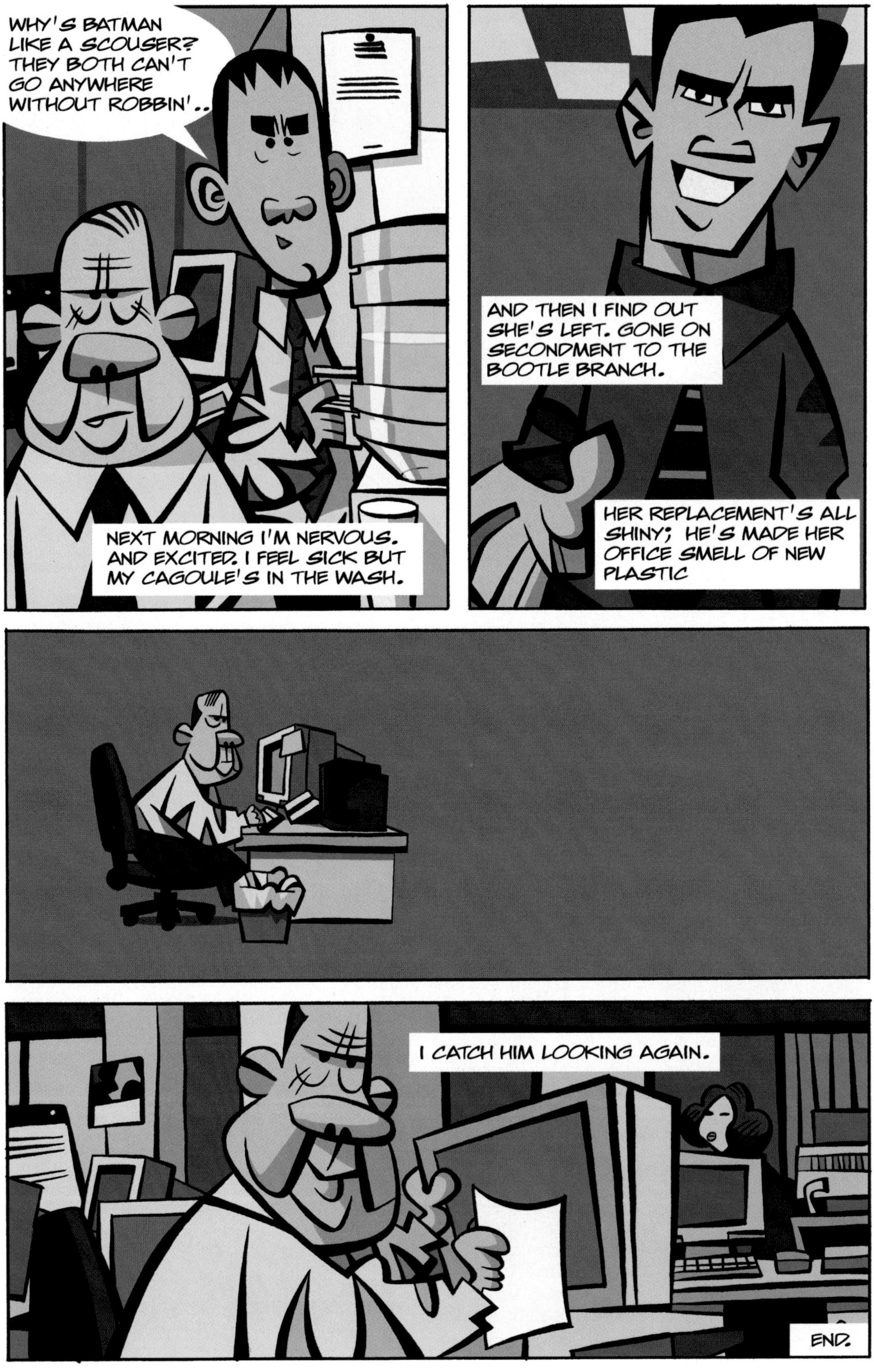
WHY'S BATMAN LIKE A SCOUSER? THEY BOTH CAN'T GO ANYWHERE WITHOUT ROBBIN'..
NEXT MORNING I'M NERVOUS. AND EXCITED. I FEEL SICK BUT MY CAGOULE'S IN THE WASH.
AND THEN I FIND OUT SHE'S LEFT. GONE ON SECONDMENT TO THE BOOTLE BRANCH.
HER REPLACEMENT'S ALL SHINY; HE'S MADE HER OFFICE SMELL OF NEW PLASTIC
I CATCH HIM LOOKING AGAIN.
END.

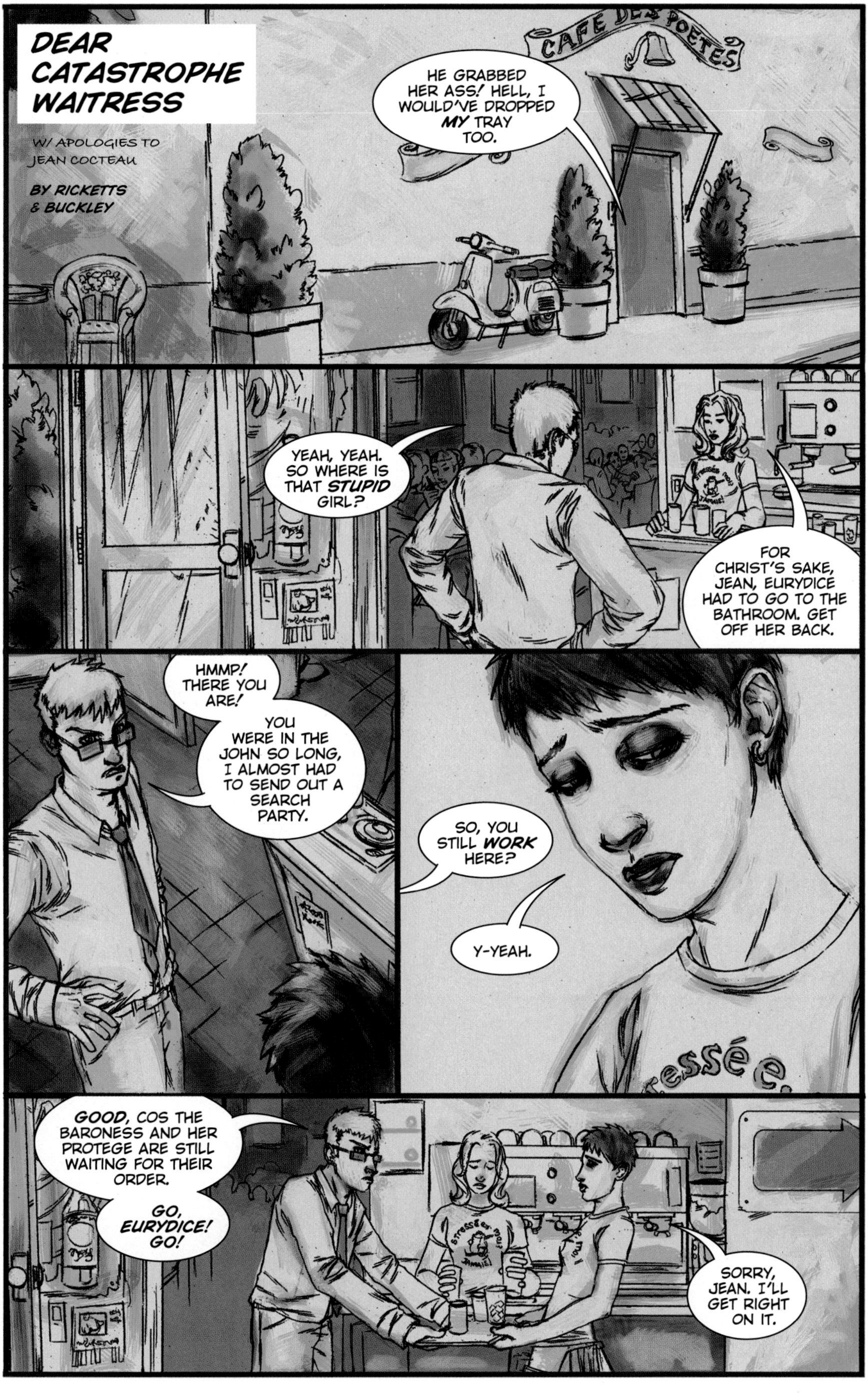
DEAR CATASTROPHE WAITRESS
W/ APOLOGIES TO JEAN COCTEAU
BY RICKETTS & BUCKLEY
CAFE DES POETES
HE GRABBED HER ASS! HELL, I WOULD'VE DROPPED MY TRAY TOO.
YEAH, YEAH. SO WHERE IS THAT STUPID GIRL?
FOR CHRIST'S SAKE, JEAN, EURYDICE HAD TO GO TO THE BATHROOM. GET OFF HER BACK.
HMMP! THERE YOU ARE!
YOU WERE IN THE JOHN SO LONG, I ALMOST HAD TO SEND OUT A SEARCH PARTY.
SO, YOU STILL WORK HERE?
Y-YEAH.
GOOD, COS THE BARONESS AND HER PROTEGE ARE STILL WAITING FOR THEIR ORDER.
GO, EURYDICE! GO!
SORRY, JEAN. I'LL GET RIGHT ON IT.

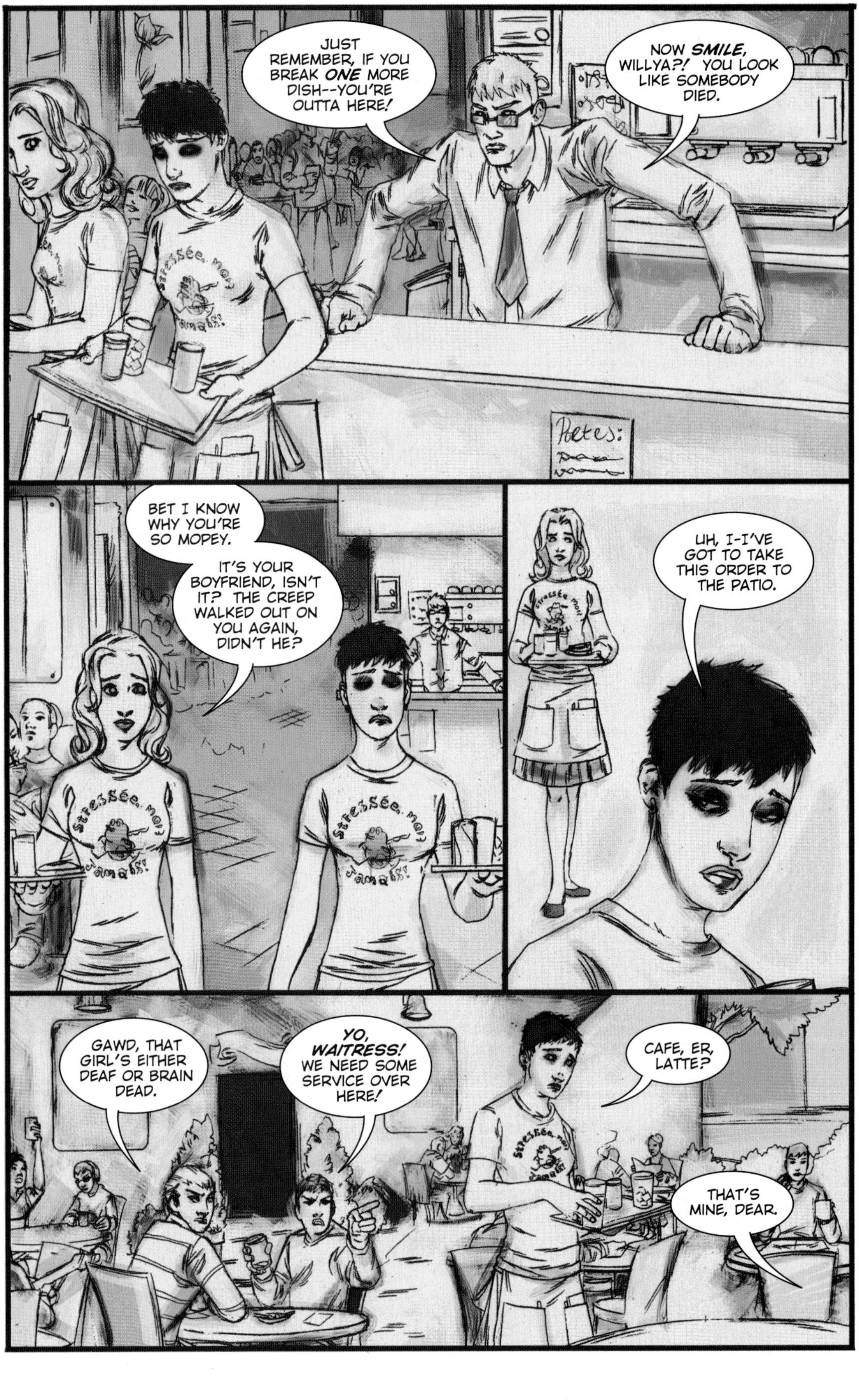
JUST REMEMBER, IF YOU BREAK ONE MORE DISH--YOU'RE OUTTA HERE!
NOW SMILE, WILLYA?! YOU LOOK LIKE SOMEBODY DIED.
Petes:
BET I KNOW WHY YOU'RE SO MOPEY.
IT'S YOUR BOYFRIEND, ISN'T IT? THE CREEP WALKED OUT ON YOU AGAIN, DIDN'T HE?
UH, I-I'VE GOT TO TAKE THIS ORDER TO THE PATIO.
GAWD, THAT GIRL'S EITHER DEAF OR BRAIN DEAD.
YO, WAITRESS! WE NEED SOME SERVICE OVER HERE!
CAFE, ER, LATTE?
THAT'S MINE, DEAR.

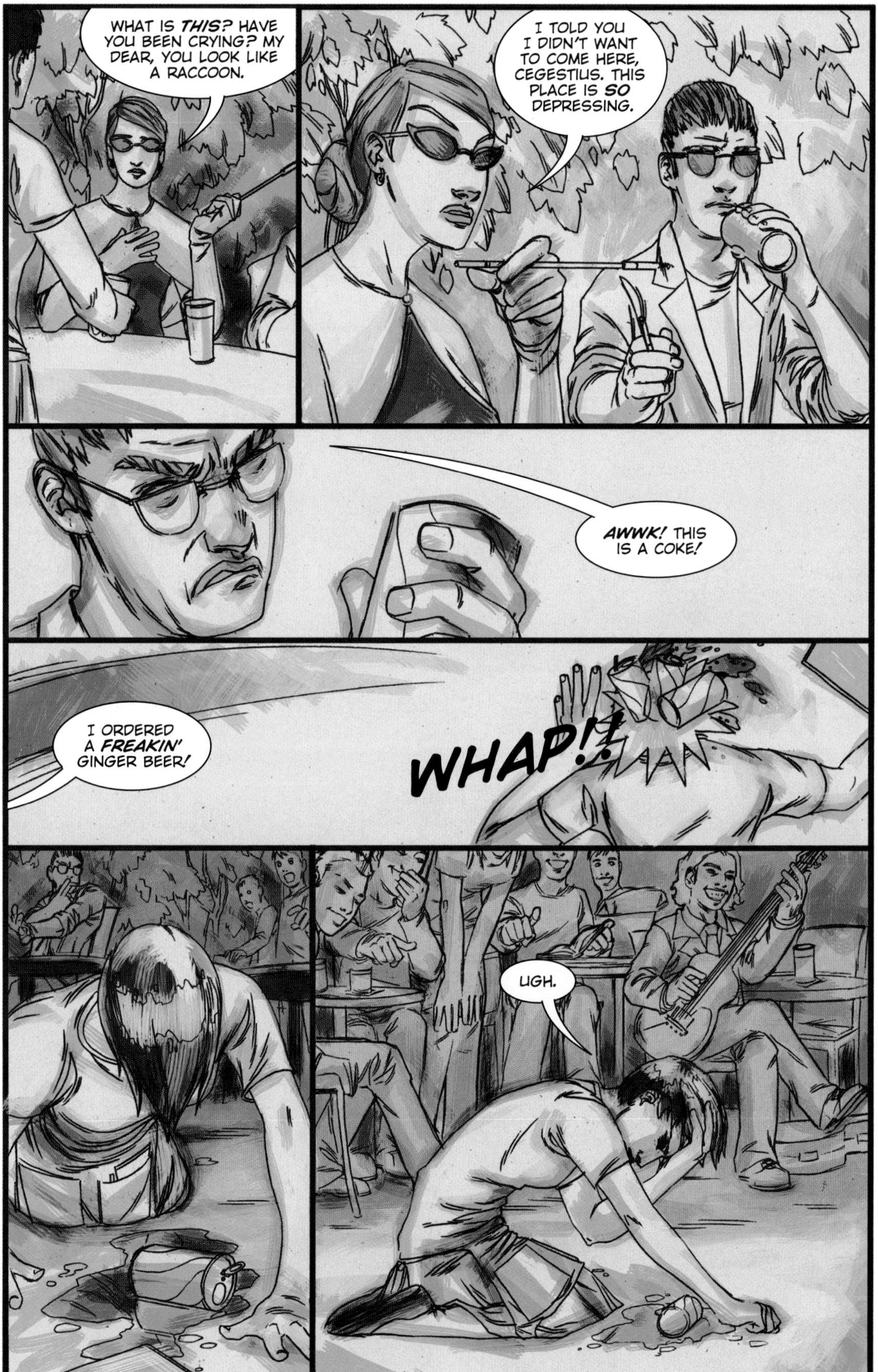
WHAT IS THIS? HAVE YOU BEEN CRYING? MY DEAR, YOU LOOK LIKE A RACCOON.
I TOLD YOU I DIDN'T WANT TO COME HERE, CEGESTIUS. THIS PLACE IS SO DEPRESSING.
AWWK! THIS IS A COKE!
I ORDERED A FREAKIN' GINGER BEER!
WHAP!!
UGH.

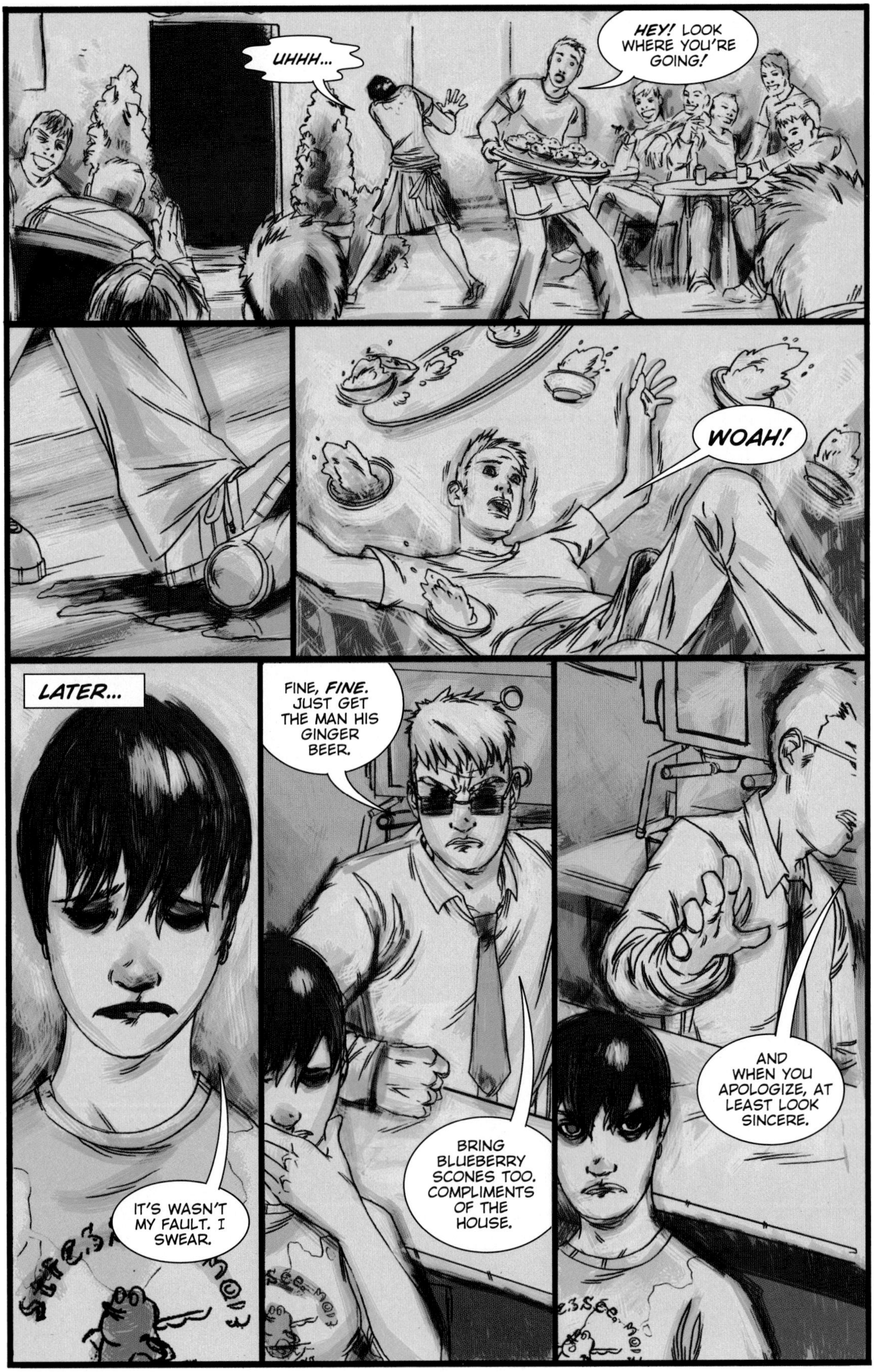
UHHH...
HEY! LOOK WHERE YOU'RE GOING!
WOAH!
LATER...
IT'S WASN'T MY FAULT. I SWEAR.
FINE, FINE. JUST GET THE MAN HIS GINGER BEER.
BRING BLUEBERRY SCONES TOO. COMPLIMENTS OF THE HOUSE.
AND WHEN YOU APOLOGIZE, AT LEAST LOOK SINCERE.

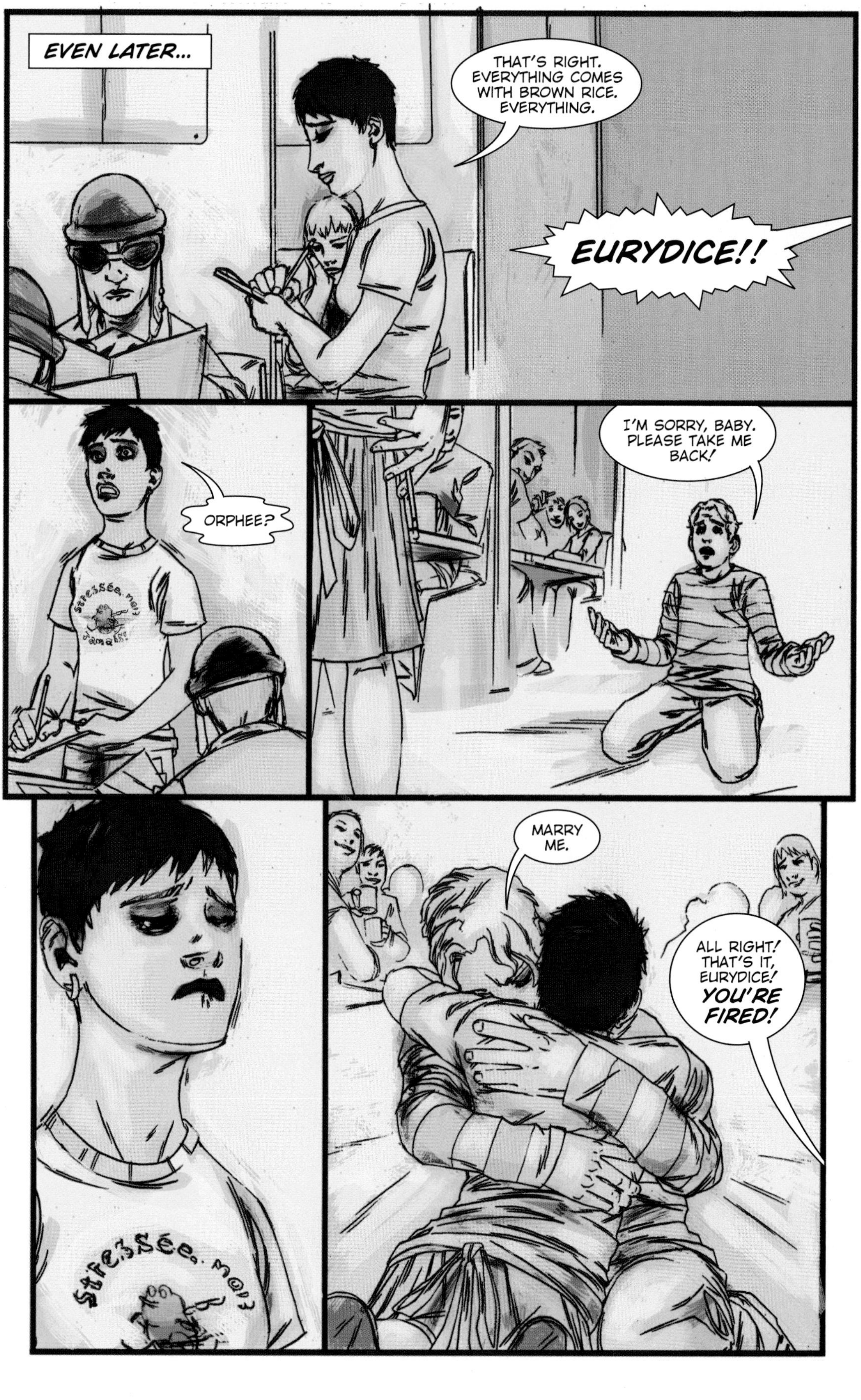
EVEN LATER...
THAT'S RIGHT. EVERYTHING COMES WITH BROWN RICE. EVERYTHING.
EURYDICE!!
ORPHEE?
I'M SORRY, BABY. PLEASE TAKE ME BACK!
MARRY ME.
ALL RIGHT! THAT'S IT, EURYDICE! YOU'RE FIRED!

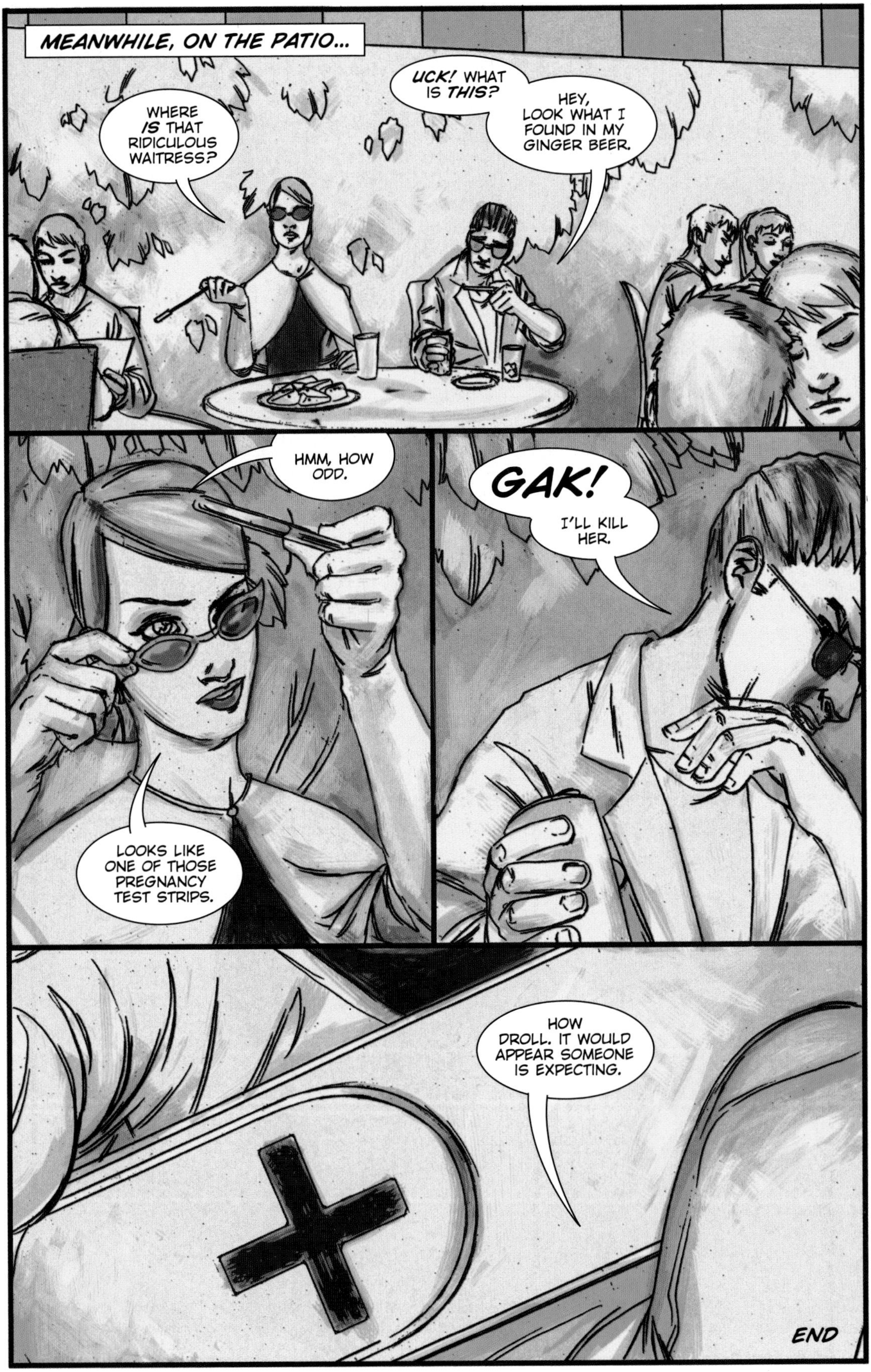
MEANWHILE, ON THE PATIO...
WHERE *IS* THAT RIDICULOUS WAITRESS?
UCK! WHAT IS *THIS?*
HEY, LOOK WHAT I FOUND IN MY GINGER BEER.
HMM, HOW ODD.
LOOKS LIKE ONE OF THOSE PREGNANCY TEST STRIPS.
GAK!
I'LL KILL HER.
HOW DROLL. IT WOULD APPEAR SOMEONE IS EXPECTING.
END

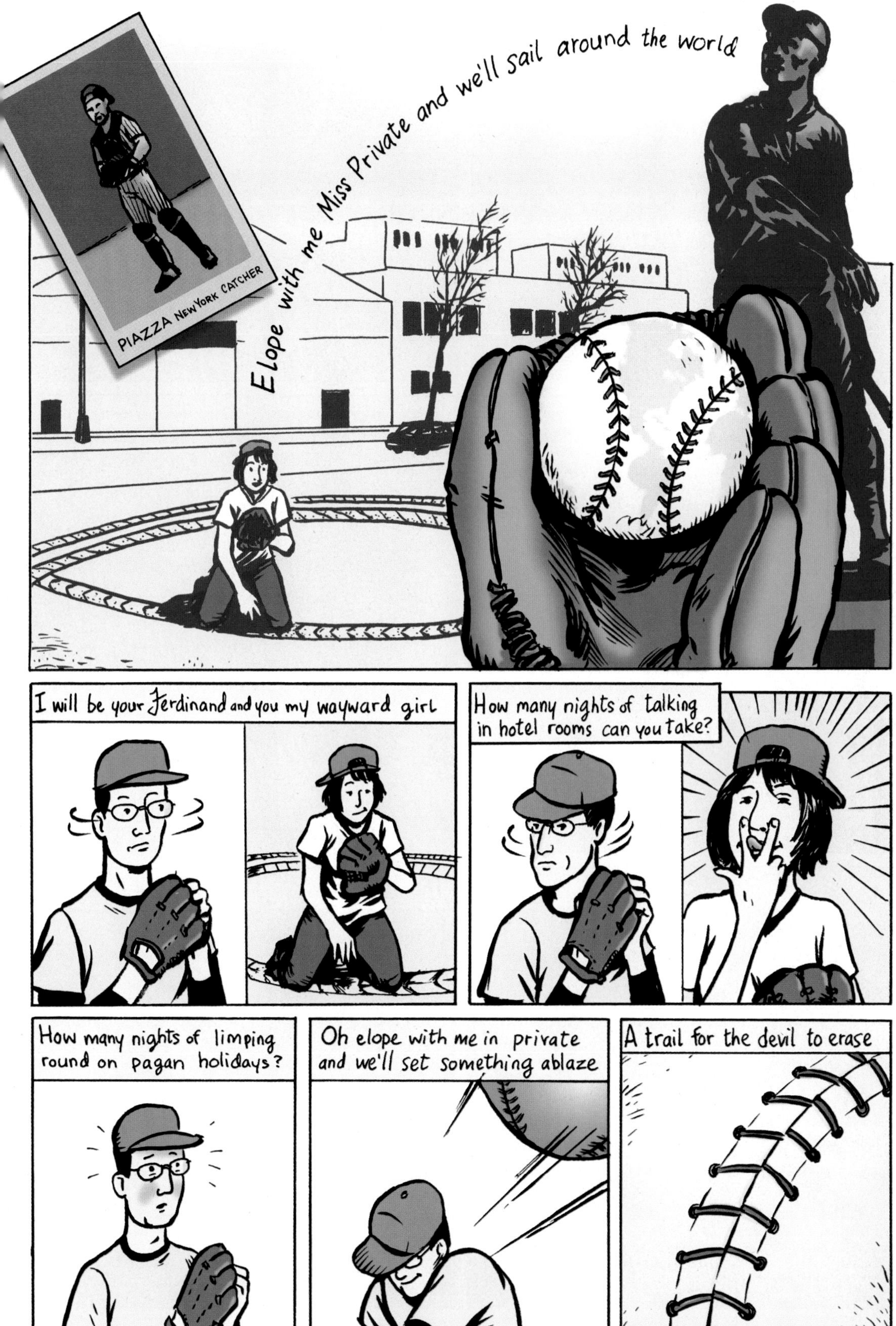

PIAZZA NEW YORK CATCHER
Elope with me Miss Private and we'll sail around the world
I will be your Ferdinand and you my wayward girl
How many nights of talking in hotel rooms can you take?
How many nights of limping round on pagan holidays?
Oh elope with me in private and we'll set something ablaze
A trail for the devil to erase

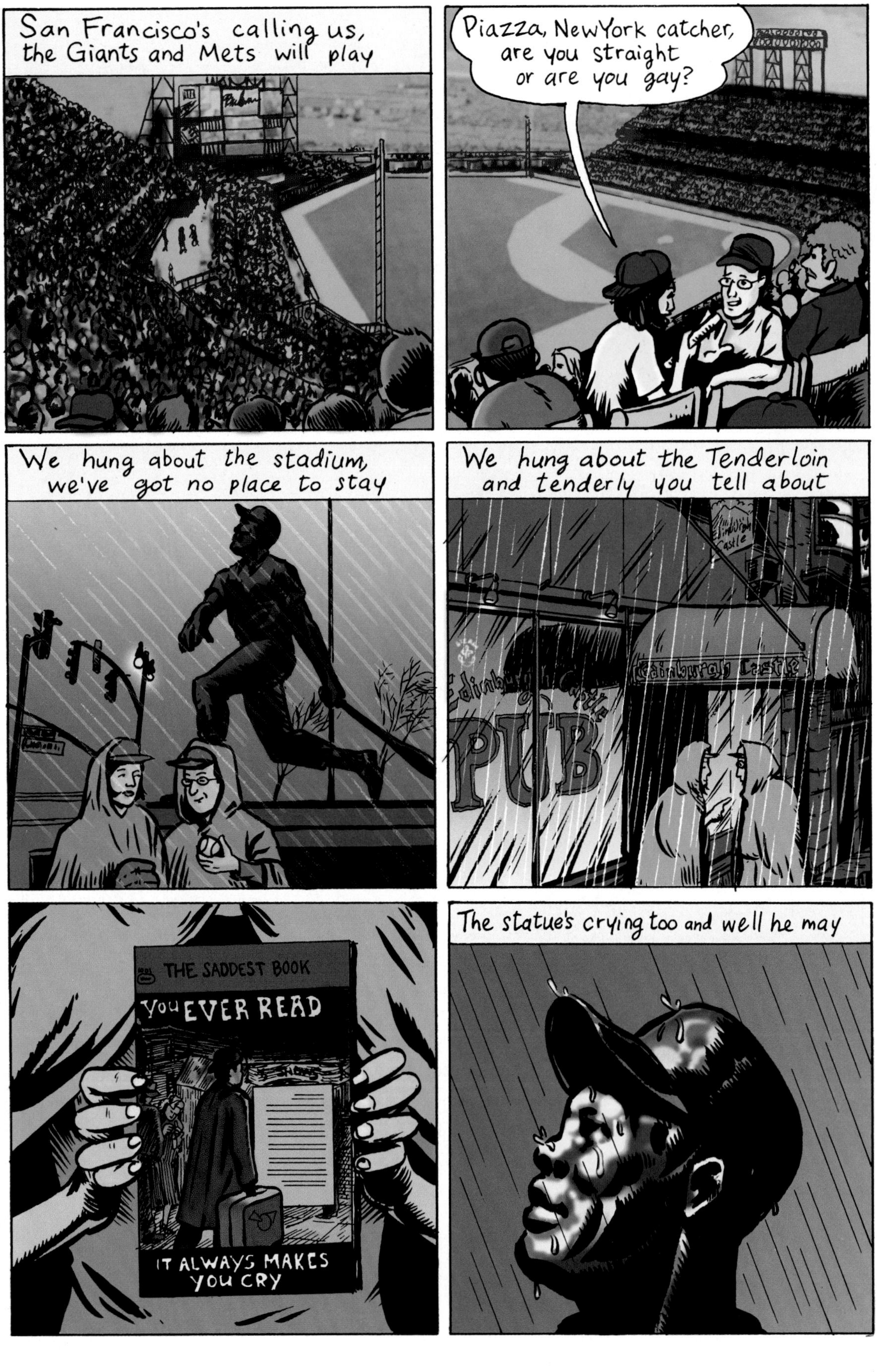
San Francisco's calling us,
the Giants and Mets will play
Piazza, NewYork catcher, are you straight or are you gay?
We hung about the stadium, we've got no place to stay
We hung about the Tenderloin and tenderly you tell about
Edinburgh Castle
PUB
THE SADDEST BOOK
YOU EVER READ
IT ALWAYS MAKES YOU CRY
The statue's crying too and well he may

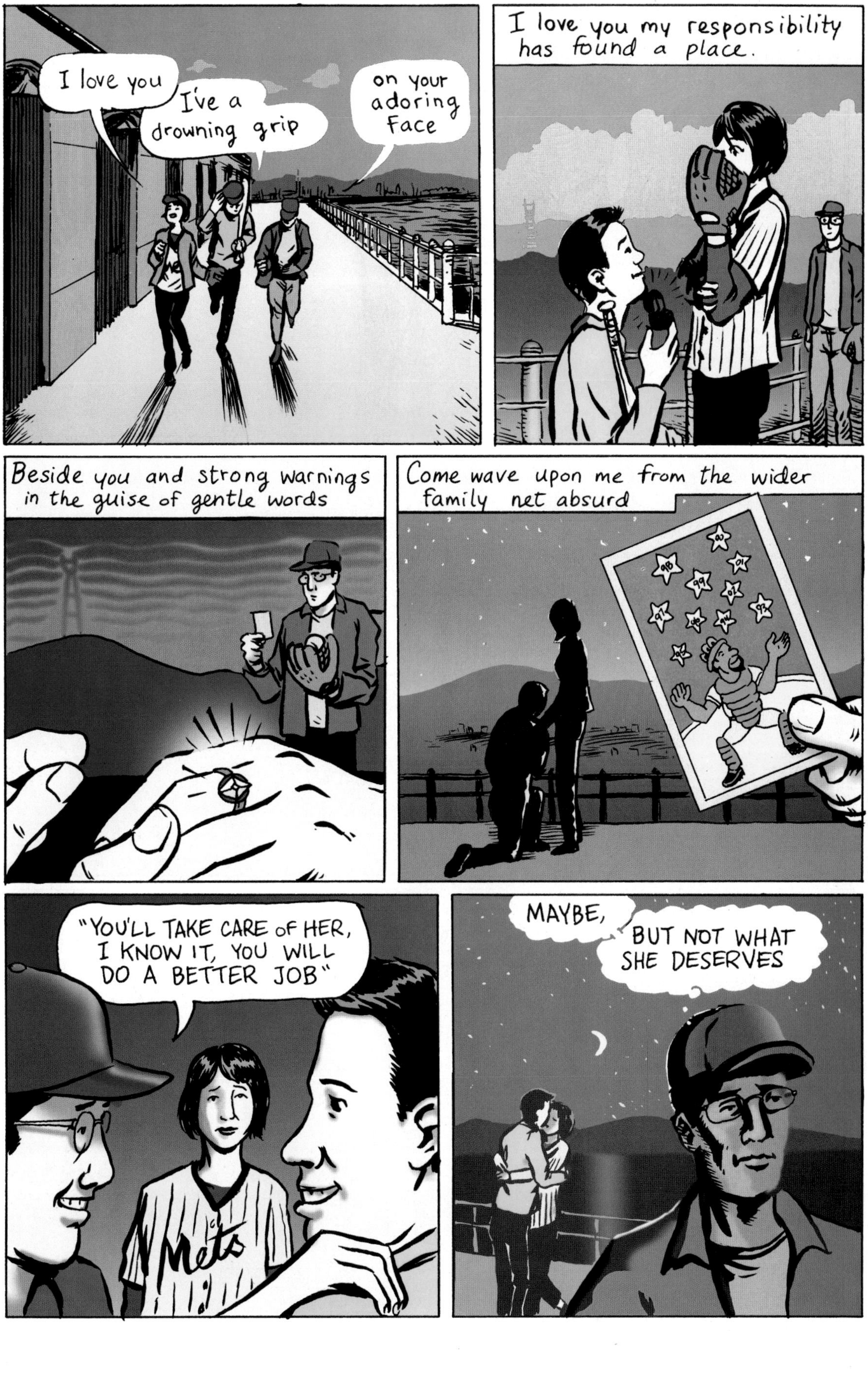
I love you
I've a drowning grip
on your adoring Face
I love you my responsibility has found a place.
Beside you and strong warnings in the guise of gentle words
Come wave upon me from the wider family net absurd
"YOU'LL TAKE CARE OF HER, I KNOW IT, YOU WILL DO A BETTER JOB"
MAYBE,
BUT NOT WHAT SHE DESERVES

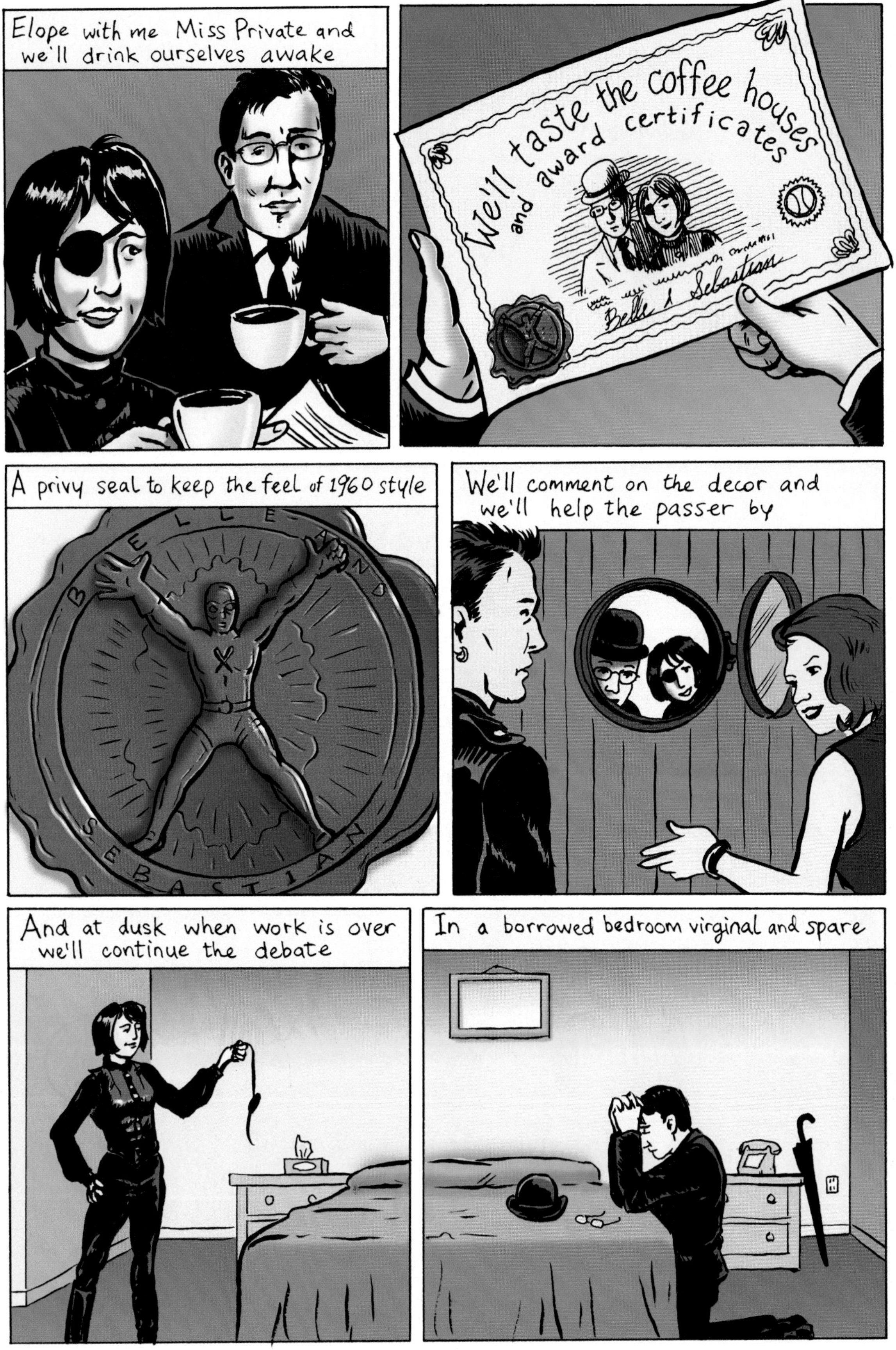
Elope with me Miss Private and we'll drink ourselves awake
We'll taste the coffee houses and award certificates
Belle & Sebastian
A privy seal to keep the feel of 1960 style
BELLE AND SEBASTIAN
We'll comment on the decor and we'll help the passer by
And at dusk when work is over we'll continue the debate
In a borrowed bedroom virginal and spare

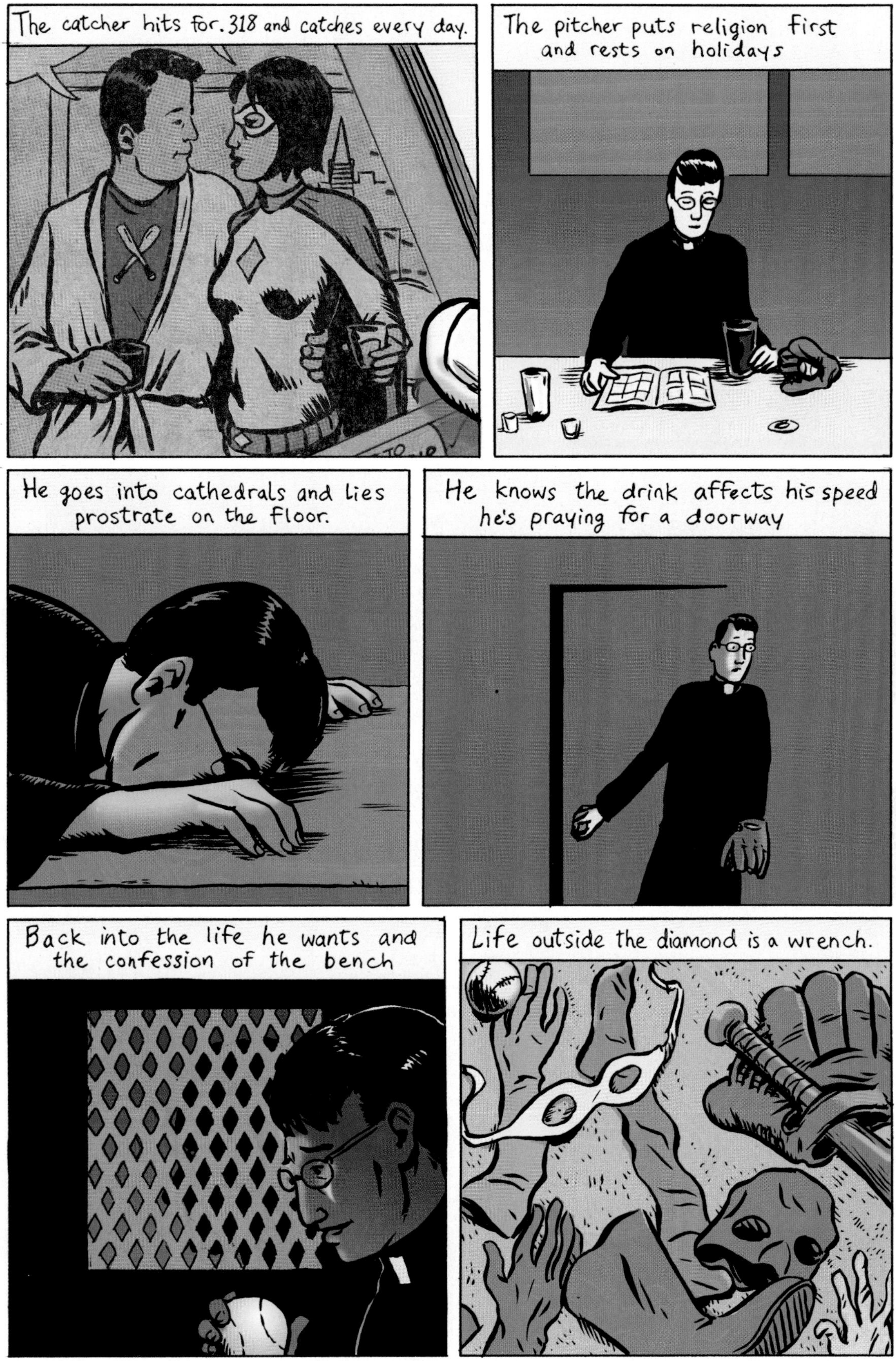
The catcher hits for .318 and catches every day.
The pitcher puts religion first and rests on holidays
He goes into cathedrals and lies prostrate on the floor.
He knows the drink affects his speed he's praying for a doorway
Back into the life he wants and the confession of the bench
Life outside the diamond is a wrench.

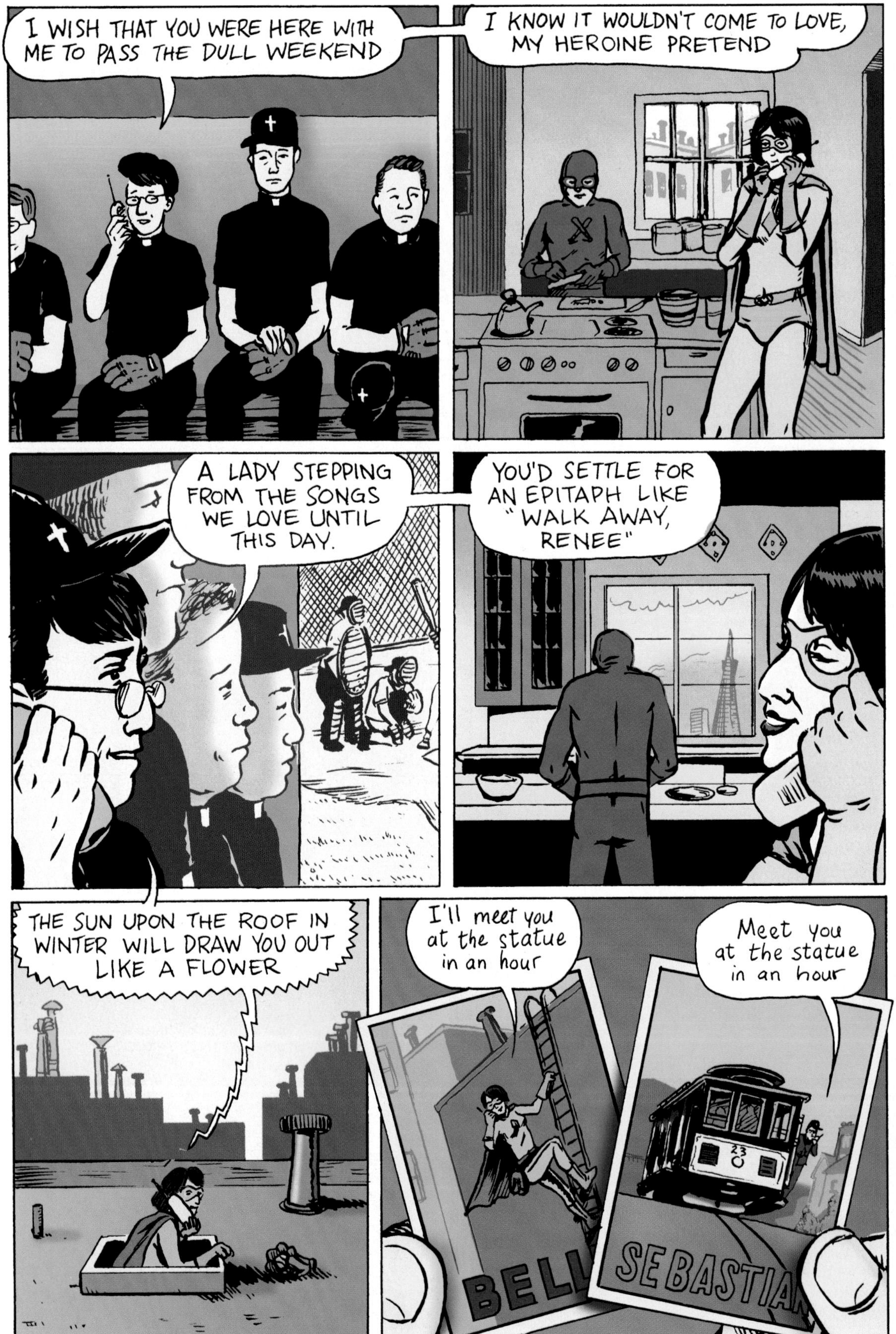
I WISH THAT YOU WERE HERE WITH ME TO PASS THE DULL WEEKEND
I KNOW IT WOULDN'T COME TO LOVE, MY HEROINE PRETEND
A LADY STEPPING FROM THE SONGS WE LOVE UNTIL THIS DAY.
YOU'D SETTLE FOR AN EPITAPH LIKE "WALK AWAY, RENEE"
THE SUN UPON THE ROOF IN WINTER WILL DRAW YOU OUT LIKE A FLOWER
I'll meet you at the statue in an hour
Meet you at the statue in an hour
BELL
SEBASTIAN

ADAPTED BY DAVID LASKY   EMBELLISHED BY SCOTT FAULKNER

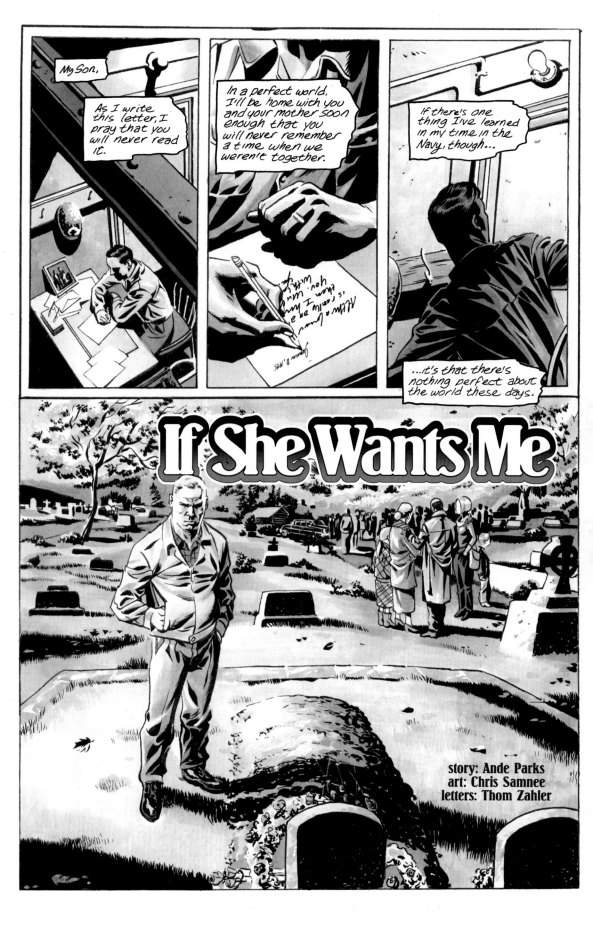

My Son,

As I write this letter, I pray that you will never read it.

In a perfect world, I'll be home with you and your mother soon enough that you will never remember a time when we weren't together.

If there's one thing I've learned in my time in the Navy, though...

...it's that there's nothing perfect about the world these days.

If She Wants Me

story: Ande Parks
art: Chris Samnee
letters: Thom Zahler

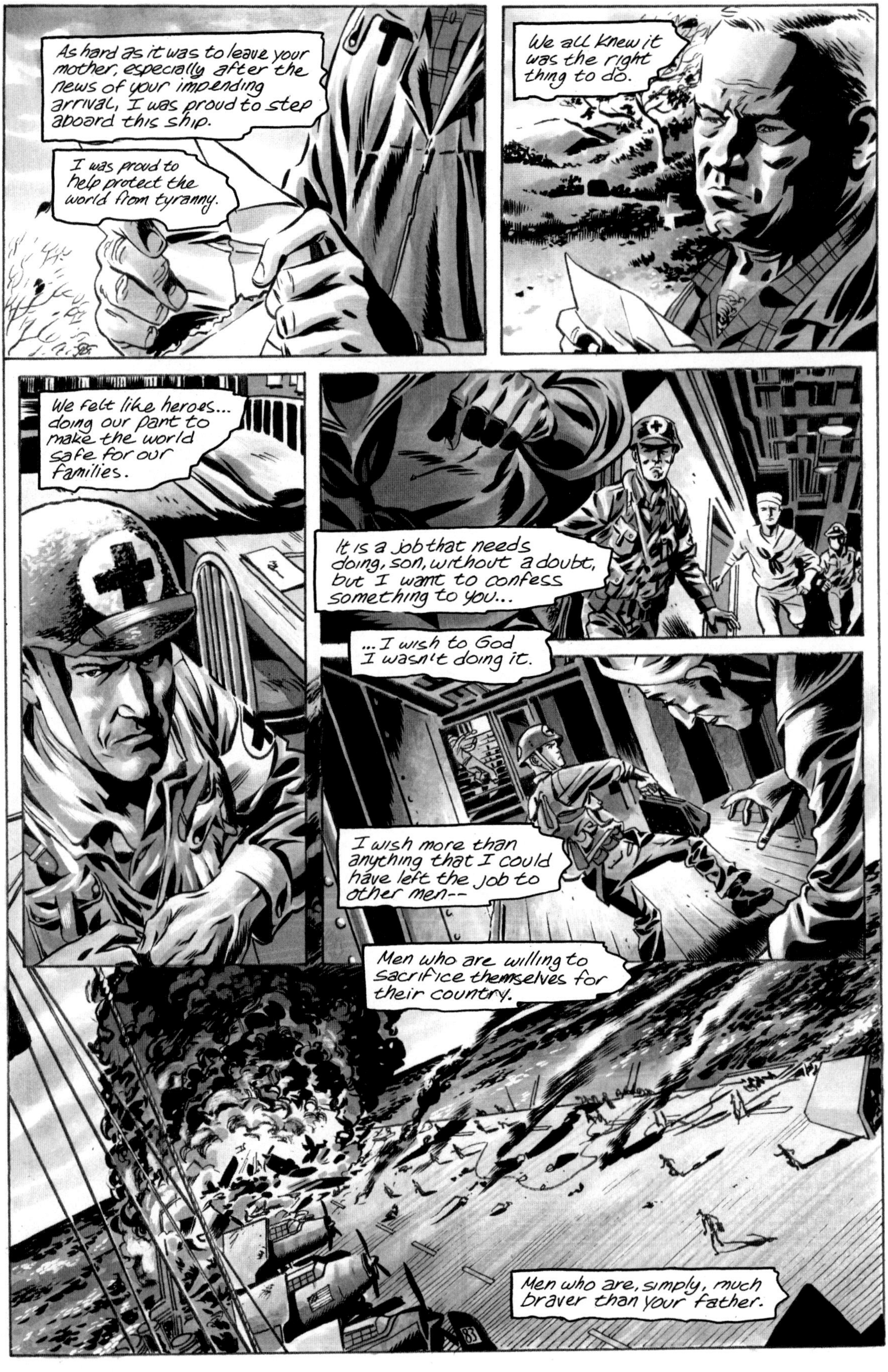
As hard as it was to leave your mother, especially after the news of your impending arrival, I was proud to step aboard this ship.
I was proud to help protect the world from tyranny.
We all knew it was the right thing to do.
We felt like heroes... doing our part to make the world safe for our families.
It is a job that needs doing, son, without a doubt, but I want to confess something to you...
...I wish to God I wasn't doing it.
I wish more than anything that I could have left the job to other men--
Men who are willing to sacrifice themselves for their country.
Men who are, simply, much braver than your father.

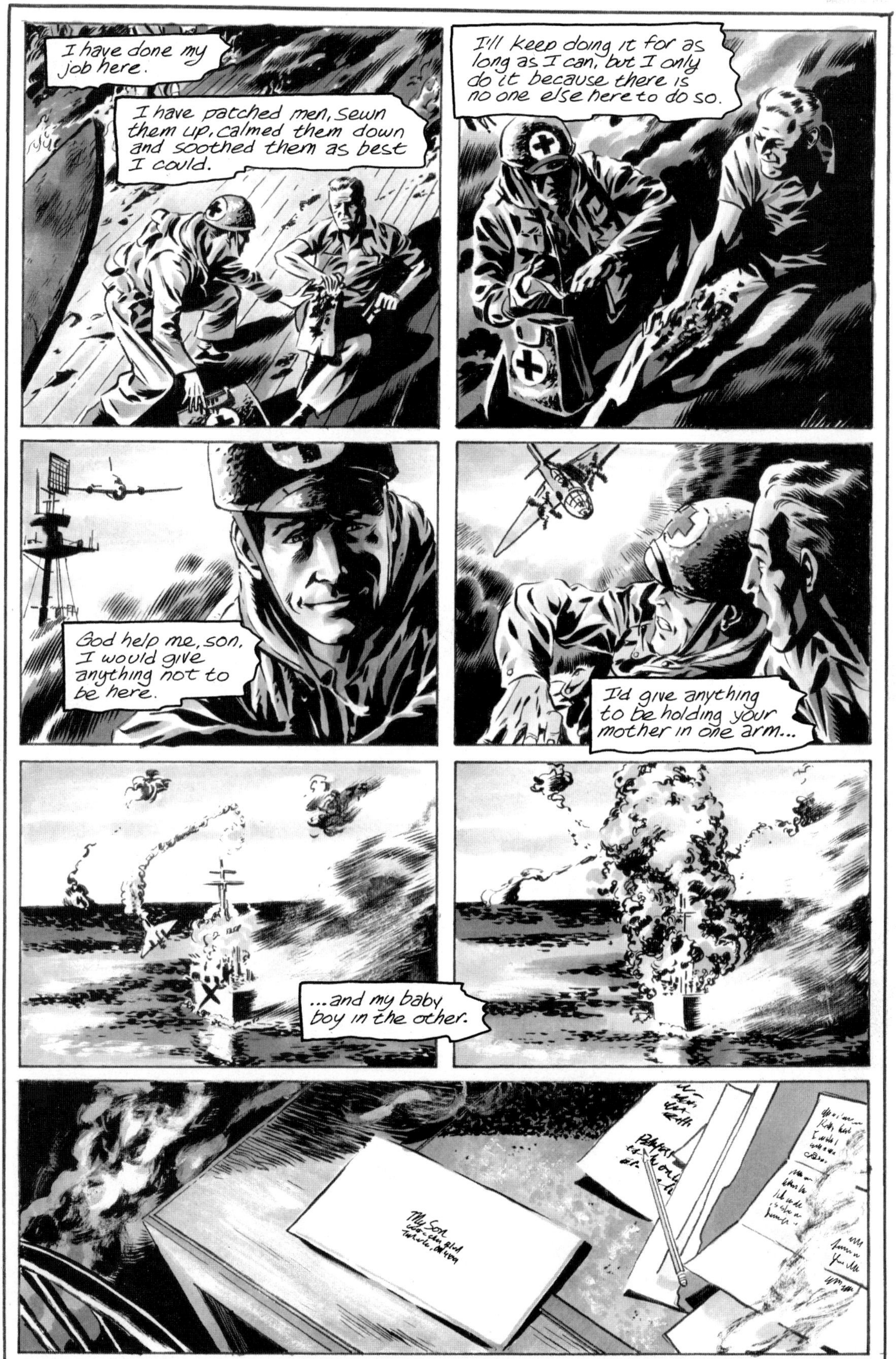
I have done my job here.
I have patched men, sewn them up, calmed them down and soothed them as best I could.
I'll keep doing it for as long as I can, but I only do it because there is no one else here to do so.
God help me, son, I would give anything not to be here.
I'd give anything to be holding your mother in one arm...
...and my baby boy in the other.
My Son

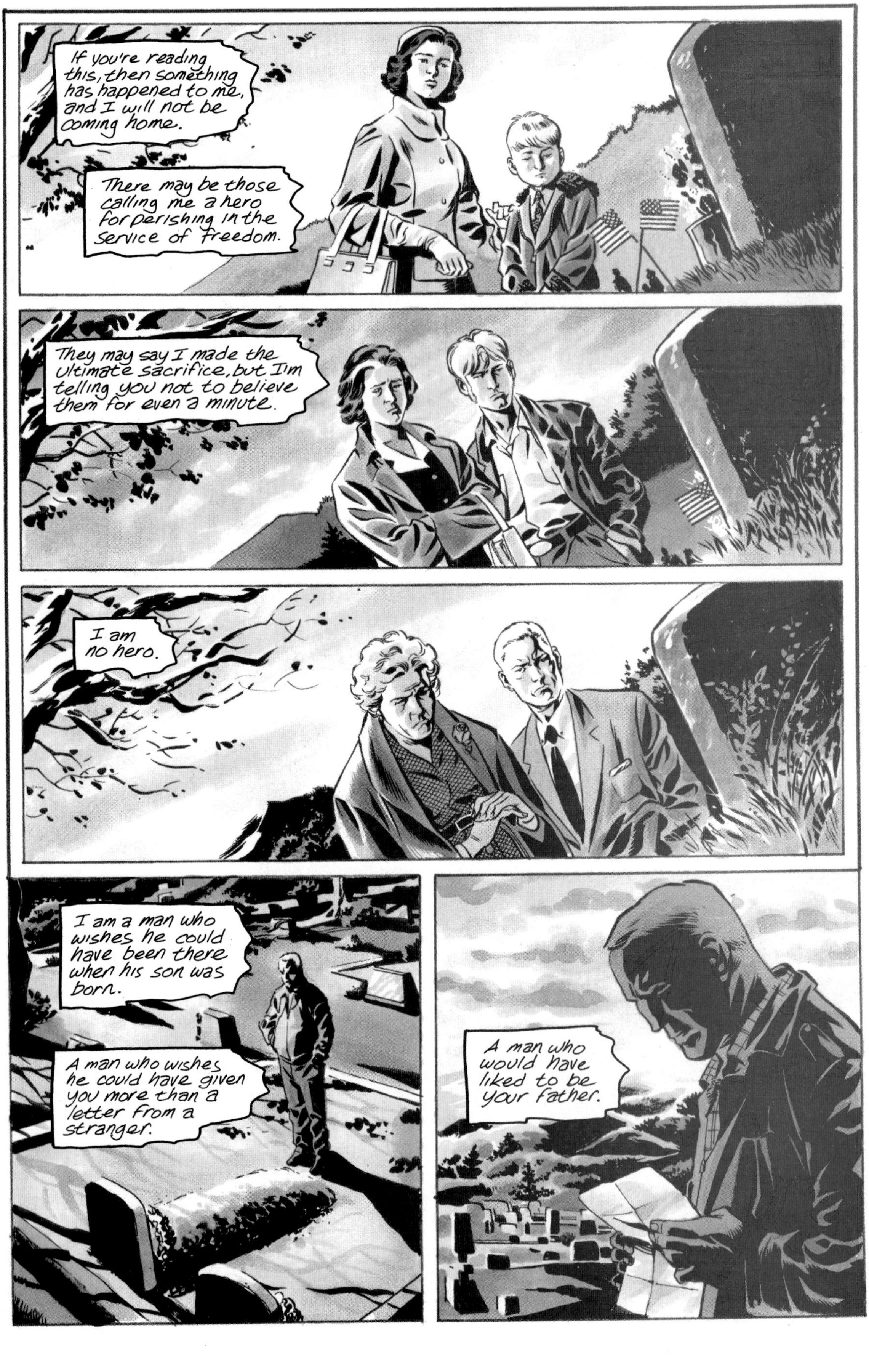
If you're reading this, then something has happened to me, and I will not be coming home.
There may be those calling me a hero for perishing in the service of freedom.
They may say I made the ultimate sacrifice, but I'm telling you not to believe them for even a minute.
I am no hero.
I am a man who wishes he could have been there when his son was born.
A man who wishes he could have given you more than a letter from a stranger.
A man who would have liked to be your father.

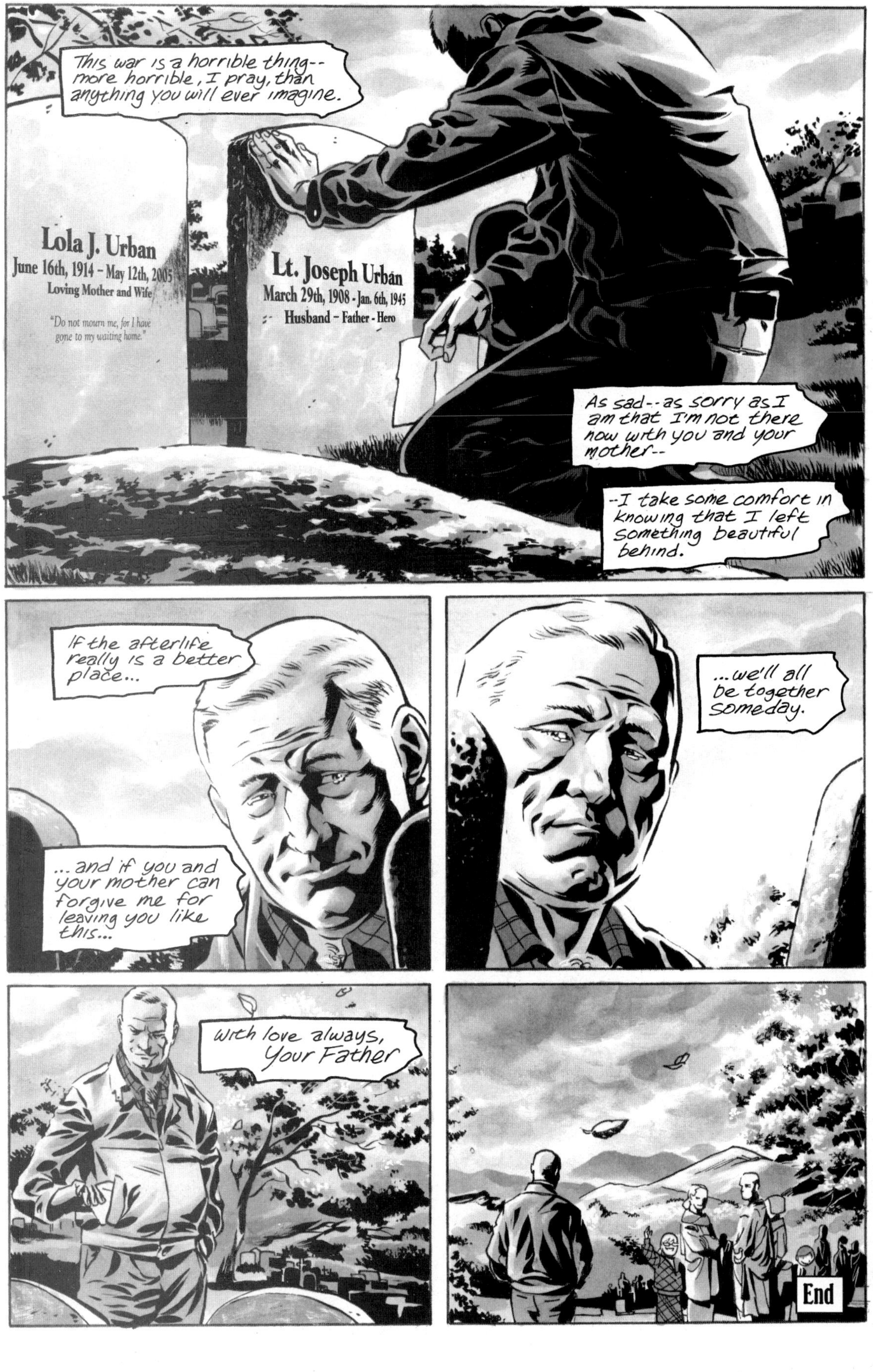
This war is a horrible thing-- more horrible, I pray, than anything you will ever imagine.
Lola J. Urban
June 16th, 1914 - May 12th, 2005
Loving Mother and Wife
"Do not mourn me, for I have gone to my waiting home."
Lt. Joseph Urban
March 29th, 1908 - Jan. 6th, 1945
Husband - Father - Hero
As sad--as sorry as I am that I'm not there now with you and your mother--
--I take some comfort in knowing that I left something beautiful behind.
If the afterlife really is a better place...
...and if you and your mother can forgive me for leaving you like this...
...we'll all be together someday.
With love always, Your Father
End

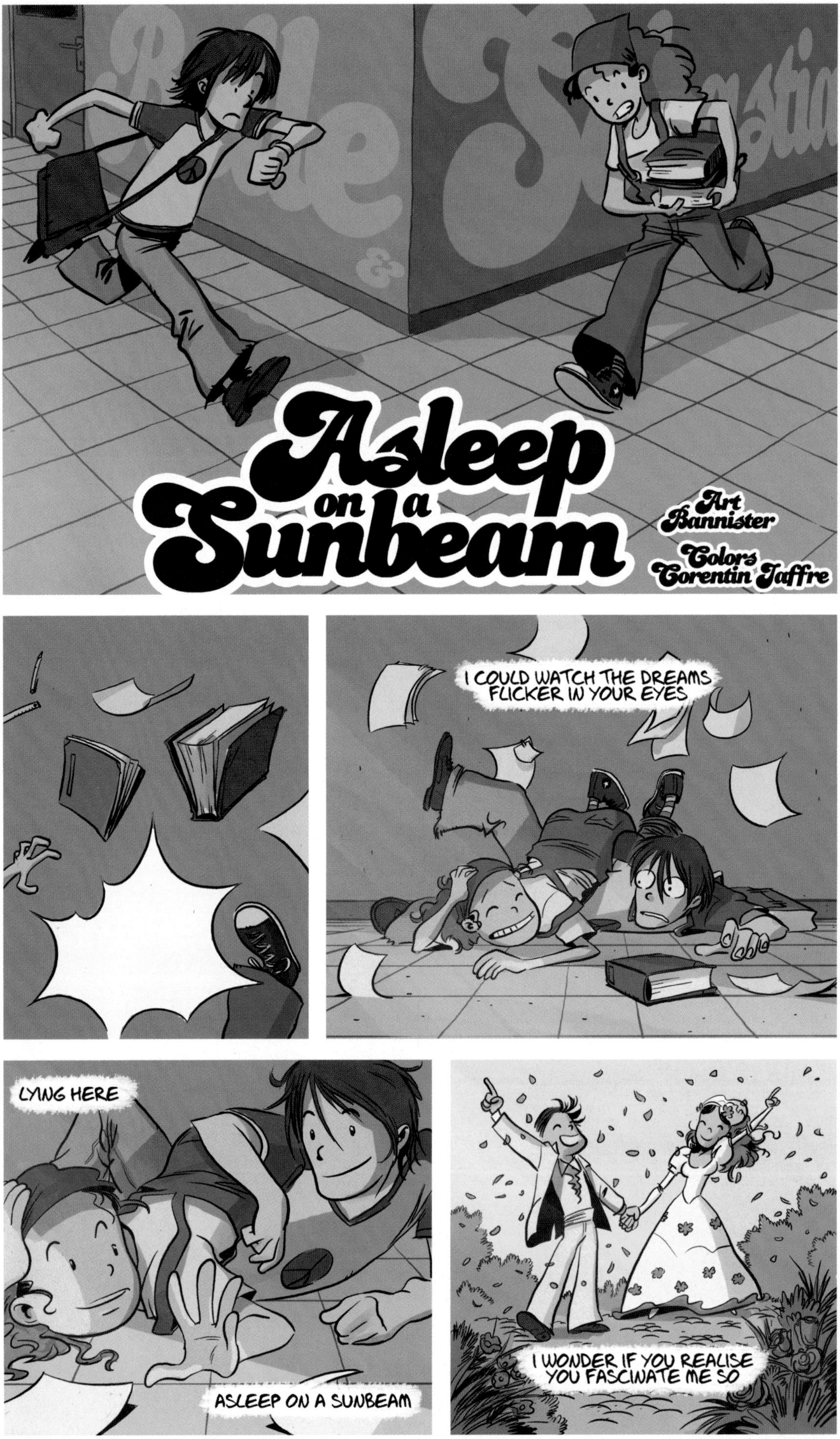
Asleep on a Sunbeam
Art Bannister
Colors Corentin Jaffre
I COULD WATCH THE DREAMS FLICKER IN YOUR EYES
LYING HERE
ASLEEP ON A SUNBEAM
I WONDER IF YOU REALISE YOU FASCINATE ME SO

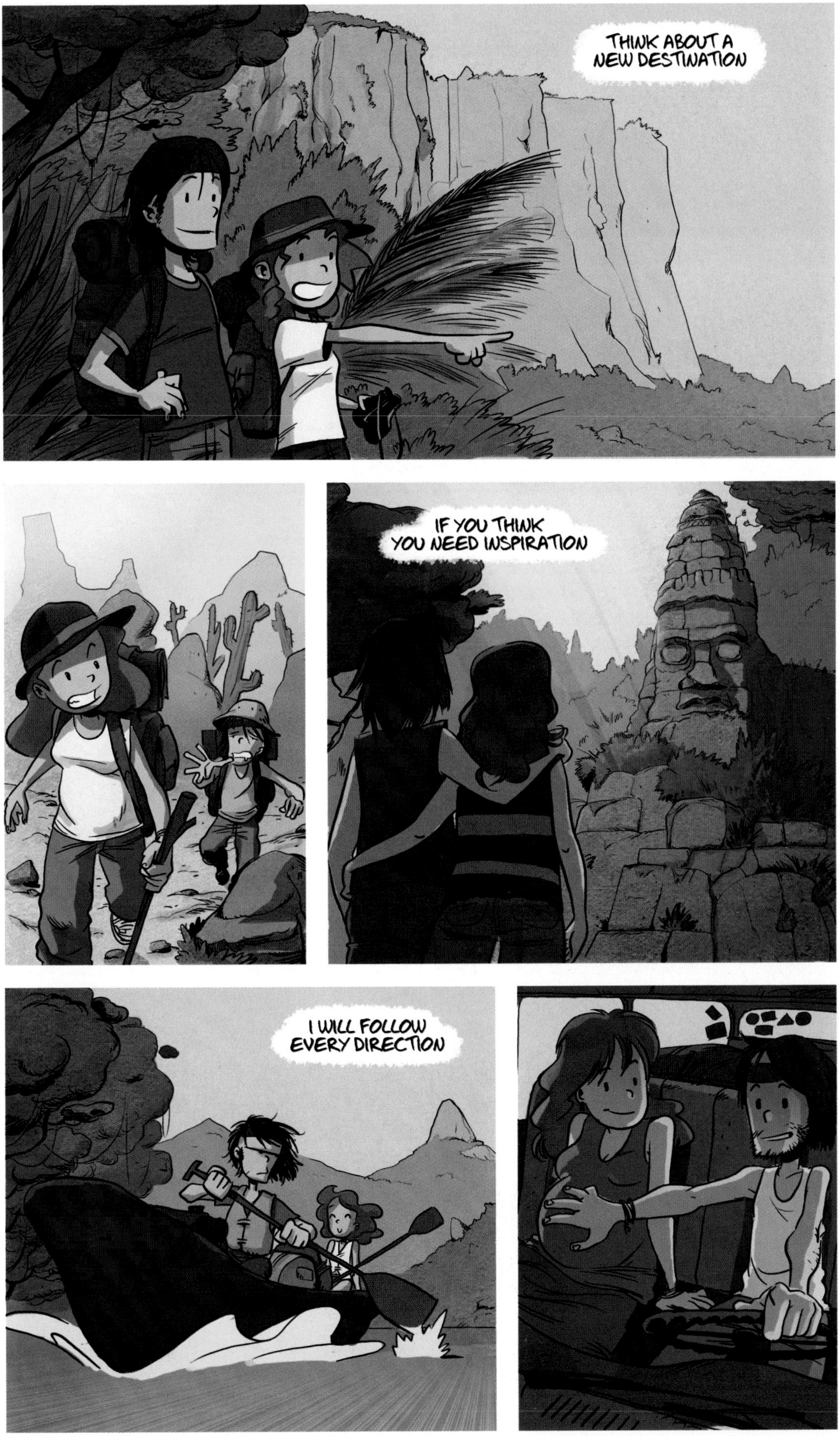
THINK ABOUT A NEW DESTINATION
IF YOU THINK YOU NEED INSPIRATION
I WILL FOLLOW EVERY DIRECTION

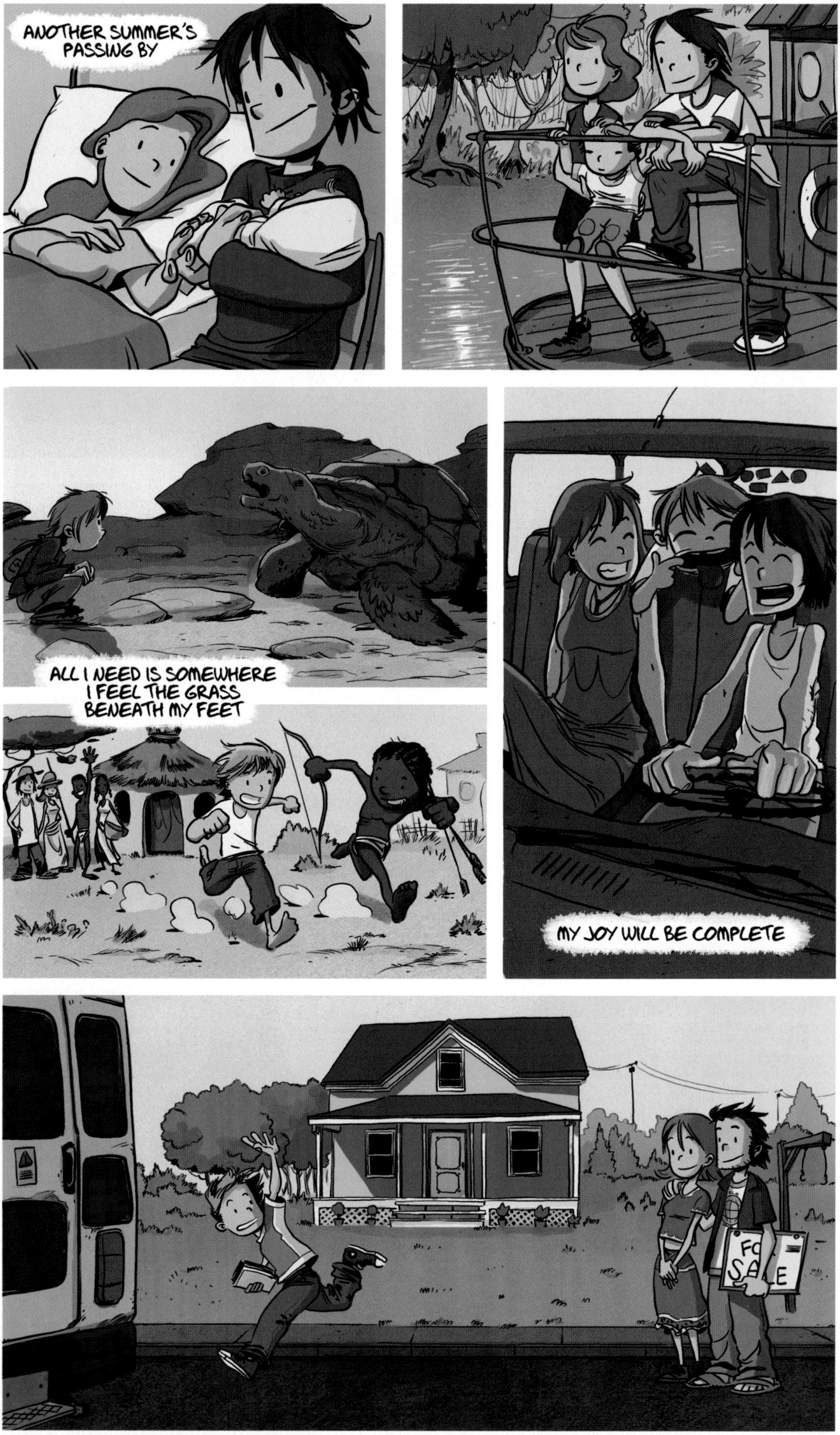
ANOTHER SUMMER'S PASSING BY
ALL I NEED IS SOMEWHERE I FEEL THE GRASS BENEATH MY FEET
MY JOY WILL BE COMPLETE
FOR SALE

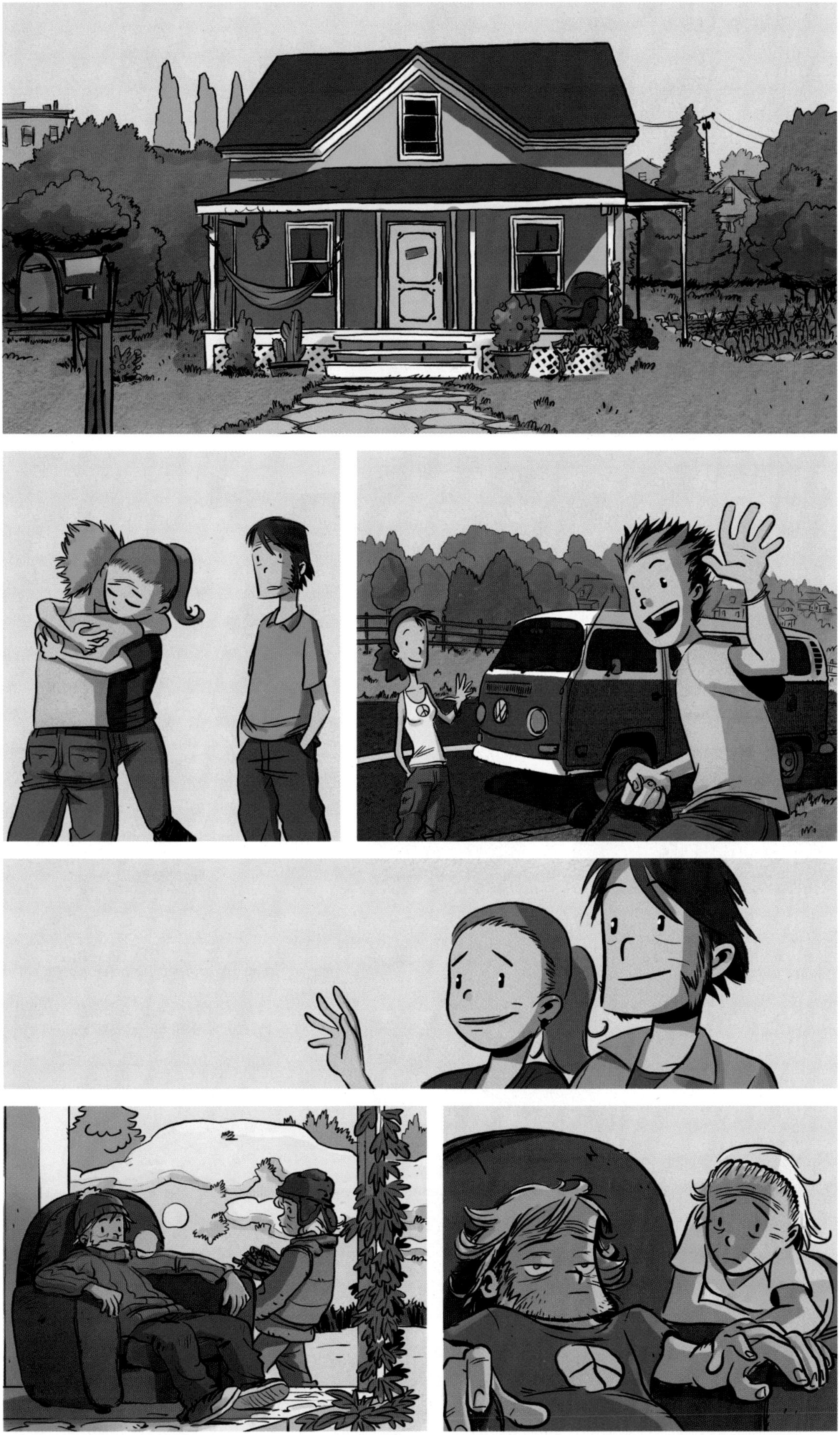

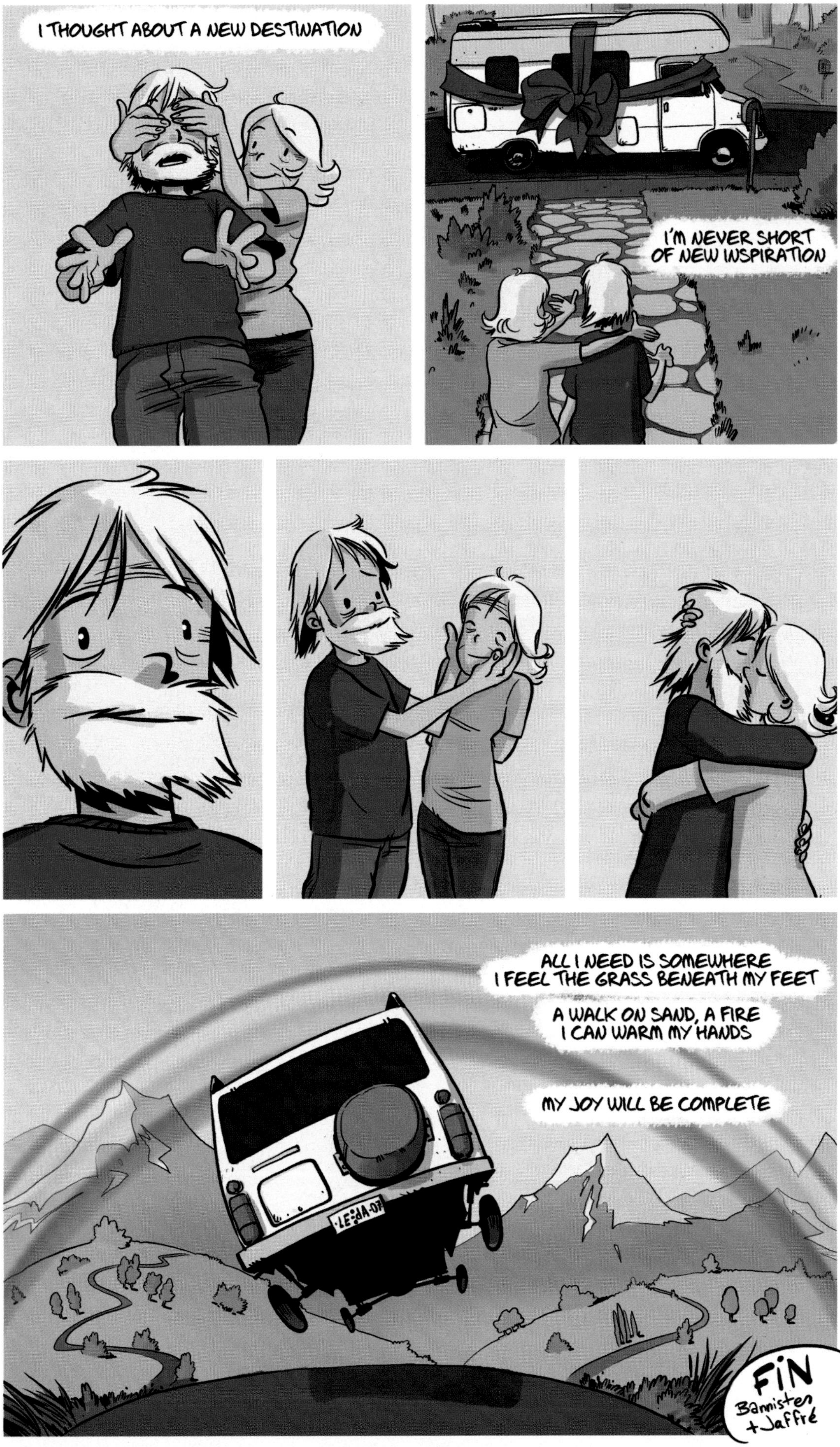
I THOUGHT ABOUT A NEW DESTINATION
I'M NEVER SHORT OF NEW INSPIRATION
ALL I NEED IS SOMEWHERE I FEEL THE GRASS BENEATH MY FEET
A WALK ON SAND, A FIRE I CAN WARM MY HANDS
MY JOY WILL BE COMPLETE
FIN
Bannister + Jaffré

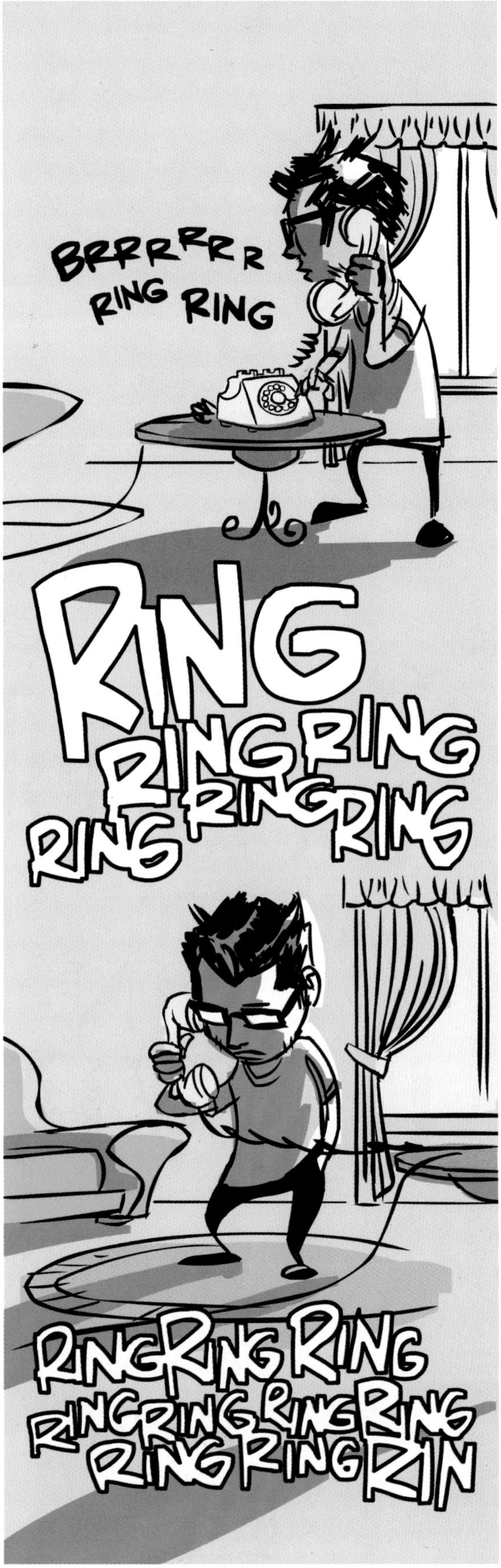
BRRRRRRR
RING RING
RING
RINGRING
RINGRINGRINGRING
RINGRINGRING
RINGRINGRINGRING
RINGRINGRIN

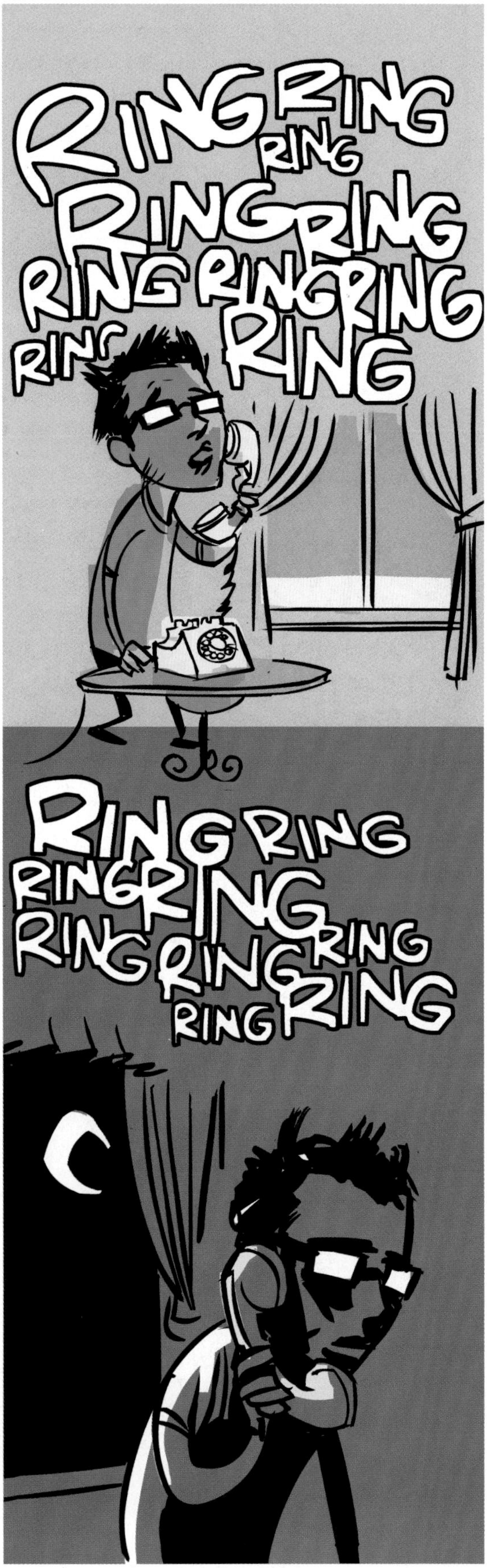
RINGRING
RING
RINGRING
RINGRINGRING
RIN RING
RINGRING
RINGRING
RINGRINGRING
RINGRING

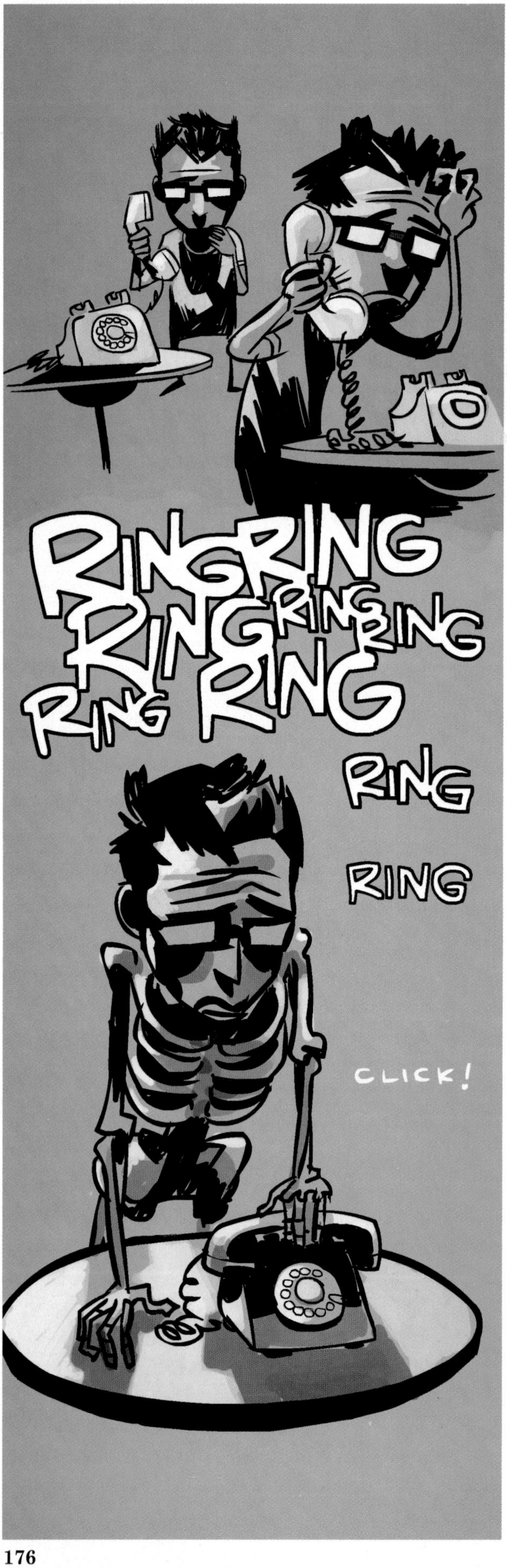
RINGRING
RINGRINGRING
RING RING
RING
RING
CLICK!

IF YOU find YOURSELF CAUGHT IN LOVE

by
Steven Griffin

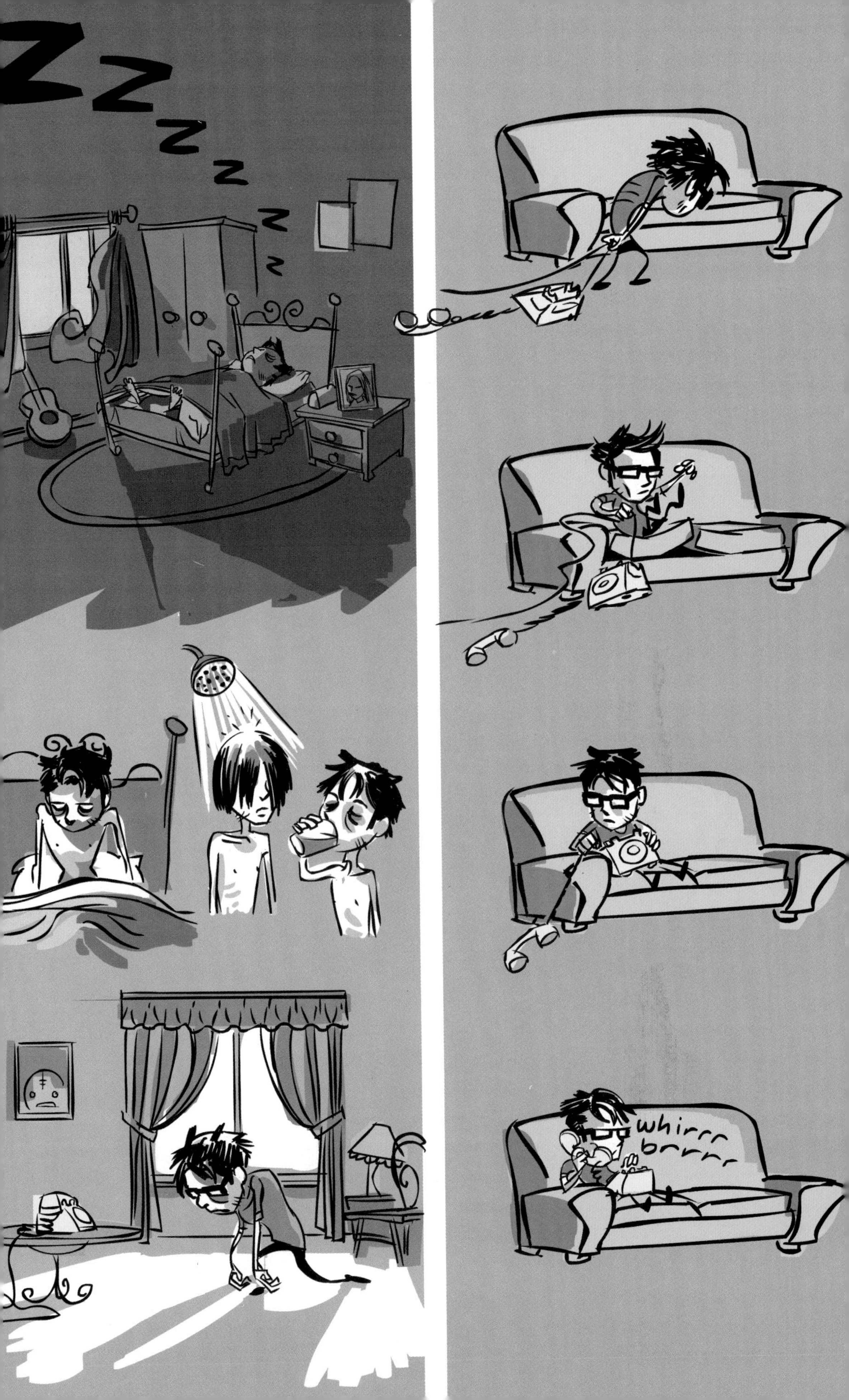
ZZZZZZ
whirrr
brrrrr

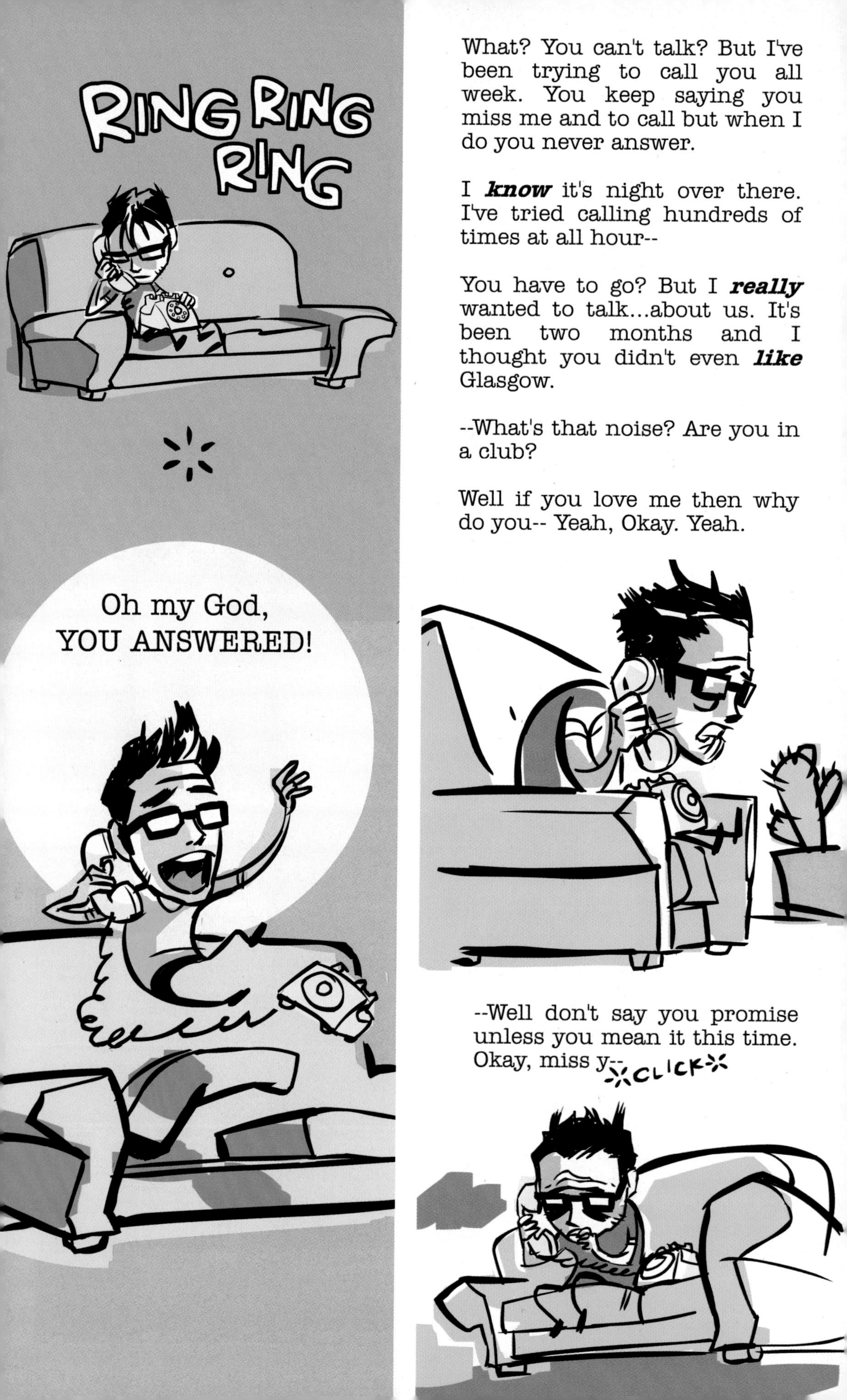
RING RING RING
Oh my God, YOU ANSWERED!
What? You can't talk? But I've been trying to call you all week. You keep saying you miss me and to call but when I do you never answer.
I ***know*** it's night over there. I've tried calling hundreds of times at all hour--
You have to go? But I ***really*** wanted to talk...about us. It's been two months and I thought you didn't even ***like*** Glasgow.
--What's that noise? Are you in a club?
Well if you love me then why do you-- Yeah, Okay. Yeah.
--Well don't say you promise unless you mean it this time. Okay, miss y--
CLICK

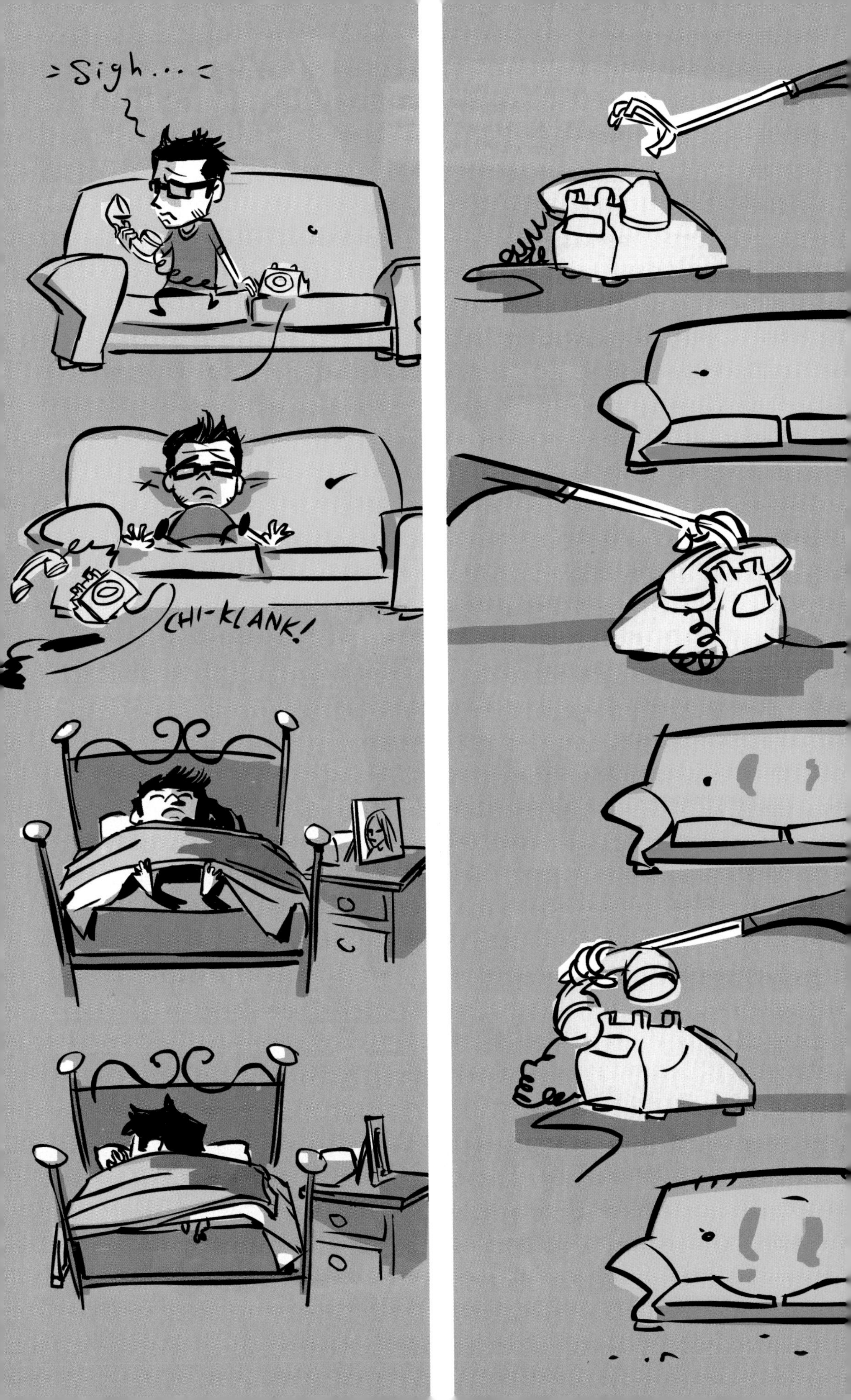

Sigh...
CHI-KLANK!

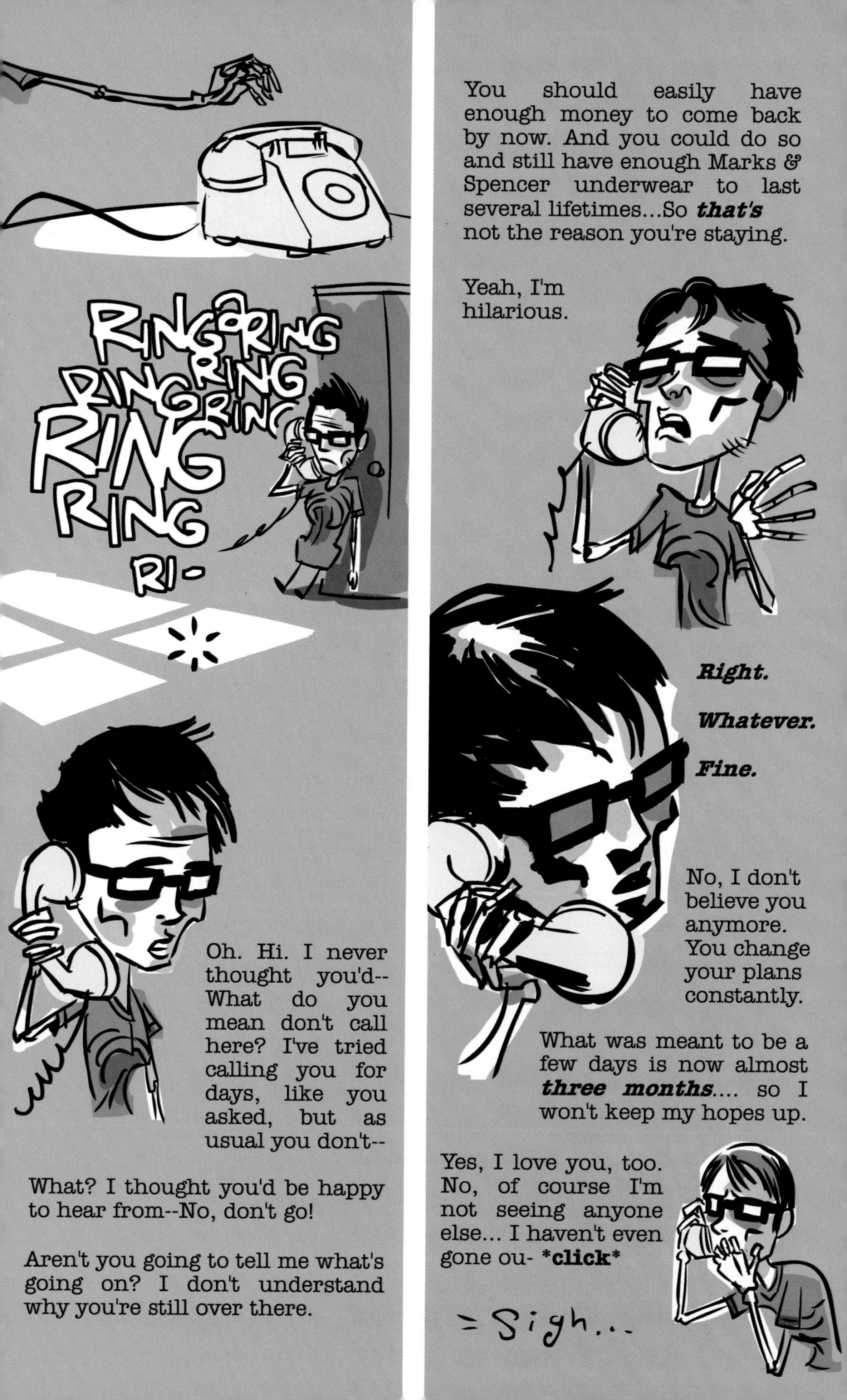
RINGaRING
RINGaRING
RINGaRING
RING
RING
RI-
Oh. Hi. I never thought you'd-- What do you mean don't call here? I've tried calling you for days, like you asked, but as usual you don't--
What? I thought you'd be happy to hear from--No, don't go!
Aren't you going to tell me what's going on? I don't understand why you're still over there.
You should easily have enough money to come back by now. And you could do so and still have enough Marks & Spencer underwear to last several lifetimes...So ***that's*** not the reason you're staying.
Yeah, I'm hilarious.
Right.
Whatever.
Fine.
No, I don't believe you anymore. You change your plans constantly.
What was meant to be a few days is now almost ***three months***.... so I won't keep my hopes up.
Yes, I love you, too. No, of course I'm not seeing anyone else... I haven't even gone ou- ***click***
= Sigh...

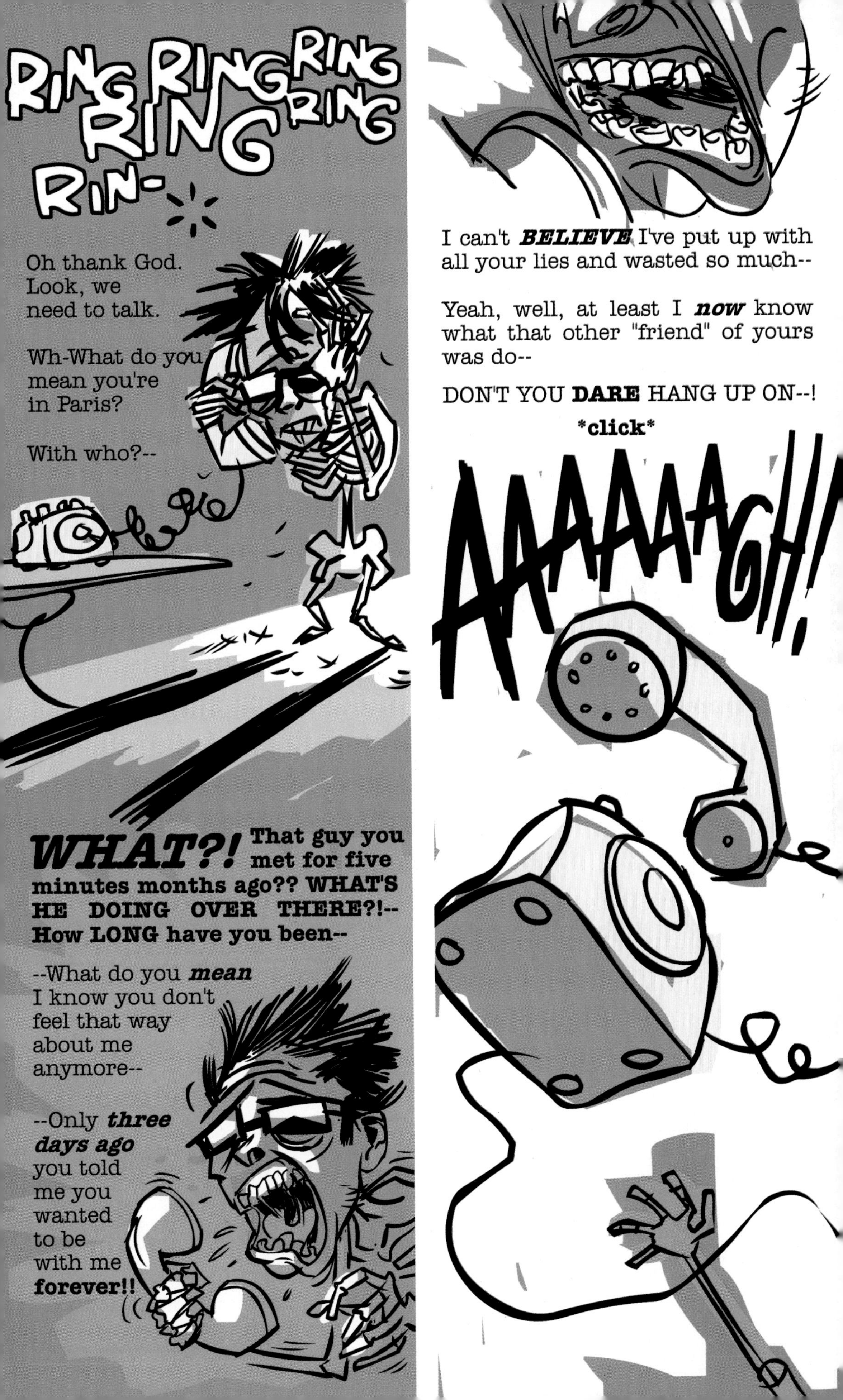

RING RING RING RING RING
RIN-
Oh thank God. Look, we need to talk.
Wh-What do you mean you're in Paris?
With who?--
WHAT?! That guy you met for five minutes months ago?? WHAT'S HE DOING OVER THERE?!-- How LONG have you been--
--What do you *mean* I know you don't feel that way about me anymore--
--Only *three days ago* you told me you wanted to be with me **forever!!**
I can't ***BELIEVE*** I've put up with all your lies and wasted so much--
Yeah, well, at least I ***now*** know what that other "friend" of yours was do--
DON'T YOU **DARE** HANG UP ON--!
click
AAAAAAGH!!

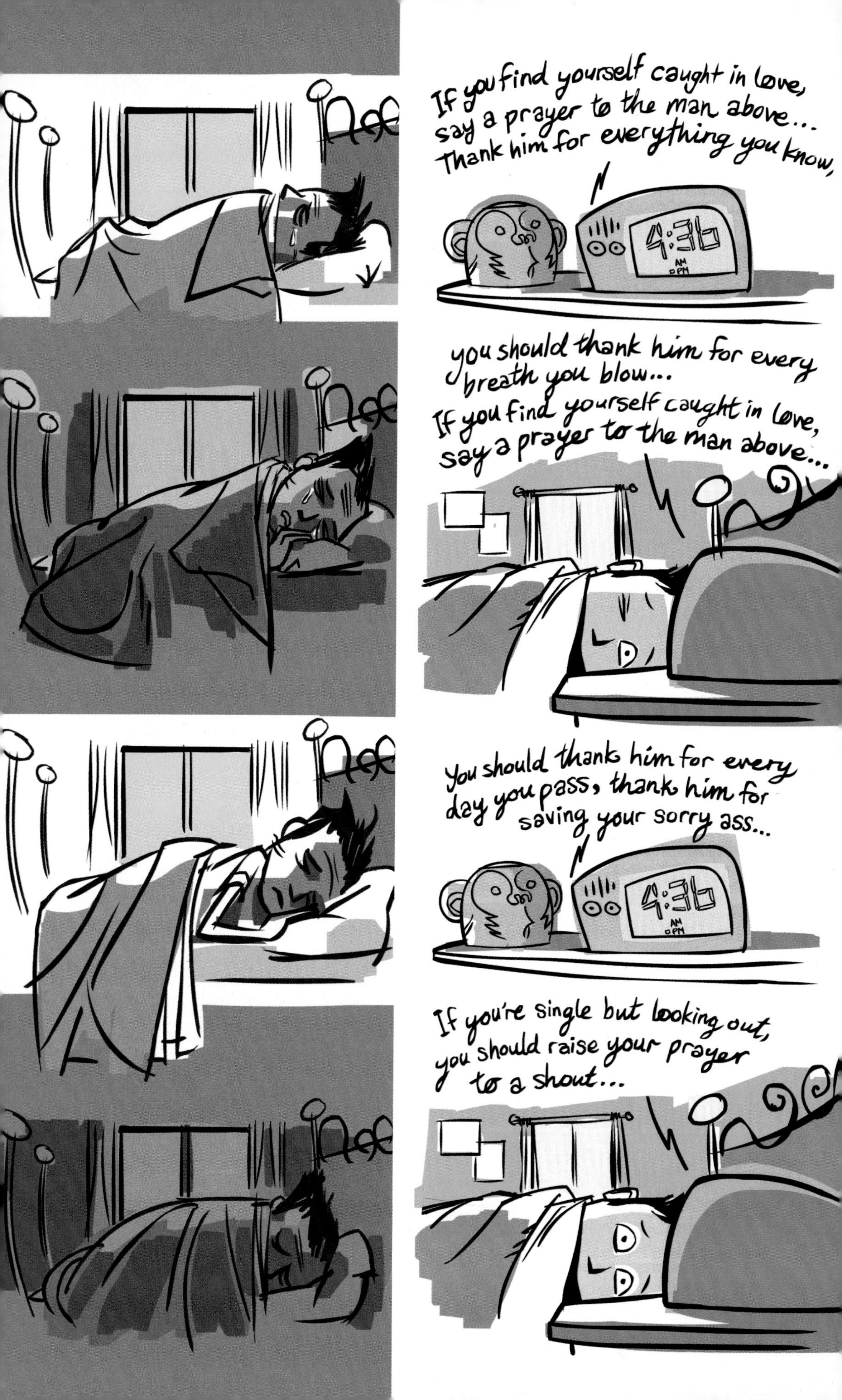

If you find yourself caught in love, say a prayer to the man above... Thank him for everything you know,
4:36
AM
PM
you should thank him for every breath you blow... If you find yourself caught in love, say a prayer to the man above...
You should thank him for every day you pass, thank him for saving your sorry ass...
4:36
AM
PM
If you're single but looking out, you should raise your prayer to a shout...

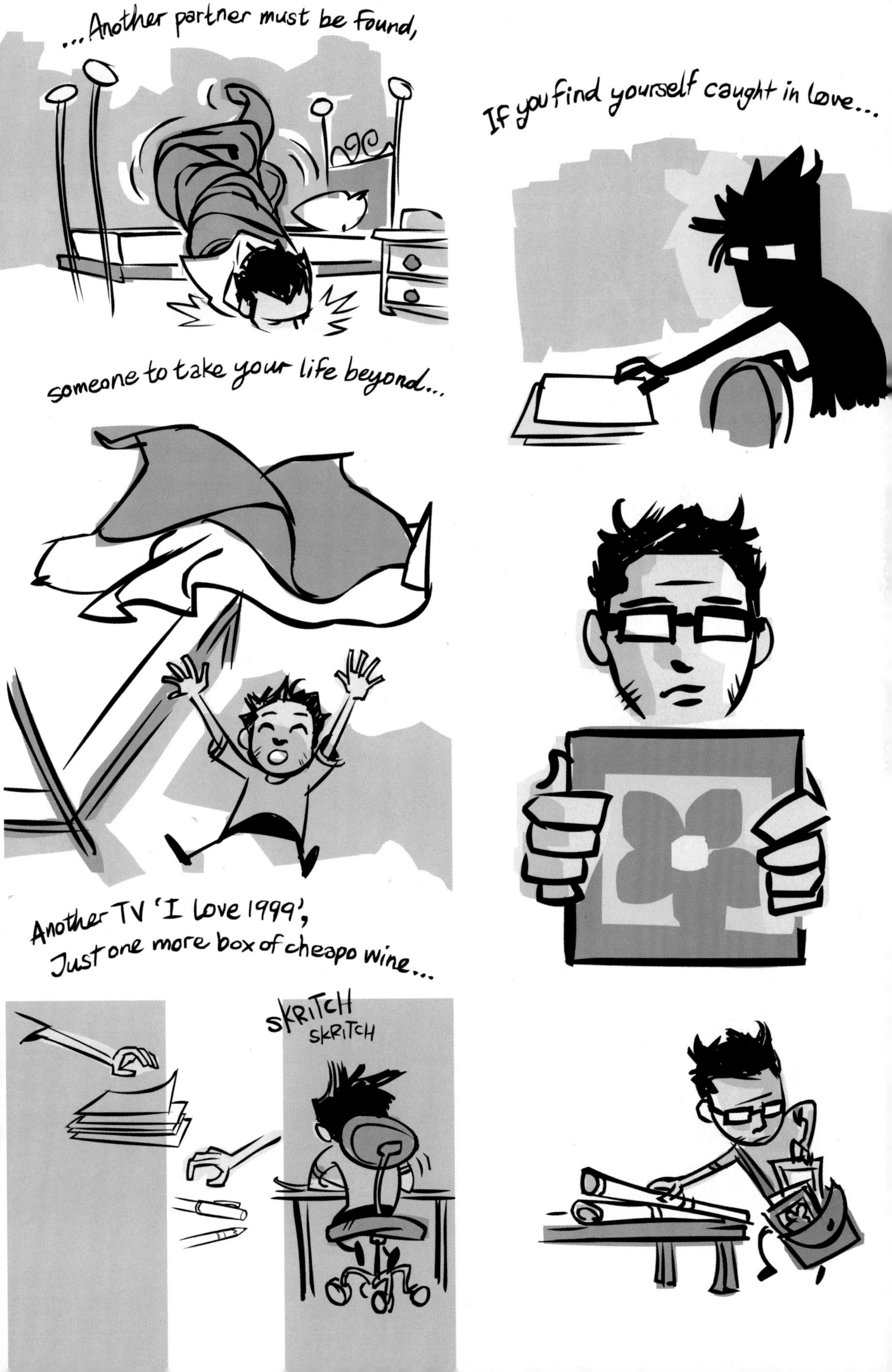
...Another partner must be found,
someone to take your life beyond...
Another TV 'I Love 1999',
Just one more box of cheapo wine...
SKRITCH
SKRITCH
If you find yourself caught in love...

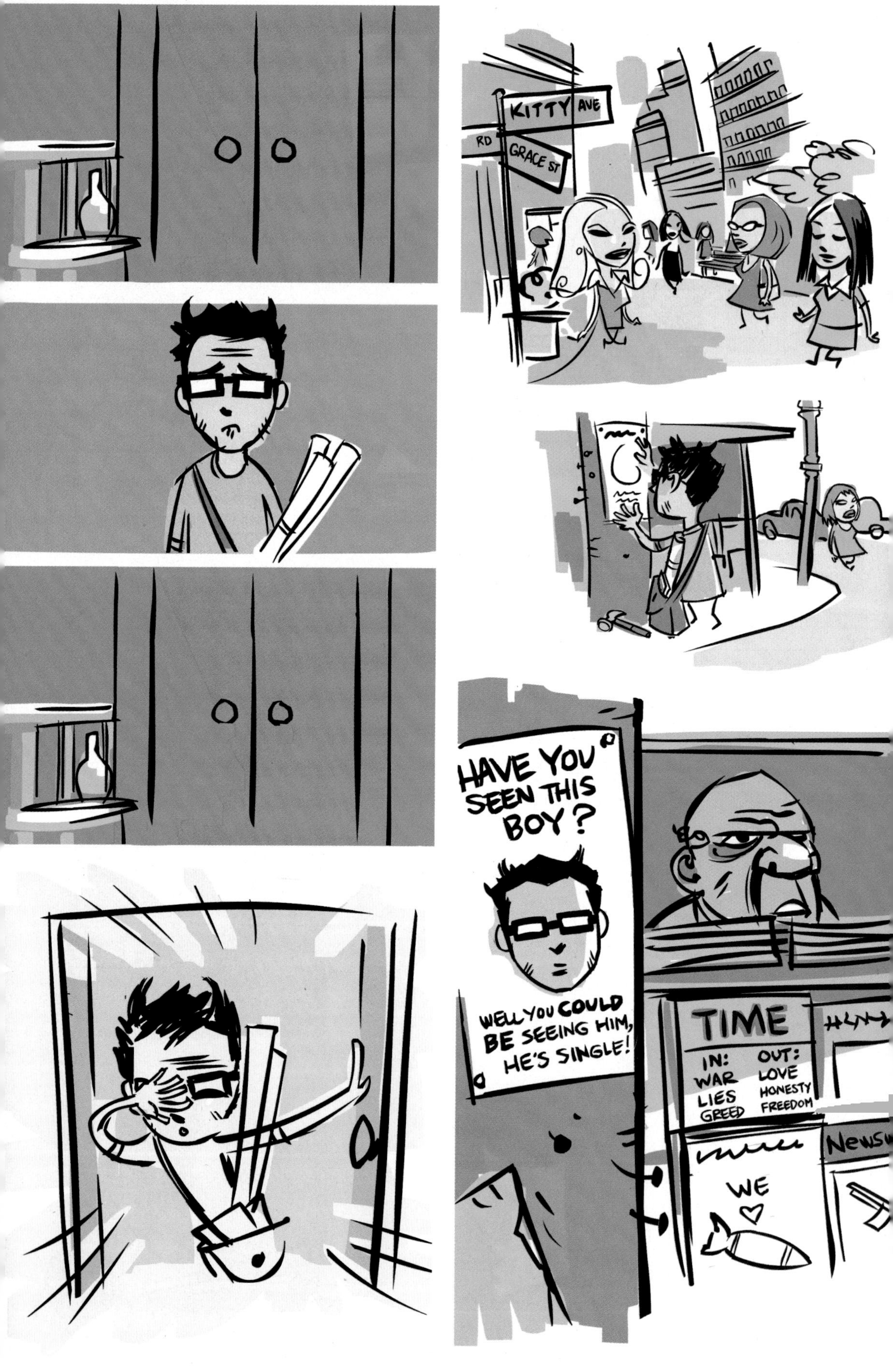
KITTY AVE
RD
GRACE ST
HAVE YOU SEEN THIS BOY?
WELL YOU COULD BE SEEING HIM, HE'S SINGLE!
TIME
IN: WAR LIES GREED
OUT: LOVE HONESTY FREEDOM
WE ♥

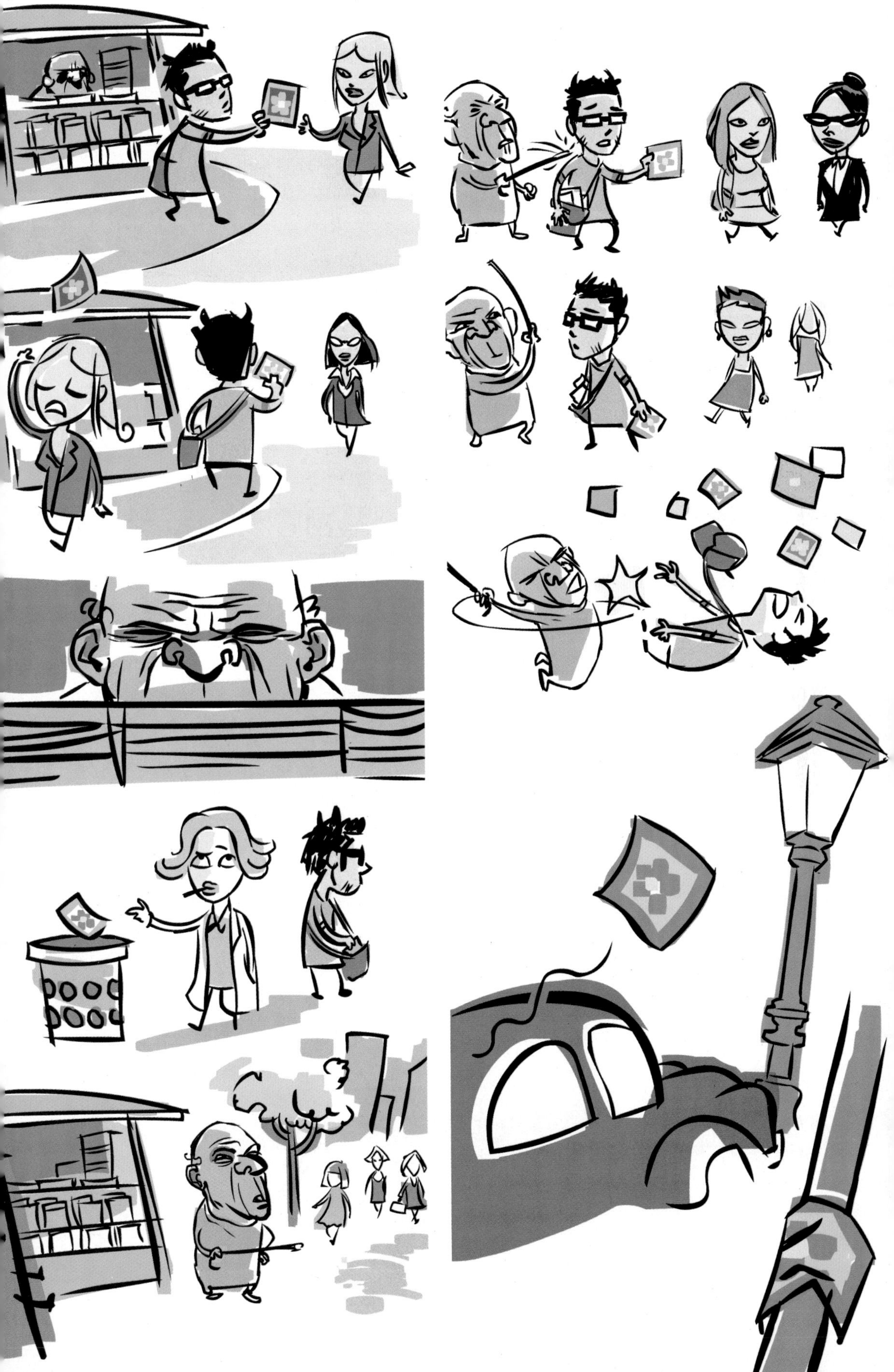

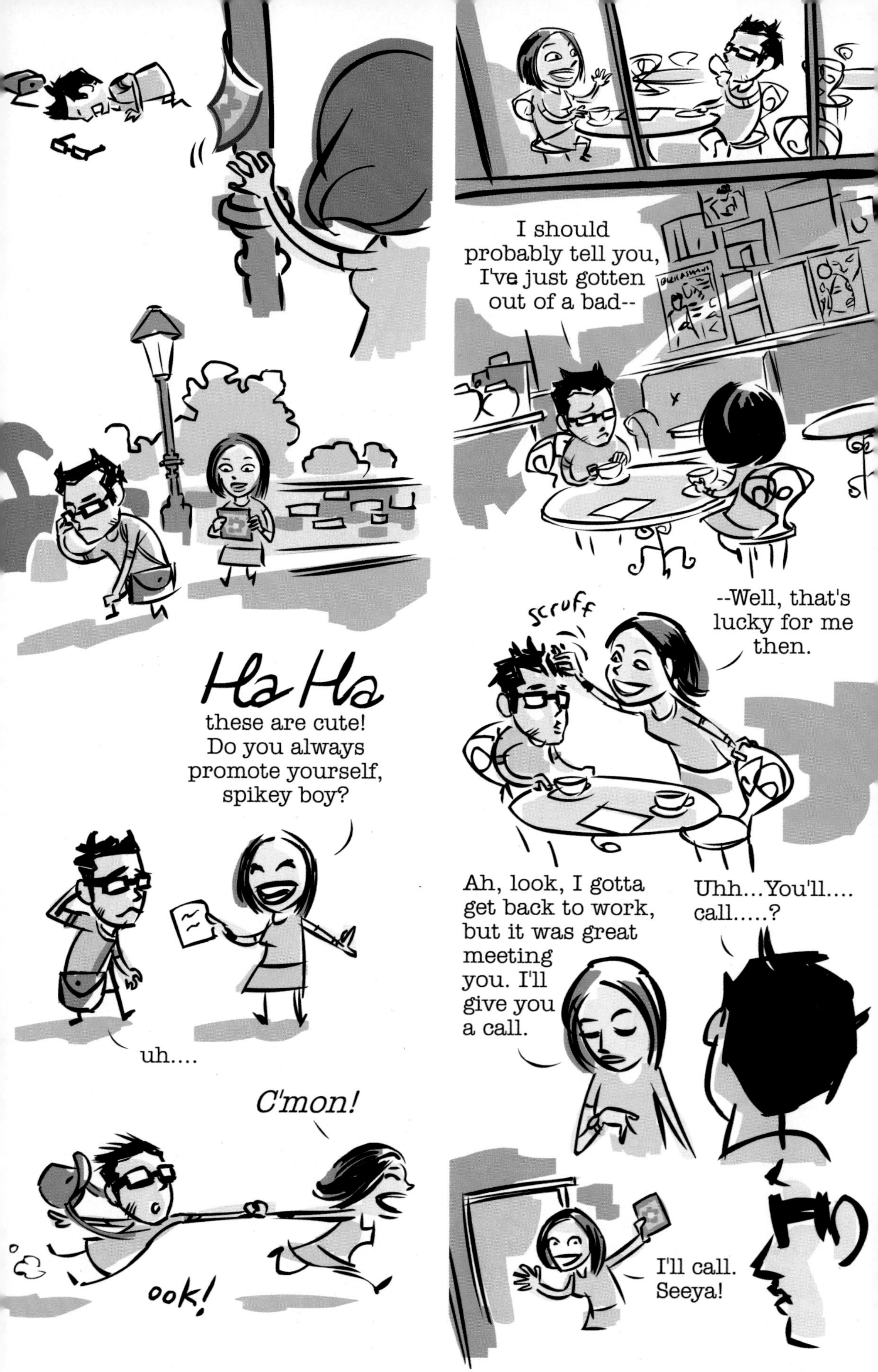

Ha Ha
these are cute!
Do you always
promote yourself,
spikey boy?
uh....
C'mon!
ook!
I should probably tell you, I've just gotten out of a bad--
scruff
--Well, that's lucky for me then.
Ah, look, I gotta get back to work, but it was great meeting you. I'll give you a call.
Uhh...You'll.... call.....?
I'll call. Seeya!

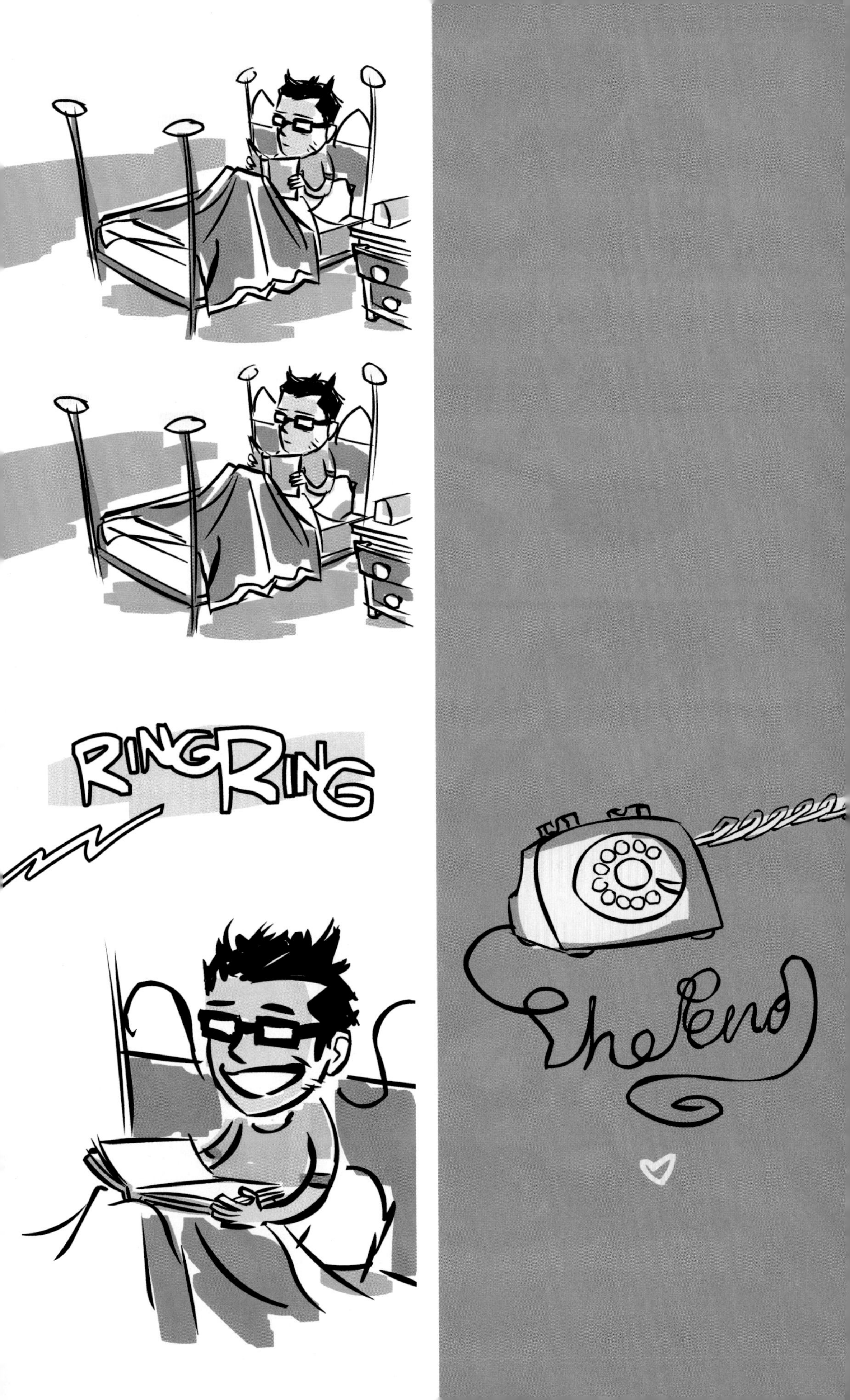
RING RING
The End

RICK SPEARS & ROB G have been conspiring together since 2000 to bring the comics industry to its knees. They are responsible for work from several companies, including DC Comics, Humanoids Publishing and AIT/Planet Lar. They continue to further their evil plans through Gigantic Graphic Novels. They both live in Brooklyn with their wives, who keep them out of trouble.

CHRISTOPHER BUTCHER is a writer at comics212.net and is manager of The Beguiling Books & Art in Toronto and the co-founder of the Toronto Comic Arts Festival, visit it online at www.torontocomics.com.
KALMAN ANDRASOFSZKY loves to draw. He's drawn comic books, for magazines and roleplaying games too. He lives in Toronto, likes cats, and finally has his own studio; which means he gets to see the sun sometimes. You can find out more about Kalman at www.horhaus.com. RAMON PEREZ is the co-creator of the online comic Butternutsquash.net and freelance artist on such comic books as Spellgame (artist), The Incredibles (inker) and Hulk: Gamma Games (penciller) as well as a multitude of Role-Playing Game publications. For more, mosey on over to ramon-perez.com

ANDI WATSON is the creator of Skeleton Key, Breakfast After Noon and most recently Little Star for Oni Press. He's tone deaf and while at college inadvisably bought an acoustic guitar which he couldn't tune because he's tone deaf. He lives in Staffordshire with his wife, daughter and cat, without a guitar. www.andiwatson.biz

MARK ANDREW SMITH is the writer and co-creator of the Amazing Joy Buzzards at Image Comics. He loves Ninjas, Giant Sea Monsters and Luchadores.

PAUL MAYBURY, born in 1982, raised in Boston MA. Wishes he could draw comicbooks.... oh wait... www.deliciousbrains.com

TOM HART won a 1994 Xeric grant for his book, Hutch Owen's Working Hard. Two collections of Hutch Owen have been published by Top Shelf Productions. He is the editor of serializer.net and is a founding member of Oubapo-america. Tom teaches cartooning in New York City where he lives with his wife and fellow cartoonist, Leela

JACOB MAGRAW was born in Seattle. He has two sisters and five cousins.

KAKO is never up before noon and never in bed before dawn. www.kakofonia.com

CATIA CHIEN was raised in Brazil and read comics ever since she was a wee little girl. Now she lives on the West Coast painting for gallery shows, sketching concept artwork and illustrating children's books. She feels lucky to be doing what she truly loves. To see more of her work: www.catiachien.com

JANET HARVEY is a writer and award-winning filmmaker living in Los Angeles. Her work includes the first adventure of the new Batgirl in Batman #569, and most recently, the Hi Hi Puffy Ami Yumi Special from DC Comics. She really enjoys saying "award-winning filmmaker."
LAURENN McCUBBIN is the writer and illustrator of the Xeric grant winning XXXLiveNudeGirls (with Nikki Coffman) and the artist of Rent Girl (with Michelle Tea). Her work has appeared everywhere from On Our Backs to McSweeneys to the New York Times. You can see more of her work at laurennmccubbin.com

MATTHEW S. ARMSTRONG is a self taught artist, who is now trapped in a life of his own making along with his lovely wife and daughter.

CHARLES BROWNSTEIN is an occasional writer and the full-time Executive Director of the Comic Book Legal Defense Fund. He lives and works in New York City.
A natural born softie, DAVE CROSLAND can be found getting drunk off two beers and stumbling into monkeyshines at www.hiredmeat.com.

BRUNO D'ANGELO published his first comic mini-series, Drakken's Awakening, in 1997. A prolific artist, he produces comics, animation, storyboards, paintings, cover illustrations and work as the Art Director of Brazil's premier car magazine. He is the artist of Rock'n'Roll (Image), Prey, Lord Takeyama, Horns of Hattin and Gunned Down (Terra Major). Bruno also practices Kenjutsu and lives in São Paulo, Brazil, with his wife Graziela.

JENNIFER DE GUZMAN has left behind a past life of glorious piracy to write fiction and edit comic books in the San Francisco Bay Area. She is at work on a novel and an MFA degree and is editor-in-chief at Slave Labor Graphics.
BRIAN BELEW's previous comic book work can be found in Haunted Mansion #1, in which he inked, coincidentally, a story about piracy. He works as a graphic and packaging designer in the San Francisco Bay Area.
MATT FORSYTHE is an illustrator and comic-book creator from Toronto, Canada. He currently lives in Montreal where he is working on his his Eisner-nominated comic, Ojingogo. www.comingupforair.net
ERIN LAING is a writer/director from Montreal, Canada, where she is currently developing her first feature film, Welcome To My World. www.apartment304.com

RICK REMENDER writes comics such as Strange Girl, Fear Agent, Sea of Red and Black Heart Billy. Everything he touches becomes a solid gold dancer with a tall afro of quality. He lives in the Bay Area with his wife, Danni.
JOHN HEEBINK has drawn comics for Image, Fantagraphics, AIT, Claypool and others. He is an instructor at San Francisco's Academy of Art.

LEELA CORMAN is an illustrator and bellydancer. She lives in Brooklyn, New York with her husband, Tom Hart. She is currently at work on a graphic novel that she refers to as "the Yiddish Telemundo".

JOEY WEISER is a recent graduate of the Savannah College of Art & Design. His work can be seen in Flight 3 as well as online at www.tragic-planet.com where he is serializing his first graphic novel, The Ride Home.

JAMIE S. RICH is the author of the musically obsessed prose novel Cut My Hair and its forthcoming sequel, The Everlasting, due from Oni Press in the summer of 2006. It will be followed by his full-length comics debut, 12 Reasons Why I Love Her, illustrated by Joelle Jones, and more collaborations with Marc Ellerby. He once wrote a cheeky—yet positive review—of a Belle & Sebastian album that angered fans in Portland, OR, and those still smarting should consider this his mea culpa. www.confessions123.com

MARC ELLERBY's next project will be illustrating Jamie S. Rich's new Oni Press series, Love the Way You Love. He gets easily distracted by muffins.

IAN CARNEY is the writer and co-creator of the 'hit' comic books Sugar Buzz, Pants Ant and Where's It At, Sugar Kat? By day he is an animation scriptwriter and has worked on shows for Cartoon Network, Nickelodeon, BBC, Aardman, ITV and Hensons.

JONATHAN EDWARDS started his comics career working for Deadline and has recently collaborated with Ian Carney on A Bag of Anteaters. He also works as an illustrator and designs record sleeves.

DAVID LASKY has produced a number of experimental comic books, including a nine page mini-comic adaptation of Joyce's Ulysses. His work appears in a wide variety of anthologies, including Moxie, My Sweet (www.finecomix.com) and the newspaper called Arthur.

MARK RICKETTS is not your father, no matter what was revealed in those DNA tests. He IS a graphic novelist whose works include Nowheresville, Lazarus Jack, Dioramas, Whiskey Dickel, Int'l Cowgirl and the upcoming Night Trippers.

LEANNE BUCKLEY has illustrated for various role-playing companies, comics and magazines. She spends more time messing around in Photoshop than she probably should and has way too many pens in her collection.

CHRIS SAMNEE is living out his dream of drawing comics from his home in St. Louis, where he always has a cup of coffee or his wife Laura at his side. Visit him at www.chrissamnee.com.

NICHOLAS BANNISTER was born in 1973. He lives with his girlfriend as a freelance artist/comicker near the French Alps. His new book will be published in 2007, and it's going to be a nice book, at least that's what people says. A very little bit of his work can be seen at www.bannister.fr.

STEVEN GRIFFEN is the Eisner-nominated co-creator of the acclaimed HAWAIIAN DICK and lives and breathes in Sydney, Australia.

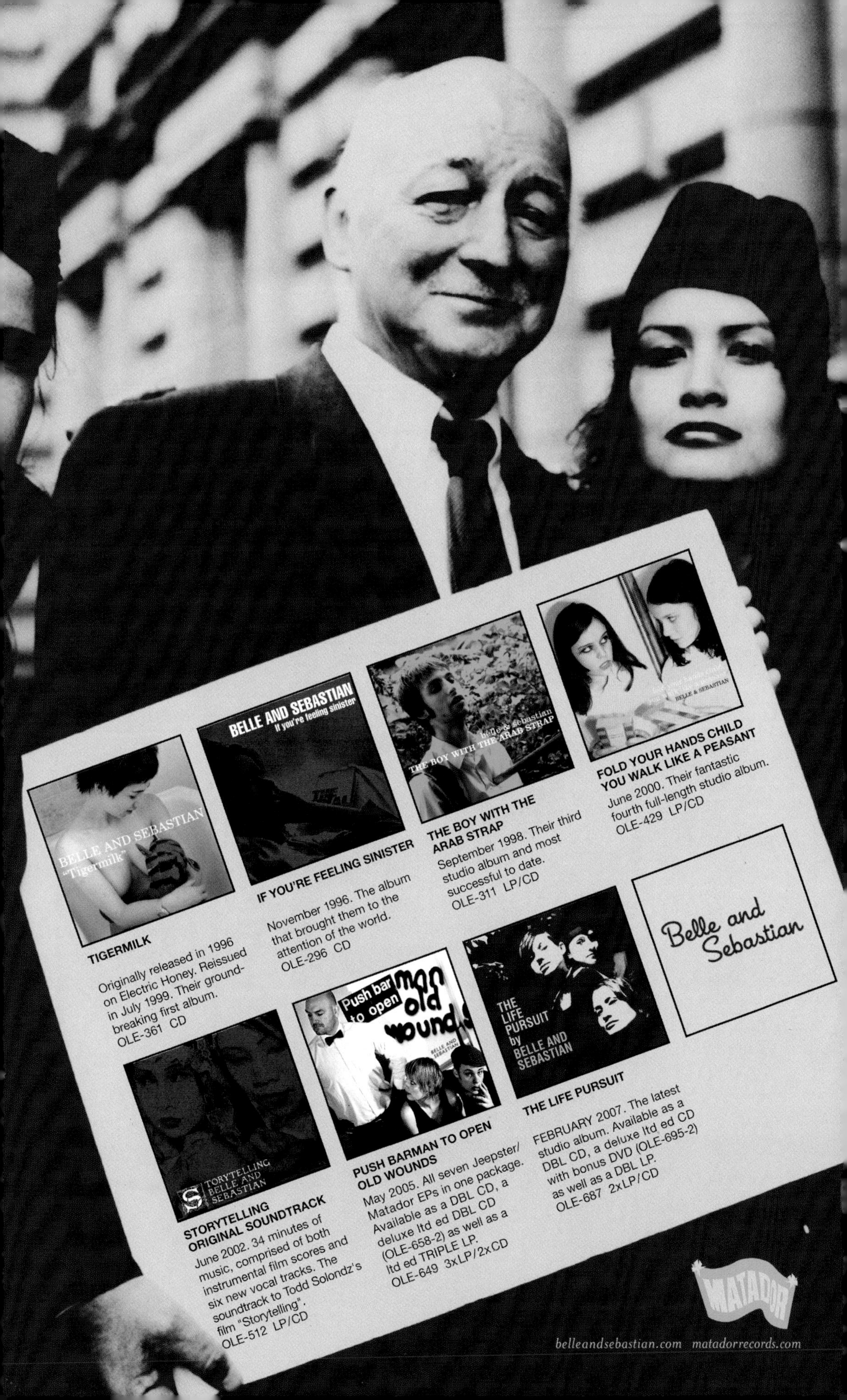

TIGERMILK
BELLE AND SEBASTIAN "Tigermilk"
Originally released in 1996 on Electric Honey. Reissued in July 1999. Their ground-breaking first album.
OLE-361 CD
BELLE AND SEBASTIAN If you're feeling sinister
IF YOU'RE FEELING SINISTER
November 1996. The album that brought them to the attention of the world.
OLE-296 CD
belle & sebastian THE BOY WITH THE ARAB STRAP
THE BOY WITH THE ARAB STRAP
September 1998. Their third studio album and most successful to date.
OLE-311 LP/CD
BELLE & SEBASTIAN
FOLD YOUR HANDS CHILD YOU WALK LIKE A PEASANT
June 2000. Their fantastic fourth full-length studio album.
OLE-429 LP/CD
Belle and Sebastian
STORYTELLING BELLE AND SEBASTIAN
STORYTELLING ORIGINAL SOUNDTRACK
June 2002. 34 minutes of music, comprised of both instrumental film scores and six new vocal tracks. The soundtrack to Todd Solondz's film "Storytelling".
OLE-512 LP/CD
Push bar to open man old wounds
BELLE AND SEBASTIAN
PUSH BARMAN TO OPEN OLD WOUNDS
May 2005. All seven Jeepster/Matador EPs in one package. Available as a DBL CD, a deluxe ltd ed DBL CD (OLE-658-2) as well as a ltd ed TRIPLE LP.
OLE-649 3xLP/2xCD
THE LIFE PURSUIT by BELLE AND SEBASTIAN
THE LIFE PURSUIT
FEBRUARY 2007. The latest studio album. Available as a DBL CD, a deluxe ltd ed CD with bonus DVD (OLE-695-2) as well as a DBL LP.
OLE-687 2xLP/CD
MATADOR
belleandsebastian.com matadorrecords.com

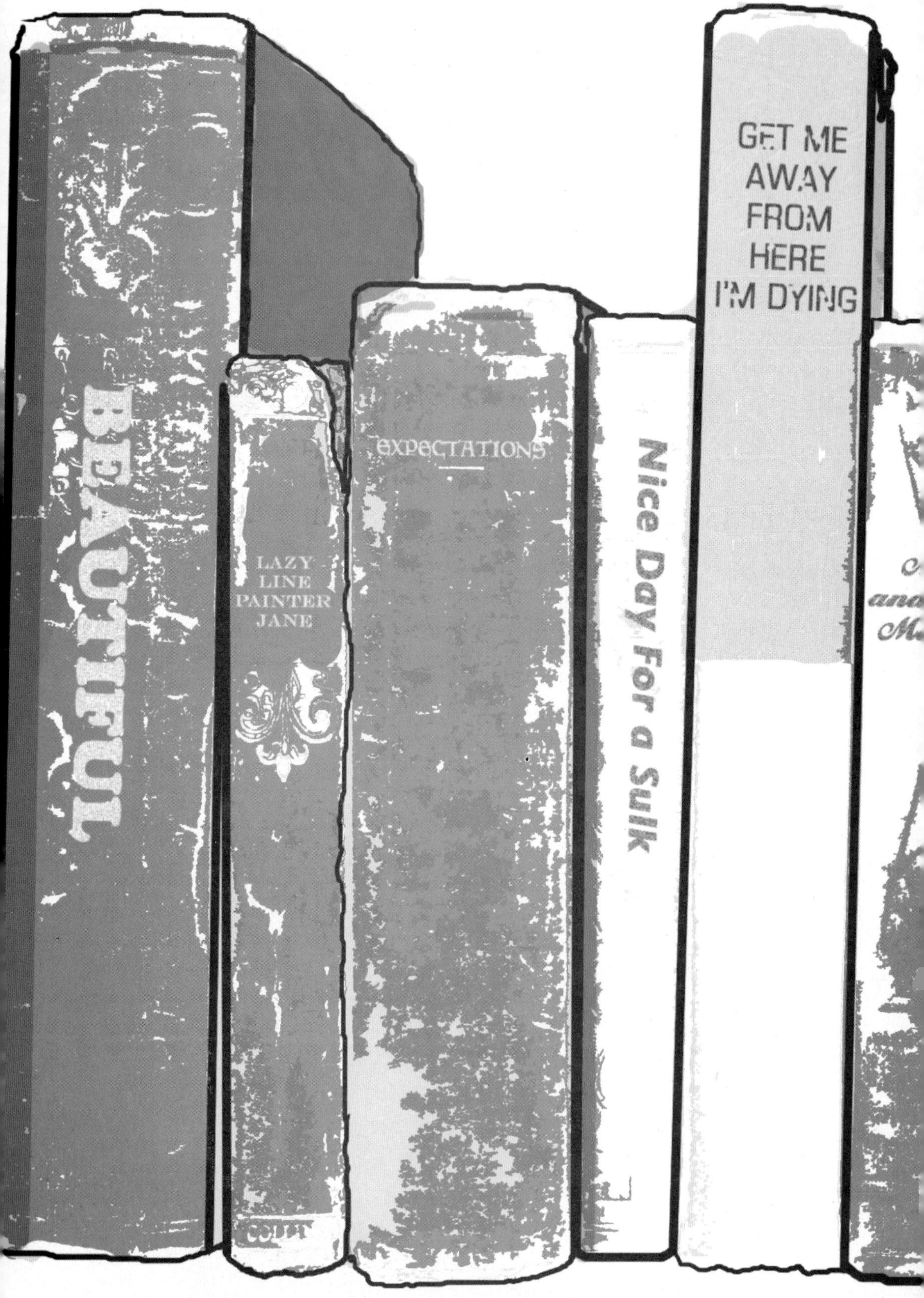
BEAUTIFUL
LAZY LINE PAINTER JANE
EXPECTATIONS
Nice Day For a Sulk
GET ME AWAY FROM HERE I'M DYING